No entry without strategy

No entry without strategy: Building the rule of law under UN transitional administration

Carolyn Bull

United Nations University Press

TOKYO · NEW YORK · PARIS

© United Nations University, 2008

The views expressed in this publication are those of the authors and do not necessarily reflect the views of the United Nations University.

United Nations University Press
United Nations University, 53-70, Jingumae 5-chome,
Shibuya-ku, Tokyo 150-8925, Japan
Tel: +81-3-3499-2811 Fax: +81-3-3406-7345
E-mail: sales@hq.unu.edu general enquiries: press@hq.unu.edu
http://www.unu.edu

United Nations University Office at the United Nations, New York
2 United Nations Plaza, Room DC2-2062, New York, NY 10017, USA
Tel: +1-212-963-6387 Fax: +1-212-371-9454
E-mail: unuona@ony.unu.edu

United Nations University Press is the publishing division of the United Nations University.

Cover design by Maria Sese-Paul

Cover photograph by REUTERS/AFLO

Printed in the United States of America

ISBN 978-92-808-1151-3

Library of Congress Cataloging-in-Publication Data

Bull, Carolyn Gardner, 1969–
  No entry without strategy : building the rule of law under UN transitional
administration / Carolyn Bull.
    p.   cm.
  Includes bibliographical references and index.
  ISBN 978-9280811513 (pbk. : alk. paper) 1. Nation-building—Case studies.
2. United Nations. Transitional Administration in East Timor. 3. United
Nations. Transitional Authority in Cambodia. 4. United Nations Interim
Mission in Kosovo. I. Title.
JZ6300.B86 2008
341.5′23—dc22

For my mother, Nancy
Always interested, she nurtured my love of learning and taught me
many things

Contents

Acknowledgements

For their intellectual guidance and support, I am indebted to my PhD supervisors, Professors David Lovell and William Maley. I would also like to thank Professor James Cotton for reviewing sections of the draft and Professors Ramesh Thakur, Hilary Charlesworth and Duncan Chappell for their invaluable suggestions. I am also grateful to the staff and students of the School of Humanities and Social Sciences at the University of New South Wales at the Australian Defence Force Academy for their assistance and collegiality during my studies. Thanks are also due to the Centre of Asian Studies at The University of Hong Kong for providing a visiting scholar position, and to Professor Chris Reus-Smit and Dr Ron May at the Research School of Pacific and Asian Studies, Australian National University, for advice during the early phase of my research.

I am grateful to the many experts in the field who offered their time and opinions, especially UN mission staff who were very helpful, candid and constructive. I would also like to thank James McCormack, Lynn Peever, Connor, Tiffany, Sokchea and Neary for giving me a home in Phnom Penh. Likewise, Sandra Knowles pointed me in all the right directions in East Timor. I also owe much to the staff of the Interim Office of the Commission for Reception, Truth and Reconciliation in Dili for the opportunity to work with and learn from them. Many others gave generously of their time, experience and networks to assist my fieldwork, including colleagues at AusAID, the Australian Federal Police and the Department of Foreign Affairs and Trade, Manuel Abrantes, Jacinto

Alves, Peter Bartu, Alex Bellamy, Bob Bradley, Lima Castro, Simon Chesterman, Mac Darrow, Natalie David, Jim della Giacoma, Virginia Dumnica, Helena Fraser, Kek Galabru, Euan Graham, Aniceto Guterres Lopes, Michael Hartmann, Kao Kim Hourn, Lao Mong Hay, Scott Leiper, Michael Maley, David Marshall, David Mearns, Eirin Mobekk, Eva Mysliewisc, Kassie Neou, Mark Plunkett, Ed Rees, Rita Rowland-Jones, Lt Gen. John Sanderson (on whose archives I drew extensively), Thun Saray, Nick Thomas, Chea Vannath, Sergio Vieira de Mello, Joao Vincente, Pat Walsh and Nick Wheeler. Finally, the staff at UNU Press made the publishing process easy and enjoyable and taught me a lot about their craft.

This study would not have been possible without the financial support of an Australian Postgraduate Award, a scholarship and fieldwork funding from UNSW@ADFA and a bequest from my Aunt Marion.

Most especially, I would like to thank Rob, for his love, enthusiasm and support during the long slog, and Eliza and Liam, for bringing much cheer.

Abbreviations

AAK	Alliance for the Future of Kosovo
ADHOC	Cambodia Human Rights and Development Association
CARERE	Cambodia Resettlement and Reintegration project
CAVR	Commission for Reception, Truth and Reconciliation (Commissao de Acolhimento Verdade e Reconciliacao)
CHR	Commission on Human Rights
CIVPOL	Civilian police
CNRT	National Council of Timorese Resistance (Conselho Nacional de Resistencia Timorense)
CPP	Cambodian People's Party
CRP	Community Reconciliation Procedure
EJS	Emergency Judicial System
ETPS	East Timor Police Service
ETTA	East Timor Transitional Administration
F-FDTL	East Timor Defence Force (Falintil-Forca Defesa Timor-Leste)
Fretilin	Revolutionary Front for an Independent East Timor (Frente Revolucionaria de Timor-Leste)
FTO	Field Training Officer
FUNCINPEC	National United Front for an Independent, Neutral, Peaceful and Democratic Cambodia (Front Uni National pour un Cambodge Indépendant, Neutre, Pacifique, et Coopératif)
HPCC	Housing and Property Claims Commission
ICTY	International Criminal Tribunal for the Former Yugoslavia
IJPs	international judges and prosecutors
INTERFET	International Force in East Timor
JAC/LM	Joint Advisory Council for Legislative Matters

JIAS	Joint Interim Administrative Structure
KCS	Kosovo Correctional Service
KFOR	Kosovo Force
KJPC	Kosovo Judicial and Prosecutorial Council
KLA	Kosovo Liberation Army
KPC	Kosovo Protection Corps
KPNLF	Khmer People's National Liberation Front
KPS	Kosovo Police Service
KTC	Kosovo Transitional Council
LDK	Democratic League of Kosovo
NADK	National Army of Democratic Kampuchea (also known as Khmer Rouge)
NATO	North Atlantic Treaty Organization
NCC	National Consultative Council
NDI	National Democratic Institute for International Affairs
NGO	non-governmental organisation
OHCHR	Office of the United Nations High Commissioner for Human Rights
ONUC	United Nations Operation in the Congo
OSCE	Organization for Security and Co-operation in Europe
PDK	Democratic Party of Kosovo
PISG	Provisional Institutions of Self-Government
SCIU	Serious Crimes Investigation Unit
SCU	Serious Crimes Unit
SNC	Supreme National Council
SOC	State of Cambodia
SRSG	Special Representative of the Secretary-General
US	United States
UN	United Nations
UNAMA	United Nations Assistance Mission in Afghanistan
UNAMET	United Nations Assistance Mission in East Timor
UNBRO	United Nations Border Relief Operation
UNCOHCHR	United Nations Cambodian Office of the High Commissioner for Human Rights
UNDP	United Nations Development Programme
UNEF-I	First United Nations Emergency Force
UNGA	United Nations General Assembly
UNHCR	United Nations High Commissioner for Refugees
UNMIBH	United Nations Mission in Bosnia and Herzegovina
UNMIK	United Nations Interim Administration Mission in Kosovo
UNMISET	United Nations Mission of Support in East Timor
UNTAC	United Nations Transitional Authority in Cambodia
UNTAES	United Nations Transitional Authority in Eastern Slavonia, Baranja and Western Sirmium
UNTAET	United Nations Transitional Administration in East Timor
UNTAG	United Nations Transition Assistance Group in Namibia

UNTEA	United Nations Temporary Executive Authority
UNTSO	United Nations Truce Supervision Organization
WPU	Witness Protection Unit

Map of Cambodia

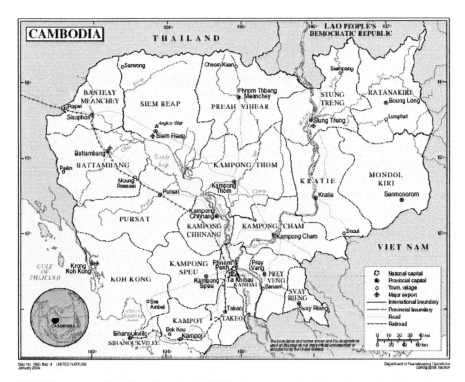

Source: UN Department of Peacekeeping Operations, Cartographic Section, 2004, at ⟨http://www.un.org/Depts/Cartographic/map/profile/cambodia.pdf⟩.

Map of Kosovo

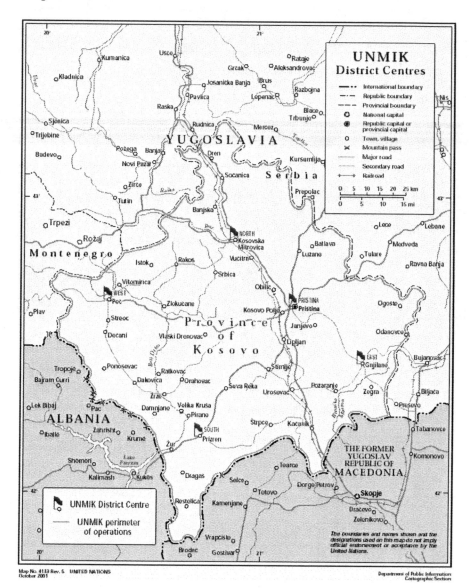

Source: UN Department of Public Information, Cartographic Section, 2001, at ⟨http://www.unmikonline.org/maps/unmik.pdf⟩.

Map of East Timor

Source: UN Department of Peacekeeping Operations, Cartographic Section, 2005, at ⟨http://www.un.org/Depts/Cartographic/map/profile/timoreg.pdf⟩.

1

Introduction: The elusive goal

[A] constellation of persons or groups among whom there existed no expectation of security against violence, of the honouring of agreements or of stability of possession we should hardly call a society at all.

Hedley Bull, *The Anarchical Society* (1977: 5)

For international actors seeking to consolidate peace and democracy in so-called disrupted states,[1] the importance of establishing the rule of law is now well recognised. Yet the goals of ensuring security against violence and building legitimate state structures to redress disputes peacefully have proven frustratingly elusive. International actors have found it even more difficult to instil principles of governance that promote accountability to the law, protect against abuse and generate trust in the state.

In championing such goals in conflict-riven states, United Nations (UN) actors have pitched against the odds. In the hostile intervention environments examined in this book, UN peace operations have pitted meagre resources against monumental aspirations for change. Not unpredictably, these aspirations have generally remained unmet. At one extreme, renewed violence in Cambodia in 1997, Kosovo in 2004 and Timor-Leste in 2006 has been a stark reminder of the frailty of the rule of law; more invidious, perhaps, has been the everyday incidence of agreements dishonoured, instability of possession and state abuse.

A threshold question of this book is whether, in the case of UN attempts to build the rule of law, such unmet aspirations derive from deficiencies in intervention strategies or from unrealistic ambition. If

No entry without strategy: Building the rule of law under UN transitional administration, Bull, United Nations University Press, 2008, ISBN 978-92-808-1151-3

establishing the rule of law requires no less than the transformation of social norms regarding conflict, power and the state, can an external actor such as a UN mission ever expect to succeed? Is the goal elusive, or impossible?

The peacebuilding agenda

Increasingly, rule of law objectives have been incorporated into post–Cold War UN peace operations as a core element of the doctrine of "peacebuilding", which transformed the traditional blue helmet role of *keeping* the peace into an imperative to *build* it. This doctrine, which emerged in the early 1990s, reasoned that the pursuit by peace operations of a particular political, social and economic order in post-conflict environments was instrumental in securing the primary objective of a stable peace. The Secretary-General's 1992 *Agenda for Peace* described peacebuilding as the "construction of a new environment" to prevent the recurrence of conflict. It stressed the obligation of UN missions to identify and support structures that consolidated peace, including disarmament, demilitarisation, repatriation, human rights protection, reform or strengthening of government institutions, and promotion of democratic political participation (UNGA 1992: paras 55, 59).

These objectives, which as Cousens (2001: 13) has observed formed a helpful but limited roadmap that covered "the entire basket of post-war needs", were reaffirmed in subsequent keynote documents, including the 2000 *Brahimi Report* and the Secretary-General's 2001 report *No exit without strategy*. The latter proposed that peace operations should seek to move conflict from the battlefield to a peaceful institutional framework and defined peacebuilding as "an attempt, after a peace has been negotiated or imposed, to address the sources of present hostility and build local capacities for conflict resolution" (UNSC 2001a: para. 11). It outlined three preconditions for successful peacebuilding: consolidating internal and external security through peacekeeping and security sector reform; strengthening political institutions and good governance; and promoting economic and social rehabilitation and transformation.

With the development of peacebuilding practice during the 1990s, it became apparent that these preconditions were linked intimately to the functions of the state or, more accurately, to its dysfunction. Accordingly, UN "peacebuilding" interventions moved increasingly to support, build or strengthen the institutions of *state*, with a view to stabilising or even creating territorial entities that fulfilled a particular conception of legitimacy and were capable of assuming their rightful place in international society. The term *state-building* entered international security lexicon and, in the context of UN peace operations, may be defined as "an intervention designed to create a stable, democratic and viable state, primarily through building the institutions of a state".[2]

Although often equated with the term peacebuilding, the concept of state-building thus extends beyond peacebuilding's central concern of preventing the recurrence of violent conflict to an explicit focus on the state and its institutions. As discussed in detail in Chapter 2, the state-building agenda of UN peace operations has focused, primarily though not exclusively, on developing those institutions of state that underpin liberal democracy, human rights protection, transparent and accountable public administration, and a free market economy.

State-building and rule of law strategies

The proliferation of costly and protracted state-building enterprises in the 1990s soon generated alarm that the international community was intervening in disrupted states, in increasingly intrusive ways, without a clear strategy for action. This was especially evident with respect to the most extensive state-building missions, such as those deployed in Bosnia-Herzegovina, Kosovo and East Timor, where UN missions found themselves over-extended, under-equipped and bereft of success stories.

Across the gamut of state-building issues, these frustrations were demonstrated no more clearly than in the rule of law arena. A central concern was the relative lack of priority being accorded to rule of law issues in complex peace operations, relative to other pressing issues on the agenda that seemed more visible and immediate. A second, related concern was that of continued disappointing results in attempts to implement rule of law reform. By the early twenty-first century, recognition of both sets of concerns by an increasingly wide range of UN actors prompted a significant increase in attention to rule of law issues across the UN system (UNSC 2004e: 3).

This sea change was encapsulated in the Secretary-General's August 2004 report on *The rule of law and transitional justice in conflict and post-conflict societies*, which catalogued a myriad of problems related not only to *what* rule of law initiatives had been implemented, but to *how* they had been implemented. Beyond the question of giving sufficient priority to the rule of law in overall mission mandates, these problems included a failure to consider country context; to identify, support and empower domestic reform constituencies and cultivate broad-based support for reforms; to recognise the political dimensions of rule of law reform; to ensure post-mission support, including long-term development assistance; to develop holistic strategies that engage all official and non-official justice institutions; and to address the issue of past crimes through appropriate institutional mechanisms (UNSC 2004e: 6–19; see also Carlson 2006 and Rees 2006).

The momentum for change thus established, at the 2005 UN World Summit more than 170 heads of state and government identified the rule of law as one of four key areas that demanded greater attention. By late 2006, in his report *Uniting our strengths: Enhancing United Nations support for the rule of law*, the Secretary-General noted that rule of law and transitional justice issues were "now being consistently integrated into the strategic and operational planning of new peace operations and Member States now almost universally recognise the establishment of the rule of law as an important aspect of peacekeeping" (UNSC 2006a: 1).

Accompanying this heightened attention to the rule of law in the UN state-building agenda has been the emergence of an extensive range of guidelines, manuals and other materials and tools aimed at strengthening the United Nations' strategic and practical capacity (UNSC 2006a 1). Notable developments included the establishment in December 2005 of the UN Peacebuilding Commission, with a mandate to advise on integrated long-term strategies for post-conflict recovery, including rule of law issues; the release in 2006 of the Office of the United Nations High Commissioner for Human Rights' *Rule of law tools for post-conflict states* (OHCHR 2006a, 2006b, 2006c, 2006d); and the launch in 2007 of integrated "model codes", to provide a legal framework for peace operations, other international missions and national governments to use to respond to justice needs in post-conflict environments.[3]

Despite these advances, in 2006 a UN self-assessment concluded that "the Organization's engagement, approach and coordination at both the Headquarters and the mission levels remained informal and ad hoc, and was poorly harmonised with that of other key external partners" (UNSC 2006a para. 36). Much remained to be done to promote formal processes to enhance "capacities, coherence and coordination" in UN doctrine and approach (UNSC 2006a para. 28). This resulted in the decision to establish in 2007 a Rule of Law Coordination and Resource Group in the UN Secretariat, to bring together key rule of law players in the UN system (Office of Legal Affairs, Department of Peacekeeping Operations, Office of the United Nations High Commissioner for Human Rights, United Nations Office on Drugs and Crime, United Nations Development Programme, United Nations Development Fund For Women and United Nations High Commissioner for Refugees) to focus on overall coordination and strategic policy response and coordination centre, and to identify and address gaps in capacity. This points not only to the need for refinements to UN state-building strategies, but to the scope and need for further research.

Lessons learnt

These challenges of rule of law promotion were by no means new. Earlier episodes in external rule of law promotion since the United Nations' inception had generated similarly lacklustre results. For example, the numerous legal education and code reform projects implemented in Latin American and African post-colonial states during the "law and development" movement of the 1960s showed little evidence of benefits to economic development or human rights protections (Merryman 1977: 459; Greenberg 1980: 134–135).[3]

Although some scholars pointed to positive outcomes from the movement (McClymount and Golub 2000; Borbely et al. 1999: 6), critics argued that the attempted transfer of American ideas and systems did not take sufficient account of cultural or political context (Merryman 1977: 483; Garth and Sarat 1998b: 14; Trubek and Galanter 1974: 1062; Franck 1972: 768, 785). Seidman's model of law and development (1978: 16–18) concluded that efforts to overlay western institutions on pre-existing indigenous systems, however weakened or transformed by the colonisation process, resulted only in dysfunction and corruption. Further, it was argued that modern western legal structures could not be assumed to be the key to social and economic development, not least because formal legal systems reached only a small segment of the population (Trubek 1972: 16; Valdez in Zagaris 1988: 558; Borbely et al. 1999: 6).

Undeterred by the demise of the law and development movement, law reform continued as a feature of foreign aid programmes, which increasingly linked legal reform with the democratisation agenda.[4] Rule of law projects gained new impetus with the end of the Cold War; this revival related strongly to the precept that good governance, the backbone of social and economic development, could not be achieved without rule of law institutions. Rule of law projects also became linked closely to the human rights and social justice movement, and with international law enforcement programmes (Carothers 2006b). Projects typically focused on code reform through "institutional strengthening" (Hammergren 1998a: 8), with some attention also to increasing access to justice, building consensus about the need for judicial independence, and building capacity in the justice system (Biebesheimer and Payne 2001: 1).

Like their predecessors, these judicial reform projects generally produced disappointing results, falling short of or even undermining their goals (Garth and Sarat 1998b: 13; Carothers 1999: 170, 2006a: 6). By the late 1990s, many scholars painted a bleak picture of failed legal reform, corruption, biased appointments, low public confidence and extrajudicial conflict resolution. Even studies that were relatively positive about the effectiveness of justice sector projects in advancing such goals as human rights protection, constitutional development and the expansion of civil society cautioned of the potential downsides: of aid projects that sheltered repressive regimes from scrutiny, wasted resources, distorted institutions and exacerbated social divisions. Wheel reinvention and the repeated application of flawed project design prevailed (McAuslan 1997; Thome 1997).

Twenty years into the movement, there remained considerable uncertainty about the long-run impact of specific rule of law initiatives, beyond an uneasy sense that their transformative impact was weak (Carothers 2006b). A growing body of literature on external rule of law promotion offered salient lessons – many of which echoed those of the earlier law and development movement – but few definitive solutions to the quandary of how an external actor may best seek to promote the rule of law.

Of these lessons, a recurring theme was the lack of a sound theoretical basis for projects. Upham (2002: 10) has described how the World Bank, the United Nations and aid agencies tended to embrace a "formalist model of law detached from the social and political interconnections that form actual legal systems anywhere". This model rested on three unproven assumptions: that the description of law as a system of rules is a reliable guide to understanding legal systems; that law's primary role in society is dispute resolution; and that such dispute resolution depends on formal legal adjudication (Upham 2002: 10–11).

These assumptions proved difficult to uphold empirically (Thome 1997: 50). Similarly, specific causal linkages such as the relationship between judicial reform and human rights protection or good governance remained unproven (McAuslan 1997: 30–31; Hammergren 1998a: 9). Moreover, concurring with law and society scholars who argued that law was deeply contextual and could not be detached from its social and political environment, judicial reform project analyses supported the view that constitutions and laws could not in themselves modify the substance of political actions, but were dependent on the political and cultural context in which they operated (Przeworski 1995: 51).

Upham (2002) demonstrated how, despite these findings, donors denied the political nature of law and continued to adopt approaches that underestimated the complexity of legal development. At the same time, some donors set impossible ideals not met in even the most advanced legal systems. As a result, institutional transfer either failed or generated unintended and sometimes negative consequences. Much of the analysis of law reform in East Germany, the Czech Republic and the Newly Independent States supported this view.[5]

Studies on legal sector reform repeatedly concluded that institutional change is dependent on the attitudes of the political élite, as well as key interest groups such as the judiciary (Hammergren 1998a; Kritz 2006). As Carothers (1998: 7) noted:

> reform that brings real change in government obedience to law is the hardest, slowest kind of assistance. It demands powerful tools that aid providers are only beginning to develop, especially activities that help bring pressure on the legal system from the citizenry and support whatever pockets of reform may exist within an otherwise self-interested ruling system. It requires a level of interventionism, political attention, and visibility that many donor governments and organisations cannot or do not wish to apply. Above all, it calls for patient, sustained attention, as breaking down entrenched political interests, transforming values, and generating enlightened, consistent leadership will take generations.

Stimulating broader public demand for rule of law reform in the institutional change equation in some ways presented an even higher degree of difficulty for external actors than "political will" issues. As Aron (2002) noted in a study of Russian legal reform:

> Perhaps even more debilitating is the deeply cynical view of the legal system held by millions of Russians. The supply of laws, no matter how excellent, must be met with an equally strong demand ... To resuscitate that [demand] after four generations of state terror, lawlessness, and fraud – while courts, judges, and laws were instruments of a totalitarian state – will take decades.

Methods of stimulating public demand for rule of law reform pursued by external actors, such as assistance for civil society development and public support building campaigns, tended to be underdeveloped in terms of defining, mobilising and introducing individual and group interests into the reform process (Hammergren 1998d: 10; Jacoby 2001).

The need for an early focus on rule of law issues as part of an overall reform package was increasingly recognised (Kritz 2006), but donors nonetheless found it difficult to coordinate reform strategies within the justice sector, across the entire reform programme and amongst a range of donors (World Bank 2002; Biebesheimer and Payne 2001: ii–iii). Hence, although programme designs increasingly recognised that reestablishing a judiciary or police service would be ineffective without proper attention to related justice sector components, such as legal education, prison reform, victim protection and property dispute resolution, poor implementation continued to weaken the overall effectiveness of reform (UNSC 2004e: 9). In other cases, the sequencing of particular justice sector projects was mistimed, or proved ineffective in the face of larger political issues. Project evaluations also found insufficiently sustained and consistent donor commitment to incremental reform (Lopez-de-Silanes 2002: 27; Biebesheimer and Payne 2001: iii; Jacoby 2001).

These "lessons learnt", like the experience of the law and development movement, underscored the complex set of challenges facing any external attempt to strengthen the rule of law. At the time of writing, external rule of law initiatives had only just begun to move beyond institutional formalism towards a broader enterprise in institutional change that considered issues of political will, incentives and social networking analysis, the usefulness of bottom-up processes such as legal empowerment as a way of potentially stimulating systemic change, and the importance of traditional or "informal" justice systems (Carothers 2006b).

UN transitional administrations and the rule of law

Given this rich pre-existing set of case studies regarding external rule of law promotion, what does an analysis of the experience of UN transitional administrations offer? As a specific mode of intervention in which the United Nations has assumed direct political and administrative authority over disrupted states or territories, transitional administrations represent unique situations in which the United Nations has pursued ambitious state-building projects and wielded extensive, even quasi-sovereign authority. In particular, Kosovo and East Timor constituted the first occasions on which UN peace operations exercised full judicial authority within a territory and were mandated specifically to establish a state justice system.

There has been comparatively little detailed academic focus on UN transitional administrations as a specific class of intervention or on the rule of law initiatives undertaken by these missions. Some studies of UN transitional administration, such as those by Chesterman (2001a, 2001b, 2002a, 2003, 2004a), Wilde (2001a, 2001b) and Caplan (2002, 2004a,b), have provided seminal insights, but rule of law issues have not been their primary focus. Other studies tend to fall into two groups: those that examine state-building under international intervention more generally;[6] and those that examine several rule of law issues in a single UN mission, or a single rule of law issue in one or two missions.[7]

In seeking to augment existing research, this book examines a broad set of rule of law initiatives pursued by three of the four UN transitional administrations deployed to date: the United Nations Transitional Authority in Cambodia (UNTAC, 1992–1993), the United Nations Interim Administration Mission in Kosovo (UNMIK, since 1999) and the United Nations Transitional Administration in East Timor (UNTAET, 1999–2002).[8] Existing studies of rule of law initiatives by these UN transitional administrations have yielded predominantly negative assessments of the effectiveness of UN actors in establishing the rule of law.[9] The primary objective of this study is to investigate further these apparent difficulties.

Kosovo and East Timor are perhaps the more important case studies, because of the extensiveness of the rule of law mandates given to the UNMIK and UNTAET missions. At the time of writing, UNMIK and a successor mission to UNTAET both remained in theatre. For the sake of practicality, only the first five years of the UNMIK mission (from June 1999 to June 2004) are considered and discussion of UN intervention in East Timor is confined to the UNTAET mission only.

Although limited in its rule of law activities, Cambodia provides a useful counterpoint to its more recent cousins. In effect, UNTAC begins the tale: deployed in the opening phase of the post–Cold War period, in the early days of "complex peacekeeping", and as the United Nations' first experiment in transitional administration, it illustrates both the detrimental effects of neglecting the rule of law and the rapid evolution of the United Nations' rule of law agenda over the past decade.

In pursuing its primary objective, this book also seeks to enhance conceptual understandings of the state-building agenda adopted by UN agencies in the post–Cold War period and, in particular, of the rule of law agenda as a subset of this broader agenda. More broadly, it seeks to add to the body of empirical studies concerned with how external actors may assist in establishing the rule of law in a disrupted state. Although aspects of "transitional justice" are considered, and important to, the study's conclusions, they are not the focus of this book. Many studies already deal with these issues comprehensively.[10]

Three key findings emerge from the study. First, at least nine distinct – and arguably foreseeable – factors appear to have contributed to the difficulties encountered by UN transitional administrations in establishing the rule of law in Cambodia, East Timor and Kosovo. UN transitional administrations failed in each of the following ways: to make the best use of their mandate; to establish effective state justice institutions; to build local commitment to the rule of law as a value system; to promote the formation or revival of social relationships supportive of the rule of law; to ensure sufficient state capacity to maintain and advance rule of law gains after the intervention; to maintain adequate levels of security; to address the existence of informal justice structures; to deal with the legacies of the past; and to ensure a level of mission performance adequate to support rule of law objectives.

Second, and more broadly, a state-based enforcement approach to establishing the rule of law proved ineffective. Although arguably an important component of the state-building agenda of UN transitional administrations, the establishment of a body of state law and judicial, police and prison services could not be equated with the establishment of the rule of law. Such an approach did not adequately account for the existence of entrenched informal justice institutions; for the fact that adherence to the desired rules system relied less on state sanction mechanisms than on the voluntary consent of local actors to bind themselves to those rules; for the profound influence of indigenous power struggles; or for the importance of appropriate institutional design choices. As a result, the UN approach tended to be formalistic and proved limited in its ability to offer real solutions to real problems faced by local actors.

Third, as with other external actors, UN transitional administrations seriously undermined their potential to contribute to rule of law development by neglecting to consider fully how they could create an enabling "space" in which internal processes of change could occur, to engage appropriately with the recipient population, to address the tyrannies of a short deployment period or to ensure that it addressed these issues systematically at the "front end" of the mission.

The absence of a nuanced strategy that addressed the above factors seriously undermined the ability of each UN transitional administration to establish the rule of law, the self-declared cornerstone of its state-building agenda. This is what may be called, for the purposes of this study, the "entry without strategy" approach to state-building. It is an approach that seems fatally flawed.

Outline of the book

Chapter 2 contextualises the case studies by defining the state-building agenda of UN transitional administrations. In tracing the evolution of internationally sanctioned administration of territories during the twentieth century, it demonstrates that this agenda is rooted in earlier League of Nations and UN experiments in international trusteeship as well as in contemporary peacekeeping doctrine. It argues that these forms of international administration have all pursued political solutions directed at maintaining a particular international order. As such, they may be viewed not merely as a tool for promoting international stability, but as a vehicle by which the international community has sought to construct a new political environment consistent with prevailing standards of governance.

Two features distinguish UN transitional administrations from other peace operations: the direct, mandated exercise of political authority by the United Nations; and the adoption of an intrusive state-building agenda as a primary rather than auxiliary objective. A set of benchmarks for statehood may be observed that includes a stable security environment, the foundations of a liberal democratic political system, the rule of law, mechanisms for human rights protection, a functioning and transparent government capable of appropriating and utilising resources, a sustainable market-based economy and stable external relations. Finally, this chapter frames this state-building agenda in the context of the post-conflict disrupted state, which it argues constituted a highly hostile intervention environment.

Chapter 3 examines UN understandings of its rule of law agenda in transitional administrations, suggesting that three key concepts defined this agenda. First, the "rule of law" was perceived as a distinct normative value scheme, based on a cluster of values invested with rights-based notions of substantive justice. Second, the act of establishing the rule of law was perceived to play a critical transformative role in moving a disrupted state towards a social order characterised by peace and stability, human rights protection, democratic institutions, sustainable development and "justice". Third, the principal means by which UN actors could hope to establish the rule of law in a disrupted state was through a state-based enforcement model constituted by publicly promulgated formal rules of behaviour with the force of law and coercive state structures to enforce those laws, namely state judicial, law enforcement and correctional structures.

This chapter argues that, although the broad thrust of this conception of the rule of law and its constitutive role has much support in the scholarly literature, it lacked substance both rhetorically and in the field. In particular, the operational emphasis on constructing courts, police services and prisons bordered on institutional formalism, in which the establishment of the rule of law was equated directly with the establishment of state justice organisations.

Finally, as the basis for scrutiny of the case studies, this chapter draws on the preceding discussion to identify nine areas of enquiry of potential relevance in understanding the success or failure of attempts by external actors such as the United Nations to establish the rule of law in disrupted states. These centre on whether the United Nations set appropriate strategic parameters; made effective choices in designing state justice bodies; succeeded in winning elite and popular commitment to the rule of law as a value system; supported the rebuilding of fragile social relationships; ensured sufficient state capacity to maintain and advance rule of law gains after the intervention; restored security to a sufficient level; took adequate account of the potential for informal structures to extract or prevent social loyalty to the rule of law; dealt with the question of past crimes; and ensured that its own performance was effective.

The book then turns to examine the three case studies. Chapter 4 argues that UNTAC's failure to lay robust foundations for the rule of law was a critical missed opportunity and one of the most serious flaws of the mission. It meant that UNTAC was ultimately unable to meet its own primary objectives of ending civil strife and human rights abuses, maintaining social order and supporting democratic transition. More than a decade after the UNTAC mission, the absence of crucial attributes of a democratic rule of law state – notably a lamentable judicial system and the continued primacy of strongmen operating above the law – pointed to a long-term failure of the UN intervention.

Key factors that contributed to this situation included an inadequate mandate that was interpreted narrowly; flaws in the design of state rule of law institutions; UNTAC's inability to build commitment for rule of law goals amongst the political elite and the broader community; insufficient state capacity to ensure that rule of law initiatives could be continued post-UNTAC; incomplete restoration of security; and mission shortcomings, including a truncated deployment period and poorly formulated exit strategy.

Chapter 5 examines the first five years of UNMIK, from its deployment in October 1999 to October 2004. It argues that, although UNMIK's comparatively lengthy deployment provided scope for a more sophisticated range of rule of law initiatives than in any other transitional administration, five years into the mission the inability of fledgling state rule of law structures to prevent or contain outbreaks of ethnic violence indicated a profound failure to consolidate the rule of law or even to stabilise the territory.

Uncertainty over Kosovo's final status undermined many of UNMIK's efforts to promote the rule of law. In addition, several avoidable shortcomings on UNMIK's part contributed to its failure. These included UNMIK's ambiguous interpretation of its mandate; its failure to develop a considered rule of law strategy until four years into the mission; poorly designed state rule of law institutions; a virtually non-existent capacity-building and localisation strategy; a failure to neutralise spoilers; insufficient attention to non-institutional facets of rule of law creation; and mission inertia and dissent. Critically, UNMIK did not develop an effective strategy to engage Kosovans in its rule of law initiatives. It disregarded its mandate to harness existing institutions and skills, and state rule of law structures remained inaccessible and irrelevant to much of the population. The resentment thus generated undermined UNMIK's legitimacy and ultimately the willingness of Kosovans to commit to the rule of law.

Chapter 6 considers the UNTAET mission, which administered East Timor[11] from October 1999 until the territory's independence in May 2002. UNTAET was also unprecedented in the history of UN peacekeeping: for the first time, the United Nations assumed sovereign control over a territory independent of any competing official authority and with the specific objective of preparing it for statehood. UNTAET attempted perhaps the most ambitious state-building programme of any UN peace operation to date.

Against considerable odds, UNTAET made progress in nurturing state rule of law institutions and assisting Timorese to reckon with a traumatic past. Nonetheless, by the time of independence, the justice system was one of the most dysfunctional elements of the new state. Comparatively good levels of law and order relied not on robust institutions but on the self-discipline of the Timorese leadership and population, which quickly proved fallible. Fundamental building blocks of the rule of law – such as separation of powers and equality before the law – were not in place.

UNTAET's strategic shortcomings included a piecemeal approach to building state rule of law institutions; a failure to manage East Timorese expectations, to bridge the disconnect between western and Timorese conceptions of justice and the rule of law and to devolve responsibility for rule of law processes; the lack of a developmental approach to establishing the rule of law; and a failure adequately to address the question of "traditional justice".

Chapter 7 concludes the book. It argues that each of the case studies confirms the relevance of the nine areas of enquiry listed in Chapter 3 to the success or failure of UN peace operations to build the rule of law, and highlights the particular importance of three factors: establishing state rule of law institutions, building local commitment, and addressing informal justice structures.

This chapter argues that the case studies back up both relevant theoretical debates and empirical studies in cautioning against an operational approach that equates building the rule of law too closely with the establishment of state laws and justice structures. This chapter then contests three key assumptions implicit in the United Nations' approach: first, that the disrupted state is a receptive environment for the liberal normative template that underlies the United Nations' state-building strategy; second, that state-based institutions are the key to establishing the rule of law; and third, that external actors are well placed to have a substantial impact on rule of law development. The chapter concludes that UN actors undermined their capacity to support the establishment of the rule of law by failing, from the outset, to develop a nuanced strategy that took these issues in hand.

This book concludes that many of the flaws exposed in the study are inherent to the institutional dynamics of the UN system and its interaction with conflict or post-conflict social and political environments. It suggests that many elements of the United Nations' self-declared state-building agenda are therefore unrealistic, and that the very statement of such a "mission impossible" risks generating expectations amongst both local and international actors that simply cannot be met. Ultimately, this dilutes the potential for UN state-building missions to deliver a more modest set of state-building objectives that might contribute more successfully to the consolidation of peace in disrupted states.

Notes

1. See Chapter 2 for a discussion of this term.
2. In its work on state-building, the International Peace Academy has advanced a similar definition of state-building as "extended international involvement (primarily, though not exclusively, through the United Nations) that goes beyond traditional peace-keeping and peace-building mandates, and is directed at building or re-building the institutions of the state". See International Peace Academy (2003a); see also Chesterman (2003, 2004a).
3. In Korea, for example, the government used modern law imposed by Japanese and US occupiers to expropriate the best farmland and to support a secret police system. The population viewed the laws as alien and continued to use traditional conciliatory mechanisms (Greenberg 1980: 136).
4. The Reagan administration's Justice Improvement Project for the Commonwealth Caribbean in the mid-1980s was a typical example. See Zagaris (1988: 569).
5. For example, see Offe's examination of attempts by East Germany and the Czech Republic to import political and economic institutions. In those cases, the lack of regard given by reformers to the ideas and traditions of the importing society demonstrably undermined the performance of new institutions (Offe 1996: 212). Similarly, Sharlet (1998) demonstrated that US constitutional advisers assisting constitution drafters in the Newly Independent States were ignorant of both historical and prevailing conditions, and as a result much of their advice was disregarded.
6. See, for example, Ignatieff (2002, 2003); Maley, Sampford and Thakur (2003b); Dorff (1999); Fukuyama (2004); Chopra (2000); Cousens and Kumar (2001); and Chesterman, Ignatieff and Thakur (2004, 2005b).
7. For examples of works that examine a single UN administration, see Marshall and Inglis (2003); Babo-Soares (2001); Donovan et al. (1993); Guterres Lopes (2002); ICG (2002); Linton (2001); and Lorenz (2000b). For examples of those that examine a single rule of law issue in one or two transitional administrations, see Clark (2002); Crosby (2000); Dziedzic (2002); Fitzpatrick (2002); Judicial System Monitoring Program (2001, 2003a); Katzenstein (2003); Mobekk (2001); Stahn (2001b); Strohmeyer (2001).
8. The fourth UN transitional administration deployed to date, the United Nations Transitional Authority in Eastern Slavonia, Baranja and Western Sirmium (UNTAES, 1996–1998), was excluded from the study because of its lesser significance with respect to state-building issues generally and the rule of law area in particular. It was a relatively short and small mission, which focused on the peaceful reintegration of existing administrative and economic structures into those of the government of Croatia and the establishment of political institutions to facilitate greater participation in Croatian political life by the region's ethnic Serb citizens. Although the UNTAES mission incorporated some rule of law elements, notably the establishment of a temporary police force that would later be integrated into the Croatian police force, these elements were more lim-

ited than those of the three case studies chosen for this book. Preliminary research indicated that the benefits to be derived from detailed examination of UNTAES rule of law initiatives did not warrant the difficulties of fieldwork and more extensive research.

9. See, for example, Linton (2001); Marshall and Inglis (2003); Chesterman (2002a); Carlson (2006); ICG (2002); and Judicial System Monitoring Program (2003a).

10. See, in particular, the case-study series and other output developed by the International Center for Transitional Justice. These include Hirst and Varney (2005); Reiger and Wierda (2006); and Perriello and Wierda (2006).

11. Now referred to officially as Timor Leste, the term East Timor is used in this book for consistency and to reflect usage during the UNTAET period.

2

Ambitions: The state-building agenda of UN transitional administrations

The exercise of political and administrative authority over a territorial entity by representatives of the "international community" is not a new phenomenon. During much of the twentieth century, such activities were the preserve of the colonial powers. On occasion, however, the international community assumed a collective role, either supervising a state apparatus with the responsibility for governing a territorial entity, or administering a territory directly through an international organisation.

There is an equally long history of outsiders seeking to transform in some way the territories over which they have presided, using acts of governance to transmit norms or principles directed at improving the status quo. As early as 1788, Edmund Burke advanced the concept of a "sacred trust of civilization" and by the late nineteenth century colonial powers began to embrace a "civilising mission" to confer European notions of order and society on their subjects. By the early 1900s, the concept of "trusteeship" was well embedded in colonial discourse, fuelled by a conviction that the more mature members of international society had a responsibility to steer the advancement of the lesser (Schneider 1999: 44).

Early episodes of international administration of states or territories involved joint political control by coalitions of states under post-war settlements. These included the Republic of Cracow (1815–1846), the International Settlement at Shanghai (1863–1943), independent Crete (1889–1913), the international city of Tangier (1923–1956) and the International Control Commission for Albania (1913–1914). They were conceived in order to accommodate and balance the respective interests of the exter-

No entry without strategy: Building the rule of law under UN transitional administration, Bull, United Nations University Press, 2008, ISBN 978-92-808-1151-3

nal powers where this could not be achieved by a sole administering state. The level of political authority assumed by the ruling coalitions varied, as did the extent of the governance activities conducted.[1]

Although small in number, experiments by the League of Nations in administering or supervising the administration of territories played an important role in advancing the concept of international accountability for the external administration of states, in developing conditions for advancing the political, economic and social development of territories, and in spreading western concepts of legitimate statehood.[2] League involvement took the form of either direct administration or, under the Mandates system, supervision of colonial rule. The Saar (1920–1935) was the most substantive example of direct League governance (Walters 1952: 91).[3] To a lesser extent, the League also exercised direct control in the Free City of Danzig (1920–1929) and in Upper Silesia (1922–1923).[4]

More common than direct League administration were arrangements under the League Mandates system, by which the victors at Versailles administered the 15 colonies of the defeated powers under League supervision. Although the Mandates system continued the existing structures of colonialism, it called for progressive political development culminating in some cases with independent statehood (Jones 1994: 84).[5] In exercising their mandatory powers, more advanced nations were to assume the dual responsibilities of filling the administrative vacuum left by the departure of the defeated colonialist from those territories "not yet able to stand by themselves under the strenuous conditions of the modern world",[6] and of engaging in nation-building under a system of tutelage intended in principle to remove the need for permanent foreign administration.

This represented a significant departure from previous thinking, as did the assumption that the governance of these territories was a matter for international concern (Jones 1994: 84). Although the concept of a "sacred trust of civilization" was not new, it had not previously been adopted as a principle by a community of states. Also unprecedented was the establishment of an international body to which powerful states were accountable (Walters 1952: 172–173; Northedge 1986: 193).

The Mandates system embodied a formal statement of what the society of states, as represented by the League, regarded as the minimum requirements for good governance in external administration of a territory. This was the first time that an international organisation possessed the authority to examine the conduct of colonial governments, as well as to institute specific regulations concerning such normative questions as slavery, minority protection and land rights (Callahan 1999: 59). In practice, the ability of the Permanent Mandates Commission to reform existing structures of empire was limited and the completion of mandates varied. The Commission did, however, enjoy some success in advancing what it considered to be progressive standards of administration (Jones 1994: 82–83; Northedge 1986: 193, 220). The upholding of democratic ideals was an important feature of these efforts. Plebiscites, the election of local assemblies and minority protection became consistent themes and formed an important early precedent for later human rights work in the UN system (Hayashi 2001: 2; Callahan 1999: 188; Northedge 1986: 208).

Progress towards independent statehood was inherently political and, in 1932, Iraq became the only mandated territory to achieve independence. The conditions under which Iraq's mandate was terminated demonstrated close parallels with later UN views on the prerequisites for independent statehood. Pursuant to a British government proposal to terminate its mandate in Iraq, in 1931 the Mandates Commission specified five conditions under which the essential machinery of a state would be deemed operative and capable of ensuring political liberty: a settled government and administration capable of maintaining key government services; the capability to maintain territorial integrity and political independence; the ability to maintain the public peace throughout the whole territory; adequate financial resources to provide regularly for normal government requirements; and the existence of laws and a judicial organisation that would afford justice to all. In addition, the Commission recommended that, on independence, the state make a treaty-equivalent declaration guaranteeing the continuation of the human rights protections acquired by the mandatory powers (League of Nations 1931: 2057).

Decolonisation, the UN trusteeship system and non-self-governing territories

The prospect that the United Nations might be called upon to administer a territory in the event of a threat to international peace and security was contemplated in the drafting of the UN Charter, but was not included in the final document (Chesterman 2004a: 56). UN involvement in international administration nonetheless developed through the trusteeship system, the direct administration of territories and the development of peacekeeping operations. This reflected a clear progression from League thinking, with some differences: self-determination became an inalienable right after 1960 and peacekeeping emerged as a new mode of intervention.

Cold War era proposals for the collective administration of territories under UN auspices were consistently vetoed by the superpowers or other hegemonic interests in the territories concerned.[7] The first case of direct

UN executive authority for administration of a territory, and the only example prior to Cambodia, was the United Nations Temporary Executive Authority (UNTEA), which administered West New Guinea for seven months in 1962–1963 under an agreement between Indonesia and the Netherlands. The bulk of UNTEA's work involved facilitating the transfer of sovereignty to Indonesia. A 100-strong UN civilian presence furnished senior administrators, established a court system, consulted with local assemblies and implemented public works projects. The United Nations held executive as well as limited legislative powers, and had primary responsibility for policing and the election of regional representative bodies. In practice, however, UNTEA demonstrated little political will to assist with an act of self-determination or to advance broader notions of governance (Saltford 2000: 379–380).

In addition to UN involvement in decolonisation plebiscites (see Ratner 1995: 113), the decolonisation period saw 11 territories[8] placed under a UN Trusteeship system, all of which subsequently became independent or voluntarily associated themselves with a state. Like the League Mandates system, the UN Trusteeship system professed under Chapter XII of the Charter to promote the political, economic and social advancement of trust territories and to support international peace and security. Under Article 76, the United Nations made an explicit commitment to the progressive development of all trust territories towards self-government and self-determination, and to encourage respect for human rights and fundamental freedoms.

Although it was envisaged that trust territories could be administered collectively or directly by the United Nations, in practice the system operated much like the League mandates, with individual states acting as administering bodies and supervised by the United Nations (Wilde 2001a: 604).[9] In supervising the administration of trust territories, the Trusteeship Council helped to raise standards of administration and to facilitate a relatively orderly process of transition to independence. Like the Mandates Commission, however, the Trusteeship Council was dominated by great power interests and had no legal powers of coercion. Occupying powers typically resisted supervision, demonstrating dubious support for genuine self-rule (Chopra 1997: 10). In practice, although the UN Trusteeship system guaranteed eventual self-determination for the territories it covered, this did not translate into robust preparations for independent self-government.[10]

Like trust territories, those states charged with administering the 80 or so non-self-governing territories were required under Chapter XI of the Charter to accept as a "sacred trust" the promotion of political and economic development and the progressive development of free political institutions of self-government. Chapter XI made no provision for the

United Nations to play an explicit supervisory role over those territories, but the United Nations nonetheless progressively assumed a greater level of interest in and supervisory role over these territories. Following East Timor's independence in 2002, 16 non-self-governing territories remained in existence.

Early peacekeeping operations

The end of the British mandate in Palestine saw the creation in June 1948 of the first UN peacekeeping operation – the United Nations Truce Supervision Organisation (UNTSO) – established to supervise the truce between Arab and Jewish parties. UNTSO later monitored ceasefires, supervised armistice agreements and assisted other UN peacekeeping operations in the region. This was followed in 1956–1957 by the first fully fledged peacekeeping operation, the First United Nations Emergency Force (UNEF-I), established to act as a buffer between Egyptian and Israeli forces. The legal and political basis of UNEF-I – consent of the parties, UN neutrality and the temporary duration of missions – became the tenets of subsequent "first-generation" peacekeeping operations established through to the late 1980s (Ratner 1995: 25). These were principally military operations, although most included some ancillary functions such as humanitarian assistance. A number of missions, including those in the Middle East and Cyprus, had political and diplomatic functions, although only in Cyprus (1964) was the United Nations involved directly in the peacemaking process.

The first truly multidimensional peacekeeping operation was the United Nations Operation in the Congo (ONUC, 1960–1964). ONUC performed some governance functions, helping to establish a functioning civilian administration, providing technical and other assistance to the administration and engaging in de facto policy-making (Thornberry 1995: 4). ONUC also established a Monetary Council and drafted a new constitution.

Cold War rivalries saw UN peace operations plateau during the 1970s and 1980s. By the late 1980s, however, the United Nations began to explore peacebuilding initiatives in situations where proxy conflicts displayed some prospect of resolution. The end of the Cold War broke the deadlock in the Security Council, giving the United Nations increased scope to act as an agent of the community of states; this, and the growing interdependence of a greater number of state and non-state actors, encouraged joint responses to international security threats. The United Nations was the only organisation approximating universality in approving or disapproving of state behaviour, and the sole universally accepted sanctioning body for intervention (Barnett 1995: 10), which greatly increased both the opportunities for and expectations of UN action (ICISS 2001). This environment created a critical turning point in UN involvement in state-building, with the deployment of so-called complex peace operations, beginning with Namibia in 1989.

Complex peace operations: The rise of a modern state-building agenda

The United Nations Transition Assistance Group in Namibia (UNTAG, April 1989–March 1990) was the first mission since UNTEA with a primarily non-military mandate, the first multidimensional peacekeeping mission since the Congo and the first mission actively to promote political change (NDI 1990: 4). Although Namibia continued to be governed by South Africa, UNTAG supervised and controlled the transition to independence and, as a result of its efforts to promote political reconciliation, significantly penetrated the political landscape. Its operational complexity eclipsed previous missions. In addition to its military mandate to supervise the ceasefire and the cantonment of South African forces, UNTAG assisted the Constituent Assembly to draft the constitution, oversaw refugee repatriation and conducted law and order duties. It negotiated with the South African government to revise its electoral law to meet basic standards of fairness, to issue an amnesty and to repeal discriminatory and restrictive laws (Ratner 1995: 120). UNTAG also oversaw the electoral process conducted by South Africa.

UNTAG's success in delivering political stability to independent Namibia was hailed as a peacekeeping triumph. This success was owing in large measure to meticulous long-term planning, which began more than 10 years before UNTAG was deployed. Ironically, a delay of more than 20 years caused by South Africa's refusal to permit UN entry into Namibia gave the United Nations significant lead time in which to organise the mission, train its officers, draft constitutional provisions for the new government and oversee extensive negotiations between South Africa and the South West Africa People's Organization (Ratner 1995: 118–19). UN efforts to promote dialogue between the parties also helped foster mutual understanding between the key players, including the reconciliation of all parties in Namibia to independence. The settlement plan encouraged participatory decision-making on the question of who would govern the country and was strongly underpinned by the interests of the major players, including South Africa. The UN Security Council endorsed the process fully. UNTAG had a strong mandate on the ground and a high degree of legitimacy with the populace (NDI 1990: 4–5).

The UNTAG experience buoyed optimism regarding the scope for further such missions and the usefulness of elections in resolving longstanding political conflict (NDI 1990: 83). Many of the 40 or so peacekeeping operations authorised during the 1990s embraced complex mandates that included functions as diverse as disarmament, military training, the creation of new police forces, human rights training, emergency relief, the conduct or monitoring of elections, constitution drafting, legislative reform and refugee repatriation.[11]

These early forays into complex peacekeeping reflected a newly sophisticated approach to questions such as how to bridge the operational gap between emergency relief and long-term development assistance, as well as how to leverage the short-term presence of peacekeepers into long-term peace (Cousens 2001: 2). They also reflected important trends in post–Cold War international relations, notably a redefining of international security norms and the deepening of an international normative consensus on democracy as the only legitimate political model. Together, these generated a paradigmatic shift in intervention doctrine that elevated state-building to the centre of international responses to intrastate conflict.

The collapse of the Soviet Union and the proliferation of intrastate conflict and "failed states" during the post–Cold War period altered perceptions about international peace and security. Intrastate conflict became a core international security concern, as reflected in the UN Secretary-General's 1992 *Agenda for Peace*, which formally linked the two. This relationship became entwined with debate on the responsibility of the society of states for "humanitarian intervention". An accumulating body of law and practice during the 1990s supported the notion that intervention by international actors to protect populations threatened by internal conflicts, state repression or collapse was potentially warranted in situations where the state could not fulfil its sovereign responsibility to do this. Accordingly, traditional concepts of state sovereignty were broadened to include the "responsibility to protect" the basic rights of the people within the state, and correspondingly for the international community to hold states accountable for their failure to do so (ICISS 2001; UNGA 2004: 66).

This redefining of security norms legitimised coercive multilateral intervention in intrastate conflict under Chapter VII of the Charter (Dunne and Wheeler 1999a: 23; Yannis 2002: 825–826), to the point where Chapter VII mandates became the standard for peace operations (UNGA 2004: 68). More generally, it broadened the interpretation of Article 2(7) of the Charter to allow for UN involvement in matters that had previously been confined to domestic jurisdiction. Although most UN interventions continued to take place either with the consent of the authorities of the state concerned or in situations where no functioning government existed (Dunne and Wheeler 1999a: 23), this created the space for the Security Council to consider and approve the intrusive types of peacekeeping seen in complex peace operations.

At the same time, the notion of democracy as the only legitimate system of governance became sufficiently entrenched in international normative discourse that its promotion by the United Nations became not only possible but, arguably, imperative. UN actors stressed that democratisation was "central to a state-building and peace-building exercise if peace is to become sustainable and post-conflict reconstruction and development is to succeed" (UNSC 2000e: 7).[12] They became increasingly active in promoting democratic processes and institutions, including in peace operations.

Similarly, with the ascendancy of human rights in the post–Cold War institutional order[13] human rights promotion activities also became integral to peace operations (Burgerman 2000: 1). This represented a radical departure from earlier peace operations, which, despite a post-war human rights regime that clearly sanctioned human rights as a universal value and saw significant advances in human rights, had remained preoccupied with issues of sovereignty and avoided a human rights agenda (Barnett 1995: 9; Donnelly 1999: 89).

A further, related, influence was the rise of the "good governance" agenda in the development debate of the 1990s (UNDP 1997). As development cooperation gradually expanded from economic and social development to a broader focus on human development and "good governance" assistance (International Institute for Democracy and Electoral Assistance 2000: 1), so too did peace operations.[14]

UN missions thus began to incorporate progressively more extensive state-building functions, most notably in the four transitional administrations in Cambodia, Eastern Slavonia, Kosovo and East Timor. In the first mission of its kind since UNTEA, the United Nations Transitional Authority in Cambodia (UNTAC) was mandated under the 1991 Paris Peace Agreements and Security Council Resolution 745 of February 1992 to stabilise the security situation in Cambodia and to supervise the demobilisation of the forces of the four Cambodian factions; to organise and conduct elections for a constituent assembly; to maintain law and order; to oversee the repatriation of refugees; to coordinate economic reconstruction; and to assume control of those parts of the bureaucracy with the potential to influence the outcome of the elections. Elections were held in May 1993, creating what was hailed as Cambodia's first democratic government since the 1960s (United Nations 1995a: 38). UNTAC's mandate ended with the creation of a new Cambodian government on 24 September 1993.

Other missions assumed state-building responsibilities more by default than by design, registering modest success in some cases and spectacular setbacks in others. The United Nations Operation in Somalia II (1993–1995) assumed de facto responsibility for governing, but without the mandate, resources or political will to fill that role. Its disastrous withdrawal greatly depleted the optimism generated by UNTAG, as did the United Nations' failure to act on Rwanda. In other cases, state-building intentions were thwarted by local political resistance. In 1991, the United Nations Mission for the Referendum in Western Sahara was authorised to exercise all necessary administrative powers to administer Western Sahara in preparation for a referendum on independence from Morocco, but, at the time of writing, the failure of the parties to agree on key issues had prevented any progress.

In other instances, missions adopted progressively more intrusive state-building functions in response to setbacks and changed circumstances. The United Nations Assistance Mission in Sierra Leone (1999–2005), for example, initially undertook only basic law and order and governance functions. With the collapse of the Lomé Agreement in 2000, however, it assumed further responsibilities and ultimately assisted with elections in 2002, conducted human rights activities, helped establish the Sierra Leone Truth and Reconciliation Commission, recruited and trained over 3,500 police, rehabilitated the police and court infrastructure, helped stem the illegal diamond trade, disarmed ex-combatants and assisted with the voluntary return of over half a million refugees and internally displaced persons. In Haiti, the failure of multiple UN missions since 1993 eventually saw the deployment over a decade later of the United Nations Stabilization Mission in Haiti, with a Chapter VII mandate and an extensive state-building agenda that included good offices support for constitutional and political processes, strengthening the capacity of national and local authorities and institutions, reforming the Haitian National Police, monitoring judicial and prison reform and disarmament and demobilisation activities.

The Balkans generated perhaps the most extensive examples of UN state-building activity during the 1990s. In Bosnia and Herzegovina, the 1995 Dayton Peace Agreement spelt out the international community's goal of building institutions that would allow all citizens in Bosnia to live in peace and without discrimination, and divided civilian authority between a number of organisations. Although the United Nations Mission in Bosnia and Herzegovina (UNMIBH, 1995–2002) did not exercise final authority in the territory,[15] it undertook a wide range of rule of law initiatives, including reforming and restructuring the local police, and monitoring the existing judicial system, the police and others in the law and order arena. It also coordinated UN efforts on humanitarian relief, demining, elections, economic rehabilitation and restructuring.

Two of the four post–Cold War transitional administrations were also established in the Balkans. The United Nations Transitional Authority in Eastern Slavonia, Baranja and Western Sirmium (UNTAES, 1996–1998) was established in January 1996 under Security Council Resolution 1037, in accordance with a political settlement between the government of Croatia and the local Serb authorities, which had assumed control of Eastern Slavonia upon Croatia's declaration of independence from Yugoslavia. UNTAES was mandated to govern Eastern Slavonia with the purpose of reintegrating it peacefully into the Republic of Croatia. Its mandate covered peace and security; demilitarisation and repatriation; the establishment of a police force; civil administration and public services, including the negotiation of agreements with the Croatian government on law, education and social welfare; the conduct of elections; reconstruction; and human rights monitoring. UNTAES conducted elections in April 1997, giving the local population its first legitimate representation in the Croatian government since the beginning of the conflict. UNTAES gradually devolved executive responsibility for civil administration in the region, ending its mandate on 15 January 1998.[16]

In June 1999, the United Nations Interim Administration Mission in Kosovo (UNMIK) was mandated under Security Council Resolution 1244 to administer Kosovo as an autonomous region under the Federal Republic of Yugoslavia until a political settlement could be reached on Kosovo's future status. UNMIK was mandated to perform civil administration functions and to establish "multi-ethnic" government structures; to facilitate the political process to determine Kosovo's future status; to undertake reconstruction; to maintain security and law and order, including by developing a local police force; to undertake democratisation and institution-building; through elections to develop provisional institutions for democratic and autonomous self-government; and to build genuine rule of law and an independent, multi-ethnic judiciary. UNMIK assumed full legislative, executive and judicial powers, although key state-building responsibilities were devolved to the United Nations High Commissioner for Refugees, the Organization for Security and Co-operation in Europe and the European Union.

The 1990s closed with the establishment of the United Nations Transitional Administration in East Timor (UNTAET) in October 1999, which under Resolution 1272 undertook the most comprehensive mandate of any UN peace operation to date. UNTAET was required to provide security; to establish an effective administration; to assist in the development of civil and social services; to coordinate development assistance; to build capacity for self-government; and to conduct elections to form an East Timorese government. East Timor was declared independent on 20 May 2002 and UNTAET was replaced with a successor mission, the United Nations Mission of Support in East Timor (UNMISET), to provide three years of phased down support to the new East Timorese government. UNMISET completed its mandate on 20 May 2005 and was succeeded by a follow-on mission, the United Nations Office in Timor-Leste (UNOTIL), comprising a small band of civilian, police and human rights advisers. A deterioration in the security situation in early 2006 led to the subsequent expansion of the UN presence with the establishment of the United Nations Integrated Mission in Timor-Leste (UNMIT), which remained in theatre at the time of writing.

Into the twenty-first century

The strategic and political environment in which recent UN and other external interventions have occurred, notably by Coalition forces in Iraq, consolidated state-building as an ongoing feature of the intervention agenda. The attacks of 11 September 2001 further transformed the international security agenda, highlighting the extent to which state failure could facilitate the emergence of non-state actors that threatened international peace and security, and alerting states to the notion that such situations could involve greater national interest than previously recognised (Chesterman 2004a: 97). By the early twenty-first century, these security interests combined with ongoing debate on multilateral humanitarian responsibilities to produce an international normative consensus on the responsibility to *rebuild* after a military intervention (UNGA 2004: 66), and state-building became integral to the intervention agenda.

In such terrain, the maintenance of the existing system of sovereign states remained central to UN concepts of international peace and security. Effectively functioning institutions of state continued to be seen as the best guarantor of stability, human rights protection and democracy (ICISS 2001), as well as the key to countering non-state threats such as terrorism. This was highlighted by the Secretary-General's High-level Panel on Threats, Challenges and Change, whose vision of collective security for the twenty-first century noted that the "erosion of state capacity anywhere in the world weakens the protection of every state against transnational threats such as terrorism and organised crime" (United Nations 2004: 1). In contrast to post-modern theories pointing to the decline of the Westphalian state,[17] in UN discourse the role of the state as the ultimate guardian of public order and stability remained unquestioned, because the state is the only force perceived capable of providing the structures of authority necessary to cope with the claims of competing societal groups and to ensure sustainable development (Milliken and Krause 2002: 762; Yannis 2002: 820–822). The UN system, including its peace operations, became increasingly focused on the threat posed by weak state institutions and the loss of state monopoly over the use of force (ICISS 2001).

Accordingly, all significant UN missions in the twenty-first century, including those in Afghanistan, Liberia, Côte d'Ivoire, Burundi, Haiti and the Sudan, incorporated extensive state-building components.[18] Missions undertook wide-ranging state-building activities, assisting with institutional and administrative reform, elections, constitution drafting, policing and law and order. The extent and intrusiveness of such missions varied widely. No new transitional administrations were authorised and in the majority of cases the United Nations assumed an advisory or "good offices" role to assist locally constituted interim administrations, either pre-existing or as part of a peace settlement.

By the time of the interventions in Afghanistan and Iraq, state-building had become an indispensable objective of most peace operations, albeit one that took a variety of forms. In particular, Afghanistan represented a major departure from the intrusive mandates of Bosnia, Kosovo and East Timor, challenging what had appeared to be a trend towards increased concentration of political authority in UN hands. After much initial discussion about the appropriate UN role in post-conflict Afghanistan, the Bonn agreement of 2001 gave the United Nations Assistance Mission in Afghanistan (UNAMA) substantially fewer formal political functions than other contemporary missions. The Special Representative of the Secretary-General, Lakhdar Brahimi, took a "light footprint" approach, which relied on as limited an international presence as possible in order to promote Afghan capacity and to allow space for Afghan leaders to participate fully in the political process. In practice, however, UNAMA remained closely involved with the Afghan Transitional Authority and the peace process, providing far more governance and development support than had earlier assistance missions (Chesterman 2004a: 89–91).

Iraq presented yet another variation of the intervention model, albeit one in which the United Nations played a minor role. As Chesterman (2004a: 97) observes, the Iraq scenario was unique in that available resources far exceeded any comparable situation since the end of the Second World War. Moreover, state institutions were neither divided (in they way that they were in Bosnia or Cambodia), nor failed (as in Namibia or East Timor). Whereas Resolution 1483 (2003) recognised the "Coalition Provisional Authority" as the occupying power, the responsibilities of the United Nations were intentionally ambiguous. The Special Representative of the Secretary-General was accorded vague powers included "coordinating", "reporting", "facilitating" and "encouraging". He was mandated to work with the Authority, the Iraqi people and others to "advance efforts to restore and establish national and local institutions for representative governance". Although the exact role of the United Nations was vague, the objective of state institution-building was very clear.

As the above overview demonstrates, complex peace operations as a class of intervention did not emerge in logical, linear progression. Instead, they have reflected an eclectic array of mandates and experiences that, over time and in spite of their often chaotic nature, displayed a greater state-building focus. From an operational perspective, the scope and intrusiveness of UN transitional administrations were as great as or greater than any other form of peace operation in the post–Cold War era. They involved greater penetration of the political landscape, larger numbers of UN and other international agencies on the ground engaged in a broader range of activities (Caplan 2002: 17), more complex organisational structures and larger contingents of civilian staff. The next section considers the state-building agenda of UN transitional administrations in further detail.

The state-building agenda of UN transitional administrations

Transitional administrations have not occupied a unique structural home within the UN system: there was no specific provision for them in the UN Charter and no dedicated bureaucracy to support them (Caplan 2002: 13). As described above, their objectives, mandates and operational functions overlapped considerably with contemporary complex peace operations and with earlier examples of international administration. However, transitional administrations may be distinguished in the spectrum of UN peace operations by two key characteristics: the direct, mandated exercise of political authority by the United Nations; and the adoption of an intrusive state-building agenda as a primary rather than an auxiliary objective.

The exercise of direct political authority

The exercise by UN transitional administrations of direct political authority in a territory involved the explicit, mandated assumption by the United Nations of some or all of that territory's powers of government, making it a fundamentally political (as opposed to military or administrative) enterprise (Caplan 2002: 10). In an operational sense, political authority was vested in a Special Representative of the Secretary-General acting as "Transitional Administrator" responsible for managing interim administrative structures to conduct the core functions of government (Caplan 2002: 38).

The sovereignty implications of this assumption of political authority have been the subject of ongoing debate.[19] This has revolved around whether the United Nations temporarily assumed or suspended partial or full sovereignty over the state or territory for the life of the transitional administration (Annan 1998: 59, Caplan 2002: 77; ICISS 2001), or whether it simply claimed the right to administer the territory and act as the agent of the legal person of that state, non-state or sub-state territorial entity (Wilde 2001b: 251–253). Either way, the assumption of governing power by the United Nations arguably challenged traditional sovereignty concepts in which only the state made authoritative decisions with regard to the people and resources within it.[20]

Critical to the establishment of all four transitional administrations was a consensus on the part of the international community that direct UN administration of the territory was necessary in the absence of other willing, capable and accepted authorities – national or international. This contrasted with other situations, such as Somalia, Western Sahara and the Democratic Republic of Congo, where the political will to establish a transitional administration-like operation did not exist (Chesterman 2003: 2).

The extent of the political authority exercised by the United Nations under transitional administration ranged from plenary executive, legislative and judicial authority (East Timor, Kosovo and Eastern Slavonia) to the more supervisory quality of the mandate in Cambodia. The nature of the governance tasks undertaken by transitional administrations varied accordingly. At one extreme, UNTAET was vested under Resolution 1272 with "overall responsibility for the administration of East Timor" and "all legislative and executive authority, including the administration of justice" (UNSC 1999h). At the other end of the spectrum, in Cambodia the Supreme National Council (SNC) was recognised under the 1991 Paris Peace Agreements as the sole legitimate governing body and source of authority. UNTAC was delegated only those powers necessary for it to fulfil its mandate. Although the SNC continued to conduct many government functions, UNTAC had direct authority over the organisation and conduct of free elections, including the establishment of laws and administrative procedures; over all administrative agencies that could influence the outcome of the elections (foreign affairs, defence, finance, public security and information); over the police force; over relevant law enforcement and judicial processes in consultation with the SNC; and over military operations.

There have been several useful attempts to categorise the nature of the political authority exercised by UN peace operations. Ratner (1995: 45) describes three types of authority: peace operations that executed aspects of the settlement itself (such as conducting an election); those that administered aspects of the governance of a state subject to the settlement (police work, running a civilian administration); and those that executed tasks outside the settlement proper (such as humanitarian relief). In practice, all three categories involved not just logistical and bureaucratic dimensions, but extensive political effort by UN officials to galvanize and implement the peace settlement (Ratner 1995: 44). Chopra's analysis offers a similar breakdown: *governorship*, where the United Nations assumes direct authority; *control*, where UN personnel are deployed in existing state structures to exercise direct control; *partnership*, where the United Nations acts as a partner in state administration; and *assistance*, where the state administration still functions autonomously but the United Nations assists it to do so (Chopra 1999: 13–14).[21] Similarly, Doyle (2001a) distinguishes four different types of authority: supervisory (such as in East Timor and Kosovo); executive (such as in Eastern Slavonia); administrative (Cambodia); and monitoring.

Building on these analyses, Chesterman (2004a) emphasises the importance of considering not only the amount of power exercised but the purpose and trajectory of that authority. He proposes five different categories of transitional administration based on local political context: a final act of decolonisation (East Timor); the temporary administration of a territory pending a peaceful transfer of control to an existing government (Eastern Slavonia); the temporary administration of a state pending the conduct of elections (Cambodia); interim administration as part of an ongoing peace process without an end state (Kosovo); and de facto administration or responsibility for basic law and order in the absence of a governing authority (Chesterman 2004a: 56–57). This characterisation underscores the very different political context in which each UN transitional administration operated and cautions against assuming too much similarity between them.

As Chesterman (2004a: 127) and others have emphasised, this assertion of direct political authority by the United Nations raised fundamental dilemmas about how to exercise this authority in trust for the recipient population, about consultation and accountability during the transition period, and about when and how to transfer political authority to local actors.

State-building as a primary objective

The adoption of an intrusive state-building agenda as a primary objective distinguishes transitional administrations from complex peace operations with a primarily military focus,[22] where state-building, if pursued at all, was an "auxiliary" objective. As described above, the distinction between UN transitional administrations and other complex peace operations with a strong state-building focus was less obvious. Nonetheless, the state-building mandate of transitional administrations was arguably more extensive, more explicit and, by virtue of the political authority exercised by the mission, more direct.

The mandate extended to transitional administrations to transfer governing authority from UN to local authorities during or on completion of the mission required UN agents to play a direct role in creating state institutions where these were absent or deficient. There was no coherent, unified vision or operational blueprint for state-building in transitional administrations or other peace operations, but an examination of the mandates of these missions nonetheless reveals a remarkably consistent articulation of values associated with western liberal democracy as the basis of the state-building agenda.

The state-building agenda of the four transitional administrations had in common four principal elements associated with transforming disrupted states into strong liberal ones: security, humanitarian relief, governance, and economic reconstruction. The security objective involved the establishment and maintenance of external and internal security, including the disarmament and demobilization of local security forces, the rebuilding of armies and police forces, and de-mining. The humanitarian objective encompassed emergency aid and the resettlement of refugees and displaced persons. The governance objective involved three main functions: administration of the territory and provision of essential government services by the United Nations during the transition period; oversight of the political transition; and the creation or strengthening of institutions of governance for the post-transition period. Central to the governance objective was the establishment of constitutional independence (or autonomy) through the creation of a single "legitimate" governing authority. In all cases this occurred through the holding of "free and fair elections" for a constituent assembly, which drafted a new constitution or quasi-constitution and transmuted into a legislative assembly to form the new government.[23] The economic reconstruction objective involved the rebuilding of essential physical infrastructure, the development of markets and economic and financial institutions, and the promotion of sustainable economic growth.

The scope of state-building activities undertaken by transitional administrations was thus enormous. Equally so were the transformative aspirations of the normative agenda that drove these activities. In overseeing a process of political transition, transitional administrations purported to create the conditions for legitimate statehood based on western liberal democratic principles and a free market economy. This normative agenda was driven by the United Nations' assessment that the western capitalist democratic model was the prevailing and only legitimate political system (Chopra 1997: 1) and by the "democratic peace" premise that democracies would support the overarching goal of international peace and security. What was acceptable or achievable on the ground appears to have been of far less significance (Chopra 1997: 2).

Although many, if not most, actors in the UN system might arguably have settled for the less ambitious goal of stabilisation, transitional administrations, alongside other recent peace operations, therefore advocated at least rhetorically the creation of a democratic, viable and stable entity as a central goal.[24] In a statement marking East Timor's independence on 20 May 2002, for example, the President of the Security Council applauded the role of the United Nations in "restoring peace to East Timor, and in building a solid foundation for a democratic, viable and stable East Timor" (UNSC 2002a). Similarly, UNMIK described its function as the "development of a viable system of democratic governance" (UNMIK 2001a).

UN benchmarking exercises to determine the minimum criteria for independence/autonomy in East Timor and Kosovo produced a similar set of prerequisites. For East Timor, the benchmarks for independence were identified as: security; a credible system of justice; a reasonable level of reconstruction of public services and infrastructure; a financially sustainable administration; and the completion of the political transition to independence, culminating in the adoption of a constitution and democratic elections (UNSC 2000i: 10). For Kosovo, the key benchmarks were identified as: representative and functioning institutions; the rule of law; freedom of movement; respect for the rights of all Kosovans to remain and return; a sound basis for a market economy; clarity of property title; normalised dialogue with Belgrade; and a reduction and transformation of the Kosovo Protection Corps (UNMIK 2002b: 3).

These objectives dovetail closely with standard definitions of the liberal state: a set of administrative mechanisms under centralised leadership within internationally recognised territorial boundaries; the authority to make, implement and enforce binding rules for the people in that territory; and a monopoly over the use of force within it.[25] Under this definition, a strong state is measured by its capacity to command the right to rule; to extract, appropriate and utilise resources to sustain itself and to maximise the economic wellbeing of its society; and to ensure security through the prevention or deterrence of intra-group conflict as well as external threats (Reus-Smit 1998: 5–6; Migdal 1998b: 4; Stohl 1998: 3–5). Further, the state is "just", insofar as it subscribes to the rule of law, free from despotic or arbitrary government (Rengger 1997: 60).

Following from this definition is the subject of the UN intervention: the "disrupted", "weak", "fragile", "failed" or "collapsed" state. Analyses of what this means precisely differ according to varying conceptions of the state,[26] as well as the extent to which state functions have deteriorated. However, most definitions of state *collapse* highlight the absence of centralised governmental authority,[27] whereas definitions of state *failure* concentrate on the inability of the state to perform core functions such as security, representation and welfare, usually as a result of weak state institutions.[28]

Maley, Sampford and Thakur (2003a: 3) adopt the more nuanced term "disrupted", which recognises a spectrum of situations in which the normal functioning of states may be impeded.[29] Similarly, Saikal (2003: 19) notes that disrupted states need not be suffering from complete "failure" or "collapse", but rather are characterised by varying degrees of incapacity, some of which may leave significant remnants of the state intact.

Although the nature of the disrupted state and the reasons for that disruption vary, a set of common characteristics may often be observed. The state, as a decision-making, executing and enforcing institution, cannot or will not make or implement competent decisions, subordinate individual social inclinations in favour of state-prescribed behaviour (Migdal 1998b: 31), sustain itself as a member of the international community or safeguard its citizens from threats to their security (Jackson 1999a: 3; Reus-Smit 1998: 5–6; Stohl 1998: 3–5). Its political institutions have collapsed or are dysfunctional (Dorff 1999: 3), its criminal justice institutions are weak (Boraine 2005: 318) and civil society is fragmented. State coercion, ideological conflict, personalised politics and denial of basic human rights may be prevalent (Stohl 1998: 6–7; Saikal 2003: 19). In extreme cases, complex emergencies may erupt, marked by public health catastrophes, large-scale people displacement and the threat of extinction to cultures or to ethnic or religious groups (Burkle 2003: 96).

Within these ideas of the state and state disruption, the key objectives of the United Nations' state-building agenda as reflected in the mandates and actions of UN transitional administrations may be thought of as follows:

1. *The creation of a stable security environment.* "Peace and security" were equated with the prevention and deterrence of internal and external threats to territorial and physical security, through measures that accorded with international human rights standards. In essence, this meant the existence of defence and police forces that both kept the peace and upheld democratic behavioural standards. Transitional administrations adopted a two-phase approach to security: provision of security by a peacekeeping force and/or UN civilian police, followed by the creation or reform of local institutions that would undertake this role after the transition.

2. *The establishment of the foundations of a liberal democratic political system.* Although UN rhetoric emphasised the existence of many different types of democracy,[30] the state-building agenda of transitional

administrations appears to have reflected the classic criteria for liberal representative democracy. This centred on the contestation of and popular participation in the selection of all positions of government power, plus a level of civil and political liberties sufficient to ensure the integrity of political competition and participation and to safe-guard against excessive government control and power.[31]

The hallmark of democratisation efforts in transitional administrations was the adoption of constitutions; the election of parliaments, other representative bodies and key office bearers; and the establishment of support agencies such as parliamentary secretariats. Transitional administrators, particularly in the later two missions, did however recognise that democratic consolidation required more than holding elections. UNMIK, for example, cited its most difficult challenge – and "the very medium of democracy" – as the building of trust between the people, their representatives and the civil service, as well as with neighbouring governments and between Kosovo's communities (UNMIK 2001a).

3. *The establishment of the rule of law.* As discussed in the next chapter, the United Nations adopted rights-based notions of the rule of law under which the term was equated with the notions of good governance, democracy and human rights (Bouloukos and Dakin 2001: 149) and with the legal order existing in modern liberal democratic states (Brownlie 1998: 212; Carothers 1998: 96). Transitional administrations pursued this goal primarily through the establishment of law enforcement and judicial systems, court and prison systems, police services and reconciliation, as well as support mechanisms such as judicial training institutes.

4. *Human rights protection.* The UN agenda increasingly conceptualised human rights as social and economic as well as political. UN transitional administrations formulated objectives to end human rights violations, impunity and discrimination, and to provide basic rights such as housing, social welfare, property ownership and a standard of living adequate for health and well-being. On the ground, transitional administrations tended to follow a pattern of monitoring human rights abuses, guaranteeing rights in the constitution and legislation, releasing political prisoners, establishing administrative bodies such as an ombudsman, and conducting human rights training.

5. *The establishment of a functioning and transparent public administration.* This objective was informed by the principle that bureaucracies should be professional, non-discriminatory and depoliticised, as well as financially viable. The focus in practical terms was on building administrative machinery – such as civil service departments – and recruitment, training and capacity-building to make these public administrations "professional and effective" (UNSC 2002b: 2).

6. *Ensuring the capacity of government to appropriate and utilise resources sustainably and transparently.* In attempting to establish sound fiscal management practices, mature public expenditure systems and sustainable budgets, transitional administrations made efforts to establish centralised fiscal, banking and payments authorities, to set and supervise budgets, and to build capacity through recruitment and training.

7. *The creation of a sustainable, market-based economy.* The economic objectives of transitional administrations were strongly informed by the principles of economic liberalism, under which they sought to ensure employment and economic growth, regional integration and a regulatory environment that conformed to regional and global standards. To varying extents, transitional administrations adopted measures to establish fiscal and regulatory institutions, to stabilise the currency, to stimulate the development of the private sector and to establish liberal banking, trade and customs regimes.

8. *The stabilisation of external relations.* The United Nations' objective in this respect was the creation of stable borders and interstate relationships within a statist international system. This became a matter of some preoccupation for transitional administrators, given the centrality of inter- or intrastate conflict to the intervention. These issues were mainly addressed through regulatory measures (such as border demarcation), diplomatic activity and the application of pressure on local actors to engage productively with their neighbours.

It is beyond the scope of this book to comment extensively on this state-building agenda, or on the United Nations' success in pursuing it through transitional administration. However, several observations may be usefully be made here.

First, although an examination of the United Nations' state-building activities in transitional administration reveals an identifiable goal of creating liberal democratic states and a broad set of benchmarks through which this was to be achieved, the United Nations' approach was conceptually and methodologically ambiguous. There did not exist in the UN system a coherent, unified state-building policy or framework, or A codified set of standards establishing concrete benchmarks for independent statehood or self-government. Much like the League of Nations with Iraq, such benchmarks tended to be formulated on an ad hoc basis, well into each individual mission. Senior UN officials admitted that the nature of the state-building agenda became clear only as the mission itself unfolded. Indeed, in response to accusations of "blueprinting" and contextual insensitivity, they were quick to deny the existence of any state-building "model", stressing that the fundamental differences between each mission necessitated nuanced responses (S. Vieira de Mello, personal communication, 21 November 2001). In each of the four transitional administrations, as well as in other operations with significant state-building components, state-building was thus a fluid activity whose agenda shifted alongside events on the ground.

Second, the United Nations' strategic thinking about state-building recognised the state as, first and foremost, a set of institutional components and the institutions of state as the primary means by which important functions, such as security, could be provided to the population. The primary goal of state-building was thus to reform or rebuild those institutions, placing the UN approach amongst state-building strategies that privilege a top-down approach of strengthening the central institutions of state, as distinct from "bottom-up" strategies aimed at assisting the development of democratic civic rule by fostering a functioning civil society (Von Einsiedel 2005: 25–26).

Third, the state-building agenda outlined above represented a highly ambitious undertaking. The disrupted states in which UN transitional administrations were deployed thus represent an extreme and, in many ways, hostile intervention environment characterised by high levels of state incompetence, social trauma and violence. Seeking to move disrupted states emerging from, or even remaining in, conflict towards peaceful democratic statehood required no less than massive transformation in social attitudes towards conflict management, as well as towards the role of the state in providing basic social goods. Moreover, the expectation appeared to be that the United Nations would be able at least to lay the foundations for this liberal normative template in a relatively short period of time. As Ottaway (2002: 1004) points out, the externally led state-building model as adopted by the United Nations in effect amounted to an attempt to produce a "short-cut to the Weberian state, an attempt to develop such an entity quickly and without the long, conflictual and often brutal evolution that historically underlies the formation of states".

In order to highlight the high degree of difficulty of the task thus set for UN transitional administration, several aspects of state disruption are worth further consideration here. First, the issue of low state capacity poses particular challenges. Low state capacity may be thought of in terms of the state's inability to extract, appropriate and use the resources necessary to sustain the state and to maximise the well-being of society (Reus-Smit 1998: 5–6; Migdal 1998a: 4; Stohl 1998: 3–5). This may depend in large part on the effectiveness of state institutions in making policy and administering resources, providing stable government, and using fair and transparent methods of control rather than those, such as corruption, that directly undermine the rule of law.

Low state capacity may also be thought of in terms of low levels of social control, such that the state is unable to establish an effective relationship with the society it governs and hence cannot effectively regulate social relationships or command the right to rule (Sorensen 1998). This may have resulted from a cataclysmic event (such as war), from the structure of society[32] or from lack of trust in the state stemming from oppression or abuse. In such situations, the state lacks legitimacy, where this depends on a mutually constitutive relationship between state and society in which society accepts and complies with the rules of the state and the state responds and adapts to societal demands (Migdal 1998b: 23–33; Dauvergne 1998a: 2; Sorensen 1998). Leaders may resort to the "politics of survival", such as over-centralised control or tolerating trade-offs with strongmen. These tactics may help it keep control in the short run but may also compound state failure (Migdal 1998a: 264).

Low levels of social control make it difficult to establish any regular formalised pattern of behaviour – such as rules-based interactions that support the rule of law – and may impede the delivery of external assistance. Moreover, constructing a mutually constitutive relationship between the state and society where this has been absent requires not only the construction of appropriate linking institutions but a transformation in the way in which the state and its institutions are perceived. This equates to the somewhat ethereal challenge of building trust in the *idea* of the state (Chesterman 2004a: 154).

Second, disrupted states may experience ongoing hostilities or face the threat of a return to hostilities. Arms may be prevalent and minority communities may feel insecure. Human rights abuses, impunity for political violence and state coercion may damage collective relationships at all levels of society and undermine trust in the state. Strong undercurrents of instability and insecurity may have a profound effect on state-building efforts, both practically and psychologically. Ongoing conflict may disrupt elections or other key processes; and refugee movements may make it impossible to engage large segments of the population in key processes. In situations where elements of the state have been involved in the conflict, restoring trust becomes even more difficult.

Third, disrupted states frequently contain divided societies, characterised by unreconciled grievances and low prospects for reconciliation; large numbers of people in need of psychological or physical care; disruption to the normal social patterns of communities, which may be unable, for example, to conduct day-to-day commercial transactions; and massive people displacement.

Relationships between individuals familiar to one another – such as family members – may be ruptured, and those between strangers may be even weaker. Relationships may be characterised by a narrow "radius of trust", where strong bonds sustain families or other small social groupings but civic or anonymous trust is weak (W. Maley 2001: 4). A breakdown of trust between social groups or between society and the state creates "unworkable political communities" in which it becomes very difficult to sustain a political order (M. Maley 2000: 114). Interest representation systems tend to be weak, with few or no institutional channels or incentives for people to process their interests or to confront violence or other criminal acts in a re-integrative way (Przeworski 1995: 55–64; Braithwaite 2000: 128). Political corruption tends to be more prevalent (Fukuyama 2002: 28) and certain sorts of kinship groups – such as militia groups – may resist change or perpetuate violence (W. Maley 2001: 4).[33]

The literature on social capital provides a useful starting point when considering the challenge of rebuilding shattered social relationships.[34] Societies with deep social capital are characterised by inclusive, flexible and voluntary association amongst individuals, which may be critical to long-term strategies for peacebuilding and development.[35] Fukuyama (2002) has argued that social capital, and the anonymous trust on which it rests, generally originates in religion, shared historical experience and other deeply embedded cultural traditions. It is therefore difficult to generate in societies that lack it. States may, however, play a role in widening the radius of trust to build cooperative relationships between disparate groups. They may also foster the creation of social capital by providing public goods, especially property rights and public safety; education may also help inculcate shared norms and values. Fukuyama argues further that the key to extending the radius of trust is to strengthen the rule of law:

> No one will volunteer to work for a neighbourhood organisation if the police cannot guarantee public safety; no one will trust the government if public officials are immune to prosecution; no one will sign a business contract with a stranger in the absence of tort law and enforceable contracts. (Fukuyama 2002: 33)

This line of argumentation recognises that the problem of fragile social relationships is both related to and compounded by deficits in the political development of the country: unclear or unstable divisions of power, transitory or immature political institutions, and poorly developed civil society (Wartorn Societies Project c2000: 2).

Fourth, it is well recognised that, despite appearances, disrupted states do not constitute a political or institutional *tabula rasa*.[36] Political relationships continue, but are more likely to be fluid, unpredictable and personalised. Non-state actors, not all of them benevolent, may exercise political authority to varying degrees. Informal structures may burgeon as local actors seek to capitalise on changing political and institutional dynamics by carving out new roles and authorities for themselves. They may use informal political and legal structures to compete for influence or resources, and may see the establishment of formal state alternatives as a direct threat.

In some contexts, access to power and resources may have been channelled not primarily through state institutions but through informal mechanisms such as traditional patronage structures (Thier and Chopra 2002: 6). The concept of the state as provider of basic public services may not be fully understood, and social actors may not be familiar with the idea that state institutions can provide solutions to real problems (Ottaway 2002: 1004).

In situations where political and institutional life occurs outside state structures, there is no guarantee that emerging informal power structures will be supportive of the transition. Spoilers or conflict entrepreneurs who profit politically or economically from violence may pose a significant threat to transition processes. They may mobilise support through appeals to ethnic, religious and/or ideological solidarity, patronage or promises of essential services such as security (Lyon 2002). They may continue in politically or economically powerful positions long after the transition process is under way, with the power to reignite violence if their vested interests are threatened.

Such scenarios complicate efforts to construct state-based alternatives to informal institutions. Any attempt to do so is likely to confront the challenge of how to transform political life from informal to formal institutional structures or to create the conditions under which a positive relationship may exist between the two. This may require consideration of how to deal with residual power bases, how to consult or otherwise include non-state actors in any transitional structures, and how to neutralise, exclude or win over spoilers. It also involves considering whether informal institutions are likely to be a resource or an impediment to the establishment of formal alternatives. Finally, there is a challenge in recognising that any intervention in such a situation is unlikely to be politically neutral and will inevitably change existing power balances.

Observations

Comparing the League's conditions for Iraqi independence in 1931 with the benchmarks for independent statehood laid down by the United Nations for East Timor 70 years later, one might be forgiven for thinking that not much has changed. Although the progression was by no means seamless, various incarnations of international administration pursued identifiably similar agendas. They had in common the goal of preventing or removing threats to the international order and generally focused on political, social and economic development through prevailing normative prisms. That said, the historical trends that influenced the development of UN transitional administrations and other complex peace operations reflected an evolution in the normative underpinning of international responses to intrastate conflict.

The basic paradigm that came to inform UN peace operations by the mid-1990s was that the international community could and should play a role in consolidating peace in disrupted states, by seeking to transform them into stable, human-rights-based democracies within a state-based system. Over time, UN peace operations – and transitional administrations in particular – attempted to perform increasingly dynamic and transformative functions. The state-building experiments of Kosovo and East Timor were thus a far cry from the limited trusteeship arrangements of the League and the early UN period, and represent a new chapter in the history of attempts by external actors to transform the internal conditions of states.

Inevitably, the question arises as to whether this ambitious normative agenda was genuine, or whether ultimately, the international community was prepared to settle for the narrower objective of conflict stabilisation. The answer is possibly somewhere in between. "Security" arguably sits foremost in the hierarchy, as exemplified by the Security Council's agreement to East Timor's independence in the presence of relative stability, but the absence of many if not all of the other benchmarks listed above. However, clearly observable efforts to achieve other benchmarks for statehood suggest aspirations beyond mere stabilisation. As described above, such benchmarks have, in practice, directed state-building efforts at strengthening the institutions of state, as the primary receptacle of state strength and the means by which key governance functions may be delivered to the population. The next chapter examines in further detail the features of the rule of law 'benchmark' and the conceptual approach to the rule of law applied in UN transitional administrations and other state-building missions.

Notes

1. The International Settlement at Shanghai, for example, had its own government run by members of an international council, and it enjoyed independent legislative, administrative and judicial powers quite separate from those of the Chinese municipal government. Hands-on international involvement was more limited in Albania, where the Ambassadors Conference was responsible only for settling boundaries and appointing the Prince.
2. Direct League administration proved difficult to get off the ground. The Allies did not trust the League to administer territories of strategic significance (Ratner 1995: 97), and the League Council avoided this responsibility owing to insufficient financial or military

resources (Walters 1952: 109). Proposals were floated, but never implemented, for the League to administer the ports of Fiume (Dalmatia, 1919), Memel (Baltic, 1921–1923) and Alexandretta (Syria, 1937) (Wilde 2001a: 586). In Memel, the League appointed the chairperson of the Memel Harbour Board and administered a treaty on Memel's status.

3. The League also administered Leticia, Colombia (1933–1934), through a commission and a military contingent, during its transition from Peruvian to Colombian rule. For further details on the Saar, see Ratner (1995: 92) and Walters (1952: 241–242).

4. For further details, see Wilde (2001a: 586); Ratner (1995: 95); and Walters (1952: 157).

5. Mandates were ranked A, B or C on the basis of their presumed readiness for independent statehood, with explicit commitment to independence made only for Class A.

6. Article 22(2) of the League Covenant.

7. These included plans for a Free Territory of Trieste, which would have bestowed some powers of government on the United Nations, and for UN administration of Jerusalem under the 1948 UN Truce Supervision Organization. Although the United Nations established a Temporary Commission on Korea (1947), charged with supervising elections and assisting elected delegates to establish a government, this ultimately operated only in a limited fashion in South Korea. Similarly, the United Nations' limited oversight of Libya's transition to independence in 1949 was dominated by UK, French and US interests (Shalom 1990).

8. Nauru, New Guinea, Ruanda-Urundi, Cameroons (French), Togoland (French), Somaliland, Western Samoa, Cameroons (British), Togoland (British), Tanganyika, and the Trust Territory of the Pacific Islands. The last Trusteeship Agreement was not terminated until 1994, when the US Trust Territory of the Pacific Islands (Palau) chose self-government in a 1993 plebiscite. Although there was provision for it, no other dependent territories were put under trusteeship and, with the exception of Somaliland, the Trusteeship system was never extended beyond the territories that had previously been League mandates.

9. There were two exceptions. In South West Africa (Namibia), the United Nations terminated South Africa's mandate in 1966 and adopted direct responsibility for the territory (Wilde 2001a: 592), although South Africa's refusal to cooperate meant the United Nations was unable to assume this responsibility in practice. Nauru was administered jointly by the United Kingdom, Australia and New Zealand from 1947 to 1968, although Australia acted on behalf of the other two states.

10. Papua New Guinea's experience under Australian trusteeship is indicative; see Denoon (2005).

11. For further details, see Barnett (1995: 8).

12. See also Commission on Human Rights Resolution 2000/47 of 25 April 2000 on "Promoting and Consolidating Democracy" (CHR 2000), which highlighted the links between democracy and human rights and the responsibility of member states to promote and protect human rights by consolidating democracy. General Assembly Resolution 55/489 noted that democratisation had taken root as a "universal norm and practice at national and local levels" (UNGA 2000e), and General Assembly Resolutions 53/31, 54/36 and 55/43 encouraged member states to promote and consolidate new or restored democracies (UNGA 1999b, 2000f, 2001).

13. For a discussion of this, see Donnelly (1999: 89–91).

14. See also Chopra (1997) and Fitzpatrick (1980: 47) for a discussion of the influence of modernization doctrines on international assistance and UN missions.

15. The High Representative for Implementation of the Peace Agreement held final authority, with UNMIBH mandated to work in conjunction with the High Representative and the NATO-led multinational Implementation Force to implement the peace agreement.

16. For a comprehensive analysis of UNTAES, see Dobbins et al. (2005: 107–128) and Boothby (2004).
17. See, for example, Ohmae (1995); O'Donnell (1993); Van Creveld (1999); Evans (1997); and Spruyt (1994).
18. Chesterman (2003: 4) summarises the responsibilities of state-building missions since 1945.
19. See, in particular, work by Wilde (2001a) and Chesterman (2001a).
20. In Cambodia, Kosovo and Eastern Slavonia the United Nations explicitly reaffirmed the sovereignty and territorial integrity of, respectively, the State of Cambodia, the Federal Republic of Yugoslavia and the Republic of Croatia. East Timor was a more ambiguous case, given disputed Indonesian sovereignty, and was simply classed by the United Nations as a non-self-governing territory until it gained independence.
21. See also Caplan (2002: 13–14), who draws on Chopra's work to categorise international administrations according to whether they exert supervisory authority or direct governance.
22. Recent peacekeeping operations with a primary focus on ceasefire monitoring/ demilitarization have included: the United Nations Mission in the Democratic Republic of Congo (MONUC), the United Nations Mission in Ethiopia and Eritrea (UNMEE), the United Nations Military Observer Group in India and Pakistan (UNMOGIP), the United Nations Peacekeeping Force in Cyprus (UNFICYP), the United Nations Observer Mission in Georgia (UNOMIG), the United Nations Mission of Observers in the Prevlaka Peninsula (UNMOP), the United Nations Disengagement Observer Force in the Golan Heights (UNDOF), the United Nations Iraq-Kuwait Observation Mission (UNIKOM), the United Nations Interim Force in Lebanon (UNIFIL) and the United Nations Truce Supervision Organization in the Middle East (UNTSO).
23. Except in the case of UNTAES, where elections were held for representatives in the Croatian government, not for the formation of a regional government.
24. See Security Council Resolution 1037 (1996) establishing UNTAES, Resolution 745 (1992) establishing UNTAC, Resolution 1272 (1999) establishing UNTAET and Resolution 1244 (1999) establishing UNMIK.
25. See Weber (1922: 156); Dauvergne (1998a: 2); Hinsley (1986: 3–7); Migdal (1998a: 19); Lawson (1993: 187); and Fishman (1990: 428).
26. Von Einsiedel (2005: 15) gives a useful summary of the social contract, as well as Weberian and juridical definitions of the state.
27. Yannis (2002: 821–822), for example, describes state collapse as the descent of a state into Hobbesian anarchy, signified by the violent collapse of government and the implosion of the domestic structures of authority.
28. Milliken and Krause (2002: 756) define state failure as a failure of the state to perform the three core functions of providing security, representation and welfare. See also Von Einsiedel (2005: 15), who draws on Zartmann's work to define state collapse as a situation in which basic state functions are no longer performed. Under this definition, the collapsed state maintains few or no functioning state institutions, has lost its power to confer identity, cannot ensure security and has lost its legitimacy. See also Ghani, Lockhart and Carnahan (2005: 6), who define state failure in terms of failing to fulfil the core functions of the state, and Chesterman, Ignatieff and Thakur (2005a: 2).
29. See also Saikal (2003: 19–23), who provides a useful discussion of the different forms of disrupted state and types of disruption.
30. See, for example, UNGA (2005a: 30), which recognises the diversity of models of democracy.
31. For a discussion of the conditions for liberal democracy, see Dahl (1998); Diamond, Linz and Lipset (1998: 6–7); Diamond (1993a: 39); Huntington (1991: 7); Ratner (2000: 449); Schedler (1998: 92); and Inoguchi, Newman and Keane (1998: 6).

32. As Migdal (1998a 36) argues, highly fragmented societies, such as those with a high degree of ethnic or linguistic differentiation, make political mobilisation difficult.
33. In this respect, Putnam (2000: 22) distinguishes between kinship groups that reinforce exclusive groupings and may be detrimental ("bonding" social capital) and "bridging" social capital that connects people across social divides such as religion or socio-economic status.
34. Social capital may be thought of as an informal norm that promotes cooperation in pursuit of collective goals between two or more individuals on the basis of shared values (Fukuyama 2002: 27; see also Putnam 2000: 19; Cohen and Prusak 2001: 4). It refers to people's ability to work together in groups, and is thus a functional way of looking at culture – how individuals communicate, cooperate and pursue particular collective goals (Fukuyama 2002: 25).
35. See, for example, Putnam's work comparing civic involvement in northern and southern Italy, which showed that higher levels of social capital improved governance and institutional performance (Putnam 1993).
36. See, for example, Pugh (1998); Chesterman (2004a: 128); and Schabas and Kritz (n.d.).

3

Concepts: The rule of law in UN state-building missions

The protection and promotion of the universal values of the rule of law, human rights and democracy are ends in themselves. They are also essential for a world of justice, opportunity and stability ...

... Through hard experience, we have become more conscious of the need to build human rights and rule of law provisions into peace agreements and ensure they are implemented.

... decisions should be made ... to help strengthen the rule of law internationally and nationally ... we must also move towards embracing and acting on the "responsibility to protect" potential or actual victims of massive atrocities.

(UNSC 2006a: paras 128, 129, 132)

Conceptually, UN actors have increasingly recognised the establishment of the rule of law as integral to state-building missions. This chapter considers three core concepts that appear to have shaped UN understandings of its rule of law agenda. These three concepts may be summarised as follows:

1. The rule of law is viewed as a distinct normative value scheme, based on a cluster of values characteristic of the order perceived to exist in modern liberal democratic states.
2. The rule of law is deeply constitutive of the political and social order that state-building missions have sought to promote. The act of "establishing the rule of law" is seen to play a critical *transformative role* in achieving a social order characterised by peace and stability,

No entry without strategy: Building the rule of law under UN transitional administration, Bull, United Nations University Press, 2008, ISBN 978-92-808-1151-3

human rights protection, democratic institutions, development and "justice".

3. The principal means by which the rule of law may be established in a disrupted state is through state-based enforcement structures. The upholding of the rule of law is a core state function that should be delivered by the state. This may be achieved through publicly promulgated formal rules of behaviour with the force of law, supported by state-based structures for enforcing those laws. This equates to the creation or strengthening of a state legal system supported by judicial, penal and law enforcement bodies.

The rule of law as a distinct normative value scheme

It was not until 2004 that the United Nations developed a considered formulation of how the rule of law should be conceived of in the context of conflict or post-conflict environments. Prior to this, according to UN officials working in the rule of law field, no coherent policy direction existed publicly or privately. At the overarching strategic level, UN missions such as those examined in this book thus operated in something of a policy vacuum. Security Council mandates and missions themselves typically compiled lists detailing the constituent elements of the "rule of law", without articulating a clear conceptual understanding of the term.

An August 2004 report by the UN Secretary-General, *The rule of law and transitional justice in conflict and post-conflict societies*, remedied this by defining the rule of law as

> a principle of governance in which all persons, institutions and entities, public and private, including the State itself, are accountable to laws that are publicly promulgated, equally enforced and independently adjudicated, and which are consistent with international human rights norms and standards. It requires, as well, measures to ensure adherence to the principles of supremacy of law, equality before the law, accountability to the law, fairness in the application of the law, separation of powers, participation in decision-making, legal certainty, avoidance of arbitrariness and procedural and legal transparency. (UNSC 2004e: 4)

This conception of the rule of law is strongly invested with substantive aims and, in expressly binding it to international human rights norms and standards, is both a normative and a fundamentally political concept. It reflects longstanding efforts across the UN system to promote a rights-based conception of the rule of law as a universal normative standard. The Secretary-General's 2004 *Rule of law* report noted that the normative foundation for UN work in advancing the rule of law was the set of "universally applicable standards" adopted under the auspices of the United Nations since its inception and reflected in the UN Charter, international human rights law, international humanitarian law, international criminal law and international refugee law (UNSC 2004e: 5). The 2005 UN General Assembly World Summit reaffirmed the commitment of member states to an international order based on the rule of law and international law, and accepted language regarding the international community's collective "responsibility to protect" populations from genocide, war crimes, ethnic cleansing and crimes against humanity (UNGA 2005b: 29). As quoted at the beginning of this chapter, this was further reaffirmed in the Secretary-General's 2006 report, *In larger freedom.*

These notions are reflected in numerous other UN documents;[1] in enabling documents for peace operations such as peace agreements and Security Council mandates;[2] in statements by mission leaders concerning their rule of law objectives;[3] in national constitutions and laws promulgated under UN auspices directed at institutionalising human rights objectives;[4] in provisions relating to the establishment of judiciaries;[5] in standards of judicial conduct for UN missions;[6] and in statements regarding the progress of UN operations in meeting rule of law objectives.[7]

This "universal" conception of the rule of law is not contested in this book, which focuses instead on the manner in which the United Nations has sought to operationalise its particular conception. It is worth highlighting briefly, however, that the substantive quality of the UN conception distinguishes it from narrower positivist legal definitions, which emphasise the absolute supremacy of law without placing conditions on its content (Bouloukos and Dakin 2001: 147). It also distinguishes it from definitions that stress the role of law in protecting the rights of individuals from arbitrary government, without applying a particular doctrine or set of values about what those rights are, which rules should govern or what form of government might be recommended (Dicey 1889: 175–184; Hayek 1976: 54; Dworkin 1986: 96–98; Raz 1979: 210–229).

In distinguishing between "thick" (substantive) and "thin" (instrumentalist) conceptions of the rule of law, Peerenboom (2004: 2–4) notes that even "thin" definitions may mask considerable differences in interpretation of the term. For "thick" or substantive definitions that incorporate elements of political morality, such as the United Nations', the scope for debate on the meaning of "rule of law" is even greater. The potential for alternative conceptions of the rule of law to exist and pose a fundamental obstacle to UN efforts to establish this particular conception must therefore be acknowledged. In this context, the discussion below on "legitimacy" is relevant.

The UN conception aligns with those definitions stipulating that laws must conform to a particular notion of justness. Such conceptions became prevalent during the Cold War period, notably at the 1955 International Commission of Jurists conference, and were gradually linked inseparably with the legal order existing in modern liberal democratic states (Brownlie 1998: 212; Carothers 1998: 96). Under such conceptions, the rule of law may be said to exist not just when legal process leads to procedurally just outcomes, requiring the consistent and transparent application of a complete set of decisional and procedural rules that are pre-fixed and pre-announced, but when the legal process leads to substantively just outcomes that reflect particular ideals of "justice" or "fairness".[8]

Of further note in the UN conception is the emphasis given to notions of protection against state abuse. The rule of law is perceived to shield against state tyranny, or, in the words of the *Agreements on a Comprehensive Political Settlement of the Cambodia Conflict* (Paris Agreements 1991), against a "return to the policies and practices of the past". The importance of this in disrupted states was highlighted by the United Nations Transitional Administrator in East Timor, who observed:

> Security means more than physical safety from militia and criminals. It also means protection from the state; history shows clearly that those in power can commit more abuses, more widely, than any private individual or groups. Without this security, without someone in East Timor understanding clearly what his or her rights are – and without those rights being respected – you will not truly have won your independence.... Consequently, we have tried to set up a system of laws and a system of justice that does just that. (Vieira de Mello 2001c)[9]

These notions were also embedded in the growing focus of the international community during the 1990s on principles and actions to combat impunity for human rights abuses committed by state agents, first through the creation of the ad hoc international criminal tribunals for Rwanda and Yugoslavia and later through the principle of "universal justice" for "serious crimes of concern to the international community" enshrined in the Rome Statute of the International Criminal Court (1998).

The constitutive role of the rule of law

In UN state-building missions, the rule of law has also been assumed to be deeply constitutive of a liberal democratic political and social order – the overarching state-building objective has been the establishment of a "society based on the rule of law" (Vieira de Mello 2001b; see also UNSC 2002b: 1 and UNTAC Human Rights Component 1992: 22). In the missions to Cambodia, Kosovo and East Timor, it was consistently stressed that the rule of law was an essential prerequisite for transforming the post-conflict situation into a stable and democratic society.[10] In Kosovo, for instance, the Special Representative of the Secretary-General Michael Steiner described the rule of law as the basis for every "modern European society":

> we want the rule of law instead of the rule of the jungle. We want to build here a civil society after the model we see everywhere in the rest of Europe ... If one wants to join the club of European democracies one has to accept the fundamental rules ... And part of the fundamental rules is the rule of law. (UNMIK 2002c)

Although the interconnectedness, or even indivisibility, of human rights, democratisation, peace and the rule of law has been stressed in UN peacekeeping doctrine,[11] the presumed causal linkages have seldom been explained and were noticeably absent from the 2004 report. Nonetheless, a set of generic propositions characterising key linkages that appear regularly in the discourse of a variety of UN agencies and actors may be identified as follows:

- *Constituting peace and stability*. The absence of the rule of law as understood in a democratic society is viewed as a root cause of violent conflict, whereas its presence creates peace by moving conflict into a peaceful institutional framework, protecting human rights and, through ending impunity, helping to create a climate of trust. This promotes reconciliation and ultimately a society in which all people can live without fear.[12] Strong institutions within the justice sector are critical for peace and stability.[13]
- *Developing democratic institutions*. In this view, the absence of the rule of law, specifically judicial and law enforcement structures, impedes the development of democratic institutions. The presence of the rule of law provides the necessary political stability and human rights protections to allow for free and open democratic participation.[14]
- *Protecting human rights*. In the generic UN conception, the absence of the rule of law as understood in a democratic society allows human rights abuses to occur, because there are inadequate legal restrictions on violent conflict or state abuse, or because the pre-existing legal order condones such abuse. The presence of the rule of law ensures the protection of human rights by punishing and/or deterring abusers, including the state.[15]
- *Supporting development*. The absence of the rule of law is seen to impede the delivery of development assistance and other key objectives relating to the development agenda, such as the creation of an investment-friendly environment. The presence of the rule of law pro-

vides the stability and certainty necessary for development to proceed.[16]

- *The concept of justice.* Societies where the rule of law is absent are characterised by endemic acts of injustice. The rule of law is essential to ensure a "fair" and "just" society, because all members have reasonable confidence in their own safety and that all members of society will be treated equally.[17] Closely related to this is the perceived transformative significance of delivering justice for past human rights abuses. Achieving a sense of "justice" for past human rights abuses is perceived to send powerful signals about what will be tolerated in the future and to assist in reconciliation processes. This became a well-recognised principle in UN discourse.[18]

Hence, in UN transitional administrations and other state-building missions, the rule of law was viewed both as an essential component of the social order that UN actors were trying to create and as a tool for that social transformation. The primary value of the rule of law derived from the belief that institutionalised legal rules structure, constrain and regulate both the state apparatus and the broader society, establishing and maintaining social order. Social order was generally equated with "peace" or "peaceful management of conflict" based on normative principles of human rights and democracy. The state justice system was seen as a crucial institutionalised force for coordinating behaviour and maintaining social order, because of its ability to both indicate and enforce acceptable patterns of behaviour.

This view of the constitutive powers of the rule of law conforms uncontroversially with contemporary democratisation, conflict studies and development discourse. The literature on democratic transitions supports the United Nations' contention that establishing the rule of law is critical in enabling a society emerging from conflict to make the transition to liberal democratic statehood.[19] In this view, the rule of law defines, reflects and enforces the basic principles of democracy.

At least five key arguments in the literature support this view.

1. Establishing the rule of law is seen to perform a symbolic function in signalling regime change, and in democratic transitions is more appropriately thought of as a legitimising "rite of passage" than as a strictly juridical or legal process. It allows the new regime to convey publicly and authoritatively the material differences between it and the old regime and to fashion an identity based on peace (Huntington 1991: 220; Teitel 2000: 8, 230; Mendez 1997a: 1, 9). Measures to provide accountability for past human rights abuses help constitute a shared vision of "justice" because of the high levels of public interest that characterise them (Teitel 2000: 225). Measures to construct a new legal order perform a similar function.

2. The rule of law provides an ordering system for social interaction, whose primary function is to mitigate conflict through the peaceful resolution of disputes. The dominant western jurisprudential view of law is that its basic function is conflict resolution (Seidman 1978: 15; Parsons 1962: 58), a view heavily reflected in the democratic transitions literature. Democracies are successful because the remedy they propose for conflict resolution is not coercion but the creation of rules, built into the political process, that allow people to reconcile their differences peacefully (Hampton 1992: 41). As a public institutionalised mechanism for norm enforcement or social control (Hart 1961; Raz 1979: 105; Weber 1946: 180), the law is thus an essential component of that set of rules. It renders decisions in an orderly fashion, resolving conflict or preventing violent manifestations of conflict. A well-functioning justice system may thus help restore divided societies, through addressing disputes between hostile communities (Widner 2001: 2), helping curb criminal conduct (Goldstone 1996: 490) and protecting the freedoms essential for participation in democratic processes (Linz and Stepan 1996b: 19).

3. The rule of law provides a barrier against arbitrary and excessive state power. The rule of law regulates the actions of the state, keeping the entire governmental mechanism running in conformity with the constitution and checking illegal tendencies by embedding the state in mechanisms for accountability and transparency (Neou and Gallup 1997: 8; Krygier 2000: 61). In this context, both the establishment of justice systems and the pursuit of retrospective justice are viewed as necessary precursors to peaceful democratic consolidation.[20]

4. The rule of law helps reconstruct trust. Judicial processes may help reconstruct trust in broken societies by restoring confidence in procedural justice (Rotberg 2000: 10). If the courts prove successful in resolving disputes, for example, this lessens the prospect that contestants will resort to violence or other actions that spread instability and undermine trust in the community (Widner 2001: 5).

5. The rule of law makes possible individual rights, which are at the core of the concept of democracy. Under the rule of law, the government is forced to respect the sovereign authority of the people and to treat every individual equally (Carothers 2006a: 4).

Again, I do not contest the validity of these arguments – although, as argued below, there remains a high degree of uncertainty about precisely what kinds of societal effects stem from specific changes in rule of law institutions, and this uncertainty makes it dangerous to assume that specific rule of law activities will promote specific democratisation goals (Carothers 2003: 7).

A state-based enforcement model for establishing the rule of law

UN doctrine, as reflected in key policy statements by the Security Council, the General Assembly and other UN bodies, has consistently advanced "institution- and capacity-building" as the primary means by which the rule of law may be established or strengthened in post-conflict situations.[21] This approach is principally one of institutional enforcement, based around state-sanctioned enforcement structures such as arrest, detention and prosecution mechanisms. The state, which has the means of coercion to control social actors, is seen as the primary agent of justice, which is delivered through the state justice system. Law means state law, and it derives its legitimacy and authority from the state.

Under this approach, the rule of law may be established in two main steps: establishing formal rules of behaviour with the force of law, and establishing mechanisms for enforcing or otherwise supporting those laws. The first component, *formal rules of behaviour*, codifies the desired value system and may be used to determine and deal with breaches of that value system. In practical terms, this equates to a constitutional and legislative framework that guarantees a set of rights and values, sets constraints on behaviour and defines punishment for breaches of those constraints. This framework, which is arguably the single most important organising principle of the state, formally distributes powers and prescribes norms to govern behaviour across a wide range of activities. The second component, *mechanisms for enforcing the constitutional and legal framework*, generally takes the form of judicial, law enforcement and penal systems. These systems establish an ordered and stable means for resolving disputes over the interpretation of the constitutional and legislative framework and for enforcing such resolutions.

The basic thrust of this approach has remained consistent over the past decade, as reflected in the two keynote UN documents on the rule of law that framed this period. The first, the 1994 *Report of the Secretary-General to the General Assembly on strengthening the rule of law*, listed 12 constituent elements essential to the development of a legal and institutional framework able to entrench the rule of law in society (UNGA 1994a: 5–8). These comprised a strong constitution that incorporates internationally recognised human rights and fundamental freedoms, establishes remedies at law for violations of those rights, and defines the powers of government; a strong electoral system that enshrines the will of the people as the basis for the authority of government; a strong legal framework to protect human rights and democracy; strong national human rights institutions; an independent and adequately empowered judiciary; a national training regime for justice sector officials; a military with ultimate allegiance to the constitution and to the democratic government; effective and accessible mechanisms for conflict resolution between and among citizens and groups in society and state organs; full incorporation into the international human rights system; a society educated in its rights and responsibilities; a strong civil society; and free, responsible and flourishing mass media.

These elements formed the basis of UN programmes of technical and advisory services to strengthen the rule of law and were used as reference points in UN peace operations.[22] Similar lists of the constituent elements of the rule of law appear in other key UN documents,[23] providing comprehensively for a rule of law regime based on the standard western liberal democratic rights-based model.

The second key document, the Secretary-General's 2004 *Rule of law* report, placed similar emphasis on the construction of a state justice sector, elaborating many of the same principles as its decade-old predecessor. It noted that effective rule of law strategies "necessarily focus on legal and institutional requirements" (UNSC 2004e: 8). It did, however, place significantly greater emphasis on additional factors, such as the need to assess country context, to develop participatory strategies, to support domestic reform constituencies, to build political will among stakeholders on the direction of reform, to attend to groups most affected by conflict, and to ensure the functioning of complementary and less formal legal mechanisms, including "indigenous and informal traditions" (UNSC 2004e: 8–12). In so doing, the report advanced the United Nations' conceptual appreciation of the complexity of its rule of law agenda and demonstrated constructive learning from inappropriate or inadequate rule of law assistance in the preceding decade. It reflected heightened, though still embryonic, interest in policy circles in so-called "political will" or "constituency-building" debates, in bottom-up approaches to rule of law promotion and in informal or "traditional" justice (Carothers 2006b).

It is as yet unclear whether this more sophisticated approach will be operationalised in the field. Restricting this analysis to the rule of law initiatives conducted by UN agencies in the decade spanning the two documents, including the case studies examined in this book, it is clear that, at the operational level, success in establishing the rule of law was seen as primarily dependent on the establishment of state legal, judicial, penal and law enforcement bodies.[24] The "rule of law" was often equated directly with the existence of a strong criminal justice system, to be created by restoring or building judicial infrastructure and improving the capacity of actors within it.[25] Accordingly, peace operations focused almost exclusively on constitution-drafting, the establishment of court systems, the training of local judicial and legal communities, and capacity-building in "support" areas such as civil society, legal aid schemes, judges' and prosecutors' associations, and so forth. Normative orders not attached to the state, such as indigenous justice systems or alternative dispute resolution structures, were given considerably lesser priority. In instances where they were recognised, they were viewed as a complement to, not a substitute for, state law.

At the operational level, the need for a holistic approach to strengthening the rule of law was often equated with the quest for better coordination of police, judicial and penal services.[26] It was also related to an education requirement in the justice sector and in the broader community, which in peace operations tended to take the form of "human rights training". Efforts to address issues such as civil society development and the question of transitional justice remained peripheral to the central focus on legal, judicial, law enforcement and correctional systems.

As detailed in the case-study chapters, the Kosovo and East Timor transitional administrations exemplified this approach. In Kosovo, the establishment of "genuine" rule of law was seen to be dependent on creating an "independent, impartial and multi-ethnic judiciary" (UNSC 1999a: para. 66; 2000b: para. 107) as the "guarantor of the rule of law" (UNSC 1999a: para. 40). It was noted that only such a judiciary would address existing security concerns and build confidence. The importance of a "comprehensive" approach – one that encompassed legal, judicial, penal and law enforcement bodies   was stressed, and transitional justice was emphasised for its contribution to reconciliation (UNSC 1999a: para. 66).

Like their counterparts in Kosovo, UN officials in East Timor did not distinguish clearly between the "rule of law" and the "justice system". Characterising the situation in East Timor at the time of the initial deployment of the United Nations Transitional Administration in East Timor (UNTAET) as a "complete vacuum of administrative authority and of policing and justice" (UNSC 2000c: para. 3; Strohmeyer 2001: 50; Traub 2000: 74), UNTAET's strategy focused on the establishment, virtually from scratch, of a "credible" system of justice (UNSC 2000d: para. 68). This involved the same tripartite approach as in Kosovo: attempting to build an "independent and impartial judiciary", a strong police service and a functioning prison system, and augmenting these with legal aid programmes and judicial and human rights training. Although UNTAET also emphasised the importance of dealing with past human rights violations, in essence both missions appeared to equate the establishment of state legal, judicial, police and prison services with the establishment of the rule of law.

It is by no means certain that this "state-based enforcement model" is the only or even the principal approach that should be adopted when attempting to establish the rule of law. As Thomas Carothers has noted, there remains too much uncertainty surrounding the fundamental assumptions of rule of law promotion for robust conclusions to be drawn. This includes uncertainty over what the rule of law *is*; over whether it resides primarily in institutional configurations or in more diffuse normative structures; over how it develops in a society; and over how such development may be stimulated beyond "simplistic efforts to copy institutional forms" (Carothers 2003: 6).

It would be counterproductive to suggest that state institutions be overlooked as a crucial mechanism for establishing the rule of law in any state-based system of social organisation. No influential state theories at present question the role of the state as the ultimate guardian of public interests, or the centrality of state institutions as mechanisms by which political power is channelled and apportioned and state objectives accomplished. The state continues to be viewed as the best placed, if not the only, political organisation to deliver the key societal demands of security, representation and welfare (Milliken and Krause 2002: 756; Yannis 2002: 820). State institutions are key agents in advancing such missions and, if they fail, so does the state. As Chesterman, Ignatieff and Thakur (2005a: 2) point out:

> The modern state is a manifestation of political power that has been progressively depersonalised, formalised and rationalised; the state is the medium through which political power is integrated into a comprehensive social order. In idealised form, the state embodies the political mission of a society; its institutions and officials express the proper array of techniques that are used in efforts to accomplish that mission. When those institutions and officials cease to function, this abstract idea of the state collapses and the political power that had been channelled through such structures finds alternative, less ordered, means of expression.

However, the adoption of formalist rather than substantive approaches to institution-building has consistently characterised external rule of law promotion, which has focused on establishing organisations such as government departments and public agencies, following models found in donor states. Often, there has been little recognition by donors that such organisations become institutions only when "relevant actors believe they provide solutions to real problems" and engage in political processes of transformation that may be complex, largely domestic and time consuming (Ottaway 2002: 1004, 1016).

Carothers (2003: 9) points to a growing body of research that argues not only against the formalist approach but against assuming that establishing the rule of law can be equated simply with developing state institutions with a direct connection to *law*:

> Clearly law is not just the sum of courts, legislatures, police, prosecutors and other formal institutions with some direct connection to law. Law is also a normative system that resides in the minds of the citizens of a society. As rule-of-law providers seek to affect the rule of law in a country, it is not clear if they should focus on institution-building or instead try to intervene in ways that would affect how citizens understand, use, and value law ... [S]ome research shows that compliance with law depends most heavily on the perceived fairness and legitimacy of the laws, characteristics that are not established primarily by the courts but by other means, such as the political process. An effort to improve compliance might more fruitfully take a completely different approach.

This point becomes even more salient when the rule of law is thought of as a normative value scheme that is constituted by both the "rules of the game" and *adherence* to those rules. The task of identifying how and where those rules are manifested and how adherence to those rules develops may be particularly complex in disrupted states where the rules are fragmented and the players diverse in motivation. Of relevance to UN and other actors undertaking rule of law promotion activities may be the following points:

First, *the "rules of the game" do not only reside in state legal institutions.* They may also be codified in informal institutions or in even more intangible forms or locations. North (1990: 4) notes that informal institutions such as convention and codes of behaviour exist in all societies and, like formal institutions, reduce uncertainty by establishing a stable structure for human interaction. Although the "law and society" debate in sociological jurisprudence is inconclusive on whether formal legal rules are essential to social order, it casts considerable doubt on whether formal law is the primary way in which people order their affairs. Thus, although Trubek (1972: 4–5) and others[27] have argued that "modern" societies depend on institutionalised legal rules to maintain social control, there is by no means a consensus on this. Other scholars have argued that formal law is not the primary way in which people order their affairs (Garth and Sarat 1998b: 1; Ellickson 1991). According to this view, most disputes are handled outside the courts, with formal rules operating only at the margins (Edelman and Cahill 1998: 15).

This is likely to be the case in disrupted states, where, as discussed above, people may turn increasingly to informal structures (Kritz 2006; Golub 2003: 16). It may also be the case in those environments where the state has traditionally played a small role and social problems are dealt with primarily through traditional modes of conflict resolution rather than the state legal system (Tamanaha 2001: 145–146). People may also favour informal structures where substantial barriers exist to the mobilisation of state law, particularly for the poor who may have limited access to legal services and perceive that the formal legal system favours those with greater social, political and economic clout (Edelman and Cahill 1998: 15).

In such environments, informal legal institutions may thus be significantly more entrenched than their state counterparts and their normative basis may clash with "western" legal principles. Seeking to replace informal systems with western-style state legal institutions may be difficult. North (1990: 6) notes that, although it may be possible radically to change formal legal rules very quickly, informal constraints embodied in customs, traditions and codes of conduct are much more resistant to deliberate policies of change. Owing to their cultural basis, informal structures are likely to be complex, stable in the absence or presence of state-based rule systems, and an important source of continuity in long-run societal change (North 1990: 37–38).

Rule of law practitioners have increasingly recognised that structures outside the formal justice system – such as customary law, community dispute resolution and restorative justice mechanisms – may play an important role in supporting efforts to build the rule of law (Pritchard 2001: 189). Indigenous societies may have effective and tested means of dealing with conflict, such as traditions of peacemaking that can work alongside or be accommodated in more formalised institutional systems. Informal rules-based dispute resolution mechanisms – such as community forums that stress mediation or arbitration – may carry out the same functions as law, but be better adapted to local conditions and enjoy more legitimacy than introduced formal models. As a result, they may have greater influence in the maintenance of social order, particularly where state legal norms are alien to or inconsistent with social norms, or where access is limited to a small elite (Tamanaha 2001: 115–117). They may also help relieve the pressure on low-capacity fledgling state institutions (Widner 2001: 2).

The question of how to deal with the phenomenon of informal justice systems, and in particular how to establish an effective relationship between formal and informal systems, remains open. Many scholars have cautioned against seeking to combine the two, given the risk that informal justice systems may undermine fundamental rule of law principles, for example by perpetuating discriminatory social norms. Others have argued that, given the resilience of informal systems and their potential to support state processes, the best approach may be to seek to create synergies between the two. The concept of "restorative justice"[28] has drawn particular attention as a potential adjunct or alternative to formal legal bodies designed to deliver retributive justice. As Braithwaite (2000: 129) has argued:

> The restorative justice ideal could not and should not be the romantic notion of shifting back to a world where state justice is replaced by local justice. Rather, it might be to use the existence of state traditions of rights, proportionality and rule of law as resources to check abuse of power in local justice and to use the revival of restorative traditions to check abuse of state power. In other words, restorative justice constitutionalised by the state can be the stuff of a republic with a richer separation of powers, with less abuse of power, than could be obtained either under dispute resolution totally controlled by local politics or disputing totally dominated by the state.

Second, *voluntary adherence to the "rules of the game" may be more easily secured than forced adherence.* As Hart noted, "the fact that a rule is a law is anything but a conclusive reason for obeying it" (Hart 1983, quoted in Flatham 1992: 320). There is, however, considerable uncertainty as to how such obedience may be secured. Some scholars have contended that an obligation to comply with the law, and to act accordingly, may arise if the subjects of a legal system believe that they have no alternative (Flatham 1992: 311). In this view, legitimacy does not derive solely from social or cultural compatibility, but may stem from such factors as a coercive apparatus. A well enforced legal rule system may thus generate its own legitimacy, and for this reason the concept of coercion or sanction is important to most conceptions of law.

It may nonetheless be argued that sanctions are not a necessary feature of legal rules and that the conception of law as a coercive social order cannot strictly be applied (Bull 1977: 127). There are compelling arguments to suggest that adherence to any rules system is reliant on the extent to which people commit voluntarily to it, which depends on the existence of supportive attitudes and habits that induce the population to agree on and abide by that set of rules. This in turn may be affected by a diffuse and poorly understood range of underlying factors, which may be political, social, cultural, historical or even economic.

Central to most efforts to address this issue is the question of legitimacy. As with broader aspects of state formation, social contract theorists have argued that the key legitimising force with respect to the acceptance of legal rules is consent or acquiescence, which rests on some form of social contract between the setters and subjects of those rules. They have hypothesised that the rule of law is underpinned by a social contract in which individuals consent to regulate their behaviour by rules with the force of law. Law is thus constituted and legitimated by the consent of individuals in society (Tamanaha 2001: 58; Parsons 1962: 58–59; Anleu 2000: 53).

In such conceptions, law's close identity with society underpins its legitimacy and the need for coercive enforcement is reduced (Tamanaha 2001: 3). Effective rule-governed activity presupposes a setting of widely shared, although not necessarily articulated, concepts, beliefs and dispositions, as well as enabling capacities and skills (Flatham 1992: 309–310). Hayek (1960: 208–209) argued that such shared understandings cannot be described explicitly but are evident as a common "sense of justice". The key implication of this argument is that, if the rule of law is to be established, it must be underpinned by shared beliefs and values (Anleu 2000: 49; Walker 1988: 24; Krygier 2000: 64; Hart 1961: 80). If it is not, ordinary citizens will neither understand it sufficiently nor be normatively committed to it. As a result, they will tend to ignore or avoid it (Tamanaha 2001: 235). Institutions grounded in coercive bases of domination are likely to end up confronted with a legitimacy crisis (W. Maley 2003: 170), or at the very least impose excessively high transactions costs in states that are typically resource poor (North 1990: 54).

The question of sources of legitimacy has arisen repeatedly in the context of research on legal transplanting in the development setting. Numerous scholars have argued that law cannot be separated from cultural meanings,[29] and that the importation of legal models from one culture to another fails to induce the desired social changes, including the maintenance of social order (Tamanaha 2001: 107). Although over time, and when socio-cultural circumstances are similar in receiving and generating countries, legal transplanting may succeed, when this is not the case the resulting legal system may be severely limited in its ability to regulate social behaviour.

In addressing these issues, the literature on institutional design therefore highlights the dangers of "off-the-shelf" importation. As discussed above, even in a post-conflict situation where the institutional landscape appears to have been razed, this is seldom the case. Past inheritances – residual institutions, social patterns and attitudes – may inhibit imported institutional formats from functioning as intended and lead to radical and possibly counter-intentional departures in outcome (Goodin 1996: 30; Offe 1996: 216–217; Coram 1996: 90). Copying of institutions may also bypass an essential period of gestation in which the institution and society interact, each shaping the other to produce a robust and sustainable system (Offe 1996: 216).

Again, however, the legal transplanting debate is inconclusive. Watson (1974) and other comparativists have observed that, throughout history, legal development has largely occurred through transplantation, with all systems of law composed of a mixture of foreign and home-grown rules

(Orucu 1996: 335; Tamanaha 2001: 108). They have argued that, if legal development were critically dependent on social context, then laws would transplant only with great difficulty and their effectiveness would be seriously limited. Watson (1993: 116) has therefore argued that legal culture, not social context, is the greatest determinant of legal development. Others have agreed that modern legal systems may be sufficiently independent of social and cultural systems to flourish irrespective of differences (Tamanaha 2001: 111).

Democratic consolidation literature steers a middle ground on social context. Political culture and socialisation theories in comparative politics have generally concluded that "culture matters", but greater credence has been given to the idea that supportive social discourse may be engineered (Kohli et al. 1996: 12; Inglehart 1988: 1203). In this view, the evolution and sustainability of democratic systems, including the rule of law, depend on the existence or emergence of supportive habits and attitudes among the public, which may be stimulated through the establishment of new structures (Schedler 2001: 81).

There is common ground, however, regarding the "attitudinal foundations" of democratic governance: that democracy is at risk unless all major political players have the normative motivations required to sustain a liberal democratic regime. How those in authority exercise their power is unambiguously seen to have strong implications for the quality and stability of the new order – if they do not obey the new laws, for example, then the laws are meaningless (Schedler 2001: 72). There seems to be less consensus, however, on whether the normative preferences of actors at both elite and mass level matter. Schedler (2001: 75), for example, has questioned whether the preferences of the masses are relevant, arguing that democratic regimes can survive despite low levels of public support.

However, there is reason to think that state rule of law institutions need to be in harmony with the normative principles of society or to be capable of supporting interactions with society that allow it to inculcate new norms and preferences and so gain support and recognition (Goodin 1996: 37, 118; Dryzek 1996: 122; Offe 1996: 201, 219). Ultimately, it seems unlikely that an institution that is not relevant or does not "make sense" to the recipient population is going to be used. Institutions that are seen to be procedurally and substantively "fair" motivate conformity (Rothstein 1998: 118; Krasner 1999: 36), as do those that are negotiated and inclusive. Przeworski (1995: 50–51) has argued, for example, that there is a crucial distinction between constitutions that result from a process of extensive negotiation and those executed by a victorious majority (or external actor); a democratically chosen constitution is more likely to be stable.

Third, *the rule of law is closely related to the balance of power in society.* It is therefore linked closely to political, social and even criminal structures that apportion power. Maley (2003: 170) has further pointed out that, in deeply disrupted societies, institutional design must address fundamental issues of political theory relating to the role of the state. These include the nature and locus of political authority, the question of to what distributive capacity the state should aspire, and the role of political power. Power structures, informal or formal, may have a profound impact on efforts to establish the rule of law, though this is often overlooked in conventional explanations for the failure of rule of law reform (Golub 2003: 13).

Kleinfeld Belton (2005: 9–10) demonstrates how rule of law reform may threaten existing power relationships through the pursuit of fundamentally political objectives. The goal of "government under the law", for example, is primarily about reining in government – that is, restricting the authority of powerful individuals and strengthening other power centres, such as the judiciary. Similarly, the goal of "equality before the law" changes the balance of power in a society by seeking to empower ordinary people at the expense of the rich and powerful, and is therefore likely to meet political resistance. In this respect, Upham (2002: 34–35) observed "the risk to existing informal means of social order".

> A legal system provides a powerful set of resources, and those who see themselves as benefited will use such resources to their own advantage ... [I]f the social context of a legal system is not able to support the individual exercise of rights or if the incentives governing utilisation of the resources are not finely calibrated, the results can be far from those intended ... In a mature system, established institutions can deal with negative consequences. However, in countries with new legal systems, especially ones imposed or imported from abroad, pre-existing institutions often lack the experience, expertise, and, most seriously, political legitimacy necessary to deal with unforeseen consequences of reform.

In practice, resistance to reform by elite actors has proved more the rule than the exception (Biebesheimer and Payne 2001: iii), underscoring the unpalatable fact that poorly performing judiciaries and corrupt judges often serve the interests of powerful actors (Carothers 2003: 10). Aron's work on Russian rule of law reform since 1991 amply demonstrates the obstacles posed by entrenched political resistance to reform; reactionaries in the parliament and a strong procuratorship continuously obstructed reform to ensure they retained unchecked powers of search and seizure, arrest and unlimited pre-trial detention (Aron 2002).

In such trying circumstances, donors have tended to privilege "soft targets" over the counter-establishment changes necessary for real reform, often avoiding the official sector and other "hard cases" owing to the high political risk or a desire to avoid associating with abusive organisations (Hammergren 1998d: 3). They have also tended to neglect to establish relationships with "minority traditions" – groups outside the dominant ideological or institutional traditions with the potential to become powerful allies for institutional change (Jacoby 2001).

Conversely, the chances of success may rise when reforms are clearly perceived as necessary and consistent with the broader reform agenda of key political players. Truth commissions, for example, have proved most successful when there was a powerful political consensus behind reconciliation, such as in South Africa (Goldstone 1996: 496). In instances where commissions lacked political backing, such as the Philippines in 1986 or Uganda in 1974, they did not function properly and ultimately made a limited contribution to the reform process (Hayner 1996: 24).

Similarly, where consultation and direct participation in decision-making and implementation gave actors a say and a stake in the process, they proved more open to change. Lehmann's (2000: 228) study of bail reform in Ukraine, for example, found that transplanting the western concept of bail to the post-Soviet system succeeded because legal reformers had a firm agenda and a clear idea of how to integrate bail into the existing legal framework, and because the Ukrainian judiciary was committed to the reforms. Such an approach also reduced the risk of donors imposing inappropriate alien models that put foreign policy priorities before local needs (Carothers 1999: 200, 316; Hammergren 1998a: 10; Borbely et al. 1999: 8).

These findings imply not only that attempts to create state rule of law institutions may be undermined by spoilers, but also that other institutions that channel power may be germane to rule of law development. In this respect, Carothers (2003: 8) has noted the lack of focus on the role of other institutions, such as legislatures or executive branch agencies, in law-making processes.

Finally, *state rule of law institutions are unlikely to be sustainable or utilised if they are not robust.* As the above discussion demonstrates, choices in the design of state rule of law institutions must confront the difficult questions of how state institutions are to be legitimated, how new institutions will interact with pre-existing, possibly informal ones, as well as with other state institutions, and how formal rules will intertwine with political, social and cultural discourses. In addition, the extent to which an institution is sustainable as an ordering system is likely to depend on its "robustness". Robust institutions are durable over time, changing only in ways appropriate to changed circumstances, and able to tolerate disharmony resulting from attempts to alter the status quo. Robustness is also enhanced when the institution is revisable, sensitive to motivational complexity, and compatible with the other institutions with which it interacts (Goodin 1996: 40–42, 118). A robust institution is able to withstand stressors, including spoiling activity by actors with vested interests in destroying or altering the process (Carothers 1999: 174–175; W. Maley 2000: 122). In this respect, institutions developed early in a transition process, before relationships between conflicting parties are clarified, are more likely to protect the eventual losers and thus extract their commitment (Przeworski 1995: 51).

Robustness may also be related to comprehensiveness. Institutions must, for example, be comprehensive enough to ensure they fully encompass the principles they are trying to implement. An effective constitution, for example, contains full protections: it incorporates internationally recognised human rights and fundamental freedoms, establishes remedies at law for violations of those rights, empowers an independent judiciary, outlaws discrimination, defines and limits the powers of government and establishes subsidiary institutions where necessary (UNGA 1994a: 5).

Reliability is also a relevant issue. The public must have confidence in the institution's capacity to accomplish the tasks for which it was designed, or it will not be trusted and may be underutilised (Offe 1996: 200–201; Przeworski 1995: 42). Institutional rules must be enforceable, which may require attention to capacity-related matters such as physical infrastructure and human resources (Carothers 1999: 173). It may also require the establishment of subsidiary institutions, such as a full set of laws to complement a new constitution. The reliability of an institution may also depend on its accessibility to users (Nagle and Mahr 1999: 70) and its compatibility with the available supply of financial and human resources, which may be scarce in a new, poorly resourced state (Offe 1996: 210). Accessibility has been a particular problem for the poor and the marginalised, prompting some scholars to propose a "legal empowerment" approach that prioritises legal services (Golub 2003: 3–7; Carothers 1999: 177).

Reliable institutions are also capable of achieving their objectives, rather than generating unintended, counterproductive outcomes – such as exacerbating social divisions. This is much easier said than done. Institutional design has been well recognised as an imprecise art, with institutions and the scenarios they create not always resembling the intended outcome (Goodin 1996: 27–28). In a detailed study of peacekeeping missions in the 1990s, Roland Paris (2004: ix) has argued that in post-conflict situations the process of economic and political liberalisation favoured by the international donor community can produce destabilising consequences. Poorly conceived international interventions thus risk exacerbating, or merely delaying, social tensions and reproducing traditional sources of violence. Paris calls for a process of careful institutionalisation before liberalising reforms are implemented, in order to ensure that these potentially destabilising effects are managed and reforms are phased in at a pace the situation can withstand (Paris 2004: 6).

Ultimately, robustness may necessitate a trade-off between practicality and normative desirability to ensure that the institution is realistically achievable and not destabilising (Goodin 1996: 37). In this respect, the choice of transitional justice mechanisms provides a particularly useful example of the complexities of such trade-offs in institutional choice. The question of whether a state in political transition should establish mechanisms to deal with past crimes, and, if so, the appropriate institutional choice, has been the subject of significant debate, including in the three case studies addressed in this book. Although the legal, moral and political arguments in favour of delivering accountability are relatively well established,[30] the relative merits of particular institutional choices, notably prosecutions versus non-punitive measures, remain contentious.

Those in favour of prosecutions have argued that they establish unequivocally a culture of accountability based on individual legal responsibility, and are more difficult for spoilers to challenge than non-legal attempts at redress (Little 1999: 68). In the post-conflict context, however, they have the potential to be destabilising and detrimental to the broader goal of reconciliation (Mendez 1997a: 1, 7). Where the residual powers of the old order oppose trials and impose serious restrictions, or where trials are used for political retribution, processes of accountability and justice may be de-legitimised (Mendez 1997a: 4, 7). There are also practical issues: the criminal justice system may be unable to handle the volume of prosecutions or to provide necessary support systems such as witness protection programmes.

The choice of prosecution system may also be relevant. International tribunals have been advocated in situations where political or legal reality precludes action by the national government. However, they may result in clashes of jurisdiction with national courts or complicate legal regimes. They may be ineffective where cooperation from the host state or other key parties – such as assistance with arrests or evidentiary matters – is not forthcoming. They are also subject to the political will of international powers and to restrictions based on principles of state sovereignty (Goldstone 1996: 498; Cassese 1998: 10–13).

Those in favour of non-punitive measures have argued that, if the real goal of a justice system is to end violence, then reconciliation or other restorative justice mechanisms might be preferable to criminal prosecutions. Restorative justice processes may assist in restoring a moral order that has been severely damaged or in building up a just political order if none previously existed (Kiss 2000: 80). They may be less likely to overwhelm transitional judicial systems, while offering the potential to include community leaders and to build upon pre-existing community processes (Goldstone 1996: 493). Truth commissions may also help create a culture of rights and accountability and highlight the character of the new political order (Du Toit 2000: 124–125; Rotberg 2000: 11).

Critics of truth commissions, however, have argued that they weaken the goal of accountability. Political compromises struck when formulating the terms of reference of a truth commission, particularly amnesties, may undermine the commission's credibility and distort the construction of justice (Rotberg 2000: 7). Moreover, if the truth commission does not deliver to victims a minimum acceptable degree of accountability, broader concepts of justice may be undermined in the future.

Ratner (2000: 488) has argued that, to avoid this, a truth commission should address the issue of accountability in a way that is seen by society as procedurally and substantively "just". The society in question may not view accountability in its narrow legalistic sense or interpret key concepts, such as the meaning of "gross human rights violation", in a way consistent with liberal democratic notions of justice. If such concepts are imposed, the commission may not be accepted (Hamber 1998: 3). At the same time, if the truth commission does not conform strictly to these concepts, it is questionable whether it will provide a successful foundation upon which to realise liberal democratic notions of justice in future (Du Toit 2000: 124).

A further design issue is the question of unintended or opposite effects – whether, for example, truth commissions produce disturbing reports that exacerbate instability in already tense and politically fragile environments. Hayner (1996: 23, 27, 176) has observed that, where violent destabilising elements remain and threaten to sabotage the process, truth commissions may fail to achieve their goals and may spark further violence. Ultimately, the question of what the community is willing to bear is crucial. In situations where communities are not willing to revisit past abuses, the public may not engage with the process, which may lead to perceptions that the commission was not fair or inclusive (Minow 2000: 240).

Observations

Contemporary UN peace operations, including the Kosovo and East Timor transitional administrations, mirrored broader UN discourse in consistent but somewhat vague rhetoric concerning the rule of law. At the policy level, there was increasingly clear direction that the rule of law was an essential component in state-building in post-conflict situations, and indeed an essential tool in social transformation. What was not reflected explicitly in UN policy statements was a sophisticated understanding of why this was believed to be the case or a comprehensive blueprint for how the rule of law was to be created.

At the operational level, the focus on "institution- and capacity-building" through strengthening the judiciary, law enforcement and prison sectors pointed to an apparent lack of clarity over the difference between "institution-building" and "organisation-building". Rather than understanding institutions as structures of social order and cooperation concerned with upholding stable, valued, recurring patterns of social behaviour (following Goodin 1996, Offe 1996 and Pettit 1996), the idea of "institution-building" was equated more closely with the organisational structures that could enforce those patterns, namely state justice bodies. The apparent melding of the two ideas in UN conceptions of "institution-building" appears to have contributed to a formalistic approach based on the replication of western organisational structures, missing the critical importance of promoting stable and legitimate patterns of social behaviour as the foundation for the rule of law.

As Douglass North describes (1990: 3; 1993), confusing institutions and organisations is akin to conflating the "rules of the game in a society" with the players of that game.[31] Although the two are intertwined – such that organisations allow groups of people to pursue opportunities created by the institutional "rules of the game", to give structure and form to institutional configurations and to influence the direction of institutional change – they are not the same thing (North 1990: 7).

Similarly, the UN approach appears not to have drawn a clear distinction between ends and means. As Kleinfeld Belton (2005: 6, 17) has observed, rule of law practitioners have commonly defined the rule of law not by the end purpose it is meant to serve but by its organisational attributes. This has resulted in the fusion of two parallel conversations – about the goods that the rule of law brings to society and about the organisations needed for society to possess the rule of law. Goals such as making the state abide by the law, equality before the law and efficient and impartial justice have thus been confused with the existence of legislatures, judiciaries, law schools, police services and prisons.

Case-study framework

Taken together, Chapters 1 and 2 point to several areas of enquiry of potential relevance to understanding the difficulties encountered by UN transitional administrations in seeking to establish the rule of law. These centre on the extent to which the administration overcame – or was overcome by – the challenges of pursuing rule of law promotion in disrupted

Table 3.1 Case-study framework

Area of enquiry	Core question	Key issues
1. Rule of law mandate	Did the mission's overall mandate and/or specific rule of law mandate give adequate strategic direction?	Was the overall mission mandate sufficient to accommodate rule of law objectives? Was specific strategic guidance given for rule of law issues at the outset of the mission? Was the mandate interpreted in a way that assisted with meeting rule of law objectives?
2. Establishing state justice institutions	Did the mission design and implement state justice institutions in a way that supported or hindered its rule of law objectives?	What institutional legacy did the UN mission inherit? Were pre-existing justice institutions intact, and, if so, were they consistent with UN rule of law objectives? To what extent did judicial, law enforcement, penal and retrospective justice bodies established by the UN mission meet the criteria for institutional robustness? Were there identifiable examples where an institutional choice clearly supported or undermined the rule of law?

3. Building commitment	Did the mission succeed in getting elite actors and the broader public behind its goal of establishing the rule of law? What factors helped or hindered this?	What was the degree of normative change attempted? Was there a political consensus behind rule of law objectives? What measures did the United Nations take to build such consensus? Were powerful individuals willing and able to influence social attitudes in the desired direction of change? What efforts did the UN mission make to inculcate a sense of ownership over processes designed to build the rule of law, and with what success? Did state rule of law bodies or other ordering mechanisms established by the UN transitional administration serve as incentives to commit to the rule of law agenda? Was alternative behaviour successfully discredited?
4. Rebuilding social relationships	Did the mission promote the rebuilding of trust and social capital in a way that supported its rule of law objectives?	Were social relationships compromised by the conflict? What social capital remained and how was trust characterised? What ramifications did this have in the rule of law arena? Did the UN transitional administration take effective steps to rebuild social relationships?
5. Strengthening state capacity	Did the UN ensure a successor administration sufficiently robust to maintain and advance rule of law gains after its departure?	What state capacity existed at the time of deployment? What indicators of improved state capacity were observable at the end of the transition period and attributable to actions by the UN transitional administration?

Table 3.1 (cont.)

Area of enquiry	Core question	Key issues
6. Restoring security	Did the UN restore and maintain security to a point where this had a positive bearing on the establishment of the rule of law?	Did the type and intensity of the conflict have a bearing on the UN transitional administration's rule of law work? Were specific linkages between the security environment and the justice sector evident? Did the UN mission neutralise violent actors or spoilers, or did it exacerbate conflict?
7. Addressing informal justice structures	Did the UN mission make effective use of informal justice structures to extract social loyalty to the rule of law?	What pre-existing informal justice structures existed? Were they compatible or incompatible with the UN rule of law agenda? Did the UN transitional administration make efforts to dismantle or promote such structures, link them with the formal justice system or otherwise incorporate them into its rule of law strategy?
8. Dealing with the past	Did the United Nations deal with "the past" in a way that made a positive contribution to establishing the rule of law for the future?	To what extent was society divided and traumatised by the preceding violence? What societal demands were there for past grievances to be addressed, and did the UN transitional administration respond effectively to these demands?
9. Performing effectively	Was mission performance adequate to support UN rule of law objectives?	Was pre-mission planning adequate and was there an appropriate exit strategy? Did operational problems such as mission coordination, resource shortfalls and deployment length impede performance?

states, such as a lack of state capacity, fragile social relationships and security dilemmas. They also focus on the extent to which the state-based enforcement model critiqued in this chapter proved effective or ineffective: whether institutional design choices relating to the state justice system were robust and effective; whether the mission took adequate account of the "rules of the game" present in informal structures and their potential role in extracting social loyalty to the rule of law; whether the mission succeeded in gaining the commitment[32] of elites, constituencies and the broader public to the rule of law as a value system; and whether it dealt with the question of justice for past crimes in a way that made a positive contribution to establishing the rule of law for the future. Finally, they relate also to more generic "performance" issues, such as whether the United Nations established rule of law promotion as an overarching strategic objective, including through an appropriate mission mandate; and whether the performance of the mission itself on the ground was adequate to support its rule of law goals.

Table 3.1 sets out a common framework of areas of enquiry and key questions as the basis for scrutiny of the case studies. The next three chapters examine the performance of UN transitional administrations in Cambodia, East Timor and Kosovo with respect to each of the areas of enquiry in Table 3.1.

Notes

1. See, for example, UNGA (2000a), the Universal Declaration of Human Rights (UDHR), the International Covenant on Civil and Political Rights, and the International Covenant on Economic, Social and Cultural Rights. See also the Basic Principles on the Independence of the Judiciary (1985), Guidelines on the Role of Prosecutors (1990), Basic Principles on the Role of Lawyers (1990), Code of Conduct for Law Enforcement Officials (1979), Principles Relating to the Status and Functioning of National Institutions for Protection and Promotion of Human Rights (1993) and Standard Minimum Rules for the Treatment of Prisoners (1955). On the substantive underpinning of the UN notion of the rule of law, see the 1993 *Vienna Declaration and Program of Action* for the World Conference on Human Rights (UNGA 1993), UNGA (1994a, 2000a). See also Farrall (2007: 2), who notes a rapid increase in references to the rule of law in Security Council resolutions, from a handful of times during the Cold War to at least 69 resolutions between 1998 and 2006.
2. For example, see McNamara (1993: 3); Agreements on a Comprehensive Political Settlement of the Cambodia Conflict (1991: Annex 1.B.5.B); and UNSC (1997: para. 3).
3. The Organization for Security and Co-operation in Europe, mandated to conduct rule of law institution-building under UNMIK, stated that its goal was to re-establish a judicial system "based on democratic principles and human rights" (OMIK 2006). It also pointed to the specific goal of establishing an ethnically and politically independent and impartial judiciary. The United Nations Transitional Authority in Cambodia (UNTAC) was mandated to supervise law enforcement and judicial processes with the

objective of ensuring impartiality and the full protection of human rights and fundamental freedoms (Agreements on a Comprehensive Political Settlement of the Cambodia Conflict 1991: Annex 1.B.5.B).

4. For example, the East Timor constitution provides for a "unitary democratic state, based on the rule of law and the principle of separation of powers" (UNSC 2002b: para. 5).

5. See, for example, the preamble of the *Provisions dated September 10, 1992 Relating to the Judiciary and Criminal Law and Procedure Applicable in Cambodia during the Transitional Period*.

6. See UNSC (2000f: Annex, para. 2).

7. For example, documents relating to the establishment of the UNTAC Special Prosecutor refer to concerns that judicial independence was not being upheld and courts were not meeting UN standards (Plunkett 1993: 10).

8. For further discussion of these principles, see Tamanaha (2001: 98); Dicey (1889: 114–115); Dworkin (1986: 96–98).

9. Similar comments were made about Kosovo. See, for example, UNMIK (2001c).

10. See, for example, UNMIK (2002b); UNSC (2001b: 11); and McNamara (1994: 165).

11. See, for example, UNGA (1992: para. 59) and UNGA (2000c: 7).

12. See UNGA (2000b: preamble); UNSC (1999a: 12; 1999b: 10; 2000b: 33; 2000f: 4); Strohmeyer (2001: 60); and Goldstone (1996: 487–488).

13. See, for example, UNSC (2006a: paras 4, 5); Vieira de Mello (2002: 5); preamble to the *Provisions dated September 10, 1992 relating to the Judiciary and Criminal Law and Procedure Applicable in Cambodia during the Transitional Period*; UNSC (1999a: para. 66). See also UNSC (2004e: 3).

14. The *Vienna Declaration* (UNGA 1993: para. 27) also speaks of the administration of justice as "indispensable to the processes of democracy and sustainable development". See also Strohmeyer (2001: 60).

15. See the Universal Declaration of Human Rights (preamble); UNGA (1994a: preamble); UNHCHR (1999: preamble; 2002: preamble); Vieira de Mello (2001b).

16. Strohmeyer (2001: 60) argues this point. See also McNamara (1993: 3–4); UNSC (1999a: para. 121); Vieira de Mello (2001b).

17. See Akashi (1992a); UNMIK (2002b); UNSC (2000b: 33).

18. UN bodies such as the Commission on Human Rights (CHR) invest accounting for the past with a high degree of transformative significance, arguing for example that justice for past crimes plays a critical role in the development of a secure, democratic future for countries in transition – that there can be "no democracy without justice" (Robinson 2000: 1). Discourse on justice tends to be imbued with human rights ideals and to reflect highly legalistic conceptions that emphasise individual accountability (Kiss 2000: 68). Reconciliation processes, truth-telling and justice processes outside the legal justice system are increasingly recognised as important components of peacebuilding packages (UNSC 2004e: 17).

19. See, for example, Puymbroeck (2001: 13); Ratner (2000: 449); and Rotberg (2000: 6).

20. The pursuit of retrospective justice appears to be more controversial than the establishment of justice systems. See Huntington (1991: 209) on the "torturer problem"; Mendez (1997a: 1–8) on retrospective justice and the democratisation process; Sieff and Wright (1999: 758) and Cassese (1998: 10) on the view that the attainment of peace cannot be divorced from the pursuit of retrospective justice; Goldstone (1996: 488–490) and Roht-Arriaza (1997: 94) on the deterrence value of justice for the past; and McHugh (1996: 1) on the role of truth commissions in contributing to post-conflict peacebuilding.

21. See, for example, the 1993 *Vienna Declaration* (UNGA 1993: para. 34); UNSC (2001a: 2, 8); UNGA (2000c: 24); and the preamble to the *Provisions dated September 10, 1992*

relating to the Judiciary and Criminal Law and Procedure Applicable in Cambodia during the Transitional Period.

22. See, for example, Office of the United Nations Special Coordinator in the Occupied Territories (1999); UNTAC (1993a).
23. These include the Basic Principles on the Independence of the Judiciary (1985), Guidelines on the Role of Prosecutors (1990), Basic Principles on the Role of Lawyers (1990), and Principles Relating to the Status and Functioning of National Institutions for Protection and Promotion of Human Rights (1993).
24. See UNSC (2000e: 10; 2002b: 16); and UNTAET (1999b: 10).
25. See, for example, OMIK (2001: 1); UNSC (2000b: 24; 2001b: 11).
26. There appears to have been increasing recognition of the relevance of the rule of law across all branches of government as well as independent actors and civil society. See, for example, Office of the United Nations Special Coordinator in the Occupied Territories (1999); UNSC (2004e: 9); and UNGA (2000b).
27. See also Kelsen (1946: 19); Ehrlich (1975); Tamanaha (2001: 3); Braibanti (1968: 3); and P. Fitzpatrick (1980: 49).
28. Following Marshall's definition, restorative justice may be viewed as "a process whereby all the parties with a stake in a particular offense come together to resolve collectively how to deal with the aftermath of the offense and its implications for the future" (quoted in Braithwaite 2000: 115). Brookes (2000) argues that the essential components of restorative justice are reconciliation between the victim and offender; reparation, whereby the offender takes responsibility for the crime by making good through an agreed form of compensation; and transformation, whereby individuals and communities experience some change in conditions perpetuating the cycle of violence exemplified in the original criminal behaviour. Braithwaite (2000: 115, 129) also notes that restorative justice is defined operationally by the use of "rituals of repentance" that allow dignified restoration of the harm resulting from wrongdoing.
29. For example, see Anleu (2000: 91–92); Merry (1988); Zerner (1994: 1115–1117); and Geertz (1983: 173).
30. There are strong legal, moral and political arguments in favour of delivering accountability for past crimes, many but not all of which favour prosecutions. Legally, an emerging principle of accountability under international law for crimes against humanity imposes the obligation to investigate, prosecute and punish human rights abusers (Mendez 1997a: 5). Morally, the general principle of accountability is well accepted, although many analysts have argued that prosecutions per se can be morally justified only if the objective of deterring future crimes is better served by punishment than by leniency (Mendez 1997a: 6). Politically, proponents of accountability argue that a culture of accountability is essential to the rule of law and democracy, whereas condoning impunity undermines these principles and stunts political reconciliation processes (Little 1999: 66).
31. More specifically, North (1993) defines institutions as the humanly devised constraints that structure human interaction, which comprise formal constraints such as rules, laws and constitutions; informal constraints such as norms of behaviour, conventions and self-imposed codes of conduct; and their enforcement characteristics. He defines organisations as groups of individuals bound together by some common purpose to achieve certain objectives. Organisations may include political bodies, such as political parties or the Senate; economic bodies, such as firms and trade unions; social bodies, such as churches and clubs; and educational bodies, such as schools and universities.
32. For the purposes of this discussion, "commitment" can be thought of as consent to regulate one's behaviour by binding oneself to a value system and the course of action prescribed by that value system.

4

The line of least resistance: The UN Transitional Authority in Cambodia

The United Nations Transitional Authority in Cambodia (UNTAC) was a landmark mission that assumed unprecedented state-building functions. It intervened with a high degree of intrusiveness in a sovereign state by assuming "direct control" over Cambodia's existing administration (Peou 1997: 98). It registered some significant successes in meeting its expansive mandate: ending full-scale civil war, repatriating 370,000 refugees and holding national elections in May 1993, the first to be fully conducted by the United Nations. For Cambodia, this broke the deadlock of civil strife, exposed the political system to a degree of opposition and opened the country to international development assistance.

UNTAC's shortcomings were equally weighty: it was not able fully to implement the ceasefire or to canton, demobilise and disarm the four factions;[1] nor was it successful in fully upholding law and order or political neutrality during the election period.[2] This meant that UNTAC was ultimately unable to meet its own primary objectives of ending civil strife and human rights abuses, maintaining social order and supporting democratic transition. More than a decade on from the UNTAC mission, the continued absence of crucial attributes of a democratic rule of law state – notably a lamentable justice system, widespread human rights abuses and the continued primacy of strongmen who operated above the law – raised questions about whether UNTAC had missed a critical opportunity to promote robust foundations for the rule of law.

No entry without strategy: Building the rule of law under UN transitional administration, Bull, United Nations University Press, 2008, ISBN 978-92-808-1151-3

UNTAC's work in the rule of law sphere was limited, but nonetheless unprecedented in UN peace operations. It undertook or attempted the following initiatives:

- *Oversight of constitutional reform*, leading to the adoption of a constitution following the election of a National Assembly.
- *legislative reform*, including the adoption of legislation relating to criminal law and procedure, an electoral law and international human rights instruments;
- *judicial reform*, consisting of limited measures to promote better court procedure, the establishment in January 1993 of a Special Prosecutor position, allowing it to prosecute cases unilaterally, and limited efforts to promote civilian jurisdiction over military cases;
- *prison reform*, focusing on releasing political prisoners, ending shackling, improving prison conditions and training prison officials;
- *police reform*, through monitoring and investigating crimes, supervising and training local police officers and improving law enforcement structures in some areas;
- *maintenance of public security* during the transition period, involving direct "supervision and control" of Cambodian security agencies;
- *human rights activities*, including investigations of politically motivated crimes and education programmes.

These measures represented the first steps toward the more sophisticated rule of law responses of later UN peace operations. UNTAC was not explicitly mandated to "establish the rule of law", yet its responsibilities under the *Agreements on a Comprehensive Political Settlement of the Cambodia Conflict* (Paris Agreements 1991) to carry out these functions in pursuit of a "just and durable peace" pointed clearly to an ambition for UNTAC to create the conditions in which a lasting rule of law could be established.

UNTAC's initiatives related to the rule of law had some positive impact. A former Special Representative of the Secretary-General for Human Rights in Cambodia, Justice Kirby, credited UNTAC with laying some foundations for the "beginnings of a rule of law state" (quoted in Morison 1996). Members of the Cambodian human rights community interviewed by me emphasised UNTAC's contribution to incremental progress towards accountability in law, greater political commitment to judicial reform, improved political freedoms and safer investment prospects, when at no period in the past had there been any level of transparency or accountability in government. Under UNTAC, the legislative framework was improved, the police and military brought under a degree of civilian discipline and human rights abuses reduced. The concept of international accountability – notably conformity with international human rights instruments – was introduced. A fledgling civil society and media were established. UNTAC helped stimulate awareness and interest amongst the international donor community in long-term justice sector projects, and provided the starting point for subsequent work by the United Nations Cambodian Office of the High Commissioner for Human Rights (UNCOHCHR).

By the end of the mission in September 1993, however, the conditions for a "just and durable" peace, national reconciliation and the protection of human rights were clearly not established. Cambodians were not protected from arbitrariness or abuse in the exercise of power by the state, whose leaders remained insubordinate to the law, corrupt and implicated in human rights violations. A comprehensive legal framework based on a liberal democratic value system was not fully established, let alone enforced. Separation of powers was not established and almost no progress had been made in creating effective, impartial and accessible criminal justice, penal and law enforcement systems. Virtually no attention had been paid to nurturing informal legal institutions or non-legal social institutions that might have supported the rule of law.

This chapter identifies several key factors that contributed to UNTAC's failure to meet, or at least to contribute significantly to, those benchmarks. These included an inadequate mandate that was interpreted narrowly, particularly with regard to UNTAC's assumption of the responsibilities of the "state"; insufficient focus on creating the conditions for genuine democratisation, including a cohesive rule of law strategy that focused on both state and non-state rule of law institutions; a failure to build commitment for rule of law goals amongst the political elite and the broader community; insufficient attention to building state capacity for rule of law initiatives to be continued after UNTAC; the incomplete restoration of security; and avoidance of the question of how to deal with past crimes. Mission shortcomings, including a truncated deployment period and a poorly formulated exit strategy, exacerbated these problems. Before elaborating on these issues, the next section places the case study in context by considering the rule of law environment into which UNTAC deployed.

Rule of law landscape

UNTAC deployed into a rule of law environment that bore little resemblance to the western liberal model. The Pol Pot era had weakened or eradicated most legal institutions. Under Democratic Kampuchea, the French civil law system established in 1863 was dismantled and customary justice systems – the exclusive source of law prior to the French and the sole rules-based justice system in most rural areas – had been weakened (Sok 1998: 17). Forced confessions and summary executions became the common mode for dispensing "justice" (Fernando 1998: 59). The absence of any urban social organisation following the mass expulsions of 1975 eroded the familiarity of Cambodians with the concept of regulating society by rules of law (Fernando 1998: 101–105). Most legal personnel were killed or fled the country and by 1990 fewer than a dozen people remained in Cambodia with any form of professional legal education (S. O. Sok, personal communication, 1 July 2002; Sok 1998: 162).

During the 1980s, the People's Republic of Kampuchea (1979–89) installed the socialist constitutional law and practices prevailing in Vietnam. Under this model, the executive dominated the judiciary, an arrangement formalised by the passage in April 1989 of the Constitution of the State of Cambodia (SOC), which did not provide for separation of powers or an independent judiciary.[3] From 1979 to 1985 there was only one level of court: where deemed necessary, judgments were reviewed by the Ministry of Justice and finalised by the Council of State (Sok and Sarin 1998: 53). Executive control over judicial review continued following the establishment of a Supreme Court in 1985, which itself claimed to be "not competent" to resolve law suits, but to be competent only to examine them "so that they may be turned over to the competent organs to be dealt with" (Fernando 1998: 60). A criminal law was introduced in 1980, but was used only to detain opponents of the Vietnamese.

Apart from executive control of the judiciary, the key characteristics of the socialist-style trial system introduced during this period were the predetermination of trial outcomes and the use of forced confessions (Wicremasinghe 1998: 75). The Ministry of Justice or provincial authorities were consulted on the verdict, which they varied at will.[4] Criminal defenders were employees of the state and subordinate to prosecutors, with their role limited in practice to arguing mitigating circumstances for sentencing (HRW Asia 1995: 76). Under this model, the actual courtroom trial was relatively unimportant compared with pre-trial investigations, and the role and prestige of the court and judges diminished (Falt 1998: 162). Substandard criminal justice procedures were commonplace, notably the arbitrary arrest and detention without trial of large numbers of political prisoners, the use of excessive military and police force, and summary execution (Shawcross 1994: 58).

UNTAC therefore inherited a damaged and rudimentary hybrid of French colonial civil law and Vietnamese legislation, influenced profoundly by the socialist model, which concentrated power in the executive and marginalised the judiciary (Sok and Sarin 1998: 18; Falt 1998: 162). Almost no judicial structures remained in the SOC, administratively the most intact of the four factions, and the zones of the Khmer People's

National Liberation Front (KPNLF), the National United Front for an Independent, Neutral, Peaceful and Democratic Cambodia (FUNCIN-PEC) and the National Army of Democratic Kampuchea (NADK or Khmer Rouge) operated under arbitrary military rule (Brown and Zasloff 1998: 113). Judicial structures, where they existed, were dysfunctional and highly politicised, with courts operating under directives from the Ministry of Justice (Tan 1995: 205; McNamara 1994: 1; Brown and Zasloff 1998: 113). The SOC police operated outside the jurisdiction of the courts and were controlled by the Ministry of the Interior or local warlords (Mackinlay, Chopra and Minear 1992: 16). Supporting organisations that might have been in a position to check abuse of power, such as a legislature, human rights bodies, civil society groups and a free press, were virtually non-existent (Brown and Zasloff 1998: 114). The rule of law was a largely irrelevant concept in Cambodia's pre-eminent political institutions: a patronage system that operated outside the law, a military that involved itself excessively in state affairs, and the "new rich", whose wealth derived from illegal activities (Berry 1997: 246; Fernando 1998: 104).

This was, to say the least, a hostile environment in which to attempt to promote the rule of law. As the next section will argue, UNTAC's rule of law mandate provided insufficient basis for the magnitude of the task.

Setting the parameters: UNTAC's rule of law mandate

Rhetorically, the architects of the Paris Agreements recognised the rule of law as constitutive of the political and social order they desired to create in Cambodia. The Agreements recognised the threat posed by political violence and lawlessness to UNTAC's primary democratisation objectives of conducting elections and safeguarding civil and political rights against state abuse. The imperative to act decisively on the rule of law was not, however, reflected in UNTAC's mandate. First, the Paris Agreements did not explicitly provide UNTAC with a rule of law mandate. Second, UNTAC's mandate to "supervise and control" existing administrative structures, not replace them, constrained its ability to make critical changes in those structures. Third, mission staff narrowly interpreted the mandate, further limiting scope for action.

UNTAC's force commander, General John Sanderson, has argued that omitting to provide specifically in the mandate for a "justice package" was one of the major weaknesses of the Paris Agreements (Sanderson n.d.: 11). As a result, justice was viewed not as a discrete operational area, but through the prism of UNTAC's three primary operational concerns: the restoration of security, the holding of elections and economic reconstruction. Rule of law initiatives found it difficult to compete for resources and attention with directly mandated objectives. Initiatives were developed in a piecemeal fashion rather than under a coherent rule of law "pillar" of the sort that emerged in subsequent peace operations.

UNTAC was mandated not to create new administrative structures but to supervise and control those that already existed. Accordingly, senior UNTAC officials made clear publicly that it was not their intention to create a new set of judicial institutions to replace bodies in the existing administrative structures, because of the difficulty of justifying this under the Paris Agreements and the even greater difficulty of implementation. UNTAC thus sought to work with existing judicial structures. This had two negative consequences. First, as described above, these structures were antithetical to the structures and values of a liberal democratic regime. Second, the "supervise and control" approach proved inadequate to assert control over the judiciary or other relevant administrative structures, undermining not only UNTAC's rule of law objectives but its own credibility. This is discussed further below.

The inadequacies of UNTAC's rule of law mandate appear to have stemmed from both theoretical shortcomings in peacebuilding techniques at that time and sovereignty considerations. Former UNTAC staff stressed that in peacekeeping circles, both intervention and development practice paradigms were relatively undeveloped at the time. The concept of "good governance" and a sophisticated awareness of the interconnections between democracy, the rule of law and the various components of peace operations were "old hat" in the human rights and development studies fields, but did not filter into the theoretical or operational basis of peacekeeping until after UNTAC.

Sovereignty considerations played a prominent role in the decision to limit UNTAC's mandate to "supervise and control" the existing administrative structures. Prince Norodom Sihanouk's 1981 proposal for some form of UN trusteeship was dismissed as legally infeasible because Cambodia was already a UN member state. The US Congressman Stephen Solarz later proposed that the United Nations limit itself to exercising only administrative and supervisory functions over existing administrative structures. This became the genesis of the Australian proposal on which the peace negotiations were based (Berry 1997: 23). In developing a framework that was acceptable to all parties, negotiators thus limited the extent to which UNTAC could assume or direct the functions of the state. UNTAC was there to assist, not take the place of, the state.

At the same time, the Paris Agreements arguably obliged and empowered UNTAC to take steps with a direct bearing on rule of law creation. Under the Paris Agreements (1991), UNTAC was

- obliged to foster an environment in which respect for human rights would be ensured (Article 16);
- mandated with direct control over all administrative agencies, bodies and offices acting in the field of public security, with the purpose of ensuring "strict neutrality" (Annex 1, Section B(1));
- accorded "supervision or control" of civil police and, in consultation with the Supreme National Council (SNC), supervisory powers over law enforcement and judicial processes to the extent necessary to ensure that law and order were maintained effectively and impartially and that human rights and fundamental freedoms were fully protected (Annex 1, Section B(5)(b));
- empowered to investigate complaints and allegations regarding actions by the existing administrative structures that were inconsistent with or undermined the settlement. UNTAC was empowered to undertake investigations on its own initiative and, where necessary, to take "appropriate corrective steps" (Annex 1, Section B(6));
- obliged to develop and implement a programme of human rights education, and granted general human rights oversight during the transitional period, including the investigation of human rights complaints and "where appropriate, corrective action" (Annex 1, Section E).

Annex 5 of the Paris Agreements also stipulated principles for a new constitution, including human rights protection, "due process and equality before the law", and the establishment of an independent judiciary. UNTAC itself was not mandated to design or implement the new constitution but it was understood that this would be the culmination of the operation.

These provisions arguably provided sufficient foundation for a more proactive approach by UNTAC in the justice area, particularly when read in conjunction with the preamble to the Transitional Criminal Law (see below), which noted deficiencies in Cambodian state structures, laws and the judiciary and stated that "UNTAC has the responsibility to assist in establishing such structures, laws and judicial institutions where they are absent and to improve them where they already exist in order to bring them up to the requirements of the Agreement".[5]

The Special Representative of the Secretary-General Yasushi Akashi confirmed this in a statement to the SNC[6] in which he undertook to discontinue those institutions and practices that fell short of UN standards and to establish uniform judicial and legal standards in all provinces and zones (Akashi 1992b). This was evidently not followed through and for the rest of the mission senior UNTAC officials continued to debate the extent to which UNTAC had been empowered to take action on rule of law issues. Of specific concern were the question of "corrective action", the role of Civilian Police (CIVPOL) and the limits of the human rights mandate.

UNTAC made very limited use of its right to take "corrective action" in the investigation of human rights complaints. This appears to have resulted from Akashi's narrow interpretation of the mandate, which he justified with respect to the "limited time period and resources and political and diplomatic constraints within which UNTAC functioned" (quoted in Findlay 1995: 64). He considered "corrective action" to be limited to actions specified in the Paris Agreements, such as the dismissal or transfer of government officials. These too were used sparingly. No Cambodian police or military officials were removed from their positions for human rights violations, even where their responsibility had been clearly established. The ongoing involvement of SOC security personnel in human rights violations could arguably have justified action, including against senior officials who were responsible if not directly involved (McNamara 1994: 20). In any event, where the Special Representative did make requests for officials to be removed from office, the SOC refused to comply (Findlay 1995: 65). "Corrective action" by the Human Rights Component was limited to the release of several hundred prisoners detained without trial (Brown and Zasloff 1998: 117). Even towards the end of the operation, as the SOC repeatedly refused to arrest individuals investigated by UNTAC, Akashi considered the arrest and prosecution of suspects to be the right of the law enforcement of the SOC and other factions, "a State responsibility which the UN can promote or facilitate but cannot replace" (quoted in Findlay 1995: 65). Although he subsequently signed off on the establishment of an UNTAC Special Prosecutor to carry out this function, his lack of support for the initiative seems to have played a key role in its failure.

Similarly, the CIVPOL mandate was inadequate. CIVPOL was not given an executive policing mandate until late in the operation and thus had no clear authority for proactive involvement in addressing criminal violence (Plunkett 1994: 70). CIVPOL viewed this as a matter for the peacekeeping force, whereas the latter was constrained by UNTAC's Chapter VI Security Council authorisation to act neutrally and to use minimum force in self-defence. The gap in violence management thus created was never fully closed. Moreover, there were large discrepancies in the interpretation and application of CIVPOL's mandate. In some areas, CIVPOL interpreted their role broadly and conducted extensive policing operations, to the point where they were criticised by other elements in UNTAC for exceeding their powers. In other locations, CIVPOL reported that the limited mandate served as an excuse for inaction.

Finally, problems formulating and interpreting UNTAC's human rights mandate had a direct bearing on rule of law issues. In the absence of a specific rule of law mandate, the Human Rights Component became the principal repository for UNTAC's rule of law activities. Although UNTAC had been given the most comprehensive human rights mandate of any peacekeeping operation to date, there was confusion within the UN system and on the part of some governments as to what rights were to be protected, and how. The mission lacked clear guidelines from New York and Geneva, and tensions developed between headquarters and the mission, and within the mission itself, over the mandate (McNamara 1995a: 168). Much of this stemmed from debate over what could realistically be accomplished in Cambodia, given the lack of political will by parties to the agreement to implement change. Akashi believed that implementing stronger human rights safeguards was an unrealistic prospect given the lack of genuine cooperation from the Cambodian parties and of credible enforcement mechanisms. The Director of the Human Rights Component, Dennis McNamara, believed a more aggressive approach not only should have been pursued but was essential to both UNTAC's success and Cambodia's future (Heininger 1994: 93).

These issues reflected ongoing tension amongst elements of UNTAC over the question of "sensitivities" in the rule of law area. Senior UNTAC personnel argued that SOC leaders, particularly Prime Minister Hun Sen, would never accept any action in the justice sector. Accordingly, they were unwilling to attempt to assert control, even where possible, and UNTAC backed away from ensuring that key constitutional provisions of the Paris Agreements, such as the establishment of an independent judiciary and the protection of non-Khmer nationals, were pursued in a determined fashion (McNamara 1994: 20–21). McNamara (1994: 21) attributes this judgement to "exaggerated sensitivities" within UNTAC over charges of colonialism made regularly by Cambodian leaders including Sihanouk. Regardless of who was correct, the consequence was the same: the constitutional requirements of the Agreements were not fully met. UN perceptions that judicial issues were "too sensitive" to raise with the Cambodian government continued after UNTAC and UN agencies did not begin to address the judiciary in earnest until after the 1998 elections.

Establishing state justice institutions

UNTAC made some progress in strengthening Cambodia's constitutional and legislative framework, but achieved little improvement in judicial, penal and law enforcement institutions. It thereby missed the opportunity to establish a basic institutional structure conducive to long-term efforts to embed effective and durable rule of law institutions. In continuing to deal with a weak, corrupt and exploited judiciary, UNTAC may unwittingly have further entrenched existing distortions. By the time of UNTAC's withdrawal, Cambodian rule of law institutions remained unjust, unreliable, inaccessible and mistrusted.

Constitutional framework

The constitution adopted by Cambodia's Constituent Assembly in 1993 was, with some omissions, consistent with UN standards. Modelled on the French judicial system, a chapter on the judiciary provided for separation of powers and set down many essential features of the western liberal model, including the creation of a public prosecutor and a Supreme Council of the Magistracy to appoint, oversee and discipline judges and prosecutors. However, key issues such as the status of judges and prosecutors and the functioning of the judiciary were left to be defined in later laws, which at the time of writing had still not been enacted.

Similarly, Chapter III of the constitution provided human rights guarantees consistent with international covenants, stressing individual freedoms and banning capital punishment, physical abuse and ill treatment by state actors. Although relatively comprehensive, there were some serious shortcomings: a vaguely worded national security caveat, inconsistencies with the Convention Against Torture and the exclusion of non-Khmer citizens from human rights protections (McNamara 1995a: 169). All were subsequently used by state actors to deny basic human rights protections, notably to limit freedom of demonstration and to discriminate against ethnic Vietnamese. Again, constitutional provisions on human rights were not supported by a full complement of laws.

Although in some senses a Cambodian product, the constitution was not fully endorsed by either the elite or the public in Cambodia. The pro forma for the constitution was set down in the Paris Agreements and drafted with little Cambodian input. The constitution itself was written by a 13-member committee of Constituent Assembly members in a series of closed door meetings, the proceedings of which were kept secret from the rest of the Constituent Assembly and the broader public (Marks 1994b: 61). Neither group was given the opportunity for input, apart from a public debate for five days before the constitution was adopted. The constitution's survival therefore rested on logic and aspirations unfamiliar to both the broader public and the political elite, most of who stood to lose from constitutionally constrained government (Brown and Zasloff 1998: 210). State and non-state actors violated its provisions routinely.

At the same time, UNTAC and its international sponsors had little influence over the drafting of the constitution (Curtis 1998: 13) and as a result lost critical leverage over one of the key outcomes of the peace process. An UNTAC draft was used (Tan 1995: 207), but Sihanouk cut off international assistance and ordered that no foreigners be involved in the drafting process, although a French professional eventually played a role (Brown and Zasloff 1998: 195). As a result, UNTAC lost influence over important issues germane to the rule of law, such as the structure of government and the question of rights for non-Khmer citizens.

Legislative framework

Pre-UNTAC legislation was minimal, with key areas of Cambodian life governed by decrees and regulations issued by government ministries rather than the legislature. This was a non-transparent process that concentrated power in the executive and provided extensive opportunities for state corruption (Donovan 1993: 95).

UNTAC closed several major gaps in Cambodia's legislative framework. Under UNTAC's direction, the SNC acceded to the International Covenant on Civil and Political Rights and the International Covenant on Economic, Social and Cultural Rights in April 1992 and signed five more human rights instruments in September of that year.[7] These instruments were translated into Khmer and disseminated widely by the Human Rights Component. UNTAC also drafted a comprehensive electoral law and code of conduct, which it used to some effect to curb irregularities during the election period (McNamara 1994: 6). Much of UNTAC's legislative work, however, contributed to serious ongoing violations of rule of law principles and resulted in a set of legislation that, while an improvement overall, was riddled with omissions and damaging provisions.

Two key pieces of legislation were enacted: the *Provisions dated September 10, 1992 Relating to the Judiciary and Criminal Law and Procedure Applicable in Cambodia during the Transitional Period* (hereafter the Transitional Criminal Law) and the *Law on Criminal Procedure* (1993). The former, adopted by the SNC on 10 September 1992, was the centrepiece of UNTAC efforts to address the politicisation of the judiciary and inadequate penal legislation. It emphasised the independence of the judiciary, incorporated the relevant provisions of international human rights instruments, and set down legal provisions relating to the judicial system, criminal procedure, trial, crimes, misdemeanours, punishments and applications. It was, however, drafted hastily by UNTAC's head of Public Security "at random without following a clear scheme and policy" (Wicremasinghe 1998: 76). Consultation on the law was limited: UNTAC held rudimentary consultations with courts and procurators then submitted it to the four factions with only a few days for comment. As a result it was viewed as an UNTAC rather than a Cambodian law. According to foreign and local individuals working in the justice sector at the time, this diminished its perceived relevance. The Khmer Rouge rejected the draft legislation, whereas the SOC and FUNCINPEC accepted it with some amendments, and then proceeded systematically to violate it (Fernando 1998: 62).

The law did not address some of the thorniest issues, such as the relationship between the courts and the police, the lower and higher courts and the trial system. The international covenants were not fully incorporated and some provisions did not meet international human rights standards on issues such as criminal defamation (AI 2002a). It did not proscribe a full list of basic criminal offences or provide for criminal defence. Assault, for example, was not a punishable offence unless it resulted in injury to the victim of at least six months' duration (Plunkett 1994: 71). Perhaps the most damaging segment of the law was Article 24(3), which implicitly recognised the admissibility of confessions as evidence, effectively institutionalising the common practice of using forced confessions as the primary or only trial evidence. In part the consequence of imprecise drafting, these oversights were also attributed to a lack of understanding on the part of the drafters of legal, police and court culture at the time the law was introduced (Wicremasinghe 1998: 71–76).

There was significant confusion over the content and interpretation of the new law. A Khmer translation was not available for several months after the law's adoption, and unresolved differences remained between the English and French versions. Additions were made to the text after its adoption by the SNC but never submitted to the SNC for approval, causing confusion over the law's content (Fernando 1998: 63). UNTAC conducted only a small number of two-week seminars to explain the new law to judges who found even basic concepts in the law alien. In the seminars, judges expressed confusion as to what they were meant to do; provincial judges stressed that, in the absence of adequate guidance, legal proceedings had come to a complete standstill in many provincial courts (Fernando 1998: 63). According to former CIVPOL officers interviewed for this study, in most areas Cambodian police were not given training regarding the new law.

Although the Transitional Criminal Law abrogated "any texts, provisions or written or unwritten rule contrary to the letter and spirit of the present text", the practices of the Vietnamese–Khmer model remained firmly intact. None of the provisions of the UNTAC code were applied in practice, except in a few cases where persistent interventions by the Human Rights Component secured the release of prisoners who had served lengthy detentions without trial (Fernando 1998: 62). It proved of little use in investigating or prosecuting cases of pre-election political violence in late 1992. UNTAC attempts to get these cases investigated merely revealed the widespread incidence of non-investigation of politically motivated or other crimes. In short, the judiciary remained under tight political control and the law made no inroads into meeting basic human rights standards in judicial or penal practice (McNamara 1994: 6).

The Law on Criminal Procedure was passed by the SOC on 29 January 1993. It provided for Justice Police, a provincial public prosecutor's department, investigating judges, provincial or municipal tribunals, appeal courts and the Supreme Court. Confusion reigned over whether it was meant to supplement or replace the Transitional Criminal Law and over whether other laws passed by the SOC during the transitional period were now invalid (Fernando 1998: 64). Article 125 further condoned the use of forced confessions, by explicitly and unconditionally recognising confessions as evidence and not requiring a test of voluntariness (Wicremasinghe 1998: 72). It also gave statutory recognition to the police dossier, under which convictions were made in the old socialist system. Standards of procedure were inadequate, with the focus mainly on the responsibilities of various court personnel rather than on how procedures such as issuing arrest warrants should be conducted (ADHOC et al. 1999: 23). The law was applied patchily: SOC courts applied some parts, such as bail provisions, following applications by the Human Rights Component and later by Cambodian defenders (Fernando 1998: 64–65). Court procedures such as the serving of notices, summons and warrants were not implemented and new bodies envisaged by the law, such as the Justice Police, were not created.

Despite the introduction of these two laws, legislative reform was incomplete. Many of Cambodia's pre-1993 laws remained in force and did not reflect the basic concepts and principles of liberal democracy enshrined in the constitution. Corruption was not addressed and no statute for judges and prosecutors was enacted. No regulations were passed governing membership of political parties or conflict of interest for judges or other legal personnel (ADHOC et al. 1999: 19). No civil service law was enacted, the consequence of which became clear in 1994 with the passage of the *Law adopted by the National Assembly on October 21, 1994 on the Common Statute of Civil Servants of the Kingdom of Cambodia*. This law sanctioned and institutionalised civil service impunity by protecting civil servants – including the police and military – from criminal prosecution without the consent of the Council of Ministers or the alleged offender's supervising ministry (ADHOC et al. 1999: 23).

By introducing an additional layer of law on top of the French and Vietnamese regimes, rather than using positive aspects of those legacies as a building block and ensuring that negative aspects were removed, UNTAC further confused the legal system. This was compounded by the introduction of commercial laws drawn from common law systems, which did not coalesce naturally with other civil law based codes.

Although intended to be temporary, UNTAC's "amateurish attempt at legal reform" (Fernando 1998: 63) remained in force in 2006. At the time of writing, the Transitional Criminal Law remained Cambodia's only criminal law.

The judiciary

Dennis McNamara (1994: 11) has argued that the "lack of attention and willingness to invest in the rebuilding of a professional judiciary with all necessary safeguards by the international community during [the UNTAC] period, was a major impediment to the establishment of a functioning democracy and civil society following the elections".

Parties to the Paris Agreements were aware of the dire state of Cambodia's judiciary, but did not make adequate provision to improve it. Article 5 of Annex 5 of the Agreements stipulated that under the new constitution "an independent judiciary will be established, empowered to enforce the rights provided under the Constitution", including the establishment of a new court system. But the Agreements did not stipulate a roadmap by which this might be achieved and, as discussed, UNTAC was neither explicitly mandated to create new judicial structures nor sufficiently focused on the issue.

UNTAC monitored the judiciary, mainly through the Human Rights Component. Executive interference continued unabated, with judges continuing to be required to seek advice from the Ministry of Justice (Fernando 1998: 97). Police routinely interfered in hearings, and during the election period a number of judges complained to UNTAC that they had been forced to campaign on behalf of the Cambodian People's Party (CPP), the political arm of the SOC (Hughes 1996: 35). UNTAC recorded many instances of well-intentioned judicial officials who wished to exercise greater independence but were afraid to do so (McNamara 1994: 11). Despite this, no concerted effort was made to remedy the situation. Judges were not forced to renounce their political affiliations, no statute for judicial conduct was enacted and no pressure was exerted on faction leaders to desist from judicial interference.

A further violation of due process was that of lengthy court delays. An UNTAC report on the situation in Kompong Thom province, for example, noted that, of 124 prisoners in the local jail, the trials of 100 had been delayed, some for as long as one year (Germanos 1992: 1).

UNTAC Human Rights officers monitored courts in both Phnom Penh and the provinces, but this proved ineffective in promoting better court process, given limited resources and time (McNamara 1994: 11). The first trial held in Kompong Thom province under the UNTAC-sponsored Law on Criminal Procedure, held on 16 March 1993, was indicative. The accused in the trial, Sao Yim, was an NADK soldier who had been captured the previous October after the destruction of a bridge and attack on nearby villages. He was initially sent to Phnom Penh for interrogation by the SOC authorities. His pre-trial confession was widely publicised in the media, after which he was thought to have been released. He was later discovered in Kompong Thom prison and, when he finally made it to court, he appeared without a defender and the prosecutor admitted there were no defenders in the province (Yahmed 1993: Annex IV).

UNTAC made no preparations for the new court system foreshadowed in the Paris Agreements and the post-UNTAC judicial structure thus inherited the deficiencies of the past. The Supreme Court, for example, had no appellate function, its power being limited to reviewing case records privately and, if necessary, requesting a retrial. Courts remained an organic part of the military-dominated executive, and civilian judges and prosecutors believed that the cooperation of military commanders was essential to the proper functioning of the justice system (HRW Asia 1995: 72). A former UNTAC official observed in 1998:

> Deviations and violations in regard to the provisions of criminal procedure are glaringly visible. The judges are, as the Minister of Justice confirms, in the habit of writing their judgement even before the cases are heard. Judges exercise their discretion, not judicially, but arbitrarily, acting on prejudices, preset opinions, extraneous facts and circumstances not established through evidence heard in court. This is more evident in cases where a political element is present ... What makes the process of adjudication even more arbitrary is the fact that judges treat the general principles of the law of evidence as alien and are not sensitive to practices of a free and fair trial. Instead, in judging cases, they adhere to the executive methodologies as strategies to which they are addicted. (Fernando 1998: 91)

Judicial professionalism

UNTAC officials were acutely aware of the scarcity of educated judges and prosecutors and of the systemic nature of professional misconduct (Yahmed 1992: 1; Germanos 1992: 1). Most judges appointed in the post-Khmer Rouge period were former teachers, with few legal credentials: as recently as 2002, only one-third of Cambodia's 200-odd judges had any legal training and only 40 per cent had reached high school (United States General Accounting Office 2002: 9). According to one prominent human rights activist, law was viewed by many as an undesirable profession because of the high level of politicisation.

UNTAC's efforts to improve judicial professionalism centred on a series of well-received but limited training courses. A five-year law degree was begun in 1992 and the first batch of 226 students graduated in 1997 (Sok 1998: 164). A two-year training course for court clerks and paralegals commenced in 1994. In the meantime, UNTAC and other organisations such as the International Commission of Jurists and international non-governmental organisations (NGOs) conducted basic training for judges, prosecutors and defenders. UNTAC conducted training sessions on the Transitional Criminal Law from November 1992 to early 1993 for approximately 200 persons representing the SOC, the KPNLF and FUNCINPEC (Porcell 1992: 3). In July 1993, the Human Rights Component ran a three-week programme for judges appointed or likely to be appointed to the Court of Appeals and Supreme Court (McNamara 1994: 15).

Education and training proved of little use in improving the conduct of judges faced with the more pressing concerns of livelihood and security. Judges did not receive a living wage, rendering corruption essential, and, despite some UNTAC assurances, judges and their families were not provided with adequate security from politically motivated violence and intimidation. According to one Cambodian national employed by UNTAC, local staff had repeatedly suggested to senior UNTAC international staff that addressing these two factors was the key to building a professional judiciary. This aroused some interest and a proposal was formulated to pay judges a salary of US$500 per month – high by Cambodian standards but low by UN standards. The proposal was rejected by the Director of Civil Administration on the grounds that UNTAC should not be seen to be paying salaries to government officials and that it would be humiliating to the prime minister, who was paid a lesser amount. The issue then appears to have been dropped.

UNTAC made some progress in establishing a supply of public defenders – of which there had been none since 1975. The Transitional Criminal Law guaranteed the right to legal assistance and, in recognition of the extreme scarcity of legally trained advocates, anyone with a high school education or who was a family member (regardless of their education level) was entitled to act as a defender. In order to provide a minimum level of competence for potential defenders, UNTAC ran a Defenders Training Program to provide basic training in Cambodian criminal law to anyone who wanted to act as a criminal defender. In so doing, however, UNTAC was criticised for further diluting the quality of the profession by opening up eligibility instead of focusing on existing legal professionals who remained from the SOC government (HRW Asia 1995: 77). Legal aid programmes were established only after UNTAC's departure through such foreign-funded NGOs as the Cambodian Defenders Project and Legal Aid of Cambodia, established in 1994 and 1995 respectively, and to this day the state provides no legal aid. Attention to the issue of access of the poor and marginalised to justice was therefore insufficient.

There was some discussion within UNTAC on the establishment of a Cambodian Bar Association in late 1992 but no action (UNTAC Civil Administration Component 1992: 3). The Law on the Bar was eventually introduced in 1995, and a bar association established in late 1995.

UNTAC Special Prosecutor

UNTAC's main initiative with respect to improving the functioning of the judiciary was the establishment on 6 January 1993 of the Office of the

Special Prosecutor. This initiative aimed to respond to the escalating political violence of late 1992 – the majority of which was perpetrated by the police and military – and UNTAC's frustration over the reluctance of the Cambodian police and judiciary to investigate and prosecute offenders (Plunkett 1994: 72). By bringing trials to Cambodian courts, the office also intended to "play a role in altering the legal and official 'culture' of the courts of the existing administrative structures" (Hughes 1996: 51). The Special Prosecutor was empowered to investigate serious offences, particularly those perpetrated by officials, police or military officers, to issue warrants for the arrest and detention of suspects and to prosecute cases before the Cambodian courts, under a prosecutions policy based on UN and Australian codes.[8] For a UN peacekeeping operation this was a radical step, and the first time that UN CIVPOL had been given powers of arrest.

The rapidity with which the initiative unravelled illustrated the chronic difficulties UNTAC confronted in discharging its responsibilities regarding law and order and human rights violations and securing the cooperation of existing administrative structures, including the judiciary. There were serious doubts as to whether the SOC courts could be considered to have been appointed by law and would therefore be appropriate to hear UN prosecutions. Judges privately expressed concerns for their own safety in trying cases brought by the Special Prosecutor (UNTAC 1993b). Politicisation of the courts was a major problem: bringing cases involving one faction before judges aligned with another faction risked biased judgements. To overcome this, the Special Prosecutor proposed that UNTAC appoint special judges from all factions under international jurists.[9] No action was taken. The initiative was swamped by other pressures on the mission (Plunkett 1994: 74) and, in the view of some human rights groups, fell victim to "legalism" and timidity (Findlay 1995: 67).

A further difficulty was that UNTAC found itself unable to live up to its own standards for detention and trial. It took six months to establish detention facilities, causing UNTAC to violate the very rule – no detention without charge for longer than 48 hours – that CIVPOL and Human Rights officers had worked to enforce with Cambodian police (UNTAC 1993o: 13). Two suspects arrested by the Special Prosecutor's office were detained for over six months.

Perhaps the greatest obstacle, however, was opposition from the SOC authorities and within UNTAC. SOC opposition appeared to stem from a fear that the initiative would increase UNTAC's power.[10] After some initial court appearances, the SOC courts refused to hear all cases brought by the Special Prosecutor. In one case brought to the court in January 1993,[11] the Minister of Justice directly instructed the Chief Justice of the Phnom Penh Municipal Court that he would be punished if he agreed to hear the case. In refusing to hear the case, the judge told the Special Prosecutor that he was required to follow the orders of the Ministry of Justice and suggested UNTAC seek the latter's agreement.[12]

In another case, the judge refused to hear the case of a SOC police-man, Em Chan, implicated in the murder of a FUNCINPEC official. He later told UNTAC officials that it was not safe for his family or UNTAC officials to bring the case to court. To break the impasse, Akashi issued a directive stating that the suspect would continue to be detained until a competent court could be identified to hear the case. In response, the Phnom Penh Municipal Court served an order on UNTAC demanding Em Chan's release on the basis that the 48-hour detention period had been exceeded. UNTAC was then forced to declare the court order void (Akashi 1993). Such clashes further eroded the relationship between UNTAC and the SOC authorities.

The office of Special Prosecutor was further emasculated by opposition from senior UNTAC officials. The Special Prosecutor and members of the Human Rights Component have argued that elements within UNTAC actively sought to obstruct the office. In particular, the Civil Administra-tion Component formed an "Action Cell" to act as a secret court of pre-view that decided which cases should be prosecuted based on whether faction leaders would be upset or implicated, condoned the non-cooperation of judges and provided tip-offs about arrests. This behaviour appeared to stem from uncertainty about the scope of the UNTAC mandate and an assessment that it was not worth compromising already fragile relations with the regime in Phnom Penh for the sake of a few prosecutions (Shawcross 1994: 59).

Ultimately, the only gains from the whole episode were the construc-tion of a prison to house suspects arrested by UNTAC and the arrest of three prison officials who were still awaiting trial by the time of UNTAC's departure. Following their transfer to the Cambodian authorities on UNTAC's departure, two were imprisoned for torture and murder – one of them was subsequently reinstated as deputy prison director at the same prison (AI 2003a). The third suspect died in custody in suspicious circumstances (Plunkett 1994: 72–73).

Law enforcement

UNTAC made few inroads into upholding its law enforcement mandate, beyond contributing to an improved level of security for the elections. This was owing not least to the incompetence of some CIVPOL deploy-ments, poorly articulated CIVPOL objectives and the structural and legal vacuum in which CIVPOL were expected to operate (Eaton 1994: 61). A further reason was that UNTAC failed to prioritise the reform of Cambodian law enforcement bodies. The lack of systems and processes within the Cambodian police was an issue that remained virtually unaddressed until 1997, with the commencement of the donor-funded Cambodian Criminal Justice Assistance Project. Police corruption and ineptitude continued to undermine basic freedoms in Cambodia after UNTAC's departure.

UNTAC's mandate did not provide specifically for the creation of a police force and the mission did not focus on improving existing police structures, which were dysfunctional in the SOC zone and virtually non-existent in the others. UNTAC thus missed an opportunity to create a cohesive policing structure across Cambodia and to promote systemic reform of a police culture that was politicised and characterised by human rights abuses and corruption. It also failed to recognise that such actions were critical in improving the integrity and independence of the judiciary, given that police officers in practice determined both whether cases went to court and the outcome of criminal proceedings (Donovan 1993: 90; Fernando 1998: 65).

Most efforts at police reform were conducted by UNTAC's 3,600-strong CIVPOL presence. Although UNTAC went further than previous missions such as that in Namibia by providing for "supervision and control" of the police forces of the four factions, this was extremely difficult given the numbers involved. CIVPOL were expected to establish effective control over 45,000 CPP police and more than 10,000 from the other three factions (Peou 1997: 190; Doyle 1995: 48). As discussed, UNTAC's mandate did not give CIVPOL executive policing powers until January 1993. This meant that CIVPOL could not conduct basic policing themselves, and in many areas their interpretation of "supervise and control" was so passive as to amount to little more than a traditional monitoring role. Senior CIVPOL officers reported that most CIVPOL had little awareness of their potential "big picture" role in moving the country from a war situation towards peace, security and community safety.

The centrepiece of police reform was training conducted by CIVPOL and the Human Rights Component, which contracted specialist police trainers to run sessions for several thousand local police in Phnom Penh and six provinces. Overall, around 9,000 police officers from the four factions participated in various courses (UNTAC 1993o: 36). These focused on preventing basic human rights abuses and did not generally extend to policing skills or to explaining the laws. Ultimately, training was ineffective given the non-functioning judicial system and continued political control of the police (McNamara 1994: 10).

UNTAC's general lack of success in utilising and developing local capacity for community policing supports Eaton's claim that UNTAC "substantially undervalued and neglected" the use of indigenous resources

(1994: 61). In areas where such resources were harnessed, CIVPOL achieved some degree of success in establishing improved law enforcement structures that made a positive impact on the rule of law. The 10-member CIVPOL contingent deployed to the north-west region of Thmar Pouk was amongst the most successful. A complete breakdown in law and order had occurred in the zone, which was controlled by the KPNLF, with neither state nor informal justice systems functioning. In conjunction with the Provincial Human Rights Officer, CIVPOL developed a community law enforcement structure by negotiating with local factions to establish a basic law and order model that included a district police patrol organisation. CIVPOL appointed 1,010 local police.

Senior CIVPOL officers interviewed for this study considered that much of the initiative's success stemmed from the ability of CIVPOL to build good relations with local faction leaders. CIVPOL included all four factions in the negotiations and, importantly, established a relationship with the Khmer Rouge even after their decision to boycott the election process (McPhedran 1993: 11). CIVPOL's negotiating clout was bolstered by a visit to the area by King Sihanouk, who convinced the local Khmer Rouge general to cooperate. Circumventing the official UNTAC policy of not remunerating Khmer Rouge, CIVPOL provided the battle-fatigued local Khmer Rouge forces with food provisions, thereby securing their cooperation with civilian structures. CIVPOL trained police recruits and ran an instructors' course to enable Cambodians gradually to take over training The participation of all four factions in the training programme made a rare contribution to national reconciliation (UNTAC 1993o: 36; Doyle 1995: 47).

Members of the CIVPOL contingent described how they also pursued a "hearts-and-mind" campaign with the local population, including English classes. In so doing, they proved good role models for Cambodian police in promoting community service and new attitudes to law and order and community safety. The support networks formed between CIVPOL and local police in Thmar Pouk were sustained long after UNTAC's departure.

Again, the ability of the Thmar Pouk CIVPOL contingent to improve the law and order situation was limited by the absence of supporting penal and judicial facilities. CIVPOL and local police could investigate and report crimes and prepare a brief of evidence, but the lack of a prosecutor or investigating judge made it difficult to go any further. Justice was often served through financial compensation determined extrajudicially (McPhedran 1993: 11). The politicisation of the police force also remained a significant problem. According to the then director of the Khmer Police Training School, most of the 1,300 police trained in the Thmar Pouk district, for example, were not allowed to join the Cambodian police force established under the new constitution because they belonged to the wrong political party. UNTAC's departure also saw a reversion to military rule in the area, and many of UNTAC's efforts to create law and order structures were reversed soon after its departure (HRW Asia 1995: 73).

Prisons

UNTAC secured modest improvements in prison conditions and the release of some political prisoners. With CIVPOL assistance, UNTAC's Human Rights Component and Public Security Service conducted visits to all known prisons in Cambodia. All fell under SOC authority – the other factions denied the existence of any prisons in their territories, although these probably existed (McNamara 1994: 7–8). All prisons failed to meet basic international standards: shackling, solitary confinement and the use of "dark cells" were standard practice, and basic health and medical care were virtually non-existent. Up to 90 per cent of SOC prisoners were detained without trial (McNamara 1994: 8). Resource shortfalls, inadequate salaries for prison staff and the politicisation of prison officials were contributing factors, and the lack of a functioning judicial system meant there was no effective means to clear the backlog (McNamara 1994: 7).

Most of UNTAC's work focused on releasing prisoners and monitoring physical conditions. These efforts were partially successful. Early in the mission, UNTAC secured the agreement of SOC authorities to establish basic guidelines for prison conditions and to release a number of prisoners. It gained ready access to prisons in most cases (McNamara 1994: 8). The Ministry of National Security established a Prisons Control Commission responsible for improving conditions and releasing political prisoners and prisoners detained without trial (Findlay 1995: 64). By the end of the mandate, most prisoners had specific charges laid against them and the prison population had been vastly reduced (Doyle 1995: 33). UNTAC also made progress towards ending the practice of shackling (UNTAC 1993c). Beyond this, UNTAC was unable to secure the cooperation of SOC officials, who used UNTAC's prison work as negative propaganda, blaming the rising crime rate on prisoner releases (McNamara 1994: 11). There were reports of a widespread belief amongst the populace that crime had increased because of UNTAC's interference with local prisons and the police (UNTAC 1992a). In turn, public perceptions that UNTAC had "let all the prisoners out of the jails" prompted a sharp decline in UNTAC's popularity (Hughes 1996: 36).

UNTAC did little to address the deeper aspects of institutional reform in ways that might have assisting in building a robust prison system that could be sustained upon UNTAC's departure. Although some human rights training of prison officials was conducted, prison officials gained no experience in democratic prison management, administrative skills or any additional resources during UNTAC's deployment. Although Article 38 of the 1993 constitution prohibited coercion and other mistreatment of prisoners, no statutory framework was established for prison management, which continued to be haphazard and wholly open to human rights abuses (Poletti 1998: 52).

UNTAC's failure to establish or lay the groundwork for creating the rule of law institutions envisaged in the Paris Agreements and the 1993 constitution can be attributed to inexperience, an unclear mandate and a preoccupation with more visible symbols of the transition, notably the elections. The long-term consequences were clear: a judicial system that remained dysfunctional, corrupt and subject to systemic executive interference; the continuation of torture, arbitrary and excessive detention in the prison system; and a deficient and corrupt police force. State-sponsored impunity for violations of civil and political rights continued and public mistrust of the judiciary made extra-judicial recourse common.

Building commitment

Few Cambodian political leaders or senior military or police actors were committed to UNTAC's goal of establishing the rule of law. Whereas in some areas, such as refugee repatriation, UNTAC was able to gain enough passive support for its policies to enjoy relative success (Doyle 1995: 70), in the justice sector it encountered outright resistance. In the case of elite actors, this was because the most powerful of the factions, the SOC, had strong vested interests in continuing to undermine the rule of law, and UNTAC was never able to assert sufficient authority over the SOC or the other factions to ensure their compliance. The Cambodian public continued to view the state justice system as illegitimate, but UNTAC did not provide them with a relevant and accessible alternative. For most groups in society, adopting the western liberal concept of the rule of law would have required a major political and cultural adjustment, for which UNTAC's minimalist response was insufficient.

Elite commitment

The above discussion has touched on the refusal of key members of the elite to cooperate with UNTAC or consent to bind themselves to the rule of law. In many instances they were actively obstructionist. Although Sihanouk gave strong rhetorical support for an independent and incorrupt judicial system and called for UNTAC's assistance to establish one,[13] the factions blocked UNTAC's rule of law initiatives at the highest levels. On occasions when UNTAC sought to build consensus on rule of law issues in the SNC, faction leaders regularly dissented.[14]

This was particularly the case with the SOC authorities, upon whom UNTAC depended. Of 1,300 UNTAC investigations of human rights violations, for example, not one measure was taken by SOC authorities against those believed responsible (McNamara 1995a: 168). In a typical example, SOC authorities ignored repeated UNTAC requests to locate four FUNCINPEC party members abducted by soldiers of the Cambodian People's Armed Forces (CPAF) or to bring the abductors to justice. Prime Minister Hun Sen ignored a written request from Akashi to confine the alleged perpetrators to their barracks and investigate the abduction or to hand them over to UNTAC. When UNTAC then sought to take the men into custody, they went missing from the barracks and the officer in charge was unable to provide any information on their whereabouts (UNTAC 1993d, 1993e).

Two factors help explain the lack of commitment by members of the Cambodian elite to UNTAC's rule of law initiatives: the existence of strong vested interests that would be threatened by the rule of law and the inadequacies of UNTAC attempts to extract commitment to changed behaviour.

Elite vested interests – particularly in the SOC administration – were well served by the absence of the rule of law, which assured them of political control and influence, as well as the fruits of corruption. Cambodia's highly politicised judicial and security structures were integral components of the CPP's political machinery, which used them throughout the peace process to gain advantage over their political competitors (Hughes 1996: 55). Non-functioning courts allowed SOC authorities to continue to operate in a climate of impunity, while a corrupt police force legitimised politically motivated crime. As Lizee (1993: 38) has argued:

> A complete transformation of the Cambodian socio-political environment through the creation of a "neutral political environment" meant ... that the social structures on which the Cambodian leaders have always relied to stay in power were going to be eroded or destroyed. They were bound, therefore, to resist all democratisation efforts.

On the second point, UNTAC's failure to assert authority over the factions had a direct bearing on its ability to influence their behaviour with respect to the rule of law. Although UNTAC was mandated to exercise "direct control" over the administrative structures, in the absence of any credible mechanism to ensure compliance this rested on the goodwill and cooperation of the factions, and particularly the SOC/CPP, which controlled 80 per cent of the state (Doyle 1995: 68). Peou's study on conflict neutralisation in Cambodia (1997: 98, 259) argues persuasively that the factions did not withhold cooperation initially. He describes how UNTAC lost their confidence and support because it failed to ensure the neutrality of the administrative structures, to deal firmly with the Khmer Rouge and to perform well during the initial stages of deployment. Lacking trust in each other and then losing confidence in the body charged with creating a neutral environment in which they might interact, the factions became increasingly critical of UNTAC and began to withhold their full cooperation (Peou 1997: 201).

This proved true with respect to rule of law initiatives. The SOC's extensive administrative structures, which could have been an asset, became a liability when it began to issue directives by word of mouth aimed at undermining UNTAC (Doyle 1995: 44, 70). The refusal of SOC courts to cooperate with UNTAC was a classic example. UNTAC's experience with the military and police is a further example of the tussle for authority between UNTAC and state institutions bent on maintaining their influence. UNTAC appears to have attempted to bring the military and police under a degree of civilian authority and to get them to abide by the law. However, it made little progress in either respect.

Military actors obstructed UNTAC efforts to press charges against military personnel One case involved an UNTAC warrant for the arrest of a deputy CPAF commander on murder charges. Although local court officials and the police complied with warrant and investigation obligations up to a point, the provincial "governor" and police commissioner refused to arrest the accused without the acquiescence of the regional military command, which declined to cooperate and concealed the accused for several months. UNTAC determined that no action would be possible without the assistance of the military command (Gantchev 1993: 3) but appears to have been unable to secure it. Cases were documented across Cambodia involving threats and attacks against judges and prosecutors who acted against military offenders (HRW Asia 1995: 75). Although by late 1993 some progress had been made in asserting civilian authority – for example the holding of civilian trials of military personnel for rape and murder (HRW Asia 1995: 72–73) – the situation deteriorated soon after UNTAC's departure.

Similarly, the few CIVPOL contingents that took a proactive approach to improving the performance of their Cambodian counterparts found it difficult to assert their authority or extract cooperation from local police. UNTAC reports describe not only police intimidation of UNTAC officers, but anti-UNTAC demonstrations sponsored and organised by SOC police, which were used to demonstrate that they, not UNTAC, were in control of the local population (UNTAC Information/Education Division 1993: 1). Police also refused to cooperate in criminal investigations. In one incident, police in Prey Veng province released a prisoner arrested by CIVPOL, refused to cooperate with a subsequent UNTAC investigation and prevented an UNTAC Human Rights Officer from inspecting a detention facility, where three prisoners were subsequently found in shackles. They then enlisted the Deputy Provincial Governor to lodge a complaint that UNTAC officials were harassing them.[15] CIVPOL complained that they had very little recourse against such actions, apart from efforts to educate the SOC administration in the province on the gravity of its offence (UNTAC 1993n).

A further factor behind UNTAC's inability to extract commitment to changed behaviour was the absence of consensus or cooperation between key players in the elite. Both the Paris Agreements and UNTAC underestimated the degree to which the absence of genuine reconciliation between the parties would have a negative impact across the mission, including on rule of law initiatives. As Roberts (2001: 38–39) argued:

> [I]t was as much hoped as assumed that a sufficient degree of cooperation would prove possible and sustainable between the four main parties and with UNTAC.... The CPP incumbents were expected to release their control of the state organs, in the context of having signed an agreement under pressure from a loss of international patronage and a wrecked economy which simultaneously politically legitimised their reviled Khmer Rouge opposition. It was naïve in the extreme to expect co-operation to the degree that the Accords anticipated in Paris ... It was naïve also to assume that a party as entrenched in political power as the CPP would relinquish that control when its political future depended largely upon securing support for itself through the labyrinthine networks that were characteristic of the communist model of bureaucracy and politics in Indochina.

Finally, UNTAC unwittingly shored up the very elite behaviour it desired to change by perpetuating power structures in the elite that undermined rule of law objectives. Its dependence on the SOC actually helped shift the balance of power in its favour, contributing to the continuation of a hegemonic power structure and attendant institutions that were not based on liberal democracy or the rule of law (Doyle 1995: 68).

Ultimately, by the end of its mandate UNTAC's lack of authority over the political elite and state agents such as the military had seen it lose influence over key strategic issues relating to the rule of law. The Cambodian parties moved rapidly after the elections to exclude UNTAC as far as possible from politics and policy-making. As described above, UNTAC had little input into the drafting of the constitution. Nor was it in a position to assist in establishing the basic institutions needed to institute democracy and the rule of law (McNamara 1995b: 59).

Commitment from the broader community

UNTAC faced an uphill battle to gain public commitment to the rule of law in a situation where public perceptions equated the judicial system with injustice and impunity for the powerful. The general populace had no confidence in the legal system, which was mistrusted and avoided (UNTAC Human Rights Component 1992: 9). The exemption of government officials from punishment under the law reinforced a perception amongst the general community and less powerful players in the political arena that the law operated not in the interests of the entire community but in the interests of the powerful at the expense of the weak. Hughes (2000: 18) has argued that this undermined the authority of the Cambodian legal system to a great degree in the eyes of those who were disadvantaged. This lack of confidence was exacerbated by institutional weaknesses that saw the law implemented ineffectively and inconsistently and hindered access to justice for the poor. UNTAC was unable to overcome perceptions that the law existed simply to reinforce a climate of impunity for the politically powerful. The director of Cambodia's most prominent legal aid agency suggested that it was unlikely to have succeeded in doing so until such time as high-ranking officials were successfully prosecuted by the courts.

The lack of community confidence that structures existed that could protect them from officially sanctioned violence eroded UNTAC's credibility (Hughes 1996: 50) and made it hard to gain community cooperation in activities that might have supported the rule of law. UNTAC had difficulty, for example, securing witnesses prepared to assist with human rights investigations because of a pervasive fear of reprisals against which UNTAC could offer no protection (Hughes 1996: 48). UNTAC did not offer Cambodians a workable alternative to relying on corrupt SOC structures to deliver justice. By not taking direct control in this area, it lost credibility vis-à-vis the SOC. An UNTAC Information Officer on a provincial visit explained this point in the following way:

> Cambodian conceptions of political power are related to ideas of patron/client relationships. "Big" people control things, collect things from the populace and redistribute these collected goods. "Big" men may be rising or falling, but they stand in a definite competitive relationship to all others who also would be "Big". The concept of an entity, UNTAC, which is not here to take control of the country, but to supervise the control of others, is so foreign as to be incomprehensible to the common person.

The Information Officer had numerous conversations where she was asked why UNTAC was not doing what it was supposed to do.... In each case, what the Cambodians thought that UNTAC should be doing involved taking direct control of a specific area or task.... [P]eople do not understand why UNTAC does not engage in military activities against the NADK. They do not understand why UNTAC does not take over the security checkpoints around the city themselves when everyone knows that they exist to extort money from the people. And some people say they do not understand why UNTAC does not make the Vietnamese leave.

... At the same time that people think UNTAC should take on more responsibilities, the SOC administrative structure is trying very hard to show that they are the ones who are in control.... With regard to the subject of crime, SOC has tried to demonstrate to the population that they can control the situation. When crime began to explode, the SOC called in troops to patrol the streets. Crime dropped, but the troops themselves stopped people to extort money for safe passage. So the price paid for having the crime rate drop was to have SOC troops on the streets acting with apparent impunity towards the local population.

... With regard to land disputes, the same problem of lack of understanding of the limits of the mandate prevails. UNTAC is turning the cases back to the SOC system to adjudicate. People do not understand why this is being done. They thought that a higher authority than SOC had arrived and that one could appeal directly to this authority. In fact, Information/Education materials told people that they could bring their allegations of injustices committed to UNTAC. People did not understand the limits of what injustices qualified and which did not. People are still coming to UNTAC with complaints about land disputes, but in some cases people are now going to the SOC structure first to see if it can be solved there. (UNTAC 1992a)

For the most part, existing justice institutions were not seen as relevant because they were unable to service the key needs of the majority of Cambodians. It was clear from the outset of the mission that property disputes in particular would be an ongoing major concern – the Human Rights Component, CIVPOL and the Civil Administration Component were inundated with complaints and requests for UNTAC to intervene.[16] UNTAC's policy on the handling of land disputes was not, however, coherent. Land disputes lacked an institutional home and responses were ad hoc, with little coordination and no guidelines (McLean 1992: 2; McNamara 1992d: 2). One UNTAC staff member asked to write a policy paper on land disputes for practical use by officers in the provinces produced what was described as a "private, political and very negative analysis" of no utility (Nyberg 1993: 2). No system was established to resolve the disputes and no staff were left behind to help advance the issue. UNTAC thus missed a critical opportunity to demonstrate the relevance of the rule of law by addressing disputes of utmost importance to ordinary Cambodians.

In addition, UNTAC did not devise incentives to motivate conformity with rule of law principles. Punishment for non-conformity was an empty threat given the dysfunctional court system. On the contrary, the threat of violent retribution was a disincentive to adhere to the rule of law: people were afraid to report crimes, for example. Moreover, Cambodians had little capacity to adhere to the rule of law. Access to the judicial system was limited by resource shortfalls in the court system, the prohibitively high cost of bribing judges, the lack of public defenders and low public awareness of how to use judicial processes.

What difference it might have made had UNTAC garnered popular support for its rule of law initiatives is open to conjecture. Heininger (1994: 131) has argued that support from the local populace could at least partially have substituted for the faltering commitment of Cambodian leaders. She points, for example, to the mitigating effect of the overwhelming desire of ordinary Cambodians for peace on the tendency of the elite to drift back into conflict. However, given Cambodia's hierarchical social structure, support from the top would have been essential in gaining public acceptance of new initiatives. UNTAC did not seek, and SOC authorities did not offer, high-profile public endorsement of the rule of law or sanction capacity-building at grassroots level. According to the managers of criminal justice projects implemented in the post-UNTAC period, such official support proved crucial to building commitment to project success.

Conferring "ownership"

A recurring motif in UNTAC's inability to extract commitment from elite groups or the public was its lack of effort to inculcate a sense of "ownership" over processes designed to build the rule of law. This was a difficult issue in the UNTAC context – for a start, with four competing factions it was difficult to know to whom ownership should be conferred. Although UNTAC made some attempt in the SNC to consult on major rule of law issues, such as legislation, at other levels of the decision-making process there appears to have been little consultation or participation at either elite or community level. Cambodians working with or in UNTAC complained that it did not seriously consider their suggestions on human rights or justice reform. Because Cambodians were not employed at the decision-making level, they depended on sympathetic foreigners to convey their ideas.

More broadly, the loss of Cambodian control over the development process during the transition period has been well documented (Curtis 1993: 16). Cambodians had relatively little opportunity to participate in the design of policies or programmes for reconstruction, a combined result of insensitivity on the part of UNTAC officers, a shortage of adequately trained Cambodians and political considerations about UNTAC's neutrality. There was also a tendency on the part of UNTAC and international agencies to create parallel structures that undermined local institutions that could have played an important role (Curtis 1993: 16).

In the few areas where efforts were made to build confidence, commitment and a sense of ownership over rule of law processes, better results were achieved. In isolated instances, for example, CIVPOL successfully established quasi-official community justice systems that helped restore and maintain order. One such success story was the United Nations Border Relief Operation (UNBRO) Site II refugee camp on the Thai border, home to 180,000 Cambodian refugees. Violence in the camps was an increasing problem. Faction leaders dispensed summary justice, including through the use of stocks, and there was no police force. In early 1989, as violence worsened, the United Nations deployed five police officers to assist UNBRO and the Thai government to improve security. The team established, trained and equipped a 1,267-member community police force composed of refugees, convinced rival camp factions to support the initiative, established prisons and a community court system and developed a basic criminal code.

Participating UN officials argued that the programme's success lay in UNBRO's ability to win the commitment of camp leaders and later to build popular confidence in the use of a tribunal to dispense justice. In lobbying each faction camp, UNBRO police encountered varying levels of hostility but a consistent desire to establish functioning rules of behaviour. Thai officials were also consulted, so that all parties were brought on board. The factions eventually agreed on a simple set of rules, with punishments, that could be applied to minor offences, although serious offences remained subject to the Cambodian judicial system. UN and Thai officials held a large public signing ceremony, and the new rule system was implemented in a matter of weeks.

The UNBRO police team conducted three-week training courses for the newly recruited police, who despite remaining factionalised nonetheless succeeded in building confidence in their respective communities. UNBRO observed but did not interfere with the appointment of tribunals composed of faction leaders and respected people in the society, including a sizeable percentage of women. Tribunal procedures were rudimentary – for example there were no rules of evidence for police – but both criminal and civil matters could be brought before them. Jails were redesigned and stocks removed, and many punishments consisted of community service. UNBRO police also enlisted the assistance of Buddhist monks – for example in delaying cremations until investigations could be carried out into suspicious deaths. As confidence grew, people began to take grievances to the new tribunals and the level of violence diminished, leaving UNBRO police convinced that, if justice structures in which people had confidence could be established, they would be welcomed and used. Where no such structures existed, people would continue to take matters into their own hands.

Inculcating "cultural change"

A further explanatory factor for UNTAC's failure to gain commitment to the rule of law was its inability to deal with the cultural change that would have been required. The extent of the requisite change in the conduct of state authorities who relied on lawlessness to ensure their political dominance has already been discussed. Society-wide, there was considerable variation in the sophistication of indigenous concepts of the rule of law and "justice". At the same time, most ordinary people did not understand the basis for UNTAC's judicial reform efforts. Groups specifically involved in the rule of law sphere described how they were also very much at sea and had difficulty absorbing rapid changes in context, roles and ideology. For example, former Khmer Rouge soldiers struggled to make a rapid attitudinal adjustment to their sudden role change to police officer, let alone to adapt to a policing culture based on western concepts of the rule of law. Such adjustments were made only incrementally over the course of at least a decade.

Even amongst groups who lobbied actively in support of the rule of law – such as Cambodian human rights activists – there was confusion about what was meant by the concept. The "rule of law" appeared to be generally conceived of as a desire for openness and positive change, which brought with it high expectations. The expectation that it would confer certain rights was not matched by a corresponding sense of duties, responsibilities or obligations on the part of both state and society.

UNTAC's efforts to build a culture of law and order in communities were limited. For example, CIVPOL generally confined their activities to monitoring, rather than taking on any educative role. UNTAC did not use corrective measures as incentive systems. The key tool for inculcating change was education. The Human Rights Component introduced human rights courses into high school and university curricula and screened human rights programmes on television and across Cambodia in mobile video units. The Information, Education and Training Unit of the Human Rights Component provided training for thousands of Cambodian school teachers, university students, doctors, government officials and judicial officers (UNTAC 1993f). Technical assistance and training were also provided to Cambodian human rights groups. UNTAC's education efforts stimulated a broader and more sophisticated human rights discourse amongst human rights groups and the general population, but the target groups were generally "soft" – human rights activists and ordinary citizens rather than the military, police and militia groups, who arguably posed the greatest threat to rule of law principles. Moreover, efforts in the human rights field were very much focused on basic human rights, rather than expanding awareness of other principles of the rule of law.

Rebuilding social relationships

Although aware of the problem on a general level, UNTAC did not sufficiently take into account the fact that it was faced with a traumatised society lacking in robust collective social relationships. State–society linkages were weak and characterised by mistrust, and the prevailing channel for interest representation was a politically biased and corrupt patronage system. This was inherently contradictory to rule of law principles and meant that the basis on which sustainable rule of law institutions might have been built was missing.

There is a paucity of research into the extent to which community-level social relationships were weakened by protracted civil war, but Curtis (1998: 123) notes a generalised lack of trust, even in traditional bonds at village and commune level. Roberts (2001: 52–53) has argued that the transformation of societal values resulting from the civil war and genocide engendered a diminished respect for human rights, a culture of violence and impunity and the breakdown of traditional values, including Buddhist precepts. Debilitating breakdowns in trust appear to have occurred as a result of disruptions to village structures stemming from the Khmer Rouge military structure, which centralised power and split communities into smaller groups. Families were fractured, communities were disrupted by large-scale population displacement and people were forced to spy on each other (Curtis 1998: 114, 160–161).

During the UNTAC period, there were signs that villagers had begun to return relatively quickly to old rituals, conceptions of status and patronage networks, but the relationships of trust embodied in these were personalised and relatively unamenable to the cognitive aspects of social capital, especially anonymous trust. Lack of trust was accompanied by feelings of powerlessness, which made it more difficult for individuals and groups to plan strategies for survival or motivate for social change (Hughes 2001: 20–21). State interest representation systems were weak, making it difficult or impossible for people to process interests within an official representative framework (Nee 1995: 57). NGO representatives active during this period described how people continued to mistrust the state and avoided interaction with state authorities, particularly the courts, at all costs.

Cambodians appear to have shown little tendency to form civic interest groups or associations outside family or traditional patronage networks, and this was reinforced by the Khmer Rouge experience. Only one NGO existed before UNTAC.[17] Traditional perceptions of authority and the legacy of a centralist socialist system meant that participation in decision-making at village level was restricted to the upper echelons of village society.

The UNTAC intervention appears to have loosened traditional control mechanisms, prompting a kind of "civil libertarianism" in which villagers increasingly resisted the orders of commune officials in apparent response to an increased awareness of individual human rights (Curtis 1998: 125). This was interpreted by some UNTAC officials as a sign that demand for civic participation could be stimulated and directed towards supporting the democratisation process. At the same time, Curtis (1998: 126) has argued that this "libertarianism" weakened traditional notions of communitarian responsibility, eroding community networks that might have been harnessed to support democratisation activities. Systems of behaviour that might have been supportive of trust-building may thus have been further eroded by the UNTAC intervention. Interviewees from civil society groups expressed the view that there was an obvious need for trust-building that UNTAC neglected to address, pointing to trauma counselling and reconciliation initiatives as areas in which UNTAC, as an outsider, could have offered some concrete assistance.

Some of the more proactive CIVPOL contingents did, however, engage in community trust-building initiatives and used personal relationships with local police to achieve policing objectives. The Thmar Pouk contingent, for example, found that using personal relationships to build trust, share knowledge and develop new attitudes was the most effective means to improve law and order. Although it was frequently the case that police were politicised, corrupt and party to human rights abuses, in many other instances Cambodian police were very closely connected to their communities and had a deep concern for their safety. Local police were often subject to the same political threats as others in their community. CIVPOL officers pointed to a strong potential to tap into those bonds and mutual concerns to improve police performance in upholding law and order. CIVPOL's 18-month deployment was, however, insufficient to allow for significant efforts to promote relations between the local police and their constituents (Hughes 2000: 34).

UNTAC gave some recognition to the importance of building supportive state–society linkages. In this respect, UNTAC's key strategy for the rebuilding of civil society was to support the establishment of NGOs, particularly through efforts by UNTAC's Human Rights Component to fund, train and build constitutional protection for unions and human rights NGOs.

Although UNTAC's tendency to equate NGOs with civil society was both inaccurate and limiting, it nonetheless gave the mission a concrete focus for its efforts that generated some successes. Importantly, UNTAC succeeded in providing a relatively secure environment in which NGOs could be established and operate, as well as an adequate legal structure and resources. For example, the founder of Cambodia's first human rights NGO, the Cambodia Human Rights and Development Association (ADHOC), described how UNTAC negotiated Hun Sen's agreement for ADHOC to commence operations relatively unharassed, whereas previously he had been intimidated by police and ministers in the SOC government. NGOs continued to have difficulty gaining approval for registration, but UNTAC was eventually able to establish a mechanism for such authorisations. UNTAC granted US$50,000 seed funding to each NGO, enabling them to get established and eventually attract other funding. Human Rights Component staff also provided training for NGO members, including on human rights principles and NGO management. UNTAC also prioritised the establishment of what proved to be lasting linkages between local and regional/international bodies.

On the downside, some NGOs criticised UNTAC for not making use of their local knowledge and for unintentionally undermining them:

> It became the standard UNTAC view that the local NGOs were weak and ineffective in the transitional period, and it was too early to consider them as working partners. The nature of the mandate also encouraged the viewing of all Cambodians as passive recipients of UNTAC programs. (Palan 1994: 19)

UNTAC gave insufficient focus to capacity-building, particularly to training in how to process complaints and deal with the authorities. During the UNTAC period, NGOs tended to function as transmitters of information on human rights abuses and the like to the Human Rights Component, which would then deal with the complaints through UNTAC's own channels and with the SOC authorities. This left NGOs without experience or their own established processes for dealing with the complaints after UNTAC's departure.

A further problem was that civil society groups were not sufficiently grounded in existing social structures. Civic associations were not perceived as local and citizens were suspicious of possible "foreign agendas". Civil society groups tended to be managed by returning Cambodians who has lost contact with local realities. UNTAC had not examined what forms of civil society already existed in Cambodia, assuming that an absence of western-style NGOs meant that civil society was non-existent. It thus ignored pre-existing institutions that had been inactive for years but were nonetheless familiar to local communities. It also ignored the question of what was acceptable to the major parties, making it more difficult for civil society to be sustainable.

That said, the long-term impact of UNTAC's NGO-building efforts appears to have been positive. With some exceptions, state tolerance of civil society groups remained relatively good after UNTAC's departure, with the state seldom inhibiting civic or business associations. At the same time, civil society was not able to provide a robust counterweight to the authority of the state, remaining largely unrecognised by the government and political parties as having a legitimate political role (Curtis 1998: 10).

Strengthening state capacity

In some respects, the Cambodian peace process contributed to a stronger, more competent Cambodian state. Some political institutions – for example the electoral system – were strengthened, and it is arguable that the UNTAC process installed a lasting and relatively stable government structure, particularly compared with previous decades. It removed the destabilising influence of regional hegemons, creating a political solution that enabled Cambodia to sustain itself as an active member of the international community. It opened the doors to useful work by the international aid community, including in the rule of law field.

However, post-UNTAC Cambodia remained a weak state reliant on coercion and the denial of basic human rights to maintain social control. As discussed above, state–society relations continued to be characterised by a profound lack of public trust in state justice processes – notably the judiciary, which continued to be perceived as the most corrupt body in the country (World Bank 2002: 19). The Royal Government of Cambodia remained chronically weak in democratic governance capability. State institutions were still factionalised along political lines, vulnerable to exploitation by powerful elites – notably the CPP – and unable to extract sufficient resources to remove Cambodia's heavy dependence on foreign aid, which continued to fund some 60 per cent of the budget. The state continued to be the key actor, undermining the rule of law: state-sponsored human rights abuses persisted unabated and cumbersome and unregulated state bodies remained the primary machinery for illegal appropriation of national resources by the CPP and corrupt state actors. To date, few accountability mechanisms have been developed to protect citizens from abuse of state power. Donor pressure has made only marginal progress (and then only since the late 1990s) in securing commitment and progress by the Royal Government on good governance and the rule of law.[18]

UNTAC addressed few of these issues, and efforts by donors to move towards capacity-building and governance did not really start until late 1993, following UNTAC's departure (UNDP 2001a: 45). UNTAC made few inroads into improving Cambodia's extremely weak state administrative structures. In accordance with its mandate, UNTAC emphasised control rather than replacement or improvement of the "existing administrative structures". It had no specific mandate to build capacity in those structures or to provide governance training for Cambodians, and it failed to develop a constructive relationship with structures that might have supported qualitative improvements in state performance.

Curtis (1998: 73) argues that the UNTAC process further diminished and handicapped already weak administrative structures. The weak SOC administration was the closest equivalent to a state structure but, in an effort to ensure political neutrality, UNTAC sought to minimise the role the SOC administration played prior to its transformation into the Royal Government. This made state agencies more demoralised and disorganised than they otherwise might have been, exacerbating already low levels of capacity and confidence. UN field workers were unclear whether cooperation with the authorities at the local level would compromise the UN mandate of neutrality. Interaction with local civil servants was kept to a minimum and helped create a high level of mistrust and tension between UNTAC and provincial and district civil servants. Civil servants themselves continued to suffer from the legacy of the Pol Pot era, operating in an environment of mistrust in which they sought to hide their skills, identities and opinions (UNDP 2001a: 45). At the same time, UNTAC set the stage for aid dependence by its strong emphasis on "substitution" technical assistance, whereby foreigners occupied jobs that might have been filled locally.

There were thus only a small number of indicators of improved governance on UNTAC's departure and many of the few gains made in rule of law areas, such as improved prison conditions and legislative framework, quickly deteriorated. The capacity and political will of the state to absorb rule of law assistance, as in other areas, remained low.

Restoring security

UNTAC demonstrated the potential for external interventions to act as "circuit breakers" in intrastate security dilemmas, thereby creating an environment conducive to the development of cooperative political and social relationships based on shared values such as democracy and the rule of law. The majority of Cambodian interlocutors interviewed by me argued that UNTAC's greatest contribution to the democratisation process in Cambodia was that it restored security to a level sufficient to create "space" for democratisation processes to occur. The Cambodian peace process successfully dislodged external support for conflict agents, particularly Chinese support for the Khmer Rouge, and restored a level of security in many parts of Cambodia that had not been seen for decades. Throughout the election process, UNTAC managed to keep three of the four factions at the negotiating table. Political opponents of the CPP were brought into the electoral system, thereby commencing the long-term process of political accommodation, which continues today. Cambodia was opened to the world and Cambodians who had fled or been exiled were able to return home.

This contribution notwithstanding, UNTAC's conflict management strategy was not fully able to contribute to the establishment of the rule of law. First, the "space" created by UNTAC was not fully secure, and this climate of insecurity continued to fuel mistrust on the part of both the political elite and the general public, which in turn undermined the potential for them to participate in democratic processes. Second, UNTAC did not make effective use of this "space" to promote non-violent routes for power acquisition and changed attitudes to conflict management that might have more fully supported democratic consolidation, including the establishment of the rule of law. The linkages between security and the rule of law were thus significantly under-recognised: ongoing security problems impeded the establishment of the rule of law, and the failure to establish conflict management processes consistent with the rule of law made it more difficult to establish public security.

Incomplete restoration of intrastate security

UNTAC did not prove able fully to neutralise the security environment in Cambodia. Political violence was a marked feature of the election campaign, and the non-cooperation of the Khmer Rouge saw the continuation of civil war in parts of the country. The Khmer Rouge and others who relied on violence enjoyed continued access to political power, while insecurity and mistrust among the factions was exacerbated by their lack of confidence in UNTAC's ability to ensure a strictly neutral political environment (Peou 1997: 201). UNTAC did not adequately remove access to conflict resources: the factions were not fully disarmed and the continued access of the broader community to firearms made it virtually impossible to restore law and order. The UNTAC military made only feeble efforts to secure weapons surrender, and firearms continued to be routinely used in robberies and in murders. In Thmar Pouk district alone, over 350 murders were carried out with firearms during the UNTAC period.

UNTAC does not appear to have accounted sufficiently for the threat that this insecurity posed to the development of political or legal modes of conflict management (Curtis 1998: 33). The insecurity of the factions fuelled mistrust at the political level and facilitated the continued, unregulated influence of the military in state affairs. Members of the judiciary were caught up in politically motivated violence, further eroding public trust. Political opponents and the broader public avoided confronting state actors in the courts, the media and elsewhere for fear of reprisals. Violent conflict continued to be viewed by many as the basic paradigm for conflict resolution, as evidenced by continued high crime rates. A climate of fear and insecurity prevailed, undermining the confidence with which people could exercise democratic rights such as election campaigning and freedom of speech.

Development of non-violent routes for power acquisition

The electoral process introduced by UNTAC did not prove completely successful as a non-violent route for the management of political conflict. In seeking to explain the reasons for this, Lizee (2000: 3) has pointed to the failure of the Paris Agreements and UNTAC to recognise or account for the scale of what was being attempted. The Paris Agreements aimed radically to alter the Cambodian model for power acquisition from absolutism to democracy. As the Agreements made clear, the route to non-violent political expression was seen to be the institutionalisation of political power through a strengthened state structure, cohesive administrative apparatus, capitalist economy and democratically elected government. In the Cambodian context, where violence had long been inseparable from political interaction, UNTAC would have had to create what amounted to a totally new social contract (Lizee 2000: 3, 10).

The Paris Agreements, however, provided little guidance on how this was to be achieved and, as discussed above, change was actively resisted by political forces intent on protecting the political and social order from which they derived power (Lizee 2000: 14).

[As a result] arch enemies were forced into a powersharing arrangement that had as its conclusion an election which might remove at least one group from political power, in a system which did not cater for the notion of opposition, or for the transfer of power, or for the possible consequences of such an event

... [T]he settlement reflected concerns at the international level which over-wrote the reality of settling a potentially zero-sum political contest in a highly-armed country where the contest for power amongst the elite was virtually absolute. (Roberts 2001: 35–36)

Confrontation was thus intensified at the ballot box and, once the reg-ulating effect of UNTAC was gone, violent political contest was reig-nited, as demonstrated by the 1997 coup. Conflict continued to be resolved in a manner clearly inconsistent with the principles of the rule of law, not the least of which was the complicity of the judiciary and po-lice in political violence.

Non-violent routes for conflict management

Looking beyond the ballot box, the lack of formal state structures to manage conflict continued to be a prominent feature of post-UNTAC Cambodia. Villagers tended to shun police and law courts, where they existed. Impersonal methods of social control remained undeveloped: an individual's character and access to patronage networks were more important than the nature of disputes themselves. Fear, rather than im-partial justice, was historically a dominant tool for social control and a re-luctance to resolve conflict peacefully continued (Hughes 2001: 8, 15, 27). As Vickery (1984: 18) has noted, "for the rural 80–90 percent of the Cambodian people arbitrary justice, sudden violent death [and] political oppression ... were common facts of life long before the war and revolu-tion of the 1970s".

In such an environment, Curtis (1998: 129) points to UNTAC's failure to promote new attitudes and behaviour in conflict resolution as one of its "signal failures". Appropriate conflict management mechanisms might have included not only active processes for adjudicating disputes, such as an independent judicial framework and the use or development of infor-mal justice structures supportive of the rule of law, but also efforts to promote cultural norms to regulate attitudes to conflict and conflict reso-lution, including relationship- and consensus-building through reconcilia-tion initiatives. When viewed as a method of conflict management, such structures might have helped build social order and bridge the gaps left by the absence of effective and neutral formal justice institutions. The relative security provided by UNTAC represented the first opportunity for decades to implement processes that might have facilitated the creation of sustainable alternatives to violent methods of conflict man-agement. The next two sections look more closely at informal justice structures and reconciliation processes as a means by which both security and rule of law objectives might have been supported.

Addressing informal justice structures

UNTAC made little effort to dismantle or promote informal justice structures, link them with the formal justice system or otherwise incorporate them into its rule of law strategy. It thus missed an opportunity to promote structures that were supportive of the rule of law and that might have provided an effective means of non-violent conflict management.

Little research has been conducted on the nature of the informal justice mechanisms in Cambodia at the time of UNTAC's deployment, or on their relationship to state institutions. Historically, the village was the focal point for dispute resolution, providing both sources of authority (the headman) and norms of behaviour, including laws, customs, local precedent, folklore and religious texts. Legal-administrative concerns such as divorce, bills of sale for property and the adjudication of serious disputes tended to be managed through informal conciliation mechanisms under the village chiefs, with little involvement by the formal political/ government structure (Hughes 2001: 6–7). Disputes tended to be localised and related to the agrarian economy. Dispute resolution stressed compromise solutions and the restoration of harmonious relations rather than win–lose scenarios (Falt 1998: 162).

By the time of UNTAC's deployment, community dispute resolution mechanisms had been significantly weakened, notably during the Khmer Rouge and Vietnamese periods (Curtis 1998: 130). They continued, however, to be used to quell disputes between neighbours and in some cases to adjudicate criminal acts. Buddhist monks appear to have been consulted frequently by disputants. They used and strengthened customary law, and tended to discourage people from going to court because of the high costs involved. UNTAC appears, therefore, to have been faced with a situation where the mores of remnant informal justice systems emphasised personal relationships and in some cases the use of fear, and where parties to disputes were deeply reluctant to use the state justice system.

UNTAC appears to have taken little of this into account. It did not seek to reinforce or replace weak informal dispute resolution mechanisms or systematically to harness or to configure formal and informal strands of justice in a mutually supportive way. Isolated conflict resolution activities were instituted, such as the establishment of the Cambodian Centre for Conflict Resolution as an independent centre to support conflict resolution practitioners. Such initiatives were limited, however, and did little to strengthen conflict resolution mechanisms.

UNTAC also largely ignored state conciliation networks, which, like informal dispute resolution systems, might have mitigated the pressure on the grossly under-resourced formal justice system. Such networks existed mostly in urban areas and in varying degrees of sophistication and attachment to the state apparatus. They operated below the court level, dealing mostly with domestic matters such as divorce and domestic violence (Donovan 1993: 92). They were relatively well resourced: 88 people worked in conciliation in Phnom Penh, the most developed network in the country, compared with 6 judges in the Phnom Penh City Court (Donovan 1993: 93). However, conciliation representatives were even less well trained and paid than judges, and allegations of corruption were frequent.

In some cases, CIVPOL successfully employed restorative justice techniques as credible alternatives to formal justice processes. According to a member of the CIVPOL contingent in Thmar Pouk,

> One case I recall was after a farmer burnt down five houses after an argument with his neighbours. He was arrested for arson, however owing to the lack of a justice system could not be tried. Victims and perpetrators were brought together and agreement was reached on him rebuilding all five houses ... Victims were happy – perpetrator not so happy – but issue resolved and neighbourhood rebuilt without further fuss.

UNTAC enjoyed some success in overseeing traditional dispute resolution mechanisms for land and property disputes. Most such disputes were settled by local people's committees. These had existed in areas administered by the SOC and had been considering land cases in accordance with SOC regulations since 1989. UNTAC's Civil Administration Component pursued a policy of not interfering with people's committee decisions unless there was evidence of problems such as unjustified intervention by the committees, arbitrary action on the part of the police or the use of force to occupy property. In these cases the matter was raised with the provincial authorities (UNTAC Civil Administration Component 1992: 13).

In other cases, solutions arrived at through a mix of informal justice, policing and mob justice were clearly inconsistent with the rule of law. In one instance, the Thmar Pouk CIVPOL officer recalled that:

> The village chief in Thmar Pouk was murdered by a husband following his involvement in resolving a divorce case. The husband subsequently barricaded himself in a house in front of our office with grenades and firearms. Whilst the Gendarmes wanted to kill him, the local police negotiated his surrender, handcuffed him and placed him in a vehicle. However a crowd gathered, overpowered the police and eventually murdered the husband with machetes. The village chief's wife exacted revenge on the body and it could not be touched or moved by police for a couple of days – a difficult issue that took us a week to resolve.

Practitioners working on conflict resolution projects in post-UNTAC Cambodia have argued that, in trying to establish the rule of law, traditional dispute resolution might have been best avoided where such practices were clearly inconsistent with western liberal concepts of the rule of law – for example, stoning robbers to death or forcing rapists to marry their victims. This begs the question of whether more appropriate "traditional" approaches to dispute resolution might have been engaged. Buddhist traditions, for example, have been an increasing focus of conflict management approaches in Cambodia (Hughes 2001: 15). In the 1990s, debate continued over the relevance of western liberal concepts such as "tolerance", "democracy" and "trust-building" for Cambodian society. Insufficient research has been conducted to ascertain whether the introduction of such concepts broadened the range of norms available to villagers, or whether the human rights industry begun under UNTAC stimulated a new rights-based approach to understandings of conflict management at the village level (Hughes 2001: 15–16).

Dealing with the past

Little systematic study has been conducted of the extent of social trauma that resulted from the Cambodian genocide. Mass post-traumatic stress syndrome is generally assumed and appears to have had a significant negative effect on Cambodian social structures and coping mechanisms. Notably, these effects included a generalised lack of trust, a related lack of community cohesion, including social safety nets, a fall in social solidarity (the "uncaring society"), a depersonalisation of societal relations, psychological problems, a generalised propensity to plan only for the short term, a tendency towards self-preservation reflected in "wild civil libertarianism" and the further entrenchment of a culture of violence (Curtis 1998: 113).

Although a central tenet of the Paris Agreements was the pledge to ensure that the human rights violations of the past were not repeated, the Agreements did not specifically address how the parties were to deal with this past. UNTAC did not have an explicit mandate to examine past human rights violations or to become involved in seeking redress for the genocide. On the contrary, the commitment in the Agreements to ensure a "non-return to the policies and practices of the past" (Article 15(2)) was a compromise to avoid more direct reference to these atrocities, which were perceived as a deal breaker for the Khmer Rouge, China and possibly Thailand (McNamara 1994: 11; Ashley 1998: 73). Although Hun Sen later called for a national tribunal to be established under UNTAC supervision, to arrest Khieu Samphan and other Khmer

Rouge leaders for trial, the CPP did not push the point in the Paris Agreements negotiations (FBIS 1993c: 36). The ensuing lack of any specific measures to address the genocide was widely criticised as undermining the principles of the Genocide Convention as well as the integrity of the whole settlement (G Robertson 2000: 283). Similarly, it has been argued that the inclusion of the Khmer Rouge as a principal party to the settlement negotiations, in its capacity as a member of the SNC, and later of both the CPP and FUNCINPEC, made a mockery of the commitment to end to Cambodia's culture of impunity (Ashley 1998: 74).

The tone was thus set for inaction. With a tribunal ruled out, UNTAC made little effort to gauge what, if anything, Cambodians wanted or were willing to bear with respect to dealing with the past. The head of the Human Rights Component, Dennis McNamara, speculated that an absence of any complaints relating to past actions by the Khmer Rouge may have reflected a collective wish among Cambodians to rebuild their country without dredging up the past (McNamara 1994: 12). Project workers involved in reconciliation work during or shortly after UNTAC did not observe any consensus on the level of community demand to proceed with some form of justice process. Discussion of a Khmer Rouge tribunal appears to have emerged only with the demise of the Khmer Rouge as a political and security force and with Prince Ranarridh's appeals to the United Nations for a tribunal in the mid-1990s. The lack of democratic channels for discourse precluded any wide-ranging debate on the issue (Ashley 1998: 74).

In the Cambodian context, the failure to seek accountability for past crimes appears to have set the tone for continued disrespect for the rule of law. Several authors have argued that not resolving the issue of genocide created longer-term problems, which surfaced as soon as the oversight of UNTAC was removed (Roberts 2001: 24). Most importantly, the lack of accountability for crimes against humanity condoned impunity, and allowed for ongoing political control by figures directly implicated in the genocide. This was clearly reflected in the controversy surrounding the Extraordinary Chambers in the Courts of Cambodia, a mixed Cambodian/international tribunal established under a 2001 law to try senior Khmer Rouge leaders for crimes committed during the period of Democratic Kampuchea. Protracted difficulties in ensuring that the tribunal met basic international standards in terms of its rules of procedure and the quality and integrity of its judicial staff meant that the Chambers were not in a position to charge their first suspect until July 2007. This not only generated concerns that the alleged perpetrators of the most heinous crimes of Democratic Kampuchea would die before they could be brought to trial, but fuelled continued uncertainty over the ability of the Chambers to deliver justice in the face of the lack of independence and integrity of the Cambodian judiciary, prosecutorial authorities and legal profession (UNGA 2007: 40). Ultimately, this undermined the authority of the judiciary and the legitimacy of the state.

Reconciliation

UNTAC did not implement any specific national-level or grassroots reconciliation projects, although some village-level reconciliation processes were conducted in conjunction with the refugee repatriation process as former resistance groups were reintegrated. These were largely carried out on the initiative of individuals and through personal relationship-building.

Cambodia's first systematic reconciliation programme, the Cambodia Resettlement and Reintegration programme (CARERE), was established by the United Nations Development Programme (UNDP) in June 1992 to assist in the reintegration and reconciliation of displaced persons in the Khmer Rouge stronghold of north-west Cambodia. Early projects in 1992 and 1993 sought to promote reconciliation between political factions and returnee and non-returnee households through shared economic development projects, but had a limited impact owing to the priority given to rapid short-term delivery of physical rehabilitation (UNDP 2001a: 17). More participatory mechanisms for development and reconciliation were really only developed after 1993 when CARERE began to tackle the question of local "ownership" of aid (UNDP 2001a: 19–21). From September 1993, CARERE helped to establish elected village development councils and to build relationships between the councils and provincial governments. Later, the programme was used to help build trust between the Khmer Rouge and the state, after a peace agreement in August 1996 in which Khmer Rouge groups agreed to integrate with the Cambodian governmental structures.

The CARERE reconciliation programme had several sources of success. First, reconciliation was combined with the development process: communities including Khmer Rouge groups had to negotiate with the provincial government to obtain development funding; in turn, the provincial government indicated its solidarity by providing money. This helped to establish a meaningful relationship between the two groups. Second, CARERE used and strengthened existing sources of social mediation such as religious networks and the input of village elders in programme implementation and to build relationships (UNDP 2001a: 44). Third, CARERE programme managers played the role of a neutral third party to assist in the negotiations, implement the eventual peace agreement and help build trust. The agreement itself was initiated by the parties themselves, rather than being imposed from outside. Like the

CIVPOL experience in establishing informal justice structures, the CARERE experience suggested an unmet demand for reconciliation in Cambodia.

Performing effectively

The litany of problems within the UNTAC mission itself has been discussed extensively in the literature.[19] In the rule of law area, these included poor coordination between components, no common vision,[20] severe resource shortfalls, a lack of strategic planning, and insufficient international pressure on Cambodian leaders to adhere to constitutional limitations on power (Hendrickson 1998: 7). As discussed above, UNTAC did not succeed in gaining local support for its policies and in many cases had a poor relationship with the Cambodian parties to the Agreements. Two key issues are discussed here: UNTAC's short deployment and the difficulties of establishing an effective post-UNTAC strategy.

Perhaps critics' most common refrain with respect to the prospects for creating the rule of law was that UNTAC's 18-month mandate was far too short to conduct serious state-building activities. As a prominent human rights lawyer observed, the "rule of law is not like instant noodles". The transitional administration proved too short to build institutions, change habits or cement relationships robust enough to promote sustained improvements in the rule of law. By the end of its mandate, UNTAC was only beginning to develop an understanding of the rule of law issues it was dealing with and to discuss potential solutions.

As with other peacekeeping missions, UNTAC's deployment length and resources were constrained by political realities. Mission officials described the pressure to focus on "deliverables" and a genuine belief that elections were the correct starting point from which to create room for a new environment in which judicial and other reforms could then take place. This ultimately proved misguided when it became evident that the CPP would not be sufficiently disabled by the elections, and the door to reform would not be opened. As the mission proceeded, there was growing support from elements in UNTAC – notably the Human Rights Component – for a complete overhaul of the judicial system to accompany the electoral process as a key element of reform. At a major human rights symposium held in late 1992, for example, speakers called for UNTAC to thoroughly reform the judicial system in order to create an independent judiciary. Speakers urged UNTAC to move fast on this issue, also cautioning that trying to transplant western structures to Cambodia would be unsuccessful, and that UNTAC should draw on alternative, village-based approaches to conflict resolution (UNTAC Human Rights Component 1992: 9–10). Ultimately, time ran out and such ideas were never followed up.

A well-planned exit strategy, including follow-through on rule of law initiatives, might have compensated somewhat for the shortness of UNTAC's mandate. The United Nations did not, however, provide for any specific continued action on the judicial front. This omission was also reflected in the international donor community's failure to mention, let alone make a financial commitment to, justice issues at its first donors' conference on the rehabilitation and reconstruction of Cambodia in July 1993.

UNTAC was, however, succeeded by a small Office of the Special Representative of the Secretary-General and by the UNCOHCHR, the first ever successor mission to a Human Rights Component.[21] The Human Rights Component had proposed the Office in recognition of the amount of work that remained to be done in the human rights field and with the awareness that institution-building had not even been attempted beyond some urgent issues such as improving prison conditions and police training.

The Office was established under Commission on Human Rights Resolution 1993/6, which mandated it to cover administration of justice, support for civil society and NGOs, treaty implementation, and technical assistance and education. The mandate was developed in cooperation with the UNTAC Human Rights Component and had a strengthened focus on institution-building. The Office allowed the continuation of UNTAC's protection mechanism for opposition and civil society groups and its protection mandate went beyond that of previous offices.

In its early phases, the Office focused on technical assistance to the courts through a largely unsuccessful judicial mentor programme. It also provided advice to the government on legislation, the structure of the judiciary, procedural aspects of the court, the Supreme Council of the Magistracy, the Constitutional Council and the Court of Appeal. Most of these were areas that had been untouched by UNTAC. Expectations were high and the Office found it difficult to convey the message that it was not as well resourced as a peacekeeping operation. The UNCOHCHR was present in no more than eight provinces at any time, for example, allowing significantly less penetration than UNTAC. The extent to which it could conduct meaningful work was also contingent on international support: objections by China and the Association of Southeast Asian Nations, for example, meant that at various times the Special Representative of the Secretary-General, Justice Kirby, encountered difficulties in gaining permission to investigate and report human rights issues (Brown and Zasloff 1998: 113).

Observations

Assessing UNTAC's rule of law work is perhaps an exercise more in identifying the impact of what UNTAC did not do than in examining the efficacy of what it did. Although in some respects UNTAC was a "circuit breaker" for Cambodia, ultimately it did not develop a concerted strategy to establish the rule of law, let alone one that encompassed a nuanced approach to the issues highlighted in the Chapter 3. An analysis of the mission reveals glimmers of what might have been achieved had more systematic, focused and consistent efforts been made and had UNTAC not been hamstrung by the limitations of the Paris Agreements. The "rule of law" emphasis was essentially new to these sorts of peace operations and UNTAC's approach must be viewed in that context.

The potential for the mission to support the establishment of the rule of law did exist. Community policing, human rights training and the beginnings of an NGO community, for example, had some sustained impact in introducing rule of law principles, but they proved to be developmental and time-dependent endeavours that exceeded the limits of UNTAC's short, restricted mandate. Similarly, some important steps were taken towards legislative reform, but these were largely ineffectual in the absence of supportive judicial, police and penal structures.

Moreover, processes were not set in train that might have provided an effective barrier against arbitrary and excessive state power or played a role in reconstructing trust in what was a deeply disrupted society. The CPP leadership retained political control despite their electoral defeat in 1993, and they daily circumvented constraints on the abuse of power set down in Cambodia's new constitution. The capacity of the political system to manage conflict, handle the regular affairs of state and respond to popular demands was not developed. Human rights abuses, extrajudicial violence and summary justice were enduring features of the Cambodian political landscape. The state remained mistrusted and weak and, ultimately, Cambodians continued to be denied access to basic rights.

UNTAC's lack of progress on the rule of law front reflects a common criticism of the Paris Agreements: that, in their eagerness to secure a quick political solution, the parties to the Agreements did not sufficiently prioritise democratic consolidation. The peace process was directed more at achieving a new and internationally acceptable political arrangement than at nurturing a post-electoral environment conducive to democratic development. The Agreements did not prioritise state-building, and UNTAC followed suit. In many senses, UNTAC avoided dealing with the inhospitable intervention environment with which it was confronted, taking the line of least resistance with powerful elites intent on retaining their political authority.

Notes

1. The National United Front for an Independent, Neutral, Peaceful and Democratic Cambodia (FUNCINPEC), the National Army of Democratic Kampuchea (NADK, or Khmer Rouge), the Khmer People's National Liberation Front (KPNLF) and the State of Cambodia (SOC).
2. For general studies of the UNTAC mission, see Brown and Zasloff (1998); Curtis (1998); Doyle (1995); Findlay (1995); Heder and Ledgerwood (1996a); Heininger (1994); Hughes (1996); Peou (1997); and Ratner (1993).
3. For details, see Fernando (1998: 96).
4. Fernando (1998: 60–61) describes the Vietnamese–Khmer trial mode in detail.
5. *Provisions dated September 10, 1992 Relating to the Judiciary and Criminal Law and Procedure Applicable in Cambodia during the Transitional Period* (1992). Sanderson (n.d.: 11) and Plunkett (1994: 66–67) both make this point, the latter with reference to Articles 15(1), 15(2)(c) and 16 of the Paris Agreements, the SNC's accession to the International Covenant on Civil and Political Rights and the International Covenant on Economic, Social and Cultural Rights, and the preamble to the Criminal Law.
6. The SNC was the negotiating group for the Paris Agreements and the Khmer governing body during the UNTAC mandate. As the "unique legitimate body and source of authority" it ostensibly delegated to UNTAC "all powers necessary" to ensure the implementation of the Agreements.
7. The Convention against Torture and Other Cruel, Inhuman or Degrading Treatment or Punishment; the International Convention on the Elimination of All Forms of Discrimination Against Women; the Convention on the Rights of the Child; the Convention Relating to the Status of Refugees and its 1967 Protocol. Cambodia was already a party to the Genocide Convention and the Convention on Racial Discrimination.
8. These were the UN Code of Conduct for Law Enforcement Officials and the Australian Commonwealth prosecution policy (UNTAC 1993a).
9. See "Proposed Amendments to the Cambodian Criminal Law that would facilitate the appointment of Special Prosecutors and Special Judges during the transitional period" (UNTAC 1993b: Attachment E).
10. The SOC representative stressed in SNC discussions that an UNTAC tribunal was outside the mandate of the agreement and the amendments to the penal code would concentrate excessive power in the hands of the Special Representative and violate the judicial process. FUNCINPEC and the KPNLF supported the introduction of a Special Prosecutor. Sam Rainsy, for FUNCINPEC, noted that numerous crimes were being committed with total impunity and that the acquisition by UNTAC of power of prosecution would generate confidence and release the people from a corrupt regime (UNTAC 1993i: 17). See also UNTAC (1993h: 10) and FBIS (1993a: 42).
11. The case was of an NADK soldier, Tham Theuan, who was accused of the murder of ethnic Vietnamese in Kompong Chhnang in December 1992.
12. UNTAC (1993b, 1993g, 1993j); Akashi (1993).
13. See UNTAC (1993k: 5); FBIS (1993b: 31).
14. Hor Nam Hong (SOC) and Khieu Samphan (Democratic Kampuchea) both rejected the Transitional Criminal Law in the SNC, for example, the latter on the grounds that the provision on non-discrimination would legalise the presence of Vietnamese in Cambodia. See UNTAC (1992b: 6–7).
15. See UNTAC (19931, 1993m).
16. Statistical information on cases involving the Complaints and Investigations Service in the provinces showed that the majority of cases concerned land disputes. According to

Nyberg (1993: 1), 539 of 1,052 cases reported in 12 provinces during the UNTAC period were land disputes.

17. Camera, established by the Minister for Women's Affairs.

18. See, for example, the 1994 *National Program to Rehabilitate and Develop Cambodia* and the February 1995 follow-up document *Implementing the National Program to Rehabilitate and Develop Cambodia* (RGC 1994, 1995), which identified as one of its key elements "the rule of law, including the need to promote good governance and the creation of a legal and institutional framework conducive to the emergence of a liberal market economy" and highlighted as one of its biggest problems "establishing a legal base and the means to enforce it" (Curtis 1998: 64–65). The government also committed to the rule of law in its 1995 position paper "Reinforcing the Rule of Law" (cited in Curtis 1998: 148).

19. See Brown and Zasloff (1998); Curtis (1998); Doyle (1995); Findlay (1995); Heder and Ledgerwood (1996a); Heininger (1994); Hughes (1996); Peou (1997); and Ratner (1993).

20. UNTAC (1993o: 10) gives an indicative account of the poor coordination between mission components on policing issues.

21. With the exception of a similar, but less extensive, operation in the United Nations Observer Mission in El Salvador (ONUSAL).

5

State-building without a state: The UN Interim Administration Mission in Kosovo

An effective rule of law requires above all that every member of every community in Kosovo is able to live, work and travel in a peaceful and secure environment. Recent events have demonstrated how far there is to go in attaining this goal. Such an environment requires not only an effective and professional police service and judiciary but above all the active cooperation of every inhabitant of Kosovo.

(UNMIK 2004a: 4)

Almost five years into the United Nations Interim Administration Mission in Kosovo (UNMIK), the communal violence of March 2004 demonstrated a profound lack of progress in consolidating the rule of law (OIK 2004: 20). Orchestrated attacks by Kosovo Albanian extremists against minorities resulted in 19 deaths and nearly 1,000 injuries, the forced eviction of some 4,500 people, the destruction of hundreds of properties and disruption to essential public services. The violence was preceded for several weeks by demonstrations against UNMIK and attacks on government officials, including President Rugova.

Neither UNMIK nor Kosovo's fledgling rule of law institutions proved able to prevent the violence or to deal effectively with its aftermath. Ethnic Albanian officers from the Kosovo Police Service (KPS) allegedly participated or were complicit in the attacks (OMIK 2004a: 6–7; AI 2004b: 2). Courts were closed for several days and court access for minority groups and court employees suffered extended disruptions (OMIK 2004a: 10). Neither the courts nor the correctional system had sufficient

No entry without strategy: Building the rule of law under UN transitional administration, Bull, United Nations University Press, 2008, ISBN 978-92-808-1151-3

capacity to absorb cases generated by the violence. Kosovo's political leaders responded with disappointing ambivalence (OMIK 2004a: 6).

Such concerns were not new. In 2003, Kosovo's Ombudsperson described UNMIK's lack of progress in establishing the rule of law as the "weak link in an aspiring democratic Kosovo" (OIK 2003: 3). His 2004 annual report described "chaos" in the dispensation of justice and concluded that, despite some improvements, Kosovo's judiciary was "still far away from attaining a level where it may be considered as a solid ally in protecting people's rights" (OIK 2004: 12). Beyond the judicial system, the Ombudsperson pointed to public sector corruption, overcrowded detention facilities, political extremism and the existence of illegal armed structures as threats to the rule of law (OIK 2004: 7–31). Although UNMIK officials interviewed by me dismissed such criticism as "unconstructive", they agreed with the basic thrust of the report.

From the outset, UNMIK had undoubtedly faced an uphill battle. Following the intervention by the North Atlantic Treaty Organization (NATO) in March 1999, Security Council Resolution 1244 of 10 June 1999 authorised a transitional civilian administration under Chapter VII under which "the people of Kosovo can enjoy substantial autonomy" (UNSC 1999d: 3). With minimal notice, UNMIK deployed on 13 June into a humanitarian crisis in which ethnic division eclipsed the discord witnessed in either Cambodia or East Timor. The expulsion of ethnic Albanians by Yugoslav and Serbian forces displaced 90 per cent of Kosovo's estimated 1.7 million inhabitants, both internally and to neighbouring countries (OSCE DIHR 1999; UNSC 1999a: 2). Although violations were perpetrated by and against all ethnic groups, Albanians suffered most. Up to 10,000 Kosovo Albanians were massacred, 20,000 were raped and half of Kosovo Albanian residences were destroyed (Villmoare 2002: 374).

Reflecting the United Nations' emphasis on state institutions, the Secretary-General attributed Kosovo's security problems to "the absence of law and order institutions and agencies", including a police force and courts (UNSC 1999a: 2). Under Resolution 1244, UNMIK was vested with all legislative and executive powers, including the administration of justice. It was charged with maintaining civilian law and order, performing civilian administrative functions, developing provisional institutions for democratic and autonomous self-government and transferring these to Kosovan responsibility pending a final political settlement. From the scant remains of Kosovo's judiciary, UNMIK was mandated to establish a "multi-ethnic and democratic judicial system" (UNSC 1999a: 4) and embarked on an unprecedented set of "rule of law" initiatives that by late 2004 included:

- the oversight of *constitutional reform* within the confines of Kosovo's indeterminate future status, culminating in the promulgation in May 2001 of a quasi-constitution;
- *legislative reform*, including the determination of applicable law during the transition period and the proclamation by late 2004 of over 220 legally binding regulations and 130 administrative directions;
- the appointment of *transitional judicial, prosecution and defence services*, including support and oversight measures;
- the provision of interim *law enforcement* through an international civilian police presence and the establishment of a 5,700-strong indigenous KPS;
- responsibility for *correctional services* and for developing a Kosovo correctional system; and
- the *investigation and prosecution of serious crimes* committed during and after the 1998–1999 conflict.

In examining UNMIK's first five years, this chapter argues that, although UNMIK's comparatively lengthy deployment and expansive mandate provided scope for a more sophisticated range of rule of law initiatives than earlier operations such as the United Nations Transitional Authority in Cambodia, it failed in most of its endeavours. Uncertainty about Kosovo's final status – an obstacle not of UNMIK's making – undermined many of its efforts to establish the rule of law. At the same time, UNMIK made several avoidable strategic errors that contributed to its overall failure. In addition to generic UN mission problems such as poor coordination, these included an ambiguous interpretation of its mandate, dysfunctional design of state rule of law institutions, a virtually non-existent capacity-building and transfer strategy, a failure to neutralise spoilers and insufficient attention to non-state institutional tools such as alternative dispute resolution and reconciliation processes. Critically, UNMIK did not develop an effective strategy to engage Kosovans in its rule of law initiatives. UNMIK did not sufficiently uphold its mandate to harness existing institutions and skills, and state rule of law institutions remained inaccessible and irrelevant to large segments of the population. The resentment this generated undermined UNMIK's legitimacy and ultimately the commitment of Kosovans at both the elite and community level to the rule of law.

Rule of law landscape

UNMIK deployed into a chaotic rule of law environment. Although NATO's Kosovo Force (KFOR) partially filled the security vacuum created by the withdrawal of Serbian forces during the summer of 1999, it proved unable to prevent crimes of revenge and retribution, primarily against Serbs. The Kosovo Liberation army (KLA) and other armed groups attacked Kosovo Serbs and Albanians as the political contest unfolded between Ibrahim Rugova's Democratic League of Kosovo (LDK) and Hashim Thaci's Democratic Party of Kosovo (PDK) (AI 2000: 2; O'Neill 2002: 16–17). Murder, arson and looting became commonplace and sophisticated organised crime networks flourished (UNSC 1999a: 2).

All pre-existing state judicial, police and prison structures had disintegrated with the exodus of officials to Serbia. Basic civic rule systems, such as road rules, had collapsed and court equipment and records were spirited to Serbia or destroyed (ICG 2002: 1). Most Kosovo Albanians who had served in public office before their expulsion in 1989 had not practised for 10 years and the extensive Kosovo Albanian parallel administration that emerged over the previous decade had mostly collapsed.[1] In any case, like their Serb counterparts, Albanian "officials" had acquired communist administrative habits antithetical to democratic principles (Kirste 2001: 3, 18–19).

Illegal parallel administrative structures emerged quickly in the rule of law vacuum. By mid-1999, the PDK had installed a self-proclaimed government in 27 of the 30 municipalities. It controlled most village councils and engaged in a range of criminal activity such as illegal taxation and property seizures (Kirste 2001: 4, 11). Belgrade also established parallel judicial and other structures, particularly in northern Mitrovica. UNMIK's slow deployment and its tolerance of and at times cooperation with such structures facilitated their growth (O'Neill 2002: 48).

Kosovo's rule of law landscape was coloured by a legacy of deep public mistrust of the discriminatory state justice machinery of the decade preceding the 1998–1999 conflict. Organs of the Serbian executive, especially state security officials, used the justice system as a tool to divide and repress, routinely manipulating the judiciary, disregarding its decisions and using law enforcement agencies to intimidate Kosovo Albanians (OSCE ODIHR 1999; Peake 2004: 11). The Yugoslav judicial system had never been independent under Tito and "telephone justice", by which the ruling party directed judicial and prosecutorial actions, was regarded as the norm (Hartmann 2003a: 5).

The vast majority of the population had been subjected to systematic state discrimination. The policies of the Milosevic era excluded most Kosovo Albanians from working in the justice system or attending law school in their own language. No Kosovo Albanians were recruited into the judicial system for a decade and by 1999 only 30 of 756 judges and prosecutors were Kosovo Albanian (UNSC 1999a: 12). This limited the available supply of trained judicial officials after Serbia's withdrawal and compounded distrust of the judicial system amongst the bulk of the population. Discrimination was deeply institutionalised in the courts and the police and prison services, generating disrespect and hostility (ICG 2002: 3). It also created a general expectation that whoever controlled these systems would be able to secure preferential treatment for their own ethnic group (OSCE ODIHR 1999).

Extensive human rights violations further undermined the rule of law during this period. The catastrophic events of March 1999 were preceded by a decade of human rights violations by Yugoslav and Serbian security and police forces and their paramilitary proxies, particularly against Kosovo Albanians (OSCE DIHR 1999; AI 2000: 2).[2]

Finally, Kosovo's pre-conflict civil law based judicial system fell significantly below international standards. The supreme court, 5 district courts and 18 municipal and lower-level misdemeanour courts were characterised by a reliance on circumstantial evidence, a lack of adequate defence, procedural violations, the mishandling or fabrication of evidence, and trials in absentia. Judicial review was almost non-existent. The two penal codes, the Criminal Code of the Republic of Serbia and the Criminal Code of the Federal Republic of Yugoslavia (FRY), did not meet international standards, as was the case with Serbian wartime emergency powers in force at the time of UNMIK's deployment (Hartmann 2003a: 4). Similarly, the police system fell well below international standards in most respects.

Setting the parameters: UNMIK's rule of law mandate

The strength of UNMIK's rule of law mandate lay in the breadth of authority extended to the Special Representative of the Secretary-General (SRSG), which offered extensive scope for action and, with it, the potential to achieve significant change. The mandate's shortcomings were typical of other UN missions: a paucity of specific guidance from the Security Council on how to implement the mandate, of guaranteed resources and of specific benchmarks to measure progress (Bolton 2001: 141). Two particular drawbacks are notable with respect to UNMIK: Kosovo's unresolved final status and ambiguities in UNMIK's rule of law mandate.

The unresolved final status undermined virtually every facet of the mission.[3] The "compromise" formula of Resolution 1244, which reaffirmed Serbian sovereignty but left open the question of Kosovo's future status, created tension between the goals of respecting Serbian sovereignty and realising meaningful self-government for Kosovans. Sovereignty guarantees for Serbia rested uneasily with the classic powers of a state vested in UNMIK and with UNMIK's statist model for developing civil institutions (Stahn 2001b: 540–542). Falk (2000b) has described how this created a "mission impossible" in which the nationalist aspirations of Kosovo Albanians were pitted against the interests of the Serbian state:

> The price paid for securing the acquiescence of China and Russia in the Security Council was the reaffirmation of the status of Kosovo as part of Yugoslavia, as well as the assurance that the Serbs would be able to retain their ethnic presence in Kosovo. Neither of these goals was ever really attainable, and the lip service that still must be paid to them insures constant tension, recurrent violent incidents (some against UNMIK people), frustration with the restoration of normal life to Kosovo and in the long run a probable perception of UN failure ... [T]he Procrustean UN mandate, which can neither accommodate the complexities of the situation nor realise the goals of humanitarian diplomacy ... remains the fundamental problem ... [A]n overwhelming majority of Kosovans are committed to full independence as a sacred cause. To deny this aspiration is to insure a return to violence in Kosovo.

From the outset, UNMIK's state-building agenda fell hostage to this uncertain political endpoint over which neither Kosovans nor UNMIK had control.

The consequences for UNMIK's rule of law work were significant. First, state-building activities became highly politicised. UNMIK interpreted its mandate according to developments in Serbia and the individual views of Special Representatives on the question of independence.[4] Kosovo Albanians, Serbs and Belgrade scrutinised UNMIK's state-building activities for signs of how they related to the question of independence (ICG 2004; Yannis 2004: 75–76), making it impossible to depoliticise the judiciary and other justice structures.

Second, Kosovo's ambiguous end status meant there was no set timeframe for UNMIK's departure, no definitive guidance on what Kosovo was in transition *to*, and no clear picture of what permanent institutions were to be developed. This made it difficult for UNMIK to plan, let alone implement, a clear rule of law strategy (Yannis 2004: 75), particularly to envisage how the transition from international to local authorities would proceed.

Third, the tension between "sovereignty" and state-building responsibilities complicated UNMIK's relations with Belgrade and resulted in inconsistent rule of law policies. On some issues, KFOR and UNMIK interpreted their mandate as essentially unrestrained by sovereignty considerations and set about restoring the autonomy revoked by Serbia[5] without consulting Belgrade, including on such sensitive issues as constitutional development (Yannis 2004: 69–70). In other cases, perceived sensitivities about sovereignty saw UNMIK prevaricate, for example over the introduction of international judges and prosecutors.

Fourth, UNMIK's concern not to pre-empt Kosovo's final status obstructed reconciliation on many levels. In some instances, UNMIK prevented Kosovo Albanians and Serbs from making political deals aimed at building a sustainable future for Serbs. In others, the existence of reserved powers in justice and policing obstructed reconciliation. A senior diplomat described, for example, how a deal reached by Kosovo Serbs and Albanians to allow for ethnically balanced local command and control of the police dissolved when the United Nations refused to cede its reserved policing powers. It thereby missed a chance to get Albanians and Serbs working together on a practical issue.

Finally, the lack of a final status brought inertia to the mission, allowing those with a vested interest in the mission continuing indefinitely to forestall transition plans. A commonly expressed view among UNMIK and other international staff was that NATO would seek to remain in Kosovo indefinitely in order to move its centre of gravity east, and many UNMIK officers sought to delay any policies that would "do them out of a job" in an "easy" and lucrative mission proximate to Europe.

By July 2007, when persistent Russian intransigence saw the Security Council discard a draft resolution proposing "supervised" independence for Kosovo, many of these problems had become an entrenched part of Kosovo's political landscape. Kosovo Albanian leaders continued to threaten unilateral independence, Kosovo Serb leaders – at Belgrade's encouragement - continued their near-total boycott of Kosovo's central institutions, and the Kosovo Serb community continued to hold negative perceptions about their own security and to rely on Serbian parallel structures (UNSC 2007b: 1–2).

Ambiguities in UNMIK's rule of law mandate compounded those introduced by the lack of a final status. First, central political tasks such as developing provisional institutions for self-government were not properly defined, and uncertainty over the distribution of authority between UNMIK and Kosovan political leaders led to problems in their relationship (IICK 2000: 100; Yannis 2004: 73–74). Second, the division of responsibility between the various mission pillars was poorly defined, causing confusion and duplication, particularly between UNMIK and the Organization for Security and Co-operation (OSCE) over training and capacity-building. Third, a lack of clarity about where the rule of law fitted into the hierarchy of priorities resulted in tensions between potentially competing elements of the mission, particularly the security and human rights components. Fourth, although Resolution 1244 referred clearly to the deployment of Civilian Police (CIVPOL) and the creation of an indigenous police force, it did not specifically identify the need to deploy international jurists or to develop an indigenous judiciary (KCL 2003).

These ambiguities contributed to UNMIK's failure to pursue the most robust intervention on rule of law available within its mandate and its political and budget constraints. In some cases, this seriously undermined its rule of law initiatives. Two examples are discussed below: the applicable law debacle, which stemmed from UNMIK's resistance to a broad interpretation of its legislative powers, and the negative consequences of UNMIK's initial failure to introduce international jurists.

Establishing state justice institutions

Although UNMIK implemented some important reforms, it introduced a catalogue of problems in the early phases of the mission that reflected poor institutional design. UNMIK's handling of the question of applicable law, the insertion of international jurists into the domestic court system, the lack of a strategy to transfer responsibility for the judiciary to Kosovans and the ineptitude of UNMIK's CIVPOL deployment resulted in state rule of law structures that five years into the mission were deeply flawed, unconsolidated and in some cases inappropriate to the Kosovan context.

Constitutional framework

Although not a constitution in the full sense (Stahn 2001b: 546), the Constitutional Framework for Provisional Self-Government in Kosovo promulgated in May 2001 provided a legal framework governing the organisation and exercise of public power.[6] Marking Kosovo's first major step towards self-government, it provided for the partial transfer of executive authority from UNMIK to interim public bodies pending a decision on Kosovo's final status. The Framework established Provisional Institutions of Self-Government (PISG), including a 120-seat Assembly, a President, a government and courts. This paved the way for Kosovo-wide elections in November 2001 and then in October 2004. It established basic principles to be observed by the PISG and outlined their responsibilities in key areas, including economic and financial policy, trade and social services and public administration. It also reserved a number of powers and responsibilities for the Special Representative, including justice and foreign relations.[7]

With respect to rule of law provisions, the Constitutional Framework required the PISG to promote and fully respect the rule of law, human rights and freedoms, democratic principles, reconciliation and the principle of separation of powers. It detailed extensive safeguards for the protection of human rights and ethnic, linguistic and religious communities and adopted most international human rights conventions.[8] It protected the independence of the judiciary, the right to judicial review and the right to have criminal charges decided promptly by an independent and impartial court. It established a four-tiered court structure, offices of the Public Prosecutor and Ombudsperson and a Kosovo Judicial and Prosecutorial Council. In dividing responsibilities between the PISG and UNMIK, the Special Representative retained full control over the judiciary, and Chapter Six of the Framework provided for the KPS gradually to assume UNMIK law and order responsibilities.

The Constitutional Framework was thus broadly consistent with international standards, including the United Nations' rule of law objectives. In a legal sense, this made an important contribution to entrenching these principles in Kosovo's legal order and guaranteeing at least nominal continuity for any successor order.[9]

The key omission of the Framework with respect to rule of law principles was the absence of executive accountability mechanisms. It imposed no constraints or accountability procedures on UNMIK or the Special Representative as the ultimate holder of virtually unlimited public authority (Stahn 2001b: 548). Legislative acts adopted by the SRSG were exempted from the jurisdiction of Kosovo courts, and the only body authorised to comment on the legality of the SRSG's actions was the Ombudsperson, who was both appointed and removable by the SRSG. A constitutional chamber of the Supreme Court was empowered to consider the compatibility of such actions with laws adopted by the Assembly, but only government organisations or the Assembly could file motions (UNMIK 2001b: 9.4.11; HRW 2002b: 384).

Although UNMIK's accountability to the Security Council provided an indirect check on its actions, these arrangements struck an uneasy balance between authority and accountability. Symbolically, UNMIK's unconstrained authority was compatible with neither the principles of democratic governance nor the rule of law (Stahn 2001b: 561). In practice, it allowed UNMIK to undermine the rule of law through such actions as repeated arbitrary and excessive detention. On several occasions UNMIK ignored the provisions of the Constitutional Framework, for example by appointing judges and prosecutors without Assembly approval in 2002 (Marshall and Inglis 2003: 107). Finally, in holding Kosovo's ultimate authority answerable to the international community rather than Kosovans, it disengaged them from the process of developing civic checks on the state.

The usefulness of the Framework in advancing rule of law objectives was also undermined by a consultation process that failed to engender Kosovan support. Principally through the Kosovo Transitional Council (KTC, see below), UNMIK established several mechanisms to consult and engage both Albanian and Serb political leaders on the draft framework.[10] This proved difficult, and ongoing disagreements, largely over the final status, prevented UNMIK from successfully brokering a consensus document. No Kosovan participants accepted the text as finally adopted, forcing UNMIK unilaterally to finalise key issues such as the election method for the President, a Constitutional Court and a sunset clause on the time period for provisional self-government (Chesterman 2001b: 6).

Reactions to the final document ranged from grudging acceptance to outright rejection. Kosovo Albanians accepted the limited transfer of powers and the omission of any referendum mechanism reservedly. Kosovo Serbs described UNMIK's rejection of their proposed amendments as a "slap in the face" (*Vecernje Novosti* 2001a) and the Serbian government declared the Framework "unacceptable", denouncing it as a reward for Albanian separatist violence.[11] UNMIK publicly declined to seek Belgrade's approval of the Framework (UNMIK 2001c), which contained no provisions concerning Kosovo's relationship with the FRY. This alienated Kosovo Serbs (Stahn 2001b: 544) and once more avoided the key question of Kosovo's status.

The Framework's legitimacy was further affected by the extent of UNMIK's reserved powers, which Marshall and Inglis (2003: 107) have argued were so extensive as to undermine the document's democratic credentials. It caused damaging showdowns, notably the Kosovo Assembly's decision on 8 July 2004 to amend the Framework to give Kosovans control of international relations, public security and the judiciary, and to provide for a referendum on Kosovo's status within Serbia. The Assembly also voted to abrogate "all constitutional, legal, and sub-legal acts, decisions and other acts issued by Serbia and Yugoslavia after 22 March 1989". This forced the Special Representative to declare the Assembly's decision beyond its competence and therefore void (UNMIK 2004c), further souring relations.

Additional problems with the Framework related to coordination and logistics, notably the transfer and division of responsibilities between UNMIK and the PISG. Substantive decision-making responsibilities were reserved for the UNMIK Department of Justice (previously the Department of Judicial Affairs), whereas responsibility for administering those policies, including budgeting, was transferred to the new PISG Ministry of Public Services. A lack of coordination between the two agencies caused a disjunction between major policy decisions and operational support (UNMIK 2003b).

Legislative framework

UNMIK brought Kosovo's legislative framework into closer conformity with internationally recognised standards. However, in the absence of a considered reform process, it promulgated legislation that could not be implemented effectively, was rejected locally or was inconsistent with international standards. In particular, UNMIK's mishandling of the question of applicable law prompted one of the most significant crises of the mission.

UNMIK Regulation 1999/1 of 25 July 1999 declared the FRY laws in force prior to the NATO campaign on 24 March of that year to be applicable, insofar as they did not conflict with international human rights standards or UNMIK regulations (UNMIK 1999). UNMIK appears to have made this decision in order to demonstrate its recognition of continued Serbian sovereignty (Lorenz 2000a; Chesterman 2001b: 11) and in accordance with an emerging UN policy to utilise existing legal regimes where possible.

The Albanian-dominated judiciary quickly rejected UNMIK's decision, viewing FRY and Serbian laws as instruments of oppression. It refused to apply the Serbian Criminal Code and ignored or wilfully misinterpreted Regulation 1999/1. Judges instead insisted on applying those laws in effect in March 1989, such as the Kosovo Criminal Code, which they viewed as illegally revoked by Belgrade and thus still in force. At the same time, they borrowed from Serbian or FRY law in situations not covered by the 1989 code, such as drug trafficking and war crimes (Chesterman 2001b: 11). This very public revolt not only undermined UNMIK's credibility but introduced further confusion into the barely functioning legal system.

To deal with the crisis, UNMIK reversed its decision in December 1999, declaring that the laws in force in March 1989 now constituted the applicable law. Rather than restoring faith, UNMIK's abrupt change in direction was interpreted by the judiciary as incompetence. It was also confusing: although it was intended to give primacy to the pre-1989 Kosovo Criminal Code, the FRY Criminal Code and Criminal Procedure Code and some Serbian laws had also been in force in 1989 and the question of applicable law thus remained unclarified (Hartmann 2003a: 4).

Confusion reigned well into the mission in the absence of an authoritative codified set of laws that identified which of the original laws were applicable and which had been revoked or replaced. Several versions of each "applicable law" existed and amendments to those laws were not publicised systematically. The destruction of legal documents and libraries meant that few judges possessed a full set of original laws. In late 2004, no supreme judicial body existed to determine the applicability or constitutionality of laws, because the constitutional court provided for in the Constitutional Framework had not been created (OIK 2004: 8).

Inexperienced judges struggled to determine the consistency of the criminal codes with international law and continued to apply laws that were potentially in breach of international standards (UNSC 2000h: 8).

The incorporation into applicable law of the European Convention on Human Rights caused further confusion. Little training was initially provided to judges and, although this situation was later rectified, it appears to have had little impact (ICG 2002: 4; Marshall and Inglis 2003: 116).

In these circumstances, decisions on applicable law were frequently inconsistent. Some courts were paralysed, with judges refusing to conduct trials until they were certain of the applicable law; in other courts, judges made individual determinations on applicable law, creating inconsistencies in practice between the courts. This was highlighted in a US Department of State Judicial Assessment Mission, which reported:

> One judge ... selects the law that is "most favorable" to the defendant. Another judge said that he chooses the law that seems to him to "best describe the crime itself". At times, police or KFOR units have initiated proceedings using one set of laws, and then the judges have continued using a different set of laws. This practice raises serious issues concerning basic human rights and due process guarantees. (United States Department of State 2000b: 18)

Against this backdrop, it is not surprising that the legislative reform process was less than smooth. UNMIK began the reform process in August 1999 within the framework of a Joint Advisory Council for Legislative Matters (JAC/LM), which advised on legal reform and prepared new legislation in coordination with the UNMIK Office of the Legal Adviser. In an effort to involve both Kosovans and international experts, the JAC/LM was co-chaired by a Kosovan jurist and an UNMIK representative and comprised 20 Kosovan and 7 international judges, as well as former judges and attorneys. Kosovo Serb members were appointed but withdrew from the process after the first meeting. The JAC/LM process proved ineffectual on several counts. The drafting process was ad hoc and, with no drafting schedule or regular public consultation mechanism, it was unclear to relevant parties what the JAC/LM was working on at any given time (United States Department of State 2000b: 24). Its role was never fully clarified and it was not given adequate legal or other support.

As the reform agenda grew, confusion increased over who was drafting laws and how they related to each other (Marshall and Inglis 2003: 117). The division of legislative responsibilities between the JAC/LM, the OSCE Department of Human Rights and Rule of Law, UNMIK's Department of Judicial Affairs and later the Kosovo Assembly was not clear (O'Neill 2002: 39). There appears to have been little systematic effort to ascertain legislative gaps or identify ways to fill them (United States Department of State 2000b: 8). As a result, significant gaps remained, including in the areas of state accountability, compensation for victims of violent crimes, public assembly and the administration of justice. This had a major operational impact on the ability of key sectors such as the judiciary and police to perform effectively. It was not until 2002, for example, that adequate legal tools on evidence collection were implemented to enable police and the courts to investigate and prosecute organised crime, terrorism and war crimes.

Drafting processes improved over time, although problems continued with legal policy-making in the Kosovo government. The establishment of a Standardisation Unit in the Office of the Prime Minister helped streamline consultation processes and improve the consistency of new laws. By 2004, an inter-ministerial working group had been established to develop a legislative strategy, although the capacity of the government to make clear and informed legal policy decisions remained poor (UNSC 2004b: 3).

Legislative reform was also delayed by a poorly conceived review and approval process. Lorenz (2000b: 136–137) provides a telling account of a six-month delay in promulgating a regulation on witness statements, owing to the need for the regulation to be reviewed by the JAC/LM, by the Council of Europe and twice by UN headquarters in New York. Ironically, the cumbersome review process was nonetheless insufficient to ensure that all new laws were consistent with existing laws and human rights standards (ICG 2002: 13; Marshall and Inglis (2003: 97).[12]

In implementing new laws, the principles of accessibility and foreseeability remained substantially unmet. This made it difficult for practitioners to be consistent and for individuals to protect themselves from arbitrary government action or to regulate their own behaviour (OIK 2004: 8).

UNMIK provided little guidance on the implementation of new laws and regulations (Marshall and Inglis 2003: 118). Translation was slow and distribution haphazard, compounding the confusion caused by the applicable law debacle. Most new laws and regulations were not subject to a *vacatio juris* period. Even when this was substantial, UNMIK was criticised for being passive in informing the judiciary and public about the changes to the laws (OIK 2004: 10). Judges often remained unaware of new regulations, or were unable to access these in their own language for months after they were promulgated (ICG 2002: 13). As of late 2004, there was no official procedure in place regarding the publication of laws. The establishment of an internet database in June 2004 improved accessibility, but for only a small percentage of the population (OIK 2004: 8).

Implementation of new legislation was particularly patchy at the local level. Elected municipal assemblies established in early 2001 were often confused about how to implement the UN regulations, partly through lack of knowledge and partly through their lack of relevance to Balkan traditions. As a result, they often ignored or circumvented the regulations (Kirste 2001: 16).

New Kosovo Criminal Code and Criminal Procedure Code

UNMIK's key legislative achievement was the overhaul of Kosovo's criminal codes, with the entry into force on 6 April 2004 of the new Provisional Criminal Code and Criminal Procedure Code.[13] The codes had a mixed reception. They were welcomed by many in the political elite and broader public as an important symbolic break with the past. However, legal practitioners were much more cautious because of what they viewed as serious legal and practical shortcomings.

The Provisional Criminal Code incorporated a wider range of criminal offences and punishments than its communist predecessor, enhancing the justice system's capacity to deter and punish offenders. Similarly, the Provisional Criminal Procedure Code introduced important improvements, such as not allowing judges who had conducted pre-trial (investigative) actions to sit on trial panels and preventing trials from proceeding without a prosecutor. It strengthened prosecutorial capacity by authorising the Public Prosecutor to undertake investigations and by making parties, rather than the presiding judge and trial panel, primarily responsible for presenting evidence and questioning. It introduced procedures to avoid unnecessary criminal proceedings and to streamline administration, including by referring cases to mediation. It also enhanced protection for employees in the criminal justice system (Borg-Olivier 2003).

Nonetheless, both Kosovan and international legal practitioners expressed concern over the new codes. First, the codes were weakened by omissions. The Criminal Procedure Code, for example, did not incorporate procedures for juveniles and the mentally incompetent or disallow retrial panels from having the same composition as the original trial. Second, some judges considered that language drawn from international instruments was too ambiguous for a civil law context and required the enactment of additional implementing legislation, a process that could not be guaranteed. Third, neither code worked well in practice because, in replicating European and US legal codes, the drafters had imposed unrealistically high standards, which were incompatible with Kosovo's logistical realities. For example, UNMIK officials found it impossible to uphold the provision disallowing judges who had already participated in case proceedings from further involvement in another capacity when the pool of available judges was so small. Fourth, despite efforts by the drafters to draw on criminal law in Slovenia, Croatia and Bosnia-Herzegovina, practitioners believed the new codes were not adequately embedded in local jurisprudence. Given the lack of expertise and resources to develop case law jurisprudence, legal practitioners believed that, instead of creating a totally new law, a better strategy would have been to reform the existing system, which was already embedded in a social and legal context. Finally, practical measures to support the new code were inadequate. For example, despite a three-year lead-time in introducing enhanced powers for prosecutors, UNMIK made little attempt to recruit more prosecutors, upgrade facilities or create a judicial police to undertake investigations under the Public Prosecutor (OIK 2004: 10).

The judiciary

> What has been learned from the international experience in Kosovo ... is that successful international intervention in the judicial arena should be immediate and bold, rather than incremental and crisis driven. (Hartmann 2003a: 2)

Although the United Nations viewed the creation of an effective and independent judicial system in Kosovo as imperative to address security concerns and build public confidence (UNSC 1999a: 12, 2000b: 24, 2000e: 10), it manifestly failed to do so.[14] As evidenced by demonstrations against the arrest of former members of the KLA in early 2003, large segments of the public perceived the judicial system as neither effective nor impartial, and it was plagued by a litany of problems well into the mission. Investigations and trials were mishandled even for the most serious crimes. For example, in the notorious Nis bus convoy attack of February 2001, which caused 11 deaths and 40 injuries, a catalogue of failures saw suspects released, re-arrested under UNMIK's executive detention powers, and eventually re-released by an international panel of judges. Allegations that the investigation was mishandled by both UNMIK and KFOR exacerbated Kosovo Serbs' mistrust of the judicial system.

Court delays and pre-trial detention of more than a year were common, with one defendant detained for over 20 months before being acquitted owing to a lack of evidence (OMIK 2002a: 9, 12). Kosovo Serbs complained of unequal treatment, in terms of both biased judgments and unequal access arising from the scarcity of Serb defence counsel and interpreters (Lorenz 2000b: 133; UNSC 2003e: 5).

UNMIK's failure to establish a functioning judicial system may be attributed to early errors and a failure to redress these or to invest resources commensurate with the challenges. Inadequate capacity-building of local judicial officials by the OSCE further threatened the sustainability of the system.

As described above, in the opening phases of the mission a hiatus existed in which there was no civilian judicial authority. KFOR's ad hoc application of military law during this period was inconsistent and confusing. Each national contingent imposed its own national laws – French civil law in French-run tribunals in the French sector and a military variant of US common law in the American sector, for example. Although UNMIK moved quickly to establish an "Emergency Judicial System" (EJS), the stage had already been set for judicial confusion.

Although, to UNMIK's credit, it had reopened the District Court of Pristina on 30 June 1999, and established mobile courts by early July and a 55-member EJS by October, it quickly became apparent to senior UN officials that they had underestimated the difficulty of establishing the judicial system. Alongside logistical problems, judicial appointments proved highly political and subject to rejection by the local elite.[15] UNMIK struggled to secure Serb appointments to the judiciary and, by October, all Serb members of the EJS had resigned as a result of intimidation and a broader Serbian policy to boycott the UNMIK administration.[16] It proved impossible to depoliticise detention and trial practices, whereby judges frequently released KLA members while detaining Kosovo Serbs for the same crime. KFOR continued to detain arrestees at its own discretion, despite protests from Kosovan judges (Hartmann 2003a: 5–6).

Alongside severely limited policing and prison capabilities, the EJS was so ineffective that a virtual judicial vacuum remained until December 1999. Criminal activity escalated, including an orchestrated campaign to kill the remaining Serbs. The situation was so bad that many called for a state of emergency to be declared (Marshall and Inglis 2003: 101). As its "honeymoon period" drew to a close, UNMIK had thus failed to shape any positive expectations about the judicial system.

In December 1999, UNMIK moved to establish a "provisional" judicial system based on the recommendations of two joint local/ international advisory commissions.[17] UNMIK appointed 301 judges and prosecutors and 238 lay judges, the first of whom were sworn in in January 2000. By June of that year, a criminal justice system was functioning throughout Kosovo and by August, a full complement of 56 courts[18] and 13 prosecutor's offices were in operation. By July 2004, a total of 310 judges and 85 prosecutors, including 16 Kosovo Serb judges and three Kosovo Serb prosecutors, had been appointed (UNSC 2004d: 8).

Despite this progress, the development of the judicial system was deeply flawed in both form and substance. The remainder of this section examines six key problems with the establishment of the state judicial system: the introduction of international judges and prosecutors; the lack of a capacity-building and transfer strategy; court conditions; security; review and accountability mechanisms; and minority representation in the courts.

The hybrid judiciary: International judges and prosecutors

The creation of a hybrid court system in 2000 staffed by international judges and prosecutors (IJPs) was one of UNMIK's most controversial policies. It represented the first time the United Nations or any other international body had inserted international jurists into a national judicial system.[19] IJPs were introduced in response to UNMIK's assessment that ethnic discrimination by Kosovan judges and prosecutors was so acute that international control of the most sensitive cases was necessary (UNSC 2000e: 21; O'Neill 2002: 90). Flagrant bias in the judicial handling of persons implicated in the violence in Mitrovica following the Nis bus attack of February 2000 had proven the final straw. The first IJPs were appointed in Mitrovica in February 2000,[20] and, following hunger strikes by Serb defendants in May, UNMIK appointed IJPs to all five districts and the Supreme Court.[21]

This was not a straightforward decision. The UNMIK advance team had decided against appointing internationals from the outset because of concerns they would not have sufficient knowledge of the Kosovan judicial system and fears of being criticised as neo-colonialist (KCL 2003; Hartmann 2003a: 4). The decision to stay "local" contrasted with operational methodology elsewhere, where police, prison and civil administration bodies were all run by internationals from the outset. Eventually, UNMIK decided on a minimalist approach that inserted international judges into the existing system rather than creating a separate international court.

The friction caused by the introduction of IJPs outweighed the improvements they brought. Over time, the use of IJPs did improve standards of fairness and reduce impunity for key groups such as the KLA (KCL 2003). But it also introduced new problems. It proved difficult to recruit suitable candidates and the quality of internationals varied. IJPs lacked adequate legal and administrative support, such as interpreters and legal officers (ICG 2002: 8; UNMIK 2003b: 14). The unlimited subject matter jurisdiction and lack of sufficiently specific guiding principles for assigning internationals to cases[22] increased case volume beyond the capacity of IJPs, impacting negatively on the quality of case management (Hartmann 2003a: 10).

The appointment of internationals to so-called "Regulation 6" panels on a minority vote basis[23] reduced their effectiveness. Because IJPs were often outvoted by their Kosovo colleagues (ICG 2002: 5), their presence on these panels often merely served to give international "legitimacy" to questionable convictions (KCL 2003). Two changes were made to address this. First, in December 2000 majority international panels (the so-called "64" panels)[24] were assigned to all cases of war crimes and to significant "payback" crimes such as terrorism, corruption and political assassinations (Hartmann 2003a: 2). Second, the authority of IJPs was extended in January 2001 to allow international prosecutors to resume cases abandoned by their Kosovo counterparts.[25] With these changes, IJPs had the broadest subject matter jurisdiction of any of their counterparts, including in East Timor, Sierra Leone and Bosnia-Herzegovina.

The use of "64" panels caused friction in the Kosovo Serb community. Not all defendants were successful in getting their cases assigned to them and the overturning by UNMIK international panels of prior convictions, regardless of the fairness of the original judgment, fuelled further uncertainty and tension between ethnic communities (Marshall and Inglis 2003: 123). The use of international judges also created perceptions of executive control, owing to their status as UNMIK employees and the fact that the UNMIK Department of Justice was responsible for assigning them to cases. Their strong ties to the executive were not matched by institutional guarantees of independence: cases were not randomly assigned and there was no disciplinary mechanism. UNMIK did not have to comply with transparent criteria and could remove any case it liked from Kosovan judges without explanation. Further, the UNMIK Department of Justice undermined the functional independence of international judges by interfering with decision-making processes (OMIK 2003a: 29).

Critically, no comprehensive phase-out plan was developed. The highest IJP staffing level was reached in 2003, with 13 international judges and 14 international prosecutors (Hartmann 2003a: 9). Although, at this time, only around 10 per cent of criminal cases and no civil cases were handled by international judges (UNMIK 2003b: 14), their presence nonetheless allowed UNMIK to avoid giving local jurists the opportunity to take on difficult cases (ICG 2002: 9). It also failed to provide more than an interim solution to the key problems of minority representation and bias in the judiciary.

Capacity-building and transfer strategy

One of the most disturbing aspects of UNMIK's judicial programme was the almost complete absence of a strategy to strengthen the capacity of a local judiciary. Poor training was a key problem. As the agency responsible, the OSCE's Department of Human Rights and Rule of Law failed to establish a comprehensive training programme for the large intake of judges and prosecutors appointed in December, prior to the opening of the first court in January 2000. This was partially addressed in March 2000 with the establishment of the Kosovo Judicial Institute, which conducted induction seminars for judges and prosecutors across Kosovo. However, this sort of classroom training generally proved ineffectual because it neglected to focus on essential practical skills such as questioning witnesses, evidence development and legal reasoning. "Experts" flown in to conduct the training lacked the requisite language, cultural, methodological and even teaching skills to be effective. Local judges and prosecutors resented "listening to Americans preach about laws we've been practising for the last 30 years". Prosecutorial training was neglected, even after the introduction of the new Criminal Procedure Code under which prosecutors assumed a much greater role. According to UNMIK and OSCE justice sector officials, no training review was ever conducted to refine the process.

Legal education at the Pristina University Law Faculty only partially improved the skills of new graduates. The parallel law faculty run by Albanian academics during the 1990s returned to the university premises relatively quickly in November 1999, but suffered from security concerns, shortfalls in physical resources, corruption, disputes with UNMIK and a difficult transition from the communist era in terms of teaching methods and curricula (Waters 2001: 7). The faculty continued to produce graduates who were assessed by UNMIK and OSCE officials as incapable of assuming duties in the real world. The OSCE tried to remedy this through assisting students to prepare for the bar exam, but enjoyed little success.

Other support efforts had some impact. UNMIK and the OSCE oversaw the establishment in June 2000 of the Kosovo Law Centre as a registered non-governmental organisation (NGO) designed to provide technical and material assistance to the legal community. It served as a research think tank, published and distributed laws, ran a scholarship programme and supported the Law Faculty at the University of Pristina. It also compiled a publication on applicable law. These initiatives were of limited use, however, in the face of the challenges at hand.

Early intentions to use IJPs in a mentoring capacity did not eventuate. One international prosecutor deployed in Kosovo in early 2000 admitted that during his four-year deployment he had not supervised, or even observed, a single local prosecutor at work. Not one local prosecutor was given the opportunity to sit in on international-run cases between 2000 and 2004. Similarly, the integration of local judges in "64" panels did not result in better training or cooperation: they were not given consistent or extensive experience, were anxious to distance themselves from internationals and had no real incentive to integrate into the international system. With few exceptions, IJPs also admitted to distancing themselves from local counterparts. The UNMIK Criminal Division, which had oversight of IJPs, did not consider this lack of contact to be problematic.

UNMIK officials avoided assigning local judicial officials to war crimes and other serious cases, not only to avoid potential bias and security risks, but because of concerns that they would be diverted from their remaining caseload for too long. This attitude exacerbated Kosovan perceptions that resources were not being used because of political considerations. One former judge cited the case of a former law faculty professor whose expertise was not utilised because he had supported Belgrade before the war.

Most disturbing of all was UNMIK's failure to develop any strategy for phasing out IJPs, based on the spurious assumption that the need for IJPs would diminish naturally over time in light of the self-limiting number of sensitive cases and gradual improvements in local attitudes towards ethnicity. Loose talk of a "transition" had not resulted in any coherent strategy by late 2004, although this was begun in a limited sense in September with the decision by the UNMIK Department of Justice to transfer two test cases of serious crimes to local judges.

After five years of transition, there was little acceptance in UNMIK circles that Kosovo was "ready" for sensitive cases to be handed to locals. According to the UNMIK Department of Justice, the key criteria for phasing out internationals were making locals more representative of the population and ensuring that the local judiciary was "competent, professional and ethical" (Manuel 2002). This was partially addressed by the establishment of a Judicial Integration Section in the Department of Justice to improve minority recruitment, but it was unable to fully overcome resistance from the Serb community and Belgrade (Manuel 2002). Others, including a Supreme Court judge, argued that the preconditions for any such transition were far more extensive and unlikely to be met in the foreseeable future. These included free media, a civil society opposed to breaching the law, elite political support and the existence of law-abiding government institutions.

Court conditions

Court administration weaknesses were in many cases debilitating. The shortage of judges and prosecutors was matched or even exceeded by that of court administration personnel. Many courts lacked legal assistants, forensic capabilities, security personnel, translators, couriers and maintenance staff. Courts suffered from extremely poor conditions and lacked even basic material needs (United States Department of State 2000b: 10–12).

UNMIK worked to improve court conditions and the terms of employment for judicial officials (UNSC 2000b: 25). It began to allow for indefinite employment terms in 2002, extending the initial three-month contracts to nine months, and then to the end of the UNMIK mandate. Continued poor remuneration made it difficult to attract judges, however. The Ombudsperson reported that the resultant "brain drain" of judges and prosecutors to the private sector was such that the courts were unable to "play a significant role in the administration of justice and the protection of the rights of individuals" (OIK 2003: 3; Knopic 2004).

Security

Perhaps the most pressing problem in the judicial sector – particularly early in the mission – was security for the courts, particularly in the Mitrovica area. As Lorenz (2001) noted:

> there will be no real security in Kosovo without the functioning courts, and the courts cannot operate without adequate security ... Right now cases in the District and Municipal courts of Mitrovica are in a status of "indefinite delay" at the request of the UNMIK administration. There has been no commitment by KFOR (the military force) to provide adequate court security, this is assumed to be an UNMIK responsibility. But the UNMIK Civilian Police maintain that they have insufficient resources to do the job. It is a vicious circle, with the danger that violence will overtake the fragile court system before it can function properly.

The judiciary's vulnerability to retaliation was in some cases enough to influence judgments (Hartmann 2003a: 7). Neither UNMIK nor KFOR provided any security for the courts in the first year; and direct threats, attacks and even murder of members of the judiciary occurred regularly (AI 2000; Latifi and Mekolli 2001; O'Neill 2002: 82–83). In the face of security risks, as well as the temptations of bribe-seeking as an important source of economic security, judicial corruption not surprisingly remained a problem.

UNMIK responded to ongoing problems with witness intimidation by creating a specialised police Witness Protection Unit (WPU) in June 2001, empowering the courts to take measures aimed at identity concealment in September of that year and establishing a Victim Advocacy and Assistance Unit in early 2002. These measures proved insufficient to counter witness intimidation (UNSC 2002g: 6), particularly in high-profile trials involving former KLA members. In January 2003, for example, a witness in a KLA trial was murdered in the presence of 40 people (AI 2004b: 6). This undermined public confidence in the ability of the authorities to provide adequate protection and, with it, the willingness of witnesses to testify (OMIK 2003a: 14–17, 18).

Lack of resources precluded witness protection in all but the most high-profile cases, leaving many witnesses in danger (OMIK 2003a: 19). No legal protections were in place for whistleblowers (Knopic 2004) and it was not until 2004 that courtroom equipment was provided to protect witness anonymity. There was no established procedure for the safe transfer of witnesses from Serbia, or to relocate witnesses internationally (ICG 2002: 13). Questions were also raised about the robustness of WPU procedures in the absence of a system to protect sensitive information and of thorough screening procedures for KPS officers deployed to the WPU (OMIK 2003a: 26). Inadequate coordination between the WPU and the police, prosecutors and the courts contributed to misunderstandings about the programme (OMIK 2003a: 20–21).

Review/accountability mechanisms

UNMIK made a rocky start in establishing judicial accountability mechanisms. Its first attempt, the Advisory Judicial Commission, failed to initiate any disciplinary action against judges or prosecutors; ironically, its only action was to remove one Kosovo Albanian District Court president who had (properly) instructed judges to conduct proceedings in both Albanian and Serbian (Hartmann 2003a: 6; Sheikhi 2001). Similarly, the Judicial Inspection Unit, established in April 2001, suffered from a number of weaknesses. It was short-staffed and local staff risked retribution when investigating the conduct of judicial colleagues. Its location in the executive branch of government and the absence of a mechanism to address complaints raised questions about its independence.

A more successful endeavour was the Kosovo Judicial and Prosecutorial Council (KJPC), established in April 2001 to advise the Special Representative on the appointment of judges and prosecutors and to hear complaints against them. Although in some respects it did not meet European standards, it was an important step in establishing institutionalised procedures for judicial review, and by 2003 had begun to function as an effective check (Marshall and Inglis 2003: 121). It disciplined Kosovo Albanian judges for conflict of interest and accepting bribes (UNSC 2001c: 11) and developed codes of conduct for judges and prosecutors in 2001, although these were poorly publicised (ICG 2002: 7). Again, the KJPC lacked full independence from the executive and the SRSG, who could appoint or remove judges unilaterally, with no recourse for judges to challenge these decisions.

Monitoring of the extent to which the judicial system met key standards was difficult in the absence of an effective trial monitoring system for the first year[26] and indeed of a clear delineation of applicable law. In 2000, the OSCE established a Legal Systems Monitoring Section in its Department of Human Rights and Rule of Law, which produced useful reports from October 2000 and became one of the largest legal monitoring systems in the United Nations' history (Marshall and Inglis 2003: 140). It was, however, prone to conflict of interest, being located in the same division that had played a significant role in establishing the court system and appointing the judiciary (AI 2000: 10). Owing to its criticism of UNMIK, it also encountered problems securing UN cooperation, including negotiating access to courts and prisons (Marshall and Inglis 2003: 140–141).[27]

Minority representation

Minority recruitment and retention remained a persistent problem. Although a Judicial Integration Section was created within the Department of Justice in late 2001 to coordinate a minority recruitment strategy, by October 2002 only four Serb judges and prosecutors were serving in Kosovo courts, and it was not until December 2003 that the minority representation rate reached approximately 10 per cent (UNSC 2002g: 6; 2004b: 8).

UNMIK's minority recruitment efforts were impeded by Belgrade, by ongoing security concerns, and by prejudice and fear in the Kosovo Albanian judicial community. Belgrade's failure to implement the provisions of a Joint Declaration signed in July 2002[28] preserving pensions and other benefits dissuaded many Kosovo Serbs from applying to work in the UNMIK system, and others were pressured to work instead in illegal parallel structures in the Mitrovica region. Yet others resigned owing to security concerns (Lorenz 2000b: 133). There was also significant resistance from the Kosovo Albanian judicial community to the appointment of Serbs, caused by fear that judges who had participated in the discriminatory Milosevic regime would return to the bench. The Kosovo Assembly also caused excessive delays in consultation on judicial appointments of minorities (CHR 2003).

Law enforcement

UNMIK was the first mission in which the United Nations assumed the dual responsibilities of international executive policing and establishing a new indigenous police force. Of a total authorised deployment of nearly 5,000, some 3,600 CIVPOL from 50 countries remained in theatre in October 2004, comprising one of the largest and longest CIVPOL deployments to date (UNSC 2004e: 20). In confronting a challenge of this proportion, UNMIK CIVPOL appeared to apply few if any of the lessons of previous peacekeeping operations (O'Neill 2002: 99). They struggled to implement an effective system of policing, across everything from traffic control to criminal justice. CIVPOL failures to investigate prominent crimes, even as late as 2004, undermined their reputation and set a poor example of due process. In 2004, for example, the Ombudsperson found that, in two important cases, the police had taken no investigative action for over a year (AI 2004b: 8). At the same time, UNMIK failed adequately to address emerging law and order threats, such as the growth of sophisticated organised crime networks, which smuggled some 80 per cent of all heroin consumed in Europe through Kosovo (UNMIK 2003b: 24).[29]

CIVPOL's slow deployment directly hindered UNMIK's capacity to fulfil its law and order responsibilities (UNSC 2000b: 9) and to meet community expectations in that respect. The first CIVPOL did not deploy until August 1999, two months into the mission, and it was not until two years later that deployment approached the authorised strength.

Confusion over applicable law remained a persistent problem. CIVPOL officers often made assumptions about applicable law based on their own national experience and, with some 53 countries involved in the mission, this resulted in numerous violations of the law (Rausch 2002: 19; Lorenz 2000b: 140; O'Neill 2002: 107). It was particularly difficult for CIVPOL from common law jurisdictions to grapple with a socialist-inspired civil law system that embodied a very different relationship between the police, prosecutor and judge (Rausch 2002: 20). As O'Neill (2002: 109) has described, local advice was not always helpful:

An Albanian judge had instructed [the police] to "beat the suspect if he doesn't give you information". The judge said this is how interrogations had always been conducted in Kosovo and it was the best and quickest way to obtain confessions. To their credit, the UN police refused to follow this order, but they still did not know what laws governed interrogations and how to respond to this judge and others who might make similar assertions.

Lack of operational guidelines was a further problem. Ten months into the mission there were still no approved policing, arrest, evidence collection or pre-trial detention guidelines in force. By mid-2000, the OSCE had prepared a draft field manual, but institutional battles and other obstacles left it unpublished. A shorter field manual made available by the Department of Judicial Affairs in September 2000 did not prove useful (Rausch 2002: 19). In one example of the practical implications of this, a major murder trial was delayed for three days because of a dispute between police of different nationalities over handcuffing policy.

CIVPOL suffered from the usual quality control problems relating to language and professionalism, compounded by a lack of pre-deployment training on applicable law, human rights standards and local culture (Marshall and Inglis 2003: 125). Teams such as the Royal Ulster Constabulary who had worked in similar environments were relatively effective (UNMIK 2001f; O'Neill 2002: 105), but few contingents had such experience and many expressed frustration at working in an alien context (Peake 2004: 18). Some contingents were so incompetent that they were sent home and, although pre-deployment screening by a CIVPOL training unit helped improve quality control, it did not fully resolve the problem. Some countries admitted to continuing to contribute CIVPOL for the principal purpose of learning from more professional units.

Specialised capacity was also wanting. Evidence collection capabilities suffered from a lack of forensic competence, the failure to establish a functioning witness protection programme and the weak performance of police and investigating judges (ICG 2002: 11). This meant that witness statements were often relied upon as the primary evidence, including in war crimes and rape cases, increasing the potential for miscarriages of justice. It also saw UNMIK resort to extrajudicial detention in cases where it could not secure adequate evidence to lay charges. The passage of a regulation in 2002 allowing police interviews to be utilised as evidence alleviated the situation somewhat, but lack of awareness of the regulation in the judicial and police structures inhibited its use.

Other problems stemmed from a passive policing approach by many officers, who proved unwilling to leave the stationhouse or their vehicles in some cases and were tentative about pushing "neo-colonialist" reforms on local communities in others. Although CIVPOL gradually became more assertive and visible in their contact with the community (O'Neill 2002: 105), their ability to perform effectively was limited by ethnic polarisation and a strong code of silence amongst many groups.

Poor communication and coordination between CIVPOL, KFOR and the judiciary further undermined the mission's ability to enforce the law. This included an absence of meaningful dialogue between experienced lawyers, police and military on what was feasible for CIVPOL in the field and institutional battles over how to make field operations consistent with international human rights standards (Rausch 2002: 18). Cooperation in the field was also lacking. For example, investigating judges were not invited to crime scenes, hindering a critical component of their work. Although cooperation between CIVPOL and KFOR was relatively constructive, KFOR appears to have been less than forthcoming in situations where it feared alienating Albanian leaders (O'Neill 2002: 107). In some cases, such as the investigation of the Nis bus bombing in February 2001, UNMIK CIVPOL appear to have been deliberately obstructed by US KFOR personnel (AI 2004b: 9).

The Kosovo Police Service

Getting the KPS on the beat was one of the most visible symbols of progress in Kosovo. As of October 2004, the KPS had grown to a strength of 6,282 officers, 9.4 per cent of whom were Kosovo Serbs, and a further 6 per cent from other minorities (UNSC 2004c: 17). This made it one of the few relatively multi-ethnic organisations operating in Kosovo and, on the whole, the service conducted itself with encouraging professionalism.

The relative success of the KPS derived at least in part from its solid sense of identity as a professional elite, backed up by decent training. Extensive pre-planning by the OSCE Kosovo Verification Mission, which deployed 500 police and developed a recruitment and training programme prior to its evacuation in March 1999, meant that the Kosovo Police Service School could begin training almost as soon as CIVPOL deployed. This training consisted of an 8-week classroom programme,[30] followed by 17 weeks in the field prior to a permanent assignment (Peake 2004: 18). The first class of 176 cadets commenced training in September 1999 (Perito 2002: 85) and by September 2001 over 4,000 recruits, including nearly 700 minority officers, had been trained. The School also trained over 2,000 UNMIK CIVPOL as Field Training Officers (FTOs).

Training appears to have made a positive contribution to professional conduct (O'Neill 2002: 114), although it proved difficult in the classroom to translate the abstract and alien concepts of democratic policing into practical instruction.[31] Field training was the key weakness of the programme, however. In the absence of a specialised CIVPOL training unit, many CIVPOL FTOs lacked the necessary aptitude, professionalism or interest to address knowledge gaps or provide effective role models (Peake 2004: 6; Dziedzic 2002: 49). Individual FTOs varied in style and recruits were often given contradictory advice about the same problem (Peake 2004: 17). The scheme was restructured in 2000 with the introduction of a special FTO contingent, which raised the quality of FTOs but not the CIVPOL:KPS ratio of around 1:15, which precluded effective mentoring. KPS officers were gradually introduced as mentors, which appears to have been successful (Peake 2004: 20).

Recruitment proved a greater problem owing to the pursuit of political objectives in recruitment policy. UNMIK appears to have agreed with local political leaders that 50 per cent of KPS recruits would be drawn from among former KLA members (Perito 2002: 95), with a further 25 per cent from the association of former Kosovar Yugoslav National Police. Once these and the 15 per cent minority and 20 per cent female quotas had been met, there was little room to accommodate those most qualified for the work, who were often ethnic Albanian males without KLA connections (Perito 2002: 95). The appointment of former KLA soldiers and members of the Kosovo Protection Corps (KPC) to the KPS also affected the KPS's neutrality, linking it politically with the nationalist struggle and causing difficulties when some KPS officers proved unwilling to participate in cases involving the KPC (Peake 2004: 27).

Ethnic division remained a problem despite the multi-ethnic character of the KPS. It was difficult to attract Kosovo Serbs to serve in the Mitrovica region and KPS officers in the north encountered significant resistance from both the general population and extremist elements (UNMIK

2003b: 9). Concerned about their security, Serb cadets at times avoided training sessions, and separate graduation ceremonies were held for each ethnic group. Ultimately there were only a handful of stations where Albanians and Serbs worked genuinely together (Peake 2004: 18).

Again, the final status issue had a detrimental impact on plans for the transfer of policing responsibilities to the KPS, making it difficult to establish a permanent organisational and rank structure (Perito 2002: 98). Although a phased transition plan was developed whereby full operational responsibility was to be handed over to the KPS in 2006, there were a number of problems with preparations for the transfer. CIVPOL remained hesitant to hand over meaningful operational independence or to elicit ideas from locals in crafting the KPS, and political influence in the selection process for leadership positions became a problem. There was little direction or coherence in the KPS development process and insufficient funding for even basic equipment, let alone democratic policing (Peake 2004: 22–23).

The correctional system

UNMIK oversaw a significant improvement in prison standards through facility upgrades, security enhancements and professional training for local staff. The prison system was almost non-existent at the time of deployment, when the only functioning civilian detention centre in Kosovo was a small CIVPOL facility in Pristina. The first prison became operational in November 1999 with the transfer of the Prizren prison from KFOR to UNMIK's Penal Management Division. In the first year, correctional development was severely under-funded and progress was minimal but, by mid-2000, 497 prison spaces had been created (UNSC 2000e: 10). Dubrava, Kosovo's largest correctional facility, was restored and five detention centres and two prisons were in operation by October 2001 (UNSC 2001c: 12).

Concurrent with the restoration of prison services, the Kosovo Correctional Service (KCS) was established in 1999 and a correctional staff training programme began at the Vushtrri Police Academy in December of that year. Authority for prison management was transferred gradually from UNMIK to the KCS, with the exception of facilities at Pristina and Mitrovica. Recruitment into the KCS suffered from the usual problems of low salaries and a shortage of candidates. Minority recruitment was relatively successful: in 2003 approximately 11 per cent of local correctional staff were Serbian, and 4 per cent were Bosnians, Roma and Turks, broadly in line with the composition of the population at large (UNMIK 2003b: 18). However, the integration of Serb officers across the correctional system remained uneven.

A number of major issues continued to plague the correctional system. Serious deficiencies in administration remained and public confidence in the penal system was undermined by several major prison escapes in 2000, including of Serb detainees accused of war crimes (UNSC 2000g: 9), and again by an outbreak of violence at Dubrava in September 2003 that left five prisoners dead (UNSC 2003g: 6). The provision of expert international staff and funding was inadequate to establish satisfactory facilities for juveniles or the disabled or to provide education, work and counselling opportunities for inmates (UNSC 2001b: 12). Prison policies were not standardised, which caused flow-on problems for the courts on issues such as the transfer of prisoners for hearings.

Again, bias against ethnic minorities was systemic, particularly with respect to pre-trial detention and prison treatment (UNSC 2000e: 8). Albanians and Serbs were imprisoned separately, generating criticism that UNMIK was reinforcing ethnic biases (United States Department of State 2000b: 19).

Prison capacity became a major problem as the mission proceeded, and had become critical by the outbreak of violence in March 2004, at which time the prison population of 1,301 exceeded capacity by 151 persons (OMIK 2004a: 13). This made it impossible for the correctional system to function effectively in the event of a sudden surge in demand.

A final problem was that of detention rights. The lack of a functioning bail system meant that arrestees were kept in pre-trial detention, burdening the KCS and risking excessive detention. Similarly, no probation or parole system was available as an alternative to incarceration. Unlawful detention remained an ongoing problem despite the establishment of a Detention Review Commission in August 2001 (OMIK 2003a: 31–32).

In the absence of appropriately designed and properly functioning state legal, judicial, police and correctional bodies, it is not surprising that five years into the mission the formal "rules of the game" were manifestly unclear, insufficient to define the limits of appropriate behaviour and often unenforceable. The next section turns to examine how this situation was exacerbated by UNMIK's failure to win the consent of both the Kosovan elite and the broader public to bind themselves to rule of law principles and to engage with state justice bodies.

Building commitment

Five years into the mission, UNMIK faced a legitimacy crisis that seriously undermined its ability to extract commitment to the rule of law. This section first examines reasons behind this lack of commitment at elite and popular levels, before considering three key general contributing factors: UNMIK's failure to address countervailing cultures, to set a good example or to meet expectations for self-rule.

Elite commitment

Members of the political elite in Kosovo were not fully committed to UNMIK's rule of law initiatives. Although some elements, particularly the moderate Rugova faction, were supportive,[32] in many instances elite actors undermined or proved ambivalent towards UNMIK's rule of law objectives. Members of the elite engaged in illegal practices, including corruption, property seizure and reallocation, tax collection, policing and discriminatory aid distribution (Kirste 2001: 14). Albanian politicians used a range of tactics to undermine UNMIK's authority, from publicly criticising UNMIK's arrest of Albanians charged with war crimes, to adopting confrontational declarations in the Kosovo Assembly that were clearly outside its legal competence, to refusing to standardise street and village names in Albanian and Serbian (UNSC 2004b: 5). Furthermore, members of the political elite failed to condemn breaches of the law where they did not perceive it to be in their interests to do so, as exemplified by their ambivalent response to the outbreak of violence in March 2004.

This lack of commitment appears to have stemmed from a number of factors. First, elite actors pitted themselves against UNMIK in pursuit of political agendas, particularly those relating to Kosovo's final status. Posturing played a major role, for example, in the Kosovo Assembly's declarations in contravention of UNMIK regulations and the refusal of Albanian judges to implement UNMIK's initial decision on applicable law. Politicians regularly used UNMIK as a scapegoat for their own political purposes. This tended to reflect an entrenched "opposition mentality" whereby political leaders were more practised at opposing state authorities than at building cooperative relationships with them.

Second, UNMIK never established its authority over local actors to the extent necessary to implement its mandate and, ultimately, to guarantee law and order (Kirste 2001: 29). For example, UNMIK's civilian administration was not consistently able to command the necessary support from the KPS to control politically motivated actions, as evidenced by the violence of March 2004. UNMIK's lack of preparedness to enforce its own rules with the political elite also undermined its credibility. UNMIK did not, for example, enforce its own requirement under the Constitutional Framework that the President of Kosovo could not also be head of a political party.

Third, influential political actors relied on organised crime for power and financing and were thus unlikely to commit to actions that denied them this resource. PDK structures and former KLA leaders, such as Hashim Thaci, were linked to organised crime networks, murder and weapons smuggling.[33] Both Thaci and the KPC head and future Prime Minister, Agim Ceku, were implicated in war crimes (House of Commons [United Kingdom] 2004). Similarly, the head of the Alliance for the Future of Kosovo (AAK), Ramush Haradinaj, was implicated in illegal weapons possession and involved in an exchange of fire with UN peacekeepers (*AFP*, 2000b). On his election as prime minister in December 2004, Haradinaj was also facing indictment at the International Criminal Tribunal for the Former Yugoslavia (ICTY) for war crimes. In the words of one UNMIK official, at the same time as UNMIK was reluctant to transfer reserved powers "so long as politicians, warlords and criminals are one and the same", it nonetheless condoned their rise to positions of power in the transitional government.

Fourth, the structure of political patronage networks ensured entrenched opposition to some rule of law initiatives, notably the prosecution of former KLA members. This saw, for example, the Kosovo government issue a press release on 19 August 2002 condemning the arrest of former KLA members and accusing UNMIK of taking "political prisoners". Although not a unanimous government position, it illustrated the dominance of former KLA members and their supporters and suggested that, had they controlled the criminal justice system, the arrests might never have taken place (KCL 2003). Nepotism and political considerations also dominated senior civil service recruitment, making it difficult to maintain political impartiality in the civil service in a way that was supportive of the rule of law.

Fifth, UNMIK was unable to overcome animosity from Serbia at all levels (Freedom House 2004: 9). Belgrade continually reiterated its strong opposition to Kosovan independence. It promoted a formula for the territorial division of Kosovo into Albanian and Serb communities (Government of Serbia 2004) that blatantly undermined UNMIK's goal of creating multi-ethnic self-governing institutions with a high degree of autonomy, by supporting a level of autonomy only marginally greater than that allowed under Milosevic's 1992 constitution (ICG 2004: 4). Belgrade sought to undermine UNMIK's authority through provocative statements by senior politicians and the state media against Kosovo Albanians and UNMIK,[34] and by supporting parallel structures in competition with UNMIK's jurisdiction. It pressured or encouraged Serbs in Kosovo not to participate in key UNMIK activities, such as the October 2004 elections.

Finally, political leaders were seldom offered real opportunities to demonstrate their commitment to the rule of law. Very little authority was ceded by UNMIK and no mechanisms were established to give leaders the opportunity to make themselves accountable for their actions. The consequences of this disempowerment are discussed below.

Commitment from the broader community

Similarly, UNMIK struggled to build community commitment to its rule of law objectives. In large part this stemmed from low public confidence in the ability of the state justice system to deliver just, reliable, relevant and accessible outcomes, despite acknowledged improvements since UNMIK's deployment.

By early 2000 there was a growing public perception that justice was not being exercised impartially under UNMIK's tutelage. Ethnicity was seen as the decisive factor in court rulings, and the disproportionate detention and sentencing of Kosovo Serbs undermined this group's confidence in the judicial system (AI 2000: 4). Perceptions that the court system was corrupt were also prevalent. In one such example, the head of a prominent, politically aligned family whose brother had been murdered claimed that a French international judge had accepted a bribe to lower the sentence on the accused. The individual had no evidence to back up this claim, but felt that corruption must have been involved because the sentence was light and because the French defence attorneys on the trial lunched daily with the judge.

An unreliable municipal court system – the level of court with which people usually had contact – undermined public perceptions of the fairness and reliability of the justice system (OMIK 2004b: 4). The administration of justice in the municipal courts in 2004 continued to suffer from excessive delays, judicial bias and denial of rights to a public hearing and to cross-examine witnesses (OMIK 2004b: 4, 25–7).

UNMIK thus constantly failed to meet its own legal standards, setting unrealistically high benchmarks that UNMIK and other UN officials acknowledged had proved impossible to meet. It also failed to manage high community expectations, and senior UNMIK officials admitted that the public did not believe in UNMIK's ability to deliver justice. Similarly, despite an apparent degree of pride in the KPS, the community lacked confidence in its ability to provide security. This was compounded by the common belief that, even if police did their jobs properly, criminals would be able to escape punishment by paying off court or prison officials. This contributed to the continuation of a culture of self-preservation in which, in the words of a UN official and former judge, "everyone has an AK-47 under the bed".

A lack of relevance also undermined public commitment to UNMIK's rule of law strategy. The UNMIK justice system was unable to deliver on issues of key concern to the public and on a day-to-day basis many Kosovans were frustrated at the difficulties they encountered meeting simple practical needs. For example, UNMIK travel documents, drivers' licences and licence plates were not recognised outside Kosovo, which meant Kosovans travelling elsewhere in the region needed to rely on Serbian parallel structures to obtain recognised documents. Anger was particularly strong amongst Kosovo Serbs, as the community most acutely affected by such problems (OIK 2004: 11).

Human rights protection was another area in which many Kosovans found UNMIK disappointing or irrelevant. Though violations were by no means limited to minorities, UNMIK's inability to protect minority rights represented a signal failure in fulfilling its commitment to the community and, in turn, extracting commitment from it. Inadequate security for minorities had profound implications for freedom of movement and for equality of access to humanitarian assistance, employment, public services and other aspects of normal life. These concerns prevented the return of displaced persons to their homes and contributed to the ongoing emigration from Kosovo of Serbs and other non-Albanians (OIK 2004: 21). Other failings included the inability of the criminal justice system to protect the rights of juveniles, women and the mentally ill (Marshall and Inglis 2003: 137); the prevalence of people trafficking; illegal policing activities such as suspect interrogation; and the continued detention of Kosovo Albanians in Serbia (UNSC 2000b: 14–15). Very few human rights violators were prosecuted, undermining confidence in the police and judiciary and reducing community willingness to report incidents or otherwise rely on these systems (UNSC 2004b: 9; AI 2004b: 19).

A third area where UNMIK did not prove its relevance was in the protection of property rights, despite having recognised from the outset an urgent need to redress property rights violations resulting from the 1998–1999 conflict and from the discriminatory property laws of the Milosevic era (UNSC 1999a: 13). Some progress was made with the establishment of a Housing and Property Directorate and Housing and Property Claims Commission (HPCC) in early 2001. By its final deadline of 1 July 2003, the Directorate had received 28,587 claims, of which it had resolved 31 per cent by September that year (UNSC 2003g: 12).

Despite this progress, UNMIK failed to contribute substantially to improved property rights protection. The legal and regulatory framework was unclear as a result of repeated amendments, imprecise delineation between UNMIK regulations and pre-UNMIK laws and the absence of an authoritative interpretation on property. Other shortcomings included insufficient resources, security problems and limited public access to the property registration system. The slow pace of claims resolution and a lack of understanding of the HPCC's mandate led to its being circumvented (OMIK 2003b: vi; OIK 2004: 24). Judicial protection of property rights through the regular courts was inadequate owing to unclear laws, poor resource management and confusion over jurisdiction issues. A further problem was the inability of police to uphold property rights in the event of evicted illegal occupants returning to threaten the rightful owners (OIK 2004: 24).

The right to equality before the law was further affected by a lack of access to justice. Physical access to the courts remained problematic, particularly for minority groups living in enclaves, who required escorted transport to the courts, or for displaced persons living in Serbia. UNMIK improved physical access by establishing escorted transport projects, opening a Municipal Court department and minor offences court in the Kosovo Serb majority area of Strpce, and establishing court liaison offices in several other Serb areas in late 2003 (UNSC 2004b: 4). However, access to the courts for minority groups, particularly Serb and Roma communities, remained severely curtailed by late 2004 (OIK 2004: 19).

A further access issue was that of defence services. By 2004 it was possible for most Kosovans to hire a defence lawyer, but the quality of defence services generally remained poor. This threatened not only the rights of defendants to access effective private or public defence counsel but also the broader objective of ensuring that violations of court and trial procedure were challenged aggressively (United States Department of State 2000b: 17). Despite some improvements, such as the establishment of a Criminal Defence Resource Centre in May 2001, an OSCE review of defence services in 2003 found that in many cases defence counsel were not adequately representing their clients.[35] The situation for Kosovo Serbs was particularly dire, often because they could not find anyone willing to represent them (United States Department of State 2000b: 19).

Another key impediment to access to justice was the poor legal literacy of the population. UNMIK made some effort to raise awareness of rights through local media and handouts, but this did not reach the many without media access.

Countervailing cultures

A major factor in UNMIK's inability to engender broad-based commitment to its rule of law initiatives was its failure to address entrenched countervailing cultures unsupportive of the rule of law. First, as discussed further below, UNMIK proved reluctant to tackle ethnic divisions and intolerance as the source of violence and other behaviour undermining the rule of law.

Second, UNMIK failed to address "socialist" mentalities, including partisanship, corruption and the lack of a concept of the separation of powers (Knopic 2004). As Kirste (2001: 22) has described, the communist legacy of the party as the dominant institution made it difficult to counter deeply entrenched power connections between the executive, legislature and judiciary or to explain the concept of separation of powers to the population at large. This was not helped by UNMIK's lack of effort to address this through training or other mechanisms, or by the poor example set by UNMIK itself. In its own operations, UNMIK ignored the principle of separation of powers, with total executive and legislative powers as well as administrative authority over the judiciary vested in the SRSG.

Third, UNMIK failed to counter popular reluctance to use the state justice system. Part of this reluctance stemmed from negative perceptions of the system's fairness and reliability, as described above. It also appears to have resulted from a general cultural reluctance to air grievances, which tended to be resolved between neighbours or by going to the village head, rather than involving the state. The atmosphere of silence that underpinned this approach also impeded police work.

Example-setting and a culture of accountability

> UNMIK fulfils the functions of a surrogate state. Nowhere in the world does a democratic state operating under the rule of law accord itself immunity from any administrative, civil or criminal responsibility. The same applies to KFOR. (OIK 2004: 15)

Affecting its ability to extract commitment from both elite and community actors, UNMIK lacked credibility as a champion of rule of law principles because of its failure to hold itself accountable for its own legal transgressions or to ensure that all UNMIK actors set an appropriate example. Elements of UNMIK, along with other international players in Kosovo, regularly engaged in unlawful actions, including excessive pretrial detention, torture and other ill treatment in detention, and ignoring lawful orders to release detainees.[36] From January 2002 to July 2003, nearly 30 KFOR members were implicated in people-trafficking offences, without any apparent disciplinary or investigative action (AI 2004a; 2004b: 22). Corruption became a problem, as evidenced by the involvement in 2003 of the UNMIK co-head of the Public Utilities Department in the embezzlement of over US$4.3 million from the Kosovo Energy Company. In another example, a former UNMIK adviser to the Post and Telecommunications Enterprise of Kosovo was arrested in April 2004 on corruption charges along with the director-general of the Post and Telecommunications Enterprise of Kosovo (UNGA 2003). A further issue that tarnished UNMIK's reputation was its employment of suspected war criminals.[37]

For several reasons, UNMIK was seldom held accountable for these and other transgressions. First, KFOR interpreted its public order mandate as condoning measures such as COMKFOR Detention Directive 42, which allowed KFOR to impose long detention periods without judicial authorisation. UNMIK did not have jurisdiction to investigate KFOR troops, who could be held accountable only for human rights violations indirectly through national contingents, a process that occurred on only one occasion (AI 2004b: 13).

Second, senior players in UNMIK perceived a policy trade-off between security and human rights. They justified the blatant contravention of human rights principles by arguing that human rights protection was the primary obstacle to establishing security.[38] This stance meant that UNMIK never legislated on the supremacy of human rights standards or established compliance mechanisms. Instead, it promulgated legislation that served its own agenda in responding to individual or isolated events, undermining the principle of a state subject to the rule of law (Marshall and Inglis 2003: 113).

Third, few accountability mechanisms were established. Although UNMIK was accountable indirectly to the international community (Yannis 2004: 72), it was not accountable to any elected power in Kosovo or to any judicial body. An office of the Ombudsperson was established in November 2000 with jurisdiction over allegations of human rights violations or abuse of authority by any person or entity in Kosovo.[39] However, the Ombudsperson had no jurisdiction over KFOR, minimal authority over UNMIK, no enforcement mechanisms and no recourse in cases where the SRSG did not adopt its recommendations (OIK 2004: 17). The Ombudsperson complained bitterly about lack of cooperation from UNMIK, especially in investigations concerning CIVPOL, and accused UNMIK and the PISG of persistently failing to respond to requests for assistance (OIK 2004: 16).

Similarly, there was no system to hold the Kosovo government accountable for abuses. An Independent Oversight Board for Kosovo was established in December 2001 to consider complaints relating to the civil service but, despite receiving thousands of complaints from the public, by late 2004 it had not processed any owing to a two-year delay by the Special Representative in signing off on the necessary paperwork.

In the interests of promoting a culture of accountable government, UNMIK could have worked to bridge this accountability gap and to promote transparency and compliance with human rights principles in the discharge of its mandate. Its failure to do so represented an important missed opportunity to demonstrate a fundamental principle of democratic governance.

The illusion of self-rule

UNMIK's efforts to devolve power consistently failed to contain local demand for greater authority, to meet expectations for self-rule and, ultimately, to engender commitment to UN objectives. As Goldstone (2002: 145–146) observed:

> In all matters of importance, including the budget, the real power is in the hands of the UN and the special representative of the secretary-general (SRSG) ... Kosovo is effectively under colonial rule. During my most recent visit to Kosovo, the distrust [by UNMIK] of the administrative and political capacity of the Albanian population was palpable. Indeed, it underlies the most recent constitutional provisions. The international community of states expects the Albanian majority in Kosovo to behave and respond to its problems and those of the region in a responsible manner. This will be a vain expectation if those people are not given responsibility. They must be allowed to learn from their own mistakes. That will not happen under the kind of colonial tutelage that the present constitutional dispensation allows.

The Kosovo Transitional Council (KTC) established in July 1999 functioned as the primary mechanism for direct local input into UNMIK decision-making and it met weekly until it was wound up in October 2001. Although a useful consultative mechanism, it did not transfer administrative responsibility and experienced difficulties maintaining local support and participation. At various times the LDK and PDK refused to attend meetings, and Kosovo Serb representatives boycotted the process after September 1999.

The KTC was superseded in December 1999 by a Joint Interim Administrative Structure (JIAS) under which UNMIK shared administration with the three main Albanian political parties. Twenty administrative departments were established, each co-headed by an international and a Kosovan. The JIAS partially succeeded in improving cooperation between UNMIK and local partners, particularly in the municipalities where international officials relied heavily on local leaders. It also met some concrete goals such as dissolving parallel security and administrative structures (KCL 2003). However, the access of Kosovans to real authority tended to depend primarily on the personal relationship between the international and local co-head (Kirste 2001: 8). Ultimately, as senior UNMIK officials themselves recognised, the JIAS model did not satisfy Kosovan aspirations for authority.

Increasing pressure to devolve power led to the adoption in May 2001 of the Constitutional Framework, which accelerated the transfer of public administration responsibilities to local control but allowed the SRSG to retain "reserved powers and responsibilities" in those areas, including justice, where there was a perceived risk that the final status would be prejudiced or where locals were not considered "mature enough to take full responsibility" (KCL 2003).

A 120-seat Assembly was elected in November 2001 and a government formed in March 2002 after an extended deadlock between the major political opponents. The JIAS departments were streamlined into 10 ministries covering the specific executive functions listed in the Constitutional Framework, which were progressively "Kosovanised". Again, the process fell hostage to the ambiguous political situation, satisfying neither Kosovo Albanian demands for autonomy nor Belgrade's for sovereignty. Poor consultation over the devolution of powers exacerbated feelings of disempowerment. The Kosovo government was not consulted on any major policy decisions relating to the transfer during 2002, prompting one study to conclude that by 2002 there was less consultation of democratically elected Kosovans than in the first days of the mission (KCL 2003).

The introduction in 2003 of UNMIK's "standards before status" exercise – explicitly linking the international community's readiness to address Kosovo's final status to the performance of the Kosovo authorities – renewed tensions between UNMIK and the PISG. This appears to have resulted from the imposed nature of the framework and perceptions that UNMIK was using it to delay a decision on status indefinitely (Cocozzelli 2003). Despite UNMIK efforts to consult the PISG through working groups for the Kosovo Standards Implementation Plan released in March 2004, Kosovo Albanian leaders participated half-heartedly and Kosovo Serbs boycotted the process (UNMIK 2003a; UNSC 2004b: 1; 2004c: 5).

Five years into the mission, the PISG remained legally part of UNMIK and had little autonomy or authority. Reserved powers continued to intrude in almost every area of governance and consultation mechanisms were shallow. As one Kosovan human rights expert observed, consultations were characterised by "politeness and diplomacy with no substance ... each side is on a different wavelength and each is afraid of the other".

This situation was demonstrated no more clearly than in the rule of law arena, in which local actors were denied a substantive role. In recognition that rule of law areas required sustained international oversight (UNSC 2001b: 11), the judiciary, police and prison services remained under tight UNMIK control even after the establishment of the PISG. "Reserved powers" included final authority over the appointment, removal and disciplining of judges and prosecutors, the assignment of international judges and prosecutors to cases, law enforcement agencies and the correctional service; the KPC; and commercial property disputes (UNMIK 2001b: Chapter 8). For "reserved" areas, legislation was promulgated not by an Assembly vote but via an UNMIK regulation. Court administration, technical support, training, monitoring and public information roles were the only "justice" areas in which the PISG were given responsibility.[40]

The Department of Justice and most elements of the justice system thus remained under UNMIK control long after responsibility for other sectors had been devolved more fully to Kosovans. The denial of a substantive role in this area not only perpetuated resentment, but also removed the prospect of comprehensive capacity-building in justice policy and administration. The PISG lobbied unsuccessfully for control of the Department of Justice, and were given responsibility for judicial administration only. This was grouped with other "public administration" responsibilities, such as waste collection, reducing its stature symbolically and distancing it institutionally from the rest of the justice sector. Having devolved responsibility, UNMIK then neglected to address shortcomings in the area. Meanwhile, Kosovan jurists complained of difficulty accessing the Department of Justice, which concerned itself almost exclusively with the 2–3 per cent of cases involving IJPs and ignored the local judiciary.

As with broader aspects of the transition, significant local resentment over lack of ownership of rule of law issues was apparent, and was shared by many frustrated UNMIK officials. This caused the legal community to resist reform. For example, OSCE efforts to reform the bar exam and the Faculty of Law at Pristina University were resisted strenuously by the academic and legal community, as well as by the PISG Ministry of Education.

The introduction of IJPs proved particularly galling, prompting the Supreme Court to send an open letter to the SRSG stating that the regulation violated "the autonomy of the Kosovo judiciary" (Manuel 2001). UNMIK's failure to consult on or even explain Regulation 64 caused widespread resentment in the legal community. IJPs themselves recognised the intrusiveness of the IJP model and the resentment it caused, particularly when the introduction of "64" panels wrested the authority to decide cases from local hands. In some prominent cases, Kosovan judges refused to sit on the panels (Hartmann 2003a: 12), although in others local judges grudgingly accepted their international colleagues in apparent recognition of their role in offsetting pressures on themselves. By late 2004, relations were still poor and the Kosovan UNMIK legal officer responsible for determining the composition of international/local panels was often refused by local judges and had to rely on personal persuasion to get them to agree to sit with internationals.

In addition to denying Kosovan actors substantive control, lack of consultation was a persistent problem. Early initiatives to negotiate major policy changes in an inclusive way quickly deteriorated. This was exemplified by the emasculation of the JAC/LM as the key consultative mechanism on legislative reform:

> The JAC became less and less relevant and [the Office of the Legal Adviser, OLA] began to bypass the consultative process altogether. By February 2001, there was no systematic consultation with the JAC on regulations and the OLA maintained that legislation that was "interventionist", i.e., of political character, did not require local consultation. Despite vocal protests from all members of the JAC, regulations were provided to the JAC as a token gesture. By the end of 2001, it was clear that what had begun as one of the only high-level forums for international and local consultation and cooperation on legal issues had become an empty shell. As with all other areas of development within the justice sector, UNMIK's consultation with local actors on legislative reform and on the legislative reform agenda diminished rather than expanded over time. (Marshall and Inglis 2003: 117–118)

UNMIK's disregard for consultation was amply demonstrated by its handling of the new Criminal Code and Criminal Procedure Code. Despite UNMIK's claim that the codes were the result of significant local input (UNMIK 2003c)[41] and assurances that the codes required the "full engagement and full involvement of the Kosovo institutions",[42] they were never endorsed through any democratic procedure. This arguably undermined the development of democratic institutions by denying the Assembly the experience of properly debating and adopting laws and resolutions in key areas.

The local judiciary was barely consulted about the new code. The drafting process was secretive and judges did not gain access to the draft until it was put before the National Assembly, which was allocated only one week to debate it. There was no official public debate on the code and members of the Kosovan legal community who did manage to obtain and comment on the draft never received any response. IJPs themselves were given only 10 days to provide comment, and although this was subsequently extended it was not enough time to examine the draft properly.

This episode reflected one of the key dilemmas of trying to conduct state-building in a situation where no final status has been accorded to the territory concerned. Given the political constraints, it is difficult to see how UNMIK could have made the judiciary fully independent during the transition phase. At the same time, the principles both of rule of law creation (a judiciary independent of the executive) and of state-building (creating sustainable local capacity) required that UNMIK develop a strategy to do just that. What is clear, however, is that UNMIK's approach to dividing responsibilities was not successful, because it was ultimately not acceptable to Kosovans. The exclusion of Kosovan jurists from sensitive cases and from a range of consultation processes implied a lack of respect and trust that ultimately undermined UNMIK's own authority.

Rebuilding social relationships

As UNMIK deployed, there were few resilient social networks that could be harnessed in support of western conceptions of democracy and the rule of law. Kosovo Albanian society had been repressed economically, politically and socially for much of the twentieth century. Under Tito, a local elite never developed that could take responsibility for developing a free civil society. Milosevic installed the elements of such an elite, but this mostly took the form of a police and paramilitary state apparatus ill suited to promoting a politically legitimate civil society (Pettifer 2002: 6–10).

In Kosovo's clan-based and largely rural society, social relationships were based on family and other personal ties. Low levels of impersonal civic trust and the prevalence of patron–client relations made it difficult to build support for bodies, such as the courts, that relied on anonymous trust (ICG 2004: 34). Further, there were no defined constituencies with a particular interest in establishing the rule of law, such as the private sector, professionals or a reform-oriented middle class (USIP 2002: 12; Pettifer 2002: 11).

Large elements of society were alienated from institutionalised life as a result of a demographic structure dominated by children, high unemployment and a dysfunctional education system (ICG 2004). These factors made it difficult for UNMIK or the PISG to reach large segments of the population. The new elites in the PISG interacted with a narrow segment of society mainly through patron–client relations channelled through the political party system (ICG 2004: 3). Moreover, the few organised elements of Kosovo Albanian society were firmly oriented towards resistance of, rather than interaction with, the state. This not only impeded the growth of productive relationships between civil society and the structures established by UNMIK but allowed extremism to survive (ICG 2004: 35–36).

Civil society groups, not surprisingly, demonstrated a poor capacity to mobilise citizens constructively or to neutralise violent traditions. As the International Crisis Group observed:

> Kosovo Albanian society is relatively closed, tries to keep secrets to itself, and does not like to show weakness. Until [the communal violence of] 17–18 March so much was bottled up: the vast numbers of people still traumatised by their experiences; a broken-down health and social care system; secondary traumati-

sation of children by parents and an unreformed, decayed and overwhelmed education system that, in the words of a local observer: "is built with the wrong history, the wrong message, and a lot of poetry and music about heroes. It produces hate: hate speech and hate diplomas".... Kosovo's thin layer of civil society is inadequate to absorb and dissipate shocks, instead, such shocks are liable to transmit immediately into violence. Much of civil society is urban, international donor-driven and unable to make a real grassroots impact. Some groups with wider, deeper grassroots networks actually amplified the shocks on 17 March – the Council for the Defence of Human Rights and the three associations "emerged from war". An acquiescent majority allows itself too easily to be led and dominated by a violent minority. (ICG 2004: 32–33)

This situation worked against UN efforts to respond effectively to incidents of violence, notably the March 2004 riots, in which civil society groups failed to take meaningful action to prevent or condemn violence and in some cases exacerbated it by making provocative statements or actively leading the violence (UNSC 2004c: 11).

Beyond the spectre of ethnic violence, there was almost no discussion in UNMIK or other circles of the nature of social institutions or social fabric, let alone of how this might affect its policies. There appears to have been little discussion of such social issues among the Kosovan political elite either, given their preoccupation with matters of political power and independence.

UNMIK did attempt to develop local partners that could connect it with the disparate Kosovo Albanian communities and resistance cells, including by co-opting warlords into the JIAS, but ultimately it created an artificial elite without strong grassroots links (ICG 2004: 34). It failed to establish any institutionalised mechanism to facilitate dialogue with civil society. Kosovans complained that UNMIK actors rarely consulted the community, including a talented pool of civil society campaigners with a decade of experience in the Albanian parallel structures (O'Neill 2002: 129). Civil society groups were seldom involved in the decision-making or drafting processes for local laws (UNSC 2004b: 4). Where UNMIK did invite input, it tended to do so late in the process (Clark 2003).

The majority of civil society development work fell to the OSCE under its institution-building mandate, which neglected its responsibilities. Although it achieved a significant increase in the number of NGOs, from 50 in August 1999 to over 1,000 in 2003 (Clark 2003), the conferring of NGO status on many of these groups was inappropriate, posing excessive administrative burdens and masking a lack of an effective purpose and work plan (Advocacy Project 2000). Few could be considered "authentic self-motivated bodies" led by experienced activists (Clark 2003) and, by late 2004, most remained entirely dependent on international aid (Freedom House 2004: 31). The establishment by the OSCE of an umbrella

NGO council failed because it was perceived as an OSCE "implant" with little local ownership (Advocacy Project 2000).

Civil society organisations working in the rule of law area were neglected. Pre-existing legal and human rights associations, such as the Kosovo Chamber of Lawyers, were significantly weakened by the conflict and, following UNMIK's deployment, received insufficient financial or other support to re-establish themselves. Many of the best NGO activists took jobs with UNMIK and other international organisations. A study by the OSCE in 2002 of the capacity of local civil society organisations to assume human rights monitoring responsibilities yielded grim results, failing to identify a single local body with the capacity or willingness to take on this role.[43]

Some local observers believed that neither UNMIK, nor the OSCE nor the local political elite had any interest in building up civil society because it was viewed as a potential threat to their authority. Others, including key players in UNMIK's Pillar III (Institution Building), believed that civil society development was an organic process that the international community had in fact obstructed by imposing constraints on political development. According to this line of thinking, UNMIK's unwillingness to devolve power to a local accountable government with real authority removed the incentive for civil society to develop, because it could see no advocacy role for itself.

Strengthening state capacity

Although UNMIK established a basic framework for government and administration, during the first five years of the mission a robust state administration was not developed, Kosovans were given few opportunities to gain administrative experience and state capacity to undertake rule of law activities remained weak. In addition to the OSCE's neglect of its capacity-building mandate, discussed above, several factors contributed to this. The first was the continuation of "reserved powers" in rule of law areas. The lack of a Kosovo Ministry of Justice severely limited the potential to develop state capacity and, when the co-head system was abolished following the introduction of the Constitutional Framework, Kosovo officials lost the opportunity to work with internationals at the highest level, as they did in other departments. Although representatives of the Kosovo Assembly argued for Kosovan authority to be extended (UNSC 2002h: 5), five years into the mission few locals were employed in management or substantive policy roles in the UNMIK Department of Justice and Kosovans had little opportunity to participate in policy-making or planning. No strategy appeared to have been developed to build managerial capacity or to hand over policy responsibilities. The exception appeared to be the Judicial Development Division, where responsibility for victim advocacy, missing persons and forensic investigations was transferred successfully to Kosovan control (ICG 2002: 15).

A second factor was generalised chaos in the public sector. OSCE officials struggled to conduct training or otherwise to build capacity in the public sector because organisational and legislative semi-chaos reduced the potential for programmes to identify appropriate recipients and to have any impact.

A third, related factor was UNMIK's inability to contain state sector corruption. A corrupt state sector not only directly contradicted the principle of a state subordinate to the law but undermined its capacity to implement policy transparently and efficiently. Corruption continued to escalate under UNMIK because of the ineffective judicial system, the inability of citizens to challenge government behaviour in civil courts, a lack of strong punishments for corruption-related crimes, poor law enforcement capacity and the overall acceptance of corruption in society (Knopic 2004; UNMIK 2003b: 28). A 2003 survey found that municipal officials, lawyers and judges were the most corrupt state actors (Knopic 2004). Unintentionally, UNMIK added to the problem by recreating the communist system of an overstaffed, underpaid public administration that apparently relied on extra-legal perks to attract good people. Further, UNMIK's own lack of transparency and accountability, coupled with perceptions that UNMIK officials abused their position and influence, was a poor role model (Knopic 2004). Steps to combat corruption, including the introduction of an Anti-Corruption Plan in July 2002 and the establishment of an Ombudsperson, a Financial Inspection Unit and an Auditor-General's office did not significantly improve the situation.

Restoring security

By late 2004, UNMIK had not fully effected a transition from violent to non-violent forms of conflict management in Kosovo. Although the security situation had improved markedly since 1999, the March 2004 riots demonstrated the continued potential for instability, and the large peacekeeping presence (over 17,500 in late 2005) underscored the extent to which this remained of concern. UNMIK had not fully co-opted elites into the peace process, established a monopoly on the use of force or marginalised political violence. Local power structures still derived political gain from criminal activity and violence, or their capacity for it, condoning the continuation of violent and illegal activity as a paradigm of Kosovo's political life. Failures in conflict management arose from three sources: unresolved conflict stemming from Kosovo's lack of a final status; UNMIK's failure to move early and robustly to dismantle security threats, particularly the Kosovo Liberation Army; and its lack of success in promoting non-violent alternatives, such as elite reconciliation, meaningful elections and a functioning justice system.

UNMIK's arrival suspended, rather than ended, the conflict. Cockell (2002: 484), Yannis (2004: 68) and Dziedzic (2002: 37) have argued persuasively that, in the absence of a resolution to the underlying dispute over Kosovo's final status, it proved difficult for UNMIK to neutralise two sources of conflict arising from incompatible aspirations: that between Albanians and Serbs, fuelled and manipulated by Belgrade, and that between rival factions in the Albanian community, notably the PDK/KLA faction led by Hashim Thaci and the moderate LDK led by Ibrahim Rugova. Although UNMIK had some success in moving intra-Albanian conflict from the brink of civil war to peaceful democratic contest, the KLA and its proxies continued to thrive as spoilers of the peace (see below). Political uncertainty persisted, fuelling violent disagreement among the parties, with attendant human rights abuses and other actions incompatible with rule of law principles (Bolton 2001: 141).

UNMIK's failure to neutralise the security threat posed by the KLA and other spoilers demonstrated the speed with which local structures developed to fill any security vacuum. KFOR's inability to ensure public security from mid- to late 1999[44] allowed crime to escalate and political extremists, notably the KLA, to move in. Very few of the 500 murders perpetrated in the first six months of the intervention were ever punished (KCL 2003). As the Independent International Commission on Kosovo noted:

> KFOR's failure in the early stages of its deployment to avert revenge acts was a profound failure of the international community to uphold the principles that had been hailed as the driving force behind the war effort. The principle of maintaining a secure environment for all citizens was part of Resolution 1244. Given the Bosnian experience ... KFOR should have prepared itself for this type of violence. (IICK 2000: 105)

UNMIK also appears to have failed to recognise and respond to the threat posed by political-criminal networks, despite their prevalence throughout the Balkans (USIP 2002). Instead of sending a clear signal to Albanian and Serb hardliners that violence would not be tolerated in the initial stages of the mission, UNMIK's "soft approach" towards Albanian and Serbian extremists "created serious obstacles to law and order, allowed an unacceptable level of violence in Kosovo, and enabled two insurgencies on its borders with Serbia proper and Macedonia to flourish"

(O'Neill 2002: 18). Extremist political factions linked to the KLA moved into the security vacuum, assuming control over political structures and sources of wealth, developing organised criminal networks in support of political objectives and exploiting ethnic tensions (USIP 2002). This almost resulted in civil war with the LDK and, although UNMIK averted this, it caused a long-term divide between the LDK and PDK. The KLA was also involved in insurrections in southern Serbia in 2000 and Macedonia in 2001 (USIP 2002: 11). Other informal networks developed in the intelligence, military and police services enjoyed a high degree of impunity (USIP 2002: 3).

The pattern thus set, throughout the mission UNMIK tolerated and made excuses for former KLA members despite their track record of "premeditated, widespread and systemic" attacks on Serbs, other minorities and moderate Albanians (O'Neill 2002: 62). Criminal activities played a key role as a resource base for the KLA's political and military struggle (USIP 2002: 3). Politically, it proved difficult for UNMIK to take steps against political or military figures with KLA backgrounds because such action was interpreted by many Kosovo Albanians as an attempt to undermine Kosovo's nationalist agenda. As described above, convictions against former KLA members sparked major demonstrations.

The Kosovo Protection Corps, established on 20 September 1999, highlighted the danger of indiscriminately enlisting demobilised combatants into a quasi police force (O'Neill 2002: 119). NATO's original idea was to defuse tensions over demobilisation by transforming the KLA into a civilian emergency response agency, but the KPC continued to view itself as an army in waiting and successfully pressured UNMIK to retain many of its military trappings. KPC members engaged regularly in criminal behaviour, including assassinations, detentions, interrogations, property seizures, tax schemes and crowd control. By November 1999, CIVPOL described the situation as "out of hand" (O'Neill 2002: 118). The KPC proved a particular obstacle to the establishment of the Kosovo Police Service as the sole legitimate policing authority, with a significant overlap in membership between the two bodies allowing the KPC to dominate the KPS.

UNMIK made some progress in bringing KPC members accused of criminal offences to account,[45] but the KPC remained a potential threat to UNMIK and KFOR into 2004 (IICK 2000: 118–119; O'Neill 2002: 117–120). Despite its awareness of possible KPC links with extremist organisations involved in the March violence (UNSC 2004c: 12–13), UNMIK and other members of the international community continued to allow it to operate independently with little oversight.

UNMIK also failed to prevent the rise of parallel security structures. Two main parallel security apparatuses began to operate in northern Mitrovica in 1999 – the "Bridgewatchers"[46] and the police of the Serbian Ministry of Interior Affairs. UNMIK's limited capacity to undertake policing in northern Kosovo allowed both the Bridgewatchers and the Serbian Ministry of Interior Affairs to expand to become the leading "law enforcement" agencies in the region (OMIK 2003c: 12). UNMIK did, however, make progress in defusing both groups. The Bridgewatchers began to suffer from internal divisions and to lose political support in 2002, and UNMIK succeeded in recruiting Kosovo Serb police into the KPS (OMIK 2003c: 6). However, security incidents continued in the area in 2003, and by late 2004 there was still some prospect that these threats could re-emerge.

Finally, UNMIK's failure to entrench non-violent methods of conflict management contributed to the continued use of violent alternatives. Again demonstrating the inverse relationship between security and the rule of law, the lack of functioning law enforcement agencies exacerbated the security situation by allowing perpetrators of violence to function with impunity. Similarly, elections did not prove a fully effective focus for non-violent political activity, particularly given the emasculation of the Kosovo Assembly and government in the absence of a decision on Kosovo's final status.

Elite reconciliation was neglected as an important potential tool. Dziedzic (2002: 38–40) provides a useful discussion of the pitfalls of UNMIK's strategy to bring Kosovo's elites into a peace process during the first 18 months of the mission, including through dialogue, confidence-building measures, inducements and sanctions against spoilers, assisting local leaders in dealing with the risks posed by hardliners in their own factions, and formalising the gains through such measures as the demilitarisation of the KLA and the holding of elections. UNMIK's contribution to the reconciliation process is discussed further below.

Addressing informal justice structures

Informal or "traditional" justice structures in Kosovo existed in the form of limited dispute resolution mechanisms and "parallel structures". In failing to either harness or defuse these structures, UNMIK allowed them to compete with and undermine its own formal structures.

Informal dispute resolution

Traditional methods of dispute resolution included engaging respected community members as mediators. These mechanisms were more prevalent outside Pristina, particularly in the west, and were used for resolving such issues as domestic violence, marital disputes and rape (Rausch 2002: 25). Little else seems to be known about such systems. UNMIK officials appeared unclear as to what informal dispute resolution mechanisms were in place and to what extent individuals resorted to traditional or alternative dispute resolution mechanisms in preference to the formal justice system. There was little interest in informal justice and it was seldom discussed.

UNMIK had no formal policy on how to deal with these systems; it never sanctioned their use officially or attempted to incorporate them systematically into the formal justice system. Some senior UNMIK officials claimed there was an informal policy to condone such structures so long as they were "non-violent", whereas others believed that the informal policy was to discourage them because they were inconsistent with modern human rights standards.

In practice, elements of UNMIK were forced to work with such mechanisms. CIVPOL, for example, permitted the use of traditional dispute resolution mechanisms in minor cases such as traffic infringements (Rausch 2002: 25). This worked in some cases but was counterproductive in others. For example, village dispute resolution mechanisms introduced bias into cases with an ethnic or gender angle, undermining human rights principles. Ultimately, in the absence of adequate research, it is difficult to say whether the lack of focus on informal dispute resolution impeded UNMIK's efforts to establish the rule of law. It does, however, further illustrate UNMIK's failure thoroughly to assess its operating environment, including the potential tools at its disposal.

Parallel structures

Two sets of parallel structures developed as alternative centres of power and justice: Albanian underground structures and those sponsored by Belgrade. The Albanian parallel justice system relied fairly heavily on traditional methods of dispute resolution (Rausch 2002: 25) and became less of a threat to the formal justice system as UNMIK expanded its reach and incorporated Albanian personnel into its own structures.

In contrast, Belgrade-sponsored parallel court and other administrative structures remained a problem throughout the mission, undermining UNMIK's attempts to establish a unified justice system (UNSC 2003g: 4; 2003e: 5). Parallel courts were most active from 1999 to 2002 in Mitrovica and the three northern-most municipalities, when UNMIK had little presence in these areas. By 2004, highly visible parallel structures still existed in Leposavic, Zubin Potok, Zvecan and Strpce, despite the establishment of UNMIK courts in those areas. Courts that had been pulled back into Serbia proper after 1999 also continued to claim jurisdiction over the whole of Kosovo.

Parallel court structures posed a dilemma for UNMIK: UNMIK was reliant on them as the only local structures able to create order and provide basic community services, but it was reluctant to sanction them (Kirste 2001: 12). Weak and understaffed UNMIK local and regional offices cooperated with the self-appointed structures and, in some areas, relied on them to deliver legal services. UNMIK's ambivalence and passivity allowed the structures to develop to the point where they harmed UNMIK's efforts to establish multi-ethnic judicial structures and, more broadly, an impartial and accountable local government system (Kirste 2001: 14).

The parallel courts employed several dozen Serbian judges at a time when UNMIK was struggling to secure Serb representation in its own judicial system, and they created an overlapping jurisdiction that confused the public and undermined the legitimacy of the official court system. This was especially the case with property rights, which were frequently the subject of parallel court judgments. Determining the validity of judgments handed down in the parallel system became a significant problem.

In some cases, UNMIK failed embarrassingly to protect high-level Kosovan individuals from Belgrade. In October 2003, for example, the head of the KPC, Agim Ceku, was detained in Slovenia under an arrest warrant issued by the parallel "district and municipal courts of Pristina" in the southern Serbian city of Nis. He was not released until the UNMIK Special Representative intervened with the Slovenian authorities to inform them of the invalidity of the warrant owing to their lack of jurisdiction (UNSC 2004b: 8). Humiliatingly, this occurred again in February 2004 (ICG 2004: 8–9).

The parallel structures seem to have survived because of their accessibility to both Serbs and Albanians. Most cases handled by the parallel courts involved administrative decisions that needed to be recognised in Serbia proper, such as inheritance and property cases, or services (such as certification) that UNMIK courts could not provide (OMIK 2003c: 19–22). The parallel structures also survived because Serbia refused to cooperate in dismantling them, sending mixed messages to Serbian judges and prosecutors about their eligibility for social benefits and failing to pass legislation in the Serbian parliament suspending Serbian jurisdiction over Kosovo. Conditions in the Serbian parallel structures also remained generally more attractive than those in the UNMIK judicial system, providing little incentive for professionals to leave those structures. Parallel courts remained active throughout 2003, under the aegis of the Serbian Ministry of Justice. One parallel court also existed in the Pristina area.

UNMIK's attention to the issue of parallel structures waxed and waned. Renewed focus on the structures in early 2004 was not accompanied by a coherent policy to reduce demand for parallel services (in the absence of official alternatives), to negotiate with Belgrade to dismantle them, or to determine and enforce which actions of the parallel structures were valid (OMIK 2003c: 9–10). Many UNMIK legal officers believed that the structures dealt efficiently and legitimately with a range of civil issues and that not recognising this merely threatened to further overburden the court system, disrupt business and provoke the Serbian community. Accordingly, the UNMIK Office of the Legal Adviser had drafted a recommendation to recognise the jurisdiction of the parallel courts over civil matters such as divorces, although by 2004 the matter had not been decided. UNMIK thus remained without a firm determination on the jurisdiction of parallel courts.

Ultimately, the presence of parallel structures reflected the overall lack of integration between Albanians and Serbs in Kosovo. Two structures, accountable to two separate authorities, coexisted with no interaction or integration. The Albanian structure was virtually Serb free in every respect, whereas the Serb enclaves, run by Belgrade, excluded Albanians.

Dealing with the past

"Here I discovered hatred deeper than anywhere in the world, more than in Cambodia or Vietnam or Bosnia".

(SRSG Bernard Kouchner, quoted in O'Neill 2002: 52)

Throughout the mission, the past remained a continuous source of grievance and tension between Albanian and Serb communities, fuelling a strong desire for revenge and an almost unassailable presumption by Albanians of the collective guilt of the Serb community.[47] UNMIK's failure to develop a comprehensive strategy to deal with the past is all the more surprising given its stated recognition of its importance in "consolidating peace through justice and in paving the way towards reconciliation" (UNSC 2000e: 10).

Although it is arguable that any progress was contingent on a sea change amongst the communities themselves, UNMIK could nonetheless have done more. It does not appear to have made any significant evaluation of Kosovo's needs or developed a comprehensive principled approach to dealing with the past. Although individual initiatives were undertaken, UNMIK made little concerted effort to influence cross-community relations through dealing with the past in a way that identified the truth, acknowledged suffering, made violators responsible for their actions, provided opportunities for name-clearing, reconciliation or rehabilitation, or promoted a culture of respecting rights. UNMIK's main initiative was the pursuit of criminal justice for serious crimes, which it viewed as the precursor to reconciliation (UNSC 1999a: 20). Panels of international judges were established in the Kosovo courts to try serious crimes, but five years into the mission the overwhelming bulk of crimes committed during the 1998–1999 conflict had not been prosecuted.

The prosecution of serious crimes

Responsibility for investigating and prosecuting war crimes was split between UNMIK and the International Criminal Tribunal for the Former Yugoslavia. By the end of 2004 there had been some, but not much, progress in dealing with these crimes. Progress was limited by the failure to expedite war crimes trials, by delays caused by a lack of capacity in both the ICTY and the Kosovo judicial system, and by the location of most suspects in Serbia, out of reach at least until the fall of Milosevic. Failure to prosecute these crimes exacerbated intolerance towards Serbs and the incidence of extra-judicial justice (Clark 2002: 9).

UNMIK prosecutions

Kosovo Serbs suspected of war crimes and crimes against humanity were initially prosecuted under the Yugoslav Criminal Code in the newly established Kosovo court system. Increased evidence of judicial bias[48] soon generated proposals to establish a special war and ethnic crimes tribunal to try the vast bulk of Kosovo crimes not handled by the ICTY. In November 1999, the Technical Advisory Commission on Judiciary and Prosecution Service voted unanimously to recommend the establishment of a Kosovo tribunal that would operate under a similar statute to the ICTY[49] and, in December, plans to establish a Kosovo War and Ethnic Crimes Court were announced. Working groups were established but, after numerous delays, the proposal was abandoned. This appears to have resulted from opposition by some Albanian representatives (who objected to the involvement of international judges and prosecutors in cases where Albanians were accused),[50] US concern that it would turn into another ICTY or be politically destabilising, financial shortfalls, uncertainty over the jurisdictional division between the special tribunal and ordinary courts, and doubts that the court could operate in a situation where reprisals were likely and witness protection difficult. It was also argued that a tribunal was unnecessary given the presence of international judges and lawyers (ICG 2002: 20; O'Neill 2002: 91).

Trials thus proceeded through the regular court system. Many of the earlier cases were subsequently retried after the introduction of international judges and prosecutors in 2000, which resulted in acquittals in some cases and harsher sentences in others.[51] Following the promulgation of Regulation 2000/64 in December 2000, defendants were able to petition to have trials held before majority international panels. Despite this, friction continued because not all offences related to war crimes qualified for "64" panel treatment. No guidelines were issued, not all defendants got an international prosecutor, and trials that straddled the promulgation period were not dealt with adequately by either system.

The first "64" panel exemplified the failure of these panels to improve perceptions about UNMIK's ability to deliver justice. With insufficient evidence to make a war crimes conviction, the Serb defendant Savo Matic was sentenced to two years' imprisonment for causing "light body injury". The immense controversy created by this decision reflected a lack of acceptance of the system by both jurists and the lay public (UN-MIK 2001d). Breaking the normal rules on judicial deliberation by speaking to the press straight after the verdict, one Albanian judge stated that this was "an absurd judgement, a masquerade. Kosovo justice has failed ... there was enough evidence to convict him of war crimes" (quoted in ICG 2002: 21).

Among the most sensitive and controversial prosecutions were those involving former KLA members. Arrests and trials of high-profile former KLA members during 2002[52] prompted mass demonstrations, reflecting a lack of acceptance by Albanian politicians and members of the public that KLA "freedom fighters" could be subject to prosecution. A statement issued by the PDK and the AAK, for example, accused UNMIK of "holding political prisoners and devaluing the liberation struggle" (quoted in ICG 2002: 21). Claims were also made that UNMIK did not have jurisdiction over the crimes committed before its arrival in June 1999.

The resentment was exacerbated by UNMIK's failure to act against Serbs in northern Mitrovica accused of organised crime and attacks against Albanians and the international community. As one journalist noted:

> More than 60 former KLA fighters have been detained in less than a year, yet Milan Ivanovic, leader of the infamous Mitrovica "Bridge Guards" has escaped arrest and at the same time humiliated the UN by freely turning up in town to hold a press conference. (Quoted in ICG 2002: 22)

Although such reactions did not deter UNMIK from continuing to arrest and try ex-KLA and Serbs accused of war crimes, public reactions became progressively harder to manage. In July 2003, an UNMIK court sentenced a former KLA commander to 17 years' imprisonment for the torture and murder of Albanian detainees; this was inevitably compared with the 7-year sentence handed down by another UNMIK court to a Kosovo Serb member of a Serbian paramilitary group for wartime murders (ICG 2004: 9). Similarly, the indictment for war crimes of the Prizren KPC commander in February 2004 was viewed as an attack on the KPC and met with demonstrations (ICG 2004: 9). The perception that UNMIK was "hell-bent" on hunting down Albanian war criminals remained widespread among its own officials in 2004.

Although many of the 200 or so war crimes cases completed by 2004 were uncontroversial, the many negative reactions reflected public distrust of the criminal justice system and UNMIK's own credibility problems. UNMIK did not implement an effective public relations strategy to handle public reactions. For example, following the arrest in January 2003 of the popular deputy leader of the PDK, Fatmir Limaj, UNMIK did not attempt to defuse local press criticism and took three days to issue a statement clarifying its stance. Moreover, instead of seeking to maintain and defend a consistent policy, it made political judgements about whether to pursue cases. For example, prosecutors were instructed not to indict Albanians for war crimes in the Mitrovica area.

The ICTY

The ICTY's competence to prosecute violations of international humanitarian law committed in the former Yugoslavia since 1991 theoretically gave it sweeping powers to investigate numerous crimes committed in Kosovo. However, it narrowed its focus to individuals at the command level and areas where the worst massacres occurred, leaving UNMIK as the body primarily responsible for the bulk of war crimes and crimes against humanity committed in Kosovo. As of late 2004, the ICTY had issued three indictments for crimes committed in Kosovo, the most prominent of which were those of Slobodan Milosevic, Milan Milutinovic, Nikola Sainovic, Dragoljub Ohdanic and Vlajko Stojiljkovic for crimes committed in May 1999 during the NATO intervention.[53] Investigations were conducted between mid-1999 and the end of 2000, including the exhumation of some 4,000 bodies from 429 sites in Kosovo and the collection of witness statements. The Milosevic trial commenced in February 2002 and ended prematurely with his death in March 2006.

The ICTY process generated mixed reactions in Kosovo. The Milosevic trial had undoubted symbolic significance for Kosovans. Bringing Milosevic before a court sent an important signal about the subordination of powerful state actors to the rule of law, while at the same time opening raw wounds for Kosovo victims, particularly when many other perpetrators remained free. Chesterman (2001b: 8–9) has described how the complex reactions by both the Kosovo Serb and the Albanian communities to the transfer of Milosevic to The Hague cut to the core of ideas about reconciliation, as well as about Kosovo's relationship with Belgrade.

An ICTY official who worked on the Kosovo investigations observed that the process had provided some closure for witnesses and victims. For example, one woman, who had been pack raped by a group of soldiers, said that testifying was her chance to confront the perpetrators and – in the face of widely publicised statements from imams that rape victims had "asked for it" – to state that she had done nothing wrong. At the same time, very few of the Kosovo public were affected directly by the ICTY trials and there was a strong perception that the ICTY was largely irrelevant to their lives. Many Kosovo Albanians did not trust the ICTY, as illustrated by public reaction to the indictment of KLA members in February 2003. Others believed that, in order to gain Belgrade's cooperation, the ICTY had deliberately sidelined Kosovo by lowering the threshold below which it would normally leave cases to national courts (ICG 2004: 9). In UNMIK itself there was a perception that the ICTY was "not interested" in Kosovo.

Truth-seeking

The suppression of history characterised much of twentieth-century Yugoslavian government, as did the use of rival nationalist interpretations for propaganda purposes. These traditions, combined with the stereotyping of Serbs, pervaded Kosovo Albanian justifications of violence against Serbs and lessened both individual and community perceptions of responsibility for that violence (Clark 2002: 26–27).

There appears to have been little or no consideration by UNMIK of the potential for a systematic effort at truth-seeking to address these trends, either by documenting the extent and nature of the suffering or by publicising positive elements in relations between Serb and Albanian communities. The possibility of a truth commission does not seem to have been contemplated seriously. As Clark (2002: 28) has observed, this again appears at least partly attributable to the dilemma of Kosovo's final status:

> Would a Truth Commission be a useful forum for such dialogue? My view is that there is little point in establishing an official Truth Commission in Kosovo until there has been more progress towards settling its future status. Otherwise this Commission would not be a mutual search for truth by people who desire a new basis for coexistence, but rather one more arena for a propaganda struggle, Albanians and Serbs again competing to make the other look bad. The idea may be worth pursuing once there is clarity about the process for deciding

on Kosovo's future status. Even then, defining its remit would raise complex issues and be fraught with difficulties. For instance, should a Truth Commission take up issues from the 1980s in an effort to reassure Serbs that the new Kosovo would be different? These subjects remain very touchy in both communities.

Given the extent to which this issue affected confidence between the two communities, it is nonetheless arguable that UNMIK should and could have made more effort to address it. UNMIK's handling of the issue of missing persons demonstrates the potential for truth-seeking initiatives to make a contribution, the challenges of the prevailing political environment for such tasks and UNMIK's own lack of effort.

Although initially handled through a Victim Recovery and Identification Commission established in May 2000, the investigation of missing persons did not gain momentum until 2002, with the establishment of the UNMIK Office for Missing Persons and Forensics. By February 2004, the Office had collated a list of over 5,000 missing persons and exhumed 643 sets of remains, of which 452 were returned to families (AI 2004b: 6). It regularly organised clothing exhibitions, launched Kosovo's first forensic medicine diploma in July 2003 and invested in other capacity-building activities such as training staff to conduct liaison, counselling and administrative practices. This was creditable progress compared with UNMIK police investigations and it made a practical contribution to social healing as well as to building a sustainable capacity for Kosovans to conduct work in this area.

However, lack of policing resources, political impediments and community resistance hindered the Office's progress. It made few inroads in investigating the disappearance of 1,200 Serbs and other minorities believed to have fallen victim to KLA or Kosovo Albanian purges after July 1999. In particular, it was obstructed by the reluctance of Albanians to provide information that implicated fellow Albanians (AI 2004b: 6; OIK 2004: 22).

Similarly, UNMIK did not make significant progress in determining the unexplained fate of some 3,000 ethnic Albanians believed to have been arrested by Serb police and paramilitary forces between 1998 and July 1999 (AI 2004b: 7), despite having identified this issue as essential to reconciliation (UNSC 2002h: 14). The Kosovo Transitional Council established a Commission on Detainees and the Missing in September 1999, but had no power to act apart from establishing dialogue with Belgrade. In this case, little could be achieved until the election of Kostunica as the Serbian Prime Minister improved cooperation from Belgrade. In February 2001 the Yugoslav parliament passed an amnesty law that freed the majority of remaining Albanians in detention (O'Neill 2002: 59).

Reconciliation

"There's no discussion of reconciliation. There's no need. Who is there to reconcile with when the Serbs have all gone? The only returns area is a zoo – an enclave near Peje guarded by Spanish KFOR, whose inhabitants need an armed escort just to run an errand".

As this UNMIK justice department official pointed out, Kosovans themselves made little progress in reconciling their differences at the political level. Although some moderate Kosovo Serb figures made conciliatory advances to their Albanian counterparts, on the whole Kosovo Serbs took their cue from Belgrade and refused to admit that Serbian forces or Kosovo Serbs had ever committed atrocities (O'Neill 2002: 54). This lack of recognition made it difficult for moderates in the Kosovo Albanian and Serb communities to begin reconciliation, and it worked to the advantage of extremists (O'Neill 2002: 54). Although the fall of Milosevic made it politically possible for Serbia to begin to acknowledge Serb responsibility for atrocities in Kosovo, Kostunica did not satisfy the demands of most Kosovo Albanians for an unequivocal apology (O'Neill 2002: 54–55).

Some reconciliation efforts were also made by religious figures, amongst whom Bishop Artemije, head of the Serbian Orthodox Church in Kosovo, and Hieromonk Sava Janjic were the most active. Although their ability to promote reconciliation was limited by political pressures from nationalist elements within the Church, the Sarajevo Statement of February 2000 signed by the heads of the Orthodox and Catholic Churches and the Chief Mufti of Kosovo was an important step in acknowledging the suffering of all communities and making a moral commitment to look to the future.

Kosovo Albanians were split between those "oriented towards revenge and expulsion and those wanting to maintain human rights standards and to support ethnic coexistence" (Clark 2002: 3). At a leadership level, despite some overtures towards Serbs and other minorities, Kosovo Albanians' links with and apparent unwillingness to restrain the KLA understandably undermined their credibility (Clark 2002: 2–3). They also failed to confront the sensitive issue of returns, making few if any public gestures encouraging minority groups to return to Kosovo. Some prominent Albanians did, however, make calls for reconciliation, including the former political prisoners Adem Demaçi and Flora Brovina and the Catholic priest Don Lush Gjergj. Nevertheless, there remained an almost overwhelming sense that Kosovo Albanians were primarily interested in ethnic domination rather than peaceful coexistence. The March riots appeared to shock both sides into a higher degree of cooperation and improved the attitudes of some politicians. President Rugova, for example, attended some Serb community meetings and spoke in Serbian for the first time.

UNMIK's lack of focus on reconciliation was one of the more surprising elements of the mission. It was not until the violence of March 2004 that it revised the Kosovo Standards Implementation Plan to include "initiatives to rebuild trust and confidence between communities" (UNSC 2004c: 5) as one of six priority actions. Even then, reconciliation continued to be seen as the responsibility of local political leaders, despite their apparent lack of commitment to it: "While the international community can promote tolerance and coexistence, it is, in the end, the responsibility of the local population to nurture the basic prerequisites for a peaceful society in which all communities can live a normal life" (UNSC 2000e: 20).[54]

In contrast to the more proactive approach taken by the United Nations Transitional Administration in East Timor, five years into the mission UNMIK continued to consider it "too early" to address reconciliation because of the risk of inflaming tensions and because it was beyond the ambit of external intervention. In some senses, continuing reluctance by some local groups to participate in its initiatives validated this view. However, signs of the potential for UNMIK to play a more active role in supporting reconciliation were evident.

One example was the potential for UNMIK to provide space for contact and accommodation between the Albanian and Serb communities in the form of mechanisms for meeting and discussing problems. The Kosovo Assembly, for example, allowed for a level of coexistence and cooperative tackling of problems that had previously been absent, and contributed to a noteworthy increase in contact between Albanian and Serb political leaders. This was particularly the case following the municipal elections of 2000 and the Assembly elections of 2001, which placed elected Albanians and UNMIK-appointed Serbs in daily contact. As demonstrated by frequent Serb boycotts, however, whether the parties chose to utilise this was beyond UNMIK's control.

Although no mechanism for dialogue was established at the community level, UNMIK oversaw some isolated reconciliation initiatives. For example, it established multi-ethnic youth projects in mixed areas and provided forums to develop civic dialogue between Kosovo Albanian NGOs and NGOs from Serbia proper. The conduct of "go and see" visits for displaced persons to view possible return sites in Kosovo also proved successful (UNSC 2002c: 7).

The United Nations Development Programme (UNDP) sponsored some reconciliation initiatives at village level in the form of community-based recovery processes to support basic needs. One project required village leaders to build a consensus and motivate villagers to reconstruct houses for people from a different ethnic group. Although primarily aimed at strengthening village leadership, the project also provided a specific framework for inter-ethnic reconciliation (UNDP 2004). Like the Cambodia Resettlement and Reintegration programme, the strength of such projects was that they identified common interests – such as development goals – and used these to promote practical cooperation.

In other cases, however, UNMIK's "reserved powers" impeded the development of practical reconciliation initiatives. One such example was a proposal by the mayor of Gjilane to offer Serb returnees employment opportunities in the electricity and water authorities. He was unable to implement the plan because UNMIK vetoed the disproportionate employment of Serbs in public utilities, over which it held reserved powers. As a result, a potentially effective means to encourage Serb returns was lost.

Critically, very few measures appear to have been taken to encourage Albanians to distinguish between those Serbs who might have been responsible for abuses and those who were not. There was minimal public discussion of the means by which this could be achieved other than bringing individuals to trial (Clark 2002: 8). For example, there was no extensive procedure for name-clearing, including in the case of the return to Kosovo of Serb refugees (Clark 2002: 12). The test case for Serb refugee returns in the village of Osojane near Istok in north-western Kosovo was illuminating:

> The choice of Osojane for return was made more than a year in advance of the actual return. Yet despite the allegations that villagers from Osojane had participated in the massacre of Albanians in the neighbouring village of Izbica, little seems to have been done to reassure local Albanians about exactly who would be coming. When the first Serb men returned to begin reconstructing the derelict buildings, they were greeted with a 2,000-strong hostile demonstration. An Albanian café-owner opined: "They have committed crimes, they have killed and burned, they don't belong here. This is provocation".... The indispensable condition for Albanians offering protection to Serbs ... is confidence that the Serbs in question were people committed to peaceful coexistence in Kosovo. Hence we return to the need for transparent, explicit and publicly-debated criteria and procedures about screening, rehabilitation and "name-clearing" – procedures that would apply to members of every ethnic group, including the majority. In the absence of such procedures in either Bosnia or Croatia, local peace and human rights groups working for return have relied instead on face-to-face trust-building contacts – meetings on neutral territory, low-profile visits. Kosovo does not yet have grass-roots initiatives such as these: its situation is more extreme and hence the need for a formal procedure is more pronounced. (Clark 2002: 12–13)

By late 2004, inter-ethnic reconciliation thus remained an inconceivable prospect for many Kosovans and the extent to which UNMIK initiatives might have been able to promote reconciliation remained almost completely untested.

Performing effectively

Despite sweeping powers under Resolution 1244, it was not until well into the mission that UNMIK developed a blueprint for action on the rule of law. Pre-mission planning was negligible and strategic oversight of rule of law activities improved only marginally as the mission wore on. This wasted time and resulted in hesitant or inappropriate policy decisions based on "best case scenarios that failed to materialise" (KCL 2003). The first five years of the mission were thus characterised by crisis management, reactive policy-making and ad hoc initiatives.

Strategic planning on the rule of law

Pre-mission planning was negligible in the rushed and under-resourced context in which UNMIK was deployed. It was constrained by ambiguity over the United Nations' role, with the OSCE remaining the preferred organisation to assume state-building responsibilities until two weeks before Resolution 1244 was adopted (Hartmann 2003a: 4). At the time of deployment, the United Nations had contingency plans for the civilian police, but no other aspect of the operation. No state-building strategy had been formulated. The initial blueprint of the UN Department of Peacekeeping Operations resembled a statement of interest more than an operational plan and significantly underestimated the scope and depth of the mission (KCL 2003). No adequate assessment was made of existing skills and structures, a problem that left one former judge "appalled at the consistent lack of understanding of Kosovo issues".

A five-phase concept of operations was developed *in situ* by the UN advance team, under which interim structures would be established, the rule of law consolidated, reconciliation promoted, provisional institutions of self-government installed, and a final political settlement arrived at (UNSC 1999a: 18–19). Although the importance of the rule of law was emphasised,[55] there remained a high degree of ambiguity as to what specific tasks would be carried out, and how. The strategy focused heavily on the tripartite framework of judiciary, police and correctional system and provided little detail on how any of the phases would be implemented.

It was not until 2002 that a "benchmarking" exercise articulated goals for ensuring and measuring compliance with Resolution 1244 and for fulfilling the conditions for self-government.[56] The "rule of law" again took high priority, with a Security Council mission to Kosovo in December 2002 declaring that the "foundation of all other standards is the rule of law" (UNSC 2002h: 16). Rule of law "benchmarks" centred on disrupting organised crime networks, ending extremist violence, promoting public respect for the police and judiciary, ensuring the impartiality of judges and the KPS, and achieving sufficient minority representation. The focus of the exercise was not on UNMIK's performance but on the actions required of local actors. Accordingly, the PISG were required to promote the "values of the rule of law" and provide budget support to encourage higher education and entrance examinations in the legal field, and the holders of public office were to abstain from extremist public statements (UNSC 2003d: 17).

Although the setting of benchmarks was an improvement over the previous lack of direction, neither UNMIK nor the PISG translated the benchmarks into concrete initiatives on the ground and ultimately the exercise proved relatively shallow. The benchmarking exercise was developed further in the December 2003 *Standards for Kosovo* paper (UNMIK 2003a), which elaborated the standards to be attained before a process to determine Kosovo's future status could begin. Again, the rule of law was given detailed treatment. As one of eight standards, the "rule of law" objective was set out as follows:

> There exists a sound legal framework and effective law enforcement, compliant with European standards. Police, judicial and penal systems act impartially and fully respect human rights. There is equal access to justice and no one is above the law: there is no impunity for violators. There are strong measures in place to fight ethnically-motivated crime, as well as economic and financial crime. (UNMIK 2003a)

The follow-up Kosovo Standards Implementation Plan[57] noted that its "immediate priority is the establishment of the rule of law, prosecution of perpetrators and public respect for law and order" (UNMIK 2004a: 3). It established a detailed set of objectives, including improving the security environment for all ethnic communities; unequivocal support by all communities to fight crime; the assumption by Kosovans of progressively greater responsibility in the justice sector and the effective and impartial demonstration of those responsibilities; effective and equally accessible justice for all communities; better witness protection; and targeting of public sector corruption. The Plan also established priority actions that included prosecution of those responsible for the March 2004 violence, strengthening police investigation capacities, improving judicial standards through enhanced training and an examinations system, the progressive transfer of serious crimes cases to local judges and prosecutors, a public sector anti-corruption strategy and the establishment of a witness protection facility (UNMIK 2004a: 27–28).

Six months after the Plan was adopted, it had delivered few results. According to a senior figure in the UNMIK Police and Justice pillar, this was because the rule of law standards set out in the document were not embedded in an overarching state-building strategy and were politically, not technocratically, driven. The exercise had not been developed with state-building objectives in mind. Rather, it was a political exercise aimed at refocusing the attention of the local political elite away from the issue of Kosovo's final status and towards the responsibilities of governance. On this front, it failed again. Rule of law standards were too detailed to be useful as a political tool and the process was interpreted by Kosovan politicians as an attempt to delay independence for as long as possible, exacerbating their discontent and frustration with UNMIK. UNMIK's policy failure was compounded by the fact that senior officials acknowledged its lack of effectiveness but took no action to remedy it.

The "pillar" structure

The novel idea of dividing the Security Council's mandate between several major international organisations proved cumbersome and confusing. In the rule of law area, responsibilities were split between UNMIK and the OSCE: UNMIK Pillar I (Police and Justice) was responsible for oversight of the judicial, police and prison systems; OSCE Pillar III (Institution Building) was responsible for human resources capacity-building in the areas of justice, police and public administration, democratisation and governance, human rights monitoring and capacity-building, and strengthening the institutions of civil society (UNSC 1999f: 2–3). Other organisations were also involved in rule of law issues, notably NATO and the United Nations High Commissioner for Refugees.

Coordination between the pillars was patchy and the "mission" deteriorated over time into a creature that one UNMIK legal officer described as "massive and lurching in all directions". There was little or no "tribal agreement" between the various mission components on how to move ahead on issues as diverse as refugee returns and human rights capacity-building. Even in the areas it tried to control, UNMIK was unable to ensure consistency: for example NATO continued to make arbitrary arrests and detentions in contravention of UNMIK rules and without informing the United Nations.

King's College London (KCL 2003) has discussed comprehensively the unwieldiness of the pillar structure and resource allocation problems. Worth highlighting here is the extremely poor relationship between Pillars I and III. In the early phases of the mission, this manifested itself in a significant overlap of responsibilities between the dozen lawyers in UNMIK's Department of Judicial Affairs and the 75 lawyers in the OSCE Department of Human Rights and Rule of Law. As roles and responsibilities became more entrenched, communication worsened. By 2004, there was no high-level policy coordination between the two pillars, and one senior official in Pillar I admitted about the OSCE that "we don't really know what they're doing".

Over time a situation developed in which UNMIK officials rejected any responsibility for capacity-building, despite acknowledging that success in this area was intimately linked to Pillar I's goals. The OSCE was refused access to mainstream judicial activities and lacked the political resources to negotiate a role for itself. The OSCE's neglect of its capacity-building responsibilities, combined with UNMIK's recalcitrance, put at risk a key aspect of the mission mandate.

Similarly, dissent between mission components arose in connection with UNMIK's human rights function. UNMIK's senior human rights adviser resigned in 1999 in protest against the way human rights issues were being dealt with and, despite an offer by the OHCHR to fund and fill the position, it remained vacant for the next four years. In 2004, an interpillar working group on human rights was established to review UNMIK legislation for human rights compliance, but it had advisory competence only. The Office of the Legal Adviser retained the power to accept or reject the working group's recommendations, but often simply ignored them. The implementation of key human rights objectives was thus completely reliant on the political bargaining capacity of individuals vis-à-vis the OLA.

Mission inertia

A further striking aspect of the UNMIK mission was its lack of effort to rectify rule of law problems it had itself identified (i.e. senior UNMIK officers often discussed these problems but did nothing to address them). The apparent inability or unwillingness of mission heads to promote change or pursue creative solutions – such as the much-discussed idea of a special court – indicated a need for management reform at the senior level. UNMIK legal officers described the incumbent leadership as "old and tired", with vested interests in maintaining the status quo. Other observers pointed to a lack of commitment at most levels of UNMIK to hand over authority, and a strong perception that remuneration was so good that no one was in any hurry to leave.

Observations

"We feel like we're still in 1999. So much has been spent for so little ... We feel like neglected lab rats. We don't have the time for this; we're tired and fed up ... someone has an interest in things not moving forward. UNMIK failed because it suited their purpose. This is another example of where development has stalled due to personal, national or outside interests. It's extremely frustrating."

Discontent of the magnitude expressed by this former judge underscores UNMIK's profound failure to meet Kosovan expectations or to build a productive partnership with local counterparts. Even top officials in UNMIK did not dispute that they had lost both these battles. As UNMIK itself acknowledged, the critical factor in building an effective rule of law was "the active cooperation of every inhabitant of Kosovo" (UNMIK 2004a: 4). In an environment gripped by frustration, sour relations and a sense of inertia, it is not surprising that UNMIK made slow progress over the five-year period from 1999 to 2004.

Without doubt, UNMIK was thrust into an immensely trying environment in which Kosovans, engaged in longstanding ethnic and political battles, were prepared to sacrifice the cooperative pursuit of development goals for uncertain political gains. For any external actor, building consensus and commitment in such an environment would be extremely difficult, let alone over as complex a value as the rule of law.

However, at least four factors over which the United Nations had some control emerge as explanations for the difficulties encountered in many of its rule of law initiatives. First, the absence of an accepted political settlement on Kosovo's final status caused policy paralysis, provoked local political agendas that ran counter to rule of law objectives and diverted UNMIK from acting as a lever of real change. This raises the question of whether, in the circumstances, such a mission should ever have been attempted.

Second, UNMIK failed to develop a considered rule of law strategy until four years into the mission. A reactive and ad hoc approach to establishing the rule of law, coupled with poor implementation, resulted in mistakes that UNMIK lacked the political or other resources to remedy.

Third, UNMIK failed to secure the cooperation of Belgrade, dismantle rival security and justice structures or fully marginalise violent extremists. Ultimately, this meant that, in spite of an extended deployment, it was unable to consolidate its own authority or to create conditions of real security for all groups in Kosovo in which they could participate in state-building processes.

Fourth, Kosovans felt deeply disempowered. This stemmed largely from UNMIK's "reserved powers" policy and the way in which it sought to consult with and build consensus among local players. Even if one accepts that the question of Kosovo's final status was irresolvable, UNMIK might have been able to devise a transition process that devolved more responsibility sooner while remaining within internationally acceptable parameters. It might also have found itself capable of a more proactive approach to winning local support for its policies, rather than passively expecting "active cooperation". In emasculating the Kosovan elite, key constituencies and the broader population, UNMIK's limited transfer policy lacked direction, satisfied no one and denied Kosovans the opportunity to commit in practice to the rule of law.

Notes

1. Parallel structures had sprung up in resistance to the abrogation of Kosovo's autonomous powers under amendments to the Serbian constitution in 1990, the subsequent dissolution of Kosovo's institutions and the establishment of an unofficial parallel government under Ibrahim Rugova with the declaration in 1992 of the "Republic of Kosovo".
2. O'Neill (2002: 21–35) provides a detailed description of this period.
3. This point has been argued widely. See, for example, Chesterman (2001b); Yannis (2004); and ICG (2004).
4. SRSG Hans Haekkerup was widely perceived to be less supportive of Kosovan independence than his predecessor, Bernard Kouchner, for example.
5. Under the 1990 Serbian constitution, Kosovo's wide-ranging autonomy had been reduced to municipal status, with no autonomous legislative, judicial or policy-making powers. For a summary of the recent history of Kosovo's constitutional rights and legal status, see Stahn (2001b: 532–534).
6. See UNMIK (2001b, 2001e).
7. For an in-depth discussion of the Constitutional Framework, see Stahn (2001b: 542–549).
8. For a summary of the provisions, see UNSC (2001b: 7, para. 23).
9. The human rights chapter did, however, fail to incorporate the International Covenant on Economic, Social and Cultural Rights and the Convention Against Torture.
10. For example, it established a working group composed of representatives of the three major Kosovo Albanian parties, a Kosovo Serb member (who ultimately withdrew and was replaced), a Bosniac member to represent other minority groups, a civil society representative, an independent expert and seven international members.
11. For example, Predrag Simic, a foreign policy adviser to the Serb government, described it as a concession to Albanian separatists; the Serbian politician Marko Jaksic called it a reward for Albanian violence and demanded that Serbs boycott the elections (*Vecernje Novosti* 2001a); and the Serbian Justice Minister, Vladan Batic, said it showed a lack of respect for Kosovo Serbs and the Serbian government (*Vecernje Novosti* 2001b).
12. One example was the promulgation, against advice from the Senior Human Rights Adviser, of a regulation (1999/26) that allowed for pre-trial detention of 12 months, in violation of the European Convention on Human Rights and the International Covenant on Civil and Political Rights (O'Neill 2002: 78; Marshall and Inglis 2003: 143).
13. Provisional Criminal Code, UNMIK/Reg/2003/25, and Provisional Criminal Procedure Code, UNMIK/Reg/2003/26, of 6 July 2003.

14. See also the OMIK (2002a) for a detailed account of deficiencies in the judicial system.
15. Who, for example, identified one Albanian judge with the old order and accused a Bosniac judge of collaborating with the Milosevic regime (ICG 2002: 4).
16. For example, one Serb judge was evicted from his apartment and threatened with death if he returned.
17. These were the Technical Advisory Commission on Judiciary and Prosecution Service, composed of 10 local and 5 international experts, which advised on the structure and administration of the new judicial system; and the Advisory Judicial Commission, the successor to the Joint Advisory Council, appointed in September 1999 with 8 Kosovan and 3 international members to recommend permanent judicial appointments.
18. Across Kosovo, 24 municipal courts, each with an individual judge, were dealing with civil cases, juvenile cases, property disputes and lower-level criminal cases (up to five years' imprisonment); 5 district courts functioned as courts of second instance; and a Kosovo Supreme Court with territorial competence over all of Kosovo functioned as the court of last instance. There were also 25 minor offences courts and a Higher Court for minor offences.
19. With the exception of the limited experiment of the Special Prosecutor in Cambodia.
20. See UNMIK Regulation 2000/6 on the Appointment and Removal from Office of International Judges and Prosecutors, 15 February 2000.
21. UNMIK Regulation 2000/34 Amending UNMIK Regulation 2000/6 on Assignment of International Judges/Prosecutors and/or Change of Venue.
22. The Department of Justice guidelines stated somewhat ambiguously that a case could be referred to an international panel where there were factors that could affect judicial or prosecutorial impartiality or where there was public demand for a judicial outcome.
23. Under Yugoslavian law, such panels were typically composed of five members — two professional and three lay judges. The typical Regulation 6 panel in 2000 was thus one international judge and four Kosovo Albanians, three of whom were lay judges.
24. These consisted of three professional judges, at least two of whom were international.
25. For details see OMIK (2002a. 6).
26. Eight trial monitors appointed by the OSCE were unable to provide regular and comprehensive monitoring, making it difficult to obtain an accurate picture of the quality of trials, at least in the early period (United States Department of State 2000b: 17). Ad hoc reports by agencies such as Amnesty International were consistently negative. A US Department of State Judicial Assessment Mission raised serious concerns in early 2000 over due process, including applicable law, the lack of detainee rights, the lack of defence counsel, and ethnic bias.
27. Tensions flared after the Legal Systems Monitoring Section's October 2000 report, *The criminal justice system (February–July 2000)*, although the report did eventually prompt some effort by UNMIK to tackle the problems (O'Neill 2002: 93).
28. Joint Declaration between the Deputy SRSG for Police and Justice and the Serbian Minister of Justice, 9 July 2002.
29. For more details see UNMIK (2003b: 27–28).
30. This was later expanded to 9 and then to 12 weeks.
31. Peake (2004: 12–13) describes the key features of the democratic policing model as a redefinition of the police mission away from the state, making it accountable under the law and to the community, restructuring institutions and reaffirming its non-political orientation by on-the-ground actions. The democratic policing model emphasizes respect for human rights and accountability and the primacy of the interests and rights of citizens over those of one ethnic group or the state.
32. See, for example, Rugova's election pledge in 2002 to uphold "good governance and the rule of law" (Islam Online 2002).

33. Thaci's brother, Gani Thaci, controlled the building and petrol station industries and was implicated in smuggling, for example. See also Walsh (1999).
34. See, for example, the Serbian Prime Minister's description of the "misguided administration" of UNMIK in Kosovo (Kostunica 2004); or the call by Serbia's Justice Minister, Vladan Batic, for the UN Prosecutor Carla del Ponte to resign for indicting only Serbs in the ICTY (Savic 2002).
35. For example, by failing to object to the admission of prejudicial evidence or evidence obtained by torture or ill treatment, or other cases where correct procedure had not been complied with (OMIK 2003a: 45).
36. See, for example, AI (2002b). AI (2004b) also details a case of CIVPOL and KPS suspected of torturing an Albanian detainee. Although UNMIK waived the immunity of the CIVPOL officer involved, he was driven across the border, the Austrian government would not extradite him and he continued to work in the Austrian police force. In another case, UNMIK and the Kenyan police, without a formal extradition proceeding, arrested and transported a Kenyan suspected of stealing in Kosovo; he was then held for over a week without being presented to a court.
37. As in the case of UNMIK interpreter Petar Topoljski, who was extra-judicially executed in 2000 after an exposé in the local newspaper *Dita*. This revealed UNMIK's lack of principled guidelines as an employer, particularly regarding returning Serbs. UNMIK had not screened the employee, and did not suspend him pending investigation, or hold an investigation, or even seek to clear its employee's name (Clark 2002: 10).
38. Marshall and Inglis (2003: 106, 113) cite an internal UN document of March 2001 that sought to justify the use of the SRSG's executive power by placing limitations on the applicable international human rights law. They go on to detail a range of examples of the misuse of executive powers.
39. OIK (2004) lists activities in detail.
40. Specifically, the PISG were given responsibilities for the appointment of judges and prosecutors, the organisation and functioning of the courts, provision of court and prosecutorial services, provision of technical, financial, personnel and other support to the judicial and prosecutorial systems, the training of judicial personnel in cooperation with the OSCE, the organisation of examinations for legal professionals, the appointment, training, discipline and dismissal of members of judicial support staff, ensuring coordination between the judicial system and correctional service, cooperating on independent monitoring of the judicial system and correctional service, providing information on the judicial system and correctional service, protecting personal data, and assisting in the recruitment, training and evaluation of correctional service personnel (UNMIK 2001b: Section 5.3).
41. Drafting of the two codes began in August 1999 and took three years, taking in a complicated consultation process. The JAC/LM prepared the initial drafts in cooperation with the Council of Europe. Consultations were held with the OSCE, UNICEF, the American Bar Association's Central and Eastern European Law Initiative, judges, prosecutors and other legal practitioners in Kosovo, and academics. The drafts were then sent to the UNMIK Legal Adviser in November 2001 for revision. In 2002–2003 the Office of the Legal Adviser consulted with the main Kosovo drafters, UN headquarters, the Council of Europe and UNMIK, then finalised the codes. These were then sent to the Kosovo Prime Minister for review by the government and Assembly. In May 2003, the Assembly's Commission for Judicial Matters, Legislative Matters and the Constitutional Framework reviewed the drafts and submitted its recommendations to the Assembly. UNMIK then received comments from the government and Assembly and reviewed/adjusted the codes before promulgation (OMIK 2003a: 53).
42. The UNMIK Legal Adviser, Alexander Borg-Olivier, noted that "a criminal code and

criminal procedure code is the reflection of the culture and history of the people and affects people's lives, so there is no question that this is an exercise that requires full engagement and full involvement of the Kosovo institutions" (UNMIK 2003c).

43. Of the two local human rights NGOs, one (the Council for Defence of Human Rights and Freedom) had a political rather than human rights agenda; the other had credibility as a human rights NGO but was small and based in Belgrade.

44. King's College London (KCL 2003) outlines some of the reasons for this.

45. UNMIK and KFOR efforts to discipline the KPC from 2000 resulted in a drop in the number of violations: 12 KPC members were suspended in late 2003 by the SRSG and 4 were detained by KFOR in February 2004 for suspected criminal links (UNSC 2004c: 12–13).

46. The Bridgewatchers were Kosovo Serbs who from mid-1999 unilaterally enforced "security" by preventing Albanians from crossing the bridge into northern Mitrovica and gathering information on KFOR, UNMIK police and Albanians living in the north.

47. The desire for revenge was illustrated in a 1999 survey of 600 Kosovo Albanian households, in which 86 per cent of men and 89 per cent of women had strong feelings of hatred towards the Serbs and 51 per cent of women and 43 per cent of men desired revenge most or all of the time (Summerfield 2002: 1105). O'Neill (2002: 51) also notes the ferocity of the desire for revenge.

48. As discussed above. See also the example of the Momcilovic case, in Marshall and Inglis (2003: 131–133).

49. The Technical Advisory Commission recommended it be established as an extraordinary court with a broad jurisdiction to try cases involving grave breaches of the Geneva Conventions, violations of the laws or customs of war, and genocide and crimes against humanity, as well as other serious crimes committed on political, racial or religious grounds after the conflict.

50. KCL (2003).

51. See, for example, the trial of Miles Jokic (Marshall and Inglis 2003: 134).

52. Three Albanians were arrested in January 2002 for war crimes and further arrests were made in August 2002, including of former KLA and KPC members. In December 2002, four senior former KLA members were sentenced to 3–15 years for the unlawful detention and murder of Albanians in 1999. In January 2003, an UNMIK tribunal indicted four ex-KLA, including Fatmir Limaj, a senior aide to Hashim Thaci.

53. In January 2003, the ICTY indicted four KLA members for crimes against humanity and violations of the laws and customs of law, including Fatmir Limaj; initial appearances were held in February 2003. Indictments were also issued against a group of Serbian Ministry of Interior officials and army commanders (Pavkovic et al.) in September 2003, though all remained at large. The ICTY also conducted investigations of Albanian war crimes suspects, including former KLA members in 2002.

54. See also UNMIK (2004a: 3).

55. See, for example, UNSC (1999a: 12).

56. See UNSC (2003d: 17; 2002c: 10; and 2002g).

57. For full details see UNMIK (2004a: 27–46).

6

Beyond the blank slate: The UN Transitional Administration in East Timor

[I]ncoming international forces secured the airport and other critical facilities, including the [UN] compound, where many Timorese had taken refuge. However, following the complete disintegration of the [police force] in Dili over the preceding days, law and order broke down across the city. Organised groups of youths and criminal gangs committed widespread acts of arson and looting. Tens of thousands more Dili residents sought refuge in churches and other public places, while thousands of others fled to the districts.

(UNSC 2006b: 3)

Four years after East Timor's independence, the parallels between the violence of September 1999 and the April–May 2006 security crisis served as a disturbing reminder of deep fault lines in East Timor's security, political and institutional apparatus. Sparked by the dismissal in mid-March 2006 of nearly 600 members of the East Timor Defence Force (Falintil-Forca Defesa Timor-Leste, F-FDTL) who had complained of discriminatory treatment, violent conflict between the military, police and general public resulted in at least 37 deaths and the displacement of 15 per cent of the population (UNSC 2006b: 21). It also saw the desertion of East Timor's Military Police Commander Alfredo Reinado and claims that the Interior Minister, Rogerio Lobato, had acted on Prime Minister Alkatiri's instructions in recruiting and arming a civilian militia to "eliminate" Alkatiri's opponents. The subsequent collapse of East Timor's defence and police forces prompted an international military intervention and the deployment of a new UN mission to assume primary responsibil-

No entry without strategy: Building the rule of law under UN transitional administration, Bull, United Nations University Press, 2008, ISBN 978-92-808-1151-3

ity for policing, the first time the United Nations had done so in a sovereign state. President Xanana Gusmao forced Alkatiri to resign, beginning a high-level political stalemate in which the President and Prime Minister did not meet for over six months (UNSC 2007a: para. 9). It also reverberated into the parliamentary and presidential elections of 2007, when some 600 houses were burned by mobs supporting Alkatiri's Revolutionary Front for an Independent East Timor (Frente Revolucionaria de Timor-Leste, Fretilin) and at least two pro-Gusmao supporters were killed. Reinado, who was initially captured, "escaped" from Becora prison with 56 others in August 2006 and remained at large a year later.

A UN Independent Special Commission of Inquiry established in June 2006 to establish the facts behind these events pointed to the extent to which the security agencies and responsible executive ministries had acted outside the law. Lobato, along with the Minister for Defence and Defence Force Chief, had acted illegally in transferring weapons to civilians; the government had failed to follow legislative procedures in calling out the defence force on 28 April; and, in distributing police and defence force weapons to civilians, the Interior Minister and Defence Chief had acted without lawful authority. The Commission found that Alkatiri had failed to use his firm authority to denounce the transfer of weapons to civilians, and was suspected of having known about the illegal arming of civilians (UNSC 2007a: para. 19).

Four years after the departure of the United Nations UN Transitional Administration in East Timor (UNTAET), such a profound lack of commitment to the rule of law by some members of the executive, the security forces and broader society threatened to undermine the extraordinary efforts of others to build a very different East Timor from that of Indonesian rule. Questions were inevitably raised about whether the seeds of these events could have been predicted, addressed and perhaps prevented during the period of UN transitional administration.

The UNTAET mission was unprecedented in the history of UN peacekeeping. For the first time, the United Nations in effect assumed sovereign control over a territory, independent of any competing official authority and with the strategic objective of preparing it for statehood. Faced with a devastated landscape and mandated with full legislative and executive powers, UNTAET adopted an even more ambitious statebuilding programme than the United Nations Interim Administration Mission in Kosovo (UNMIK). It sought to rebuild virtually from scratch East Timor's infrastructure, economy, government and administrative system, razed by the militia attacks that followed the August 1999 popular consultation and Indonesia's subsequent destructive retreat. In the justice sector, almost all infrastructure had been destroyed and most legal personnel had fled. Accordingly, UNTAET attempted a bold set of rule of law initiatives in areas where it had little prior experience. These included:

- *oversight of constitutional reform*, leading to the drafting and adoption of a constitution by an elected Constituent Assembly;
- *legislative reform*, including the determination of applicable law during the transition period and the proclamation of over 70 legally binding regulations covering criminal law and day-to-day governance;
- *the establishment of a transitional judicial system*, including the appointment of a transitional judiciary, prosecution and defence services and a court system;
- *the development of a permanent post-independence judicial system*, with the transitional judicial system as its basis;
- *law enforcement during the transition and development of an East Timorese police force*, including the recruitment and training of East Timorese police and the phased transfer of policing responsibilities from CIVPOL to the new police force;
- *responsibility for correctional services and the development of a permanent post-independence prison system*;
- *the investigation and prosecution of serious crimes* committed in 1999 through the establishment of Special Panels for Serious Crimes with responsibility for prosecuting crimes against humanity, genocide, torture, murder and sexual offences;
- *other initiatives to deal with the past and promote reconciliation*, including UNTAET-sponsored negotiations with Indonesia and militia leaders in West Timor and the establishment of a Commission for Reception, Truth and Reconciliation.

This chapter argues that, against considerable odds, UNTAET made progress in establishing the beginnings of state rule of law institutions and in assisting the East Timorese to reckon with their traumatic past. Nonetheless, by independence in May 2002, the justice system was one of the most dysfunctional elements of the new state. A crisis of confidence had developed in a state justice system that was virtually paralysed, inaccessible and confusing. Comparatively good levels of law and order relied not on robust institutions but on the self-discipline of the Timorese leadership and population, which quickly proved fallible. Fundamental building blocks of the rule of law – such as separation of powers and equality before the law – were not in place.

In his final report on UNTAET to the Security Council, the Secretary-General acknowledged frankly the unresolved problems in the justice sector "at a time when East Timorese confidence in the nascent judicial system is vital" (UNSC 2002b: 3–4). Publicly, the Security Council continued to attribute these problems to a lack of experienced personnel and limited resources:

> The functioning of Timor-Leste's justice system continues to be hampered by severe shortages of skilled and experienced professional personnel, and limited physical infrastructure. This has resulted in delays in the administration of justice, leading to prolonged pre-trial detention and detention without the necessary legal foundation, as well as overcrowding in the prisons and unrest among inmates. It has also favoured an increased reliance on the traditional dispute settlement mechanisms, even where they may not provide adequate protection for the rights of minorities, vulnerable groups and women. (UNSC 2003c: 5)[1]

There is no doubt that, like its predecessors, UNTAET was hampered by a debilitating lack of resources, experienced personnel and infrastructure, as well as the pressures of a tight mandate.[2] However, this chapter argues that several fundamental shortcomings in UNTAET's strategic approach also hindered its efforts to develop the rule of law.

First, UNTAET's piecemeal approach to building state rule of law institutions generated systemic dysfunction, confusion and lack of confidence.

Second, despite considerable efforts, UNTAET was unable to overcome key dilemmas in engaging the Timorese population. It did not meet Timorese expectations for "ownership" over rule of law issues or satisfy demands for a functioning judicial system, justice for past crimes and essential skills for Timorese. This caused resentment and challenges to UNTAET's authority and eroded support for rule of law initiatives. In eventually devolving more authority to the Timorese, critical processes fell hostage to local politics; security, police and judicial services were politicised; and UNTAET lost policy-making influence. Further, UNTAET suffered a crisis of relevance, because it was unable to bridge the disconnect between western and Timorese conceptions of justice and the rule of law or to deliver on the issues of greatest relevance to most people.

Third, a short mandate and a results-driven mentality led to insufficient investments in longer-term capacity-building in the rule of law field and in building state capacity more generally. UNTAET also gave insufficient attention to non-institutional aspects of rule of law creation that had a distinctly developmental focus, such as building trust and supportive social relationships.

Finally, UNTAET failed to develop a principled, informed approach to local justice regimes that remained as more functional competitors to the state justice system and contained elements that contradicted essential principles of the rule of law. This created confusion and undermined the legitimacy and integrity of the state justice system.

Rule of law landscape

UNTAET deployed into a rule of law environment that bore little resemblance to the western liberal model. Indonesia's failure to uphold its responsibility to maintain law and order in September 1999 and subsequent destruction of East Timor's state administration precipitated an almost total breakdown in the rule of law. What had in any case been rudimentary state justice institutions were destroyed, along with almost all physical infrastructure. Indonesian officials destroyed or removed all state legal records. Human resources were equally scant. All Indonesian judges, prosecutors, lawyers and judicial support staff had fled, leaving behind less than a dozen very inexperienced Timorese lawyers and a total pool of some 70 individuals with legal training of any description (Strohmeyer 2001: 50; Ministry of Justice/UNDP 2002: 5; Renouf 2002: 2).

The Timorese associated the state justice sector with repression and violence. The Indonesian occupation engendered a deep legacy of mistrust of the state and of all forms of legal authority, not least arising from the wholesale impunity granted to Indonesian officials for human rights violations perpetrated against East Timorese. The Indonesian administration used the courts to maintain dominance over the Timorese, including through the assertion of unpopular and repressive laws, generating an enduring perception of partiality in the judicial system (McDonald 2001: 9). Separation of powers did not exist, and village heads, the police, the military and intelligence organisations wielded and abused judicial power. Corruption in the justice system was common (Mearns 2002: 37). The Timorese thus avoided the courts, which in any case were geographically inaccessible to much of the population. They continued to rely heavily on customary community justice systems and many had had little exposure to formal state justice systems (KCL 2003: para. 219).

Timorese mistrust of "rule of law" institutions was exacerbated by the social trauma surrounding the post-ballot violence. As many as 2,000 Timorese died at the hands of Indonesian security and police forces and their Timorese proxies. A survey conducted in 2000 found that 97 per cent of respondents had experienced at least one traumatic event during the violence; 57 per cent had been tortured; 34 per cent suffered from post-traumatic stress disorder; 31 per cent had lost their father, 24 per cent their mother, 14 per cent their spouse, and 12 per cent a child (International Rehabilitation Council for Torture Victims 2000: 2). According to professionals working in the trauma response and reconciliation fields, trauma of this magnitude caused intense damage to social relationships and generated strong calls for "justice".

Initial steps by the international community to restore law and order were taken by the International Force in East Timor (INTERFET). Under its Chapter VII mandate and based on the Geneva Convention Relative to the Protection of Civilian Persons in Time of War, INTERFET established an emergency military quasi-judicial regime to handle criminal justice cases and a temporary detention facility. INTERFET personnel and UN Civilian Police (CIVPOL) deployed with the mission undertook military and policing functions. Within the limitations of mandate and circumstance, this was a generally creditable effort that avoided compromising most human rights standards and restored some basic elements of the rule of law. INTERFET was not, however, mandated to try criminal suspects and, upon UNTAET's deployment in October 1999, no civilian mechanism existed to provide even minimum judicial functions. UNTAET faced a pressing burden of pre-existing and new criminal cases relating to the atrocities of 1999 and a rising tide of lawlessness.

Setting the parameters: UNTAET's rule of law mandate

In contrast to Cambodia, from the outset the United Nations unambiguously recognised the need for a comprehensive approach to the rule of law, which it acknowledged as critical to the overall objectives of the operation (Strohmeyer 2001: 47). UNTAET was given a broad rule of law mandate under Security Council Resolution 1272 of 25 October 1999, which empowered UNTAET with "all legislative and executive authority, including the administration of justice". Top billing in UNTAET's mandate was to "provide security and maintain law and order", reflecting the high priority accorded to this function. The resolution stressed the importance of reconciliation between pro-integration and pro-independence supporters and called for justice for violations of international humanitarian and human rights law.

The Secretary-General's report to the Security Council of 4 October 1999 elaborated a concept of operations that prioritised action on the rule of law. "Judicial Affairs" and "Civilian Police" comprised two of the six core areas of UNTAET's governance and public administration component. Recognising the urgent need for action prior to the full deployment of UNTAET, the report envisaged the early deployment of CIVPOL to assume responsibility for law and order and to prepare an East Timorese police force (UNSC 1999c: 5). The report further recommended the dispatch of legal experts to East Timor to provide "immediate legal advice and to assess the legal and judicial systems, including existing laws and other information which would be necessary in devising a properly functioning administration of justice" (UNSC 1999c: 5). It highlighted the objective of creating "non-discriminatory and impartial institutions, particularly those of judiciary and police, to ensure the establishment and maintenance of the rule of law and to promote and protect human rights" (UNSC 1999c: 7).

The report elaborated UNTAET's responsibilities with respect to establishing a court administration, prosecution service and prisons, the development of legal policies, the review and drafting of legislation and the assessment of the "quality of justice" in East Timor, including training requirements. It pointed to the need for immediate action to establish an independent and impartial judiciary, through an interim judicial panel to be replaced by permanent East Timorese judicial professionals. It stressed the need to re-establish the prison system and to amend legislation to accord with international human rights standards. It tasked UNTAET to establish a land and property rights commission to review legislation and provide a mechanism for the redress of abuses (UNSC 1999c: 10–11). With respect to policing, UNTAET was charged with providing interim law enforcement services and developing a professional and impartial East Timorese police service.

UNTAET was thus given a uniquely comprehensive mandate that both strongly endorsed rule of law objectives and provided the requisite authority to pursue them. In this respect it was a vast improvement on the United Nations Transitional Authority in Cambodia (UNTAC). However, UNTAET's mandate suffered from three flaws. First, it did not provide specific guidance on how UNTAET was to meet these objectives, or guarantee the resources to do so or provide benchmarks against which progress should be assessed. Second, the mandate was not backed by political or practical support from the Security Council or other key parties to a level sufficient to achieve its core objectives. Third, by "pushing the envelope" so far, the mandate virtually set itself up to fail, creating unrealistic expectations that dissolved into disappointment, especially for the Timorese.

Establishing state justice institutions

This section examines UNTAET's efforts to steer the development of a constitutional and legislative framework and to establish judicial, law enforcement and correctional bodies. I argue that, although each of these objectives was met to some degree, UNTAET made errors in design and implementation that had the effect of institutionalising flaws and confusion in the post-transition state justice system, leaving it dysfunctional to the point of collapse.

Constitutional framework

The Constitution of the Democratic Republic of East Timor, adopted on 22 March 2002, provided for a democratic state based on the rule of law and separation of powers. It allowed for an elected president and national parliament and enshrined fundamental rights and freedoms as per the relevant international covenants. Protections related to the rule of law were comprehensive. The constitution guaranteed the independence of the courts and the judiciary and provided for the establishment of an Ombudsman, an office of the Prosecutor General and a Superior Council for the Judiciary to manage and discipline judges. In recognition of the role of traditional justice processes in East Timor, the constitution also undertook to "recognise and value the norms and customs of East Timor that are not contrary to the Constitution and to any legislation dealing specifically with customary law".

As such, the final product was broadly consistent with international standards including the United Nations' rule of law objectives, although some departures from this have been noted (Charlesworth 2003: 331). Nonetheless, UNTAET's failure to exert a positive influence over two aspects of the constitution-drafting process raised questions about the extent to which the document would prove useful in advancing rule of law objectives.

First, some rule of law provisions suffered at the hands of inexperienced drafters intent on retaining control over what was a highly sensitive political process. The drafting was overseen by the Timorese Minister for Justice and drew on an earlier draft by the National Council of Timorese Resistance (Conselho Nacional de Resistencia Timorense, CNRT), which was based heavily on Mozambique's constitution. Human rights and judicial monitoring organisations in East Timor expressed serious concerns that key issues relating to the judiciary were omitted during the initial stages of the drafting process. The court system was not even mentioned, for example. Although this was later rectified, other omissions remained in the final document. The jurisdiction of the courts was left unclear, fair trial guarantees were poorly organised and there were few safeguards on the abuse of executive power.

Second, the Timorese leadership failed to consult on the document, particularly Fretilin. This not only revealed anti-democratic tendencies but raised concerns about the future legitimacy of the document. Public outreach was virtually non-existent; less than half of respondents to a nationwide survey in 2001 knew anything at all about the existence of a constitution (Asia Foundation 2001: 28). In March 2001, the National Council rejected a bill creating a constitutional commission to consult Timorese people on the draft and in the event the only public consultation that occurred was a one-week process organised by the Constituent Assembly. The Timorese expressed frustration at Constituent Assembly members for not keeping them informed on the drafting process (NDI et al. 2002: 9). Even within the Constituent Assembly, however, consultation was poor. Fretilin's win in the 30 August 2001 Constituent Assembly elections allowed it to control the cabinet and the Constituent Assembly and to draft and pass the constitution without taking into account the views and aspirations of other political parties. It did not provide information on the drafting to other political parties and, critically, controlled the decision over how the political balance of power was to be distributed (Charlesworth 2003: 328). Fretilin thus shored up its own access to power and weakened other potential checks and balances.

Legislative framework

In responding to the legal vacuum left by Indonesia's departure, UNTAET developed a hybrid legal system that, although innovative and closer to international standards than its predecessor, was incomplete and confused. Inevitable practical and political difficulties in implementing changes to the legislative framework were compounded by UNTAET's failure to take systematic steps to ensure that the legislative framework had a solid grounding that was both understood and supported by its users. By UNTAET's departure, important legislative gaps remained and even groups such as the judiciary and police were unclear as to the applicable law.

The choice of Indonesian law as the applicable law during the transition was contentious and remained problematic after independence. Although not recognised *de jure* by the United Nations, since 1975 it had been the de facto applicable law in East Timor. With a view to providing continuity and avoiding the practical difficulties of reverting to Portuguese law or introducing a new legal code, UNTAET declared Indonesian law applicable except where it was inconsistent with international human rights standards (UNTAET 1999a). Although this was a logical response, inadequate and ad hoc implementation of this decision seriously undermined the ability of UNTAET, and later the Timorese government, to develop and apply a cohesive legal regime. Additionally, UNTAET's failure to ensure full support in both political and judicial circles for what was in fact a highly political decision caused ongoing problems.

Although several Indonesian laws, including the death penalty and the Anti-Subversion law, were repealed quickly, UNTAET never completed a full review of Indonesian laws and their consistency with international standards. Inexperienced lawyers thus lacked comprehensive guidance on how to interpret the compatibility of Indonesian law (Strohmeyer 2001: 59; McDonald 2001: 13). Where amendments were made, they tended to be knee-jerk reactions to emerging problems, creating confusion and at times suspicion about UNTAET's motives. In one instance, in August 2000 a Japanese activist who had criticised Gusmao was arrested and detained for 18 days under the defamation provisions of the Indonesian Criminal Code, before the Transitional Administrator issued an urgent executive order repealing the relevant provisions of the Code and he was released (Linton 2001). This haphazard response generated uncertainty about which other provisions might be repealed and, more importantly, fed perceptions that UNTAET could change the law at will to suit its own needs.

The Dili District Court did not obtain a full set of Indonesian legislation until December 2000 (Pritchard 2001: 188), and by late 2001 UNTAET's Legal Office still had no Indonesian legal texts, knowledge of Indonesian law or the skills to interpret it. Different components of UNTAET translated and used Indonesian laws on a needs basis, including CIVPOL, who faced enormous difficulties attempting to enforce unknown and inaccessible Indonesian laws (KCL 2003: para. 226).

UNTAET further confused the legal regime by promulgating over 70 of its own regulations covering a provisional tax and customs regime, banks and currency exchange, justice bodies and a defence force.[3] Although the regulations arguably were necessary to ensure a legal basis for basic functions of state, they were rushed through and gaps remained. UNTAET legislation on the judiciary did not, for example, provide adequately for the separation of powers between the Ministry of Justice and the judiciary, allowing the judiciary to exercise executive powers of government and, conversely, the Cabinet Member for Justice to control judicial appointments and legal aid procedures (Yayasan HAK 2001). The process of disseminating new legislation was also patchy. UNTAET legislative acts were initially disseminated via a Gazette, but this became irregular and had lapsed by 2001 (KCL 2003: 228).

Regulation No. 2000/30 on the Transitional Rules of Criminal Procedure, passed on 25 September 2000, exemplified the positive and negative aspects of UNTAET's efforts at legislative reform. The code represented a significant effort at compliance with international standards, offered detailed coverage of all stages of criminal proceedings, and provided for statutory protection of accused persons, victims and minors. It also set the parameters for the powers of investigating authorities and the courts. At the same time, the absence of a clear and sensitive strategy caused problems during drafting and implementation. In the drafting process, UN legal officers drew on those laws with which they were most familiar, which resulted in vague and contradictory terminology in early drafts and an uneasy hybrid of civil and common law in the final draft (McDonald 2001: 13).

Similarly, Timorese jurists resentful at an inadequate consultation process for Regulation 2000/15 on Panels with Jurisdiction Over Serious Criminal Offences voiced strong opposition to the draft shortly before the National Council was due to debate it (Linton 2001). They were able to force an extended consultation period that resulted in the substantial revision of the initial document, but not before further resentment had flared. Errors in translation of the regulation into Bahasa Indonesia (the official language of Indonesia) added another layer of confusion (Pritchard 2001: 189). CIVPOL and judicial officials were not advised or trained in the operation of the new law, and multiple versions of the draft continued to circulate for months after the regulation was promulgated.

The end result of UNTAET's legislative initiatives was patchy application of Indonesian law, layered with UNTAET regulations and INTERFET military codes. Other alternatives to UNTAET's "band-aid" approach have been mooted. Linton (2001) argues that, although Indonesian law is not progressive by international standards, with some modifications it would have provided a workable basis for a transitional legal code. Another option might have been to apply an off-the-shelf transitional legal regime, had one existed, to allow time for a comprehensive and consistent Timorese legal regime to be developed.

The judiciary

Despite a clear commitment by both UNTAET and the East Timorese leadership to building a reliable judiciary, UNTAET fell far short of achieving this goal. An initial clear vision for urgent judicial reform evaporated quickly in the face of poor strategic planning, piecemeal initiatives, incompetent implementation and domestic political impediments.[4] Early teething problems and "temporary" measures were not adequately addressed and became institutionalised as permanent deficiencies. This section examines the first of two parallel criminal justice systems established by UNTAET: the ordinary court system, which had jurisdiction over all criminal activity except serious crimes committed between 1 January and 25 October 1999 – these were handled through the establishment of the Special Panels for Serious Crimes, discussed below.

By UNTAET's departure, criminal justice processes fell significantly short of international standards. The UNTAET Human Rights Unit and other monitors detailed frequent violations of due process, including unlawful detention, inadequate access to defence counsel and the inappropriate release of suspects. UNTAET Human Rights officers and others working in the justice sector recorded a range of instances where the courts did not adhere to the UNTAET Transitional Rules of Criminal Procedure but continued to follow Indonesian procedures or devised their own methods. Trials commonly proceeded with little or no defence evidence, with the defendant's statement often constituting the only "proof". Detention periods were renewed arbitrarily and, in the absence of any notification system for expired detention warrants, without even the knowledge of the public defender. The courts continued to be dominated by personalities and in some cases were subject to executive interference, entrenching public perceptions that "important people" were subject to a different law from the rest. Prosecutors compromised their independence, and public defenders were extremely under-prepared and under-resourced (JSMP 2003a: 2). An overwhelming backlog of cases prevented the timely delivery of justice in most instances. The situation continued after independence and was exacerbated by the non-functioning of the Court of Appeal for 19 months between May 2002 and July 2003, owing to delays in the appointment of foreign judges and of the Court President.

The situation was worse outside Dili, where courts were non-operational for extended periods of time. In the Oecussi enclave, for example, virtually no criminal cases went before the court for the first two years of UNTAET's mandate. Although a district court was "opened" in June 2000, by late 2001 it had been unable to hear a single case because of the absence of an investigating judge and of two out of three trial judges. The Oecussi court referred cases to the Dili District Court, which, owing to an excessive workload, accepted only 4 or 5 of some 280 cases, of which only 2 were completed. All other criminal matters in Oecussi for the preceding two years had not been to court and either remained stuck in the backlog or were resolved through *adat* (customary practices or laws). CIVPOL struggled to comply with the 72-hour detention rule and to conduct investigations. Oecussi had few judicial officials and the renovated courthouse could not be used without a full complement of staff. In the absence of basic transport links, it was not possible for a panel of judges to travel to Oecussi to hear cases on a needs basis, for the Oecussi prosecutor to get to Dili for training, or for the families of prisoners transferred to Dili to visit them. An UNTAET Human Rights Officer in Oecussi reported in late 2001 that community leaders regularly raised these problems with UNTAET district staff, who felt that they could not rebuild confidence in the rule of law or persuade the community to use the formal justice system until they had at least had the opportunity to see the formal justice system working.

This situation seems to have been caused by several key factors, as follows.

Flawed and delayed structures and regulatory guidelines

No court structure was established until five months into the mission, leaving judicial and police personnel to introduce contradictory and confused practices unilaterally. A court system was finally established in March 2000, under UNTAET Regulation 2000/11, but UNTAET proved unable to implement the intended structure of eight district courts of first instance and a single Court of Appeal. It established only four district courts, which functioned sporadically, and it took until February 2001 – nearly a year after it was established – for the Court of Appeal to begin to hear cases. Regulation 2000/11 did not adequately stipulate the duties of judges, particularly of investigating judges, or procedures for pre-trial detention. This was remedied with substantial amendments to the regulation in May 2000, when the number of courts was also reduced to four.

Although guaranteed under Regulation 2000/11, the right to legal representation was similarly slow in coming. A Public Defenders Office appears to have been established as an afterthought, and its status and that of six public defenders appointed in May 2000 remained unclear until the promulgation of an enabling regulation in September 2001 (UNTAET 2001i). The Public Defenders Office remained weak, particularly compared with the public prosecution service. It initially functioned without a budget or support staff and remained the most under-resourced part of the judiciary. Timorese defenders had no experience and by late 2001 only one UNTAET-sponsored international public defender was appearing in court. The Chief Public Defender battled to provide a quality service in these circumstances, assessing that this seriously undermined a key check and balance in the judicial system and increased perceptions of its inaccessibility. UNTAET Human Rights officers were aware that the absence of legal aid, apart from limited services provided by nongovernmental organisations (UNFPA 2001: 13), tended to work in favour of the accused. UNTAET's eventual attempts to sponsor an additional two international defenders and to establish a legal aid service were resisted by the Minister for Justice (KCL 2003: para. 232).

The public prosecution service, established in June 2000 under Regulation 2000/16, was better resourced. It suffered, however, from a key regulatory weakness in that the independence of the Prosecutor General, who was responsible for the administration of the national prosecution service, was not expressly provided for. The Ministry of Justice quickly began to play an influential role in the activities of the prosecution service, fuelling public perceptions regarding state control of the judiciary (Linton 2001).

Chronic resource shortfalls partially explain these problems. Strohmeyer (2001: 53–55) describes in detail the resource burden of trying to establish an entire judicial system in the set-up phase of a resource-stretched peacekeeping operation. Inadequate harnessing of available resources compounded the resource shortfalls. With no forward budget planning or centralised coordination of donor funding, the justice sector was left to compete, unsuccessfully, for limited funding. Staff appointments were delayed. Despite the United Nations' commitment to an urgent response, UNTAET Judicial Affairs department staff did not arrive until three months into the mission, and the failure to appoint a Director until May 2000 compounded the lack of cohesion among staff from many disparate jurisdictions and legal backgrounds, causing conflicting views over how to develop judicial policy (McDonald 2001: 12). In the courts themselves, useful human resources were not harnessed appropriately. For example, Suhrke (2001: 15) argues that, although Timorese staff could not match the international staff in technical and administrative skills or experience, they possessed a range of valuable skills, such as language, that international staff failed to appreciate.

Beyond the perennial resource issue, the delays and omissions can also be explained by the mission's preoccupation with the political transition, which precluded it from giving due attention to longer term rule of law issues. There was a strong perception among UNTAET officials working in the judicial area that the "main game in town" was the National Council and the election of a Constituent Assembly, while critical "nuts and bolts" issues had to struggle for attention.

Inadequate capacity-building

Ironically, UNTAET's decision to bring in an exclusively Timorese judiciary from the outset undermined its rule of law objectives. The decision was based on the political and symbolic importance of empowering East Timorese judicially for the first time. No Timorese judges had been appointed during the entire Indonesian occupation and there was a strong desire in UN circles to place this area firmly in the hands of the Timorese from the outset (McDonald 2001: 10). The decision also stemmed from the desire to minimise later disruption, from a lack of international lawyers and from the potential benefits of limiting translation burdens (KCL 2003: para. 230; UNSC 1999c). However, the decision came at the expense of ensuring that a competent emergency judicial regime was installed and that due process and international standards of procedure were upheld. No international judges or prosecutors were appointed initially; the East Timorese appointees had no prior professional experience, were given only minimal training and did not have sufficient grounding in the fundamentals of the rule of law (KCL 2003: 240). Not surprisingly, they struggled to cope with the demands of an excessively heavy and complicated caseload.

This had obvious repercussions for the functioning of the courts, but also for UNTAET's relationship with the judiciary, which in its frustration began to react with increasing hostility. At the same time, many of the potential benefits of high-level "Timorisation" were lost when Timorese judicial officials were not consulted on key policy decisions (Katzenstein 2003: 256). UNTAET later changed its policy and moved UNTAET Judicial Affairs officers into some judicial positions. International judges, defenders and prosecutors were also appointed, particularly for appellate proceedings and for the Serious Crimes Panels. However, the bulk of the judiciary continued to comprise inexperienced Timorese unaided by essential support structures.

Training of judicial personnel was insufficient to meet both short- and long-term needs. Initial training for judges, prosecutors and public defenders consisted of one-week "quick impact" courses in Darwin followed by mandatory ongoing training and a mentoring scheme under which international jurists provided on-the-job advice to Timorese counterparts without actually exercising judicial power. UNTAET recognised this initial training as inadequate but argued that limited resources and time precluded anything better (Strohmeyer 2001: 56). In early 2000 a more comprehensive training programme was begun, combining academic-style teaching and mentoring. Several judges, prosecutors and public defenders attended training courses in Portugal, and court registry staff received some training and mentoring. No steps were taken to establish a permanent education system to begin training more lawyers. Although a Judicial Training Centre was opened after independence, with the first class sworn in in June 2006, it was open only to current judicial appointees (KCL 2003: para. 233).

UNTAET's judicial mentoring programme was an innovative approach to enabling Timorese jurists to come on stream immediately, but proved generally unsuccessful. It faltered when mentors were diverted to other jobs within the system, spending almost all their time in court and not on mentoring work. The programme also suffered from a lack of support from the Director of Judicial Affairs, language difficulties, lack of trust, inappropriate professional background and mentoring style (UNDP 2001b: 8–9; Katzenstein 2003: 269). As described by a prominent East Timorese lawyer and human rights activist,

I was one of only a few of these [Timorese lawyers] who had ever actually worked in a court ... The new judges and others needed much assistance from the mentors. However, in fact, they received very little. In a few cases good mentors were appointed and they helped a lot. But it is sad to say that in the majority of cases international mentors did not have the experience, language or desire to really help. Some were there just to earn a big salary, with little care to build the skills of our people.... Because of this situation many of the

East Timorese lawyers were forced to work and to learn alone.... they needed proper training and a serious mentor program. Without this program we are faced with a long battle to achieve acceptable standards for our lawyers. (Guterres Lopes 2002)

UNTAET's emphasis on appointing judges and building courthouses came at the expense of adequate capacity-building in court administration. The cost of not implementing basic court administration systems, including trained support staff, was that the judicial system fell further below international standards and public confidence was further eroded (JSMP 2001: 29). A problem that caused particular chaos was the lack of sufficient translation or interpreting resources for the four working languages of the courts: Tetum (the predominant indigenous language in East Timor), English, Portuguese and Bahasa Indonesia. Court staff could not necessarily speak Timorese languages and judges, particularly international judges, could not always speak Portuguese or Tetum. The language barrier also meant that the public could not follow the legal process, which weakened public confidence in the judicial system.

The deficiencies in capacity-building reflected in part the usual resource shortfalls and time pressures. Even those UN officials who professed to be dedicated to skills transfer and Timorese ownership faced time pressures and commonly found it easier to do the jobs themselves than to transfer skills. However, it also reflected an underemphasis on capacity-building that derived from UNTAET's overriding focus on the need for identifiable "deliverables" that could be ticked at donor conferences and in reports to the Security Council. This precluded a more long-term developmental focus and made it difficult for UNTAET to carry forward initiatives that were inherently developmental in nature.

Problems with the Ministry of Justice

There was a firm perception amongst UNTAET officials and other international and Timorese observers that the Ministry of Justice in the East Timor Transitional Administration, which assumed responsibility for managing the judiciary in September 2001, had impeded its development. Like other aspects of the Timorisation process (see below), this allowed the Timorese to take early responsibility for line functions but in some cases created unexpected impediments for UNTAET officials trying to oversee the establishment of fledgling organisations and services. UN-TAET legal officials described the difficulties they experienced gaining access to ministry decisions and the Ministry of Justice became notorious for a closed door approach. Senior officials within the ministry were accused of poor management and UNTAET officials felt that what little progress had been made in developing the judiciary was deliberately stymied by the ministry for political reasons.

The minister pursued a clear political agenda to install political supporters across the judicial system and to ensure that the Portuguese legal system and language prevailed. The ministry ended non-Portuguese projects and rejected major funding offers from non-Portuguese sources that it perceived would undermine its agenda. The minister purged the ministry and the judicial system of non-Portuguese elements, recruiting Portuguese speakers behind the back of English-speaking incumbents whose contracts were then shortened or not renewed. Although in one sense this alleviated the confusion caused by trying to put together a team of people from different jurisdictional backgrounds, it also eradicated experienced staff and useful projects. For example, a New Zealand court registration system project was never replaced and progress that had been made towards implementing a court registration process quickly disintegrated.

Local and international judges and prosecutors also complained of inappropriate interventions by the minister and ministry officials (Babo-Soares 2001: 14). For example, a Brazilian federal prosecutor who acted as Prosecutor General during 2000 accused the Minister of Justice of having issued illegal arrest warrants and interfered inappropriately with the work of court personnel (Vasconcelos 2001).

These problems pointed to two dilemmas faced by UNTAET. The first was how to deal with the "clash of cultures" between various nationalities or jurisdictional backgrounds in the mission – in UNTAET's case the divide between the Portuguese and the "Anglo" camps. The second was how to ensure that the devolution of decision-making power to powerful "local" individuals with different views from UNTAET on the way forward, or who did not have the requisite judgement or skills to perform appropriately, did not undermine the mission's objectives. The latter issue is discussed in more detail below.

Law enforcement

Unlike the limited powers of CIVPOL deployed in Cambodia, CIVPOL in East Timor were charged with a broad two-pronged mandate: to enforce law and order during the transition period; and to establish and train a new national police force for East Timor. UNTAET's experience demonstrated that the ability to enforce law and order depended on operational issues such as logistics, the calibre of CIVPOL contingents and the quality of strategic direction, environmental factors such as the accessibility of locations, and, critically, the extent to which the broader judicial environment was supportive of CIVPOL objectives. This section argues that the relatively good levels of law and order that prevailed in East Timor during the transition resulted more from luck than from design, with both arms of CIVPOL's mandate compromised by chronic weaknesses in other parts of the justice sector, internal weaknesses in CIVPOL, a lack of strategic planning and poor capacity-building.

The role of CIVPOL

Law enforcement functions that were initially handled by INTERFET military police were transferred to UN CIVPOL in January 2000, when 400 CIVPOL were deployed from 29 countries across East Timor's 13 districts. They had a broad mandate that included investigative powers and, eventually, the right to bear arms (UNSC 2000c: para. 50).

The shortcomings of the UNTAET CIVPOL contingents themselves in terms of skills, coordination and direction have been well documented elsewhere.[5] This section seeks to add to the literature by focusing on how CIVPOL's mandate was undermined by UNTAET's failure to adopt an integrated approach to rule of law initiatives and to overcome crippling logistical problems. Other key issues, including CIVPOL's attempts to build trust, are discussed separately below.

The chronic weakness of the legal and judicial sectors had a major impact on the ability of CIVPOL units to conduct their duties effectively and to build community confidence. CIVPOL generally did not know the applicable law or have the means to uphold it. Court delays contributed to the excessive detention of suspects, and a lack of public defenders saw the denial of rights to representation in detention. CIVPOL regularly administered justice independent of the courts, undermining due process and further confusing local communities, who found it difficult to distinguish between police and court responsibilities.

The experience of a CIVPOL team leader deployed in Bagia, Baucau, in 2000 was indicative. Heading a disparate team comprising an Austrian, a Jordanian, an Egyptian and a Nepalese, the Australian sergeant faced an uphill battle maintaining law and order in the absence of any direction from UNTAET superiors, equipment or communications. The biggest problem identified by the team leader, however, was the lack of any clear legal or juridical framework. Although aware that she was "meant to be implementing Indonesian law", she had no access to those laws. She arrested and detained suspects unaware of whether she had any legal authority to do so, without the guidance of any UNTAET basic procedures or protocols and in the knowledge that there was no functioning prison or court. The team leader made operational decisions based on "commonsense and a test of reasonableness ... if I had to explain my actions in an Australian court, would I be found reasonable?" Villagers in the Baucau area expressed confusion at the inconsistency with which CIVPOL applied various forms of law and seldom understood the basis for CIVPOL actions, which sometimes caused resentment over arrests.[6]

In these circumstances, she described the team's efforts to maintain law and order as a "bluff act", in which her team "probably breached just about every human rights issue in the book, just to get something done".

CIVPOL were further confounded by crippling logistical problems. The Baucau team lived a two-hour journey from their patrol area, and 7 of the 10 sub-districts for which they were responsible were inaccessible owing to poor roads. The team had no direct communication with these districts, responding to informal requests from the village chiefs to involve themselves in crimes. If the village chief did not want the United Nations to become involved, CIVPOL were not informed of the crime. Murder investigations were hindered because the evidence was usually lost by the time CIVPOL arrived. The team had no communications links or liaison protocols with CIVPOL headquarters or the courts. As a result, suspects were transferred to Dili District Court with no information about the nature of their crime or arrest.

The only positive contribution to improving the rule of law that the officer was able to point to during her three-month rotation was a successful road safety campaign and the opening of a jail in Baucau. Other CIVPOL expressed similar frustrations in attempting to fulfil their law enforcement mandates.

Establishment of the East Timor Police Service

UNTAET made significant strides in establishing a national police force from scratch. Training began in February 2000 with an initial class of 50 recruits, and the East Timor Police Service (ETPS) was established on 27 March 2000.[7] During the transition period, CIVPOL and the ETPS operated under the common command of an international police commissioner and police officers were deployed under the supervision of CIVPOL. Operational responsibility passed to the ETPS as officers and districts acquired certification. By independence in May 2002, the Police College had recruited and trained some 1,800 East Timorese police officers. By September 2003, the ETPS reached its full strength of 2,800 officers. It assumed full executive policing responsibility in January 2004, with CIVPOL retaining an advisory role.

UNTAET's experience in establishing the ETPS demonstrated the difficulty of developing a professional policing agency within a tight timeframe. By UNTAET's departure, the ETPS remained inexperienced and underdeveloped. It was not sufficiently prepared to maintain law and order in a manner consistent with international human rights standards and officers regularly violated these standards, including using excessive force and torture (AI 2003b: 1; OHCHR 2003: 7). Given the legacy of corrupt and abusive policing in the territory, the lack of resources and the scale of the task, this was not surprising. However, there were other, perhaps avoidable, impediments that arose through lack of strategic planning and domestic political problems.

Along with a dearth of resources, the CIVPOL Commissioner identified the biggest challenge in establishing the ETPS as the lack of adequate legal and procedural regulatory structures. Like CIVPOL, the ETPS suffered operationally from uncertainties over the question of applicable law. In addition, the legislation under which the ETPS was established was both incomplete and not fully consistent with international human rights standards, particularly with regard to the use of force. Standards for conduct and accountability in basic procedures such as arrest, custody and detention rights were not established, opening the door to violations and inconsistencies (AI 2003b: 2). In addition, UNTAET failed to secure full support for its legislation. The legitimacy of the UNTAET police laws, and later of the United Nations Mission of Support in East Timor (UNMISET) code of police conduct, was undermined because of a tendency to view them as "temporary" until a "permanent" Timorese law could be developed (OHCHR 2003: 7). The ETPS also lacked oversight and accountability mechanisms. Complaints against ETPS officers were dealt with internally by the CIVPOL Professional Standards Unit, with no legal, procedural or institutional framework established to deal with complaints against officers. As a result, complaints against police were not adequately dealt with and, despite government commitments, this remained an issue well after UNTAET's departure.

Gradual progress was made post-UNTAET in clarifying and further developing the legislative framework, operating procedures and a code of conduct. However, even after the ETPS assumed full executive policing responsibilities, there remained a high degree of ignorance among police officers of their powers and duties under the relevant legislation, including policies on arrest and detention and the use of force (OHCHR 2003: 7–8). Although this is in part attributable to inadequate training, it may also be the case that, had regulations been introduced consistently and in full from the outset, much confusion might have been avoided.

UNTAET's recruitment process was problematic and again reflected the unresolved challenge of how to harness local resources while upholding standards of neutrality and good practice. Hence CNRT's role in vetting former militia members and other criminals in the recruitment process was invaluable, but it allowed it to exert excessive influence over the choice of recruits, undermining the fairness of the process (Mobekk 2001: 43). The police force was further politicised by the recruitment of ex-combatants from the National Armed Forces for the Liberation of East Timor (Falintil), which led to violent protests against the police as candidates from competing veterans' groups battled for recruitment. A further problem was the recruitment of Timorese who had served in the

Indonesian police force, who were fast-tracked because of their policing experience but who were not versed in democratic policing techniques and had in some cases been involved in violence, human rights abuses and corruption.

Another dilemma relating to recruitment was the deployment of young police officers to patrol their home district. On the one hand, benefits were to be derived from familiarity with their environment. On the other, they remained junior actors in a very hierarchical system and were susceptible to partisanship, particularly given their reliance on family connections for food and accommodation (Mearns 2002: 36). In Liquica district, for example, all ETPS officers came from local families and were uncomfortable about asserting law and order over families and friends. They proved particularly reluctant to become involved in cases of domestic assault.

Capacity-building was again a problem. The three-month cadet training courses run by the Dili Police College fell well short of the usual time-span for training. In addition, there were not enough quality interpreters or trainers who could communicate in local languages (Mobekk 2001: 48). ETPS officers entered the field without many basic policing skills, and their CIVPOL colleagues were ill qualified to perform a mentoring role. The differnet policing styles of the various national contingents meant that on-the-job training was not consistent and, having little background in policing (let alone human rights), many CIVPOL required monitoring themselves. Language difficulties meant that the new recruits often could not even ask their CIVPOL colleagues questions about policing techniques (Mobekk 2001: 50). The training process was gradually improved after independence, but in the absence of accountability measures, and with ongoing regulatory weaknesses, it was questionable how much effect this would have.

Although there was no guarantee that good law, sufficient training and careful thought to political dilemmas of recruitment would necessarily have translated into good policing for either CIVPOL or ETPS, their absence certainly compromised UNTAET's ability to fill the security gap. It also left a legacy of problems that the fledgling East Timor government was ill equipped to resolve.

Prisons

Like other parts of the justice sector, UNTAET failed to establish a properly functioning correctional service, which continued to suffer from multiple operational weaknesses after independence. International correctional standards were seldom adhered to, even over basic issues such as the provision of clean water (UNDP 2002a: 3). Again, the interdependence of justice sector agencies and lack of strategic direction appear to have been major contributing factors.

The painfully slow rehabilitation of East Timor's three prisons, which were not operational until late 2000, seriously undermined the capacity of the justice system. Although a makeshift detention facility was installed by INTERFET, by March 2000 serious overcrowding forced UNTAET to release detainees and impose a moratorium on new arrests.

Even once prisons were up and running, the familiar problems of lack of legislative basis, poor training and the dysfunctional judicial system took their toll. A legislative basis for correctional facilities was not introduced until UNTAET Regulation 2001/23 of August 2001, almost two years after UNTAET was deployed (KCL 2003: para. 236). The regulation accorded with international standards, but key elements such as the requirement for UNTAET to issue a code of conduct for prison officials and disciplinary processes were never implemented. No independent mechanism for institutional oversight of prison conditions was established.

Again, the near paralysis of the judicial system exacerbated problems in the prison system. In particular, continued problems with the legality of detention well after UNTAET's departure contradicted notions of transparency, adherence to the law and fair play, making it very difficult for UNTAET or East Timor's post-independence government to change deeply entrenched perceptions of prisons as outside the law. The extent of the problem was evident at East Timor's largest prison, Becora. By November 2003, Becora's 242 inmates included 165 pre-trial detainees, of whom 70 were held on expired detention orders and 3 were juveniles held for over six months (OHCHR 2003: 4).

Prison guards were not well trained and prison escapes became a regular occurrence (Babo-Soares 2001: 16). The UNTAET Human Rights Unit consistently reported mistreatment of inmates, including children. The Human Rights Unit prepared a prison training manual and conducted some human rights training, but this and other assistance offered by UNTAET and donors proved ineffective in the absence of two fundamental ingredients: a clear and well-managed organisational structure and a publicly accepted strategic direction (UNDP 2002a: 6). A mission by the United Nations Development Programme (UNDP) to East Timor in August 2002 found that fundamental problems with the correctional system

> primarily stem from the absence of a coherent and publicly accepted correctional philosophy and a weak management in structure, oversight capabilities, and execution. Without a societal consensus, involving all the relevant actors, as to the purpose and objective of the [Timor-Leste Prison Service], and good management by which that consensus is actualised international assistance to the correctional system can be remedial at best, addressing narrowly defined matters of daily operational concern. (UNDP 2002a: 2)

The next section turns to look at this question more closely, by examining UNTAET's efforts to build societal commitment to rule of law objectives.

Building commitment

"The most you can do is be sensitive. If you are sensitive, you can make what you establish the property of the East Timorese."
　　　　　(Sergio Vieira de Mello, personal communication, November 2001)

UNTAET enjoyed a level of commitment from the political elite unheard of in Cambodia and Kosovo as well as a strong desire by the broader public to see a system of justice in place. Nonetheless, UNTAET was not fully successful in cementing this initial commitment because it did not meet Timorese expectations for a relevant, accessible and robust state justice system, was unable to deal effectively with the erosion of commitment within segments of the elite when this occurred, did not adequately address cultural issues, and, despite a concerted effort, had limited success in conferring ownership on the Timorese over rule of law processes.

Elite commitment

The devastation of 1999 generated misconceptions that the United Nations faced a *tabula rasa*. The reality was that East Timor remained politically complex, with long-established personalities, groupings and rivalries, a strong aspiration for self-rule forged through 25 years of resistance and considerable leadership skill despite centuries of disempowerment. Senior UNTAET officials quickly recognised the advantages and challenges this posed, but were never fully successful in engaging the political elite.

The Timorese political elite, particularly those returning from long periods of exile in the west, expressed a high degree of rhetorical support for rule of law principles.[8] This was matched in practice to a noteworthy degree, particularly given the lack of institutional checks and balances capable of restraining it. However, in some instances members of the political elite compromised rule of law goals and undermined UNTAET efforts. This generally occurred as a result of perceived political imperatives or from a desire to protect longstanding personal vested interests.

An initial threat to UNTAET's efforts to establish the rule of law came from the CNRT's frustration at the slowness with which UNTAET deployed, took action and, ultimately, devolved power. In an effort to fill the vacuum and to establish itself as the future government, the

CNRT quickly established parallel structures of governance across East Timor, directly challenging UNTAET's authority. In some areas, CNRT representatives informally exercised powers of arrest and detention, which they used to interrogate returnees suspected of militia connections (Linton 2001). This not only undermined UNTAET's already weak judicial outreach, but perpetuated popular perceptions of partiality in justice processes.

The CNRT's stranglehold over political processes was not adequately restrained by checks and balances. By 2001, signs of political interference in judicial processes had emerged. UNTAET officials identified an unreasonable level of politicisation of cases and some intimidation of Timorese judges, who did not vigorously prosecute certain community elements in positions of responsibility or respect, such as former Falintil and CNRT members (UNTAET Human Rights Unit 2001: 6; AI 2001). According to the UNTAET Human Rights Unit, individuals wearing Falintil uniforms had pressured unarmed CIVPOL to release their relatives from detention, and investigating judges linked with Falintil had declined to charge individuals with Falintil connections allegedly involved in kidnappings and rapes.

It was difficult for UNTAET to address this problem, given the expectations deriving from the Indonesian experience that cases would be resolved with recourse to political considerations and political and community pressure to ensure that former resistance fighters were "honoured". However, the shambolic state of the judicial sector ensured failure. For example, basic steps to enforce the separation of powers were not taken owing to resource constraints: the Ministry of Justice and the court shared premises, resources and personnel, for example. Moreover, lack of due process in court hearings, poor training of judges and inadequate court monitoring created opportunities for interference, which went unchecked in the absence of any mechanism for institutional oversight of judicial conduct.

The judicial elite

Although the judicial elite were to some extent politicised, they did not demonstrate strong vested interests against establishing the rule of law. Compared with UNTAC's experience, this was a major advantage in developing a relatively "clean", albeit inexperienced, judiciary. However, UNTAET eroded the potential of this resource to support its rule of law objectives. First, as described above, the judiciary was not adequately supported by resources or training, undermining its ability to make judgments consistent with the rule of law. Second, UNTAET alienated a large segment of the judiciary, which during the course of the mission increasingly resisted its initiatives.

This resistance arose from confusion and resentment over UNTAET's mishandling of judicial affairs, including a lack of strategic direction and inadequate training programmes. It was exacerbated by perceptions that UNTAET had failed properly to consult the judiciary or adequately to equip it for what was an extremely challenging portfolio (KCL 2003: para. 248). The resulting lack of respect for UNTAET's authority ultimately led to cases of flagrant judicial indiscipline.

This was highlighted in the very first substantive case heard by the Dili District Court, in which the judge refused to apply UNTAET law. The case involved murder charges against a former Falintil member, Victor Alves, who had been arrested by INTERFET in December 1999. In April 2000 his lawyers filed for his release and payment of damages on the grounds of irregularities under the Indonesian Code of Criminal Procedure, the applicable law at the time, including unlawful detention and arrest. On 10 May, the day before Alves' hearing, UNTAET responded by rushing through Regulation 2000/14, retroactively extending the time limit on detention beyond six months and validating all arrests and detentions made by investigating judges and prosecutors prior to 10 May. The judge interpreted the timing of the regulation as political interference in the outcome of the case and refused to apply it, on the grounds that it was discriminatory and violated universal human rights standards (KCL 2003: para. 235). Alves was released pending investigation by the Serious Crimes Unit (Linton 2001). No appeal could be heard because the Court of Appeal was not yet operational.

The incident set a damaging precedent for UNTAET's relations with the judiciary. UNTAET had a clear policy justification for passing the regulation: to avoid a flood of releases of militia similarly detained. However, the action revealed a failure to manage the already serious issue of excessive detention and to avoid being seen by East Timorese as abusing its legislative power by arbitrarily deciding to pass regulations to suit its own purposes. The parallels with the Indonesian administration would not have been lost on the Timorese judge (KCL 2003: para. 235).

Commitment from the broader community

UNTAET found it difficult to build community commitment to rule of law objectives. UNTAET's rule of law model rested on the formal judicial system, which was irrelevant and inaccessible to the majority of the population. It failed to address key issues of concern, was unreliable because of lengthy delays and logistical problems, and was mistrusted.

Most Timorese continued to have no contact with the formal justice system, relying instead on customary systems. This was partly because UNTAET was unable to overcome the problem of access to the court system, which remained difficult for a large percentage of East Timor's population. The idea of mobile courts was discussed early on in the operation, but not followed through. Even in Dili, people were reluctant to seek the help of police or to use the courts owing to the delays in processing and a lack of knowledge of how to mobilise their rights under the judicial system (Mearns 2002: 48).

Like Cambodians, East Timorese neither trusted nor understood the UNTAET-imposed judicial system. As Mearns (2002: 38) observed:

> [T]here was an acknowledged heavy reliance upon village processes for the administration of justice ... [T]here existed little understanding or trust of the formal system amongst many rural villagers. Local leaders expressed (an often repeated) hope that the confusion they felt at the moment regarding the lack of an "East Timorese" Law would be settled once the new independent government came into being in May 2002. Some local village heads told me explicitly that there was no law at present ... [F]or many villagers I met in my travels, the only regular authority in their lives remained these village heads ... It was understood that military power was in the hands of the UN and that a new police force was being created by the Civpol officers whom they saw on patrol, but there was little confidence or certainty in interacting with people who were outside the local system of social relationships.

UNTAET officials appreciated the need to build community commitment, but admitted to being at sea over how to do so. Some effort was made to promote support from civil society. Public outreach on justice issues was cited frequently as an important tool, but it was ineffective. Neither the Judicial Affairs Unit nor the Civic Education Unit organised public education or information dissemination on the role of the courts and Timorese did not as a rule know where to go to resolve a justice problem. CIVPOL had some success with efforts to build local capacity and ownership through the establishment of law and order committees in the sub-districts, with a view to creating district-wide structures for community leaders to discuss issues of concern. However, these structures were unable to overcome confusion about and reluctance to engage with new processes.

As in Cambodia and Kosovo, UNTAET failed to develop a system that could deliver acceptable justice on the issues of most relevance to most people. It failed to deliver justice for serious crimes committed during 1999, while nonetheless engendering a public perception that it was more interested in the serious crimes process than in the ordinary justice sector (KCL 2003: para. 254). This failure was most glaring on the two issues that affected a large proportion of Timorese: land rights and domestic violence.

Land and property rights

A major consequence of Indonesian occupation and the post-ballot violence was displacement of land and property. Portuguese and Indonesian
occupation introduced overlapping claims to land and property, on top of
traditional claims. The displacement in 1999 of almost all of East Timor's
estimated 900,000 people, including some 300,000 who were trucked or
fled to West Timor, coupled with the destruction of land and property
records, presented a major property rights challenge. It also posed a significant security threat as conflict erupted between returning refugees,
internally displaced persons and villagers over a severely depleted housing stock (Fitzpatrick 2002: 3–5). By late 2001, UNTAET's Land and
Property Unit had received over 700 complaints, particularly regarding
the issue of property transfer by non-Timorese and the restoration of
property to returnees.

Senior legal advisers in UNTAET identified the establishment of a
mechanism to address land and property ownership and disputes as one
of the key challenges in building the judicial system. From an early stage,
however, UNTAET largely disengaged from the whole issue. Fitzpatrick
(2002: 12–13) describes UNTAET's failure to develop a land registry, a
record of land transactions, regulation of foreign leases or a system to determine competing claims to land by returnees. This not only played into
continuing uncertainty, but, as the formal judicial system was established,
created problems for the courts, adding the issues of occupation and eviction to the tangle of unresolved legal issues and complicating reconciliation processes.

There appeared to be two key reasons for UNTAET's disengagement.
First, it was a complicated issue that required a massive investment of
time and resources to resolve. Second, in an effort to accommodate the
views of Timorese leaders on the National Council, UNTAET capitu-
lated to strong domestic vested interests. In particular, the powerful
Carrascalao family had amassed large landholdings under the Portuguese
and stood to lose by UNTAET's initial decision to take into account only
Indonesian titles. Joao Carrascalao threatened to quit the Transitional
Cabinet if land and property were not transferred to his portfolio. The
cabinet acceded, opening the way for massive conflict of interest (Gorjao
2002: 327). Furthermore, in December 2000 the National Council rejected a draft regulation to establish a land commission, purportedly
owing to a desire to leave legislation to a democratically elected government and to leverage reparations claims on Indonesia, and possibly to
fear of political conflict over land claims (Fitzpatrick 2002: 197). However, as Fitzpatrick (2002: 197–198) notes,

[This decision was] neither sustainable nor appropriate for a newly independent nation-state. Not only has it created, or failed to ameliorate, conflict over land and deterred the investment that is urgently needed for reconstruction and employment, it has allowed a new round of transactions and land occupations to be built on the highly uncertain foundations of opportunism and alleged ownership. This has greatly complicated the task of resolving competing claims to land ... [will] pose major challenges for institutional capacity ... [and produce a land claims framework that] will have to incorporate a bias in favour of these current occupiers.

A land dispute mediation programme instituted towards the end of UNTAET's mandate proved ineffective and, in the absence of any clear legal basis for land title and usage or a dedicated dispute resolution mechanism,[9] land ownership conflict remained a serious problem (Pritchard 2001: 188). It also opened up the potential for politicised or corrupt land decisions in contravention of the rule of law.

Domestic violence

Similarly, UNTAET did not respond adequately to community needs regarding domestic violence, and the bulk of cases continued to be dealt with outside the formal justice system. UNTAET did not attempt to enact domestic violence legislation because of perceived difficulties in overcoming cultural beliefs about the acceptability of violence against women. Although improvements were recorded in the response of judicial and law enforcement systems, with domestic violence accounting for up to 50 per cent of cases reported to the police (JSMP 2002c: 2) and 25 per cent of all cases before the courts by 2001 (UNFPA 2001: 2), the systems continued to suffer from delays, lack of sensitivity to the dynamics of domestic violence and entrenched beliefs among staff (UNFPA 2001: 6). No provision was made for legal aid for rape or domestic violence victims. Community leaders, police and judicial officials pressured victims to settle their grievances extra-judicially and there were even reports of women being turned away from police stations when they tried to file reports (UNFPA 2001: 6).

There was also no guarantee that victims would receive fair treatment in the courts or be protected from punishment for reporting the crime (Mearns 2002: 41). Reports of unequal justice relating to prominent persons further undermined trust in the court system. In one case, a prominent surgeon and Constituent Assembly candidate, Sergio Lobo, was let off by police several times for allegedly beating his wife, and subsequently was twice acquitted in court (UNFPA 2001: 3). On the second occasion, the judge overturned his conviction on the grounds that his medical skills were too valuable to waste (Fokupers 2001). At the same time, Lobo's wife was not given equal access to justice: she was not kept informed of the progress of Lobo's case or invited to appear at the review hearing (UNFPA 2001: 3).

Like the question of land rights, part of the reason for the lack of attention to domestic violence was the perceived intractability of the issue. In addition, for much of the mission, the focus was on dealing with criminal cases involving the militias, rather than issues such as domestic violence. This is understandable given the very high international profile of the militia issue and the imperative to deliver justice for the many victims of the violence. However the neglect of lower profile but equally far reaching issues missed an opportunity to reinforce the basic principles of the rule of law.

Community policing and building trust

CIVPOL's mandate to conduct "community policing"[10] was one endeavour where UNTAET directly attempted to build community trust for rule of law objectives. It registered some successes. A study by King's College London found that there had been a gradual build-up in trust between CIVPOL and the community, especially outside Dili (Mobekk 2001: 26). CIVPOL officers pointed to generally positive relationships at village level and cited a rise in the crime reporting rate as evidence of improved trust. Like their UNTAC counterparts, CIVPOL in East Timor found that providing concrete assistance to the community, such as shelter or health facilities, proved to be important both in building trust and in providing an outlet for groups, such as unemployed youth, who might otherwise be committing offences.

However, in seeking to build community commitment to and participation in its policing efforts, CIVPOL's approach was flawed in several respects. First, a clear model of community policing was not adopted and, in the absence of any implementation plans or guidelines, most CIVPOL were unclear about what the concept entailed and what they were expected to do (Mobekk 2001: 12). Different CIVPOL contingents adopted varying styles, causing confusion and contradictory behaviour that undermined trust.

Second, misunderstandings between CIVPOL and local communities impeded both policing efforts and the building of trust. Language barriers and inadequate local knowledge caused communication difficulties that resulted in reduced efficiency, underreporting of crimes, and in some cases a passive attitude by CIVPOL. In some cases the wrong people were arrested, or people were unable to report crimes because they could not make themselves understood at the police station. Most civil society groups did not understand CIVPOL's activities or how they were meant to participate in them, and formed negative images as a result (Mobekk 2001: 14, 18, 59). In interviewing Timorese leaders and other layers of the population, Mobekk (2001: 21) found universal agreement that CIVPOL needed a more extensive understanding of the culture and history of East Timor before the population would have trust and confidence in them. She also notes that CIVPOL failed to meet the two criteria that had proved crucial to the success of community policing initiatives elsewhere – public education and substantial outreach activities with community leaders (2001: 14). CIVPOL held meetings with community leaders, but these were not always successful in building an understanding of CIVPOL's role (Mobekk 2001: 18).

Third, CIVPOL did not make sufficient effort to address negative connotations regarding community policing that stemmed from the legacy of a brutal security apparatus reliant on informants (Mobekk 2001: 58). In some areas, CIVPOL was viewed as an "organ of repression" akin to the Indonesian Police (McFarlane and Maley 2001: 15). In a society that had known only destructive and corrupt policing, it was incumbent upon CIVPOL to educate the community thoroughly as to the functions of democratic policing.

A fourth factor was the failure to ensure that communities felt fully secure. In this respect, the arming of CIVPOL increased community trust levels because they were perceived as able to deal with any militia threats (Mobekk 2001: 52). However, CIVPOL did not address community discomfort about making complaints, particularly when this risked further conflict or retaliation. There was no mechanism to assure victims who made complaints that the perpetrator's family would not seek retaliation (Mobekk 2001: 35).

Fifth, CIVPOL encountered problems in gaining the support of local political structures. On the one hand, intact and strong community governance systems proved an asset in maintaining law and order, and village leaders were generally seen as approachable and eager to harness the "face of the United Nations" to help resolve community conflicts. At other times, however, CIVPOL officers struggled to overcome turf battles with village chiefs, or *liurai*, who feared they would be usurped and tried to prevent CIVPOL from becoming involved. CIVPOL made gradual progress in gaining the confidence of *liurai* and made extensive use of either the *liurai* or local priest in negotiation and mediation. In other cases, in working with local political structures CIVPOL unwittingly legitimised behaviour that contravened the rule of law. They were, for example, used by *liurai* as bargaining chips in raising bride prices.

Finally, Mobekk (2001: 53) argues that CIVPOL should have done more to assist the ETPS to build a relationship of trust that could be sustained after CIVPOL's departure. Mobekk's study found that, although civil society leaders expressed pride in having their own police force, they were cautious about trusting the ETPS because of concerns about corruption and a deep suspicion of security forces. Civil society groups believed the solution was for the ETPS to work hard to prove it was different from its Indonesian predecessor (Mobekk 2001: 54). Although it appears that much of the answer depended on allowing time for new trusting relationships to be built, CIVPOL could have assisted the process by providing more information to the public about the new police force and better training the ETPS to ensure that it did not fall into damaging patterns of behaviour.

Conferring ownership

The inclusion of Timorese in mission processes through UNTAET's "Timorisation" policy emerged as one of the key debates of the mission.[11] From the outset, UNTAET recognised that conferring "ownership" was essential to the achievement of core mission objectives, including the rule of law. Resolution 1272 and UNTAET Regulation 1999/1 obliged UNTAET to consult closely with representatives of the Timorese people and, as noted in the Secretary-General's report of 26 January 2000,

> A key objective [of the governance and public administration programme] is to ensure that the East Timorese themselves become the major stakeholders in their own system of governance and public administration, first by intensive consultation through NCC [National Consultative Council] and district advisory councils, and then through the early and progressive development of their capacity to carry out all necessary functions. (UNSC 2000c: para. 41)

It proved difficult to confer real ownership while at the same time ensuring that mission objectives were not compromised. At the elite level, the initial consultative mechanism established by UNTAET was the National Consultative Council (NCC), created in December 1999 to enable CNRT and other Timorese leaders to participate in policy decisions. The 15-member advisory body reviewed and endorsed all UNTAET regulations before their adoption. The process was extended to all 13 districts in April 2000 with the appointment of Timorese deputy District Administrators to understudy their international counterparts. District advisory councils were also established, composed of political, Church, women and youth group representatives.

These early measures proved unable to satisfy the aspirations and expectations of the Timorese political elite, who remained frustrated with UNTAET's slowness and determined to assume responsibility for running East Timor's affairs as soon as possible. As the Transitional Administrator acknowledged at the 2000 CNRT congress,

> UNTAET consulted on major policy issues, but in the end it retained all the responsibility for the design and execution of policy. What is more, the NCC came under increasing scrutiny for not being representative enough of East Timorese society, and not transparent enough in its deliberations. Faced as we were with our own difficulties in the establishment of this mission, we did not, we could not involve the Timorese at large as much as they were entitled to. (Sergio Vieira de Mello, quoted in Chesterman 2001a: 18)

UNTAET responded by establishing an innovative co-government model under which East Timorese shared direct governing responsibility in coalition with UNTAET and which created the basic structure of the post-independence government. In July 2000, a joint East Timorese–UNTAET "Council of Ministers" was established to exercise day-to-day executive functions. Four of the eight cabinet posts were allocated to Timorese and the remaining four (including political affairs, justice and police) to international staff. In August, the East Timor Transitional Administration (ETTA) was established as the "government" of East Timor, to replace UNTAET's governance and public administration pillar. In October, a 36-member, exclusively Timorese, National Council replaced the NCC. Although the Transitional Administrator retained ultimate power, these developments represented a significant shift in mission attitude and approach.

The model was problematic, however, both failing to satisfy the expectations of the Timorese elite and politicising key appointments. East Timorese cabinet members continued to express frustration at their level of involvement in key processes and decisions (Chesterman 2001a: 22). For its part, the UNTAET Transitional Administrator acknowledged the challenge of maintaining political neutrality, particularly in the lead-up to the elections, when Timorese leaders sought to prove that they, not UNTAET, were in control of the country's agenda.

"Timorisation" came to be equated with a heavy reliance on Gusmao and the CNRT and in some cases condoned the appointment of incompetent individuals to powerful positions based on political affiliation rather than merit. Gusmao essentially chose the four Timorese cabinet members (Chesterman 2001a: 20), resistance leaders were appointed to most areas of responsibility regardless of their abilities and civil service appointments were dominated by Fretilin supporters. Chopra (2002: 982–984) discusses how, in addition to institutionalising incompetence, this prejudiced the political process in the lead-up to the elections by entrenching Fretilin's position. As Prime Minister, Alkatiri established what amounted to one-party rule after the elections, controlling executive and legislative life and spawning divisiveness.

There were several negative implications for the rule of law. First, as discussed above, in the absence of sufficient checks on power, Fretilin's entrenched position enabled it to politicise the military, police and judicial systems. Second, UNTAET's poor relationship with the East Timorese Minister for Justice[12] meant it lost influence over justice sector policy and was unable to remedy problems in the justice sector before its departure. Third, UNTAET proved unable to ensure that those members of the Timorese elite to whom it had devolved power consulted with and satisfied the expectations of other sections of the elite and the broader population. Community criticism of the Constituent Assembly's failure to consult during the drafting of the constitution – the key founding document for the rule of law – is indicative. One study found that a "passionate" sense of ownership over the constitution and pride in the Constituent Assembly as "East Timorese making the basic laws for East Timor" gave way to criticism of lawmakers for not representing the people's aspirations and for using the Assembly to further their own interests (NDI, University of East Timor and Abrantes 2002: 14).

In other respects, Timorisation had a positive impact on rule of law objectives. UNTAET took an important early step towards building transparency and local ownership in judicial appointments by waiving the Transitional Administrator's power to make judicial appointments unilaterally and instead conferring this right on a Judicial Services Commission established in January 2000. The Commission was composed of representatives from the Catholic Church, human rights non-governmental organisations (NGOs), UNTAET Judicial Affairs staff and the East Timorese Cabinet Member for Justice (Strohmeyer 2001: 51). The move drew a line in the sand between the new regime and Indonesian rule, during which no East Timorese jurists were ever appointed, let alone by East Timorese.

Inculcating "cultural change"

A further explanation for UNTAET's failure to cement commitment to the rule of law was its struggle with the question of "cultural change". UNTAET demonstrated a more sophisticated understanding than UNTAC of the issues at hand, but faltered when it came to addressing them. This may partly be explained by the fact that UNTAET undertook no studies to document local cultural values or to establish whether there was a culture "gap" with respect to the rule of law. In addition, there was little strategic planning to address the question of how to build a culture of law and order. Practical steps revolved mostly around a limited education programme, conducted by the Human Rights and Civic Education Units, although these were very much focused on human rights discourse and paid little attention to other rule of law principles.

Aware of the need to avoid criticism of cultural imperialism and to sell their actions as meeting the cultural demands of the Timorese, the question of "cultural change" appears to have acquired a certain taboo element amongst the UNTAET leadership. The Transitional Administrator, for example, rejected the proposition that any major "cultural change" was required with respect to the rule of law:

> East Timorese are a simple people with an innate sense of justice not affected by colonialism. What cultural change is there to attempt? UNTAET is not trying to implement cultural change. What we are trying to achieve through the creation of courts, the Serious Crimes unit and the truth commission is to bring institutions and processes back into tune with what the Timorese expect. We are trying to restore what they lost or never had. (Sergio Vieira de Mello, personal communication, 21 November 2001)

Vieira de Mello argued that process rather than content was the critical determinant of success in "restoring" justice to East Timor. He argued that, "unlike the Kosovars", the Timorese were not "dogmatic" or "emotional" about issues such as the type of law to be introduced. Thus, for example, Timorese would not reject Indonesian law as the basis for the judicial system merely because it was Indonesian. What was critical, however, was sensitivity and close consultation in introducing a new judicial system to ensure that the Timorese felt it was their property, would be comfortable using it and would respect it.

Although the preceding analysis supports much of de Mello's argument, it was not necessarily the case that the conceptual nature of the justice system did not matter. Abstract notions of justice and equality before the law did not necessarily sit logically with East Timorese who had never lived in a democratic society and had been dominated by external actors (Portugal and Indonesia) that had enforced regimes antithetical to those values (Mearns 2002: 49). Even amongst the elite, there was a marked divide in cultural approaches between returnees and those who had stayed, with the latter generally less clear about and less supportive of western values. Amongst the broader population, a nationwide survey conducted in early 2001 found that there was little understanding of the meaning or implications of democracy: 37 per cent of respondents said that the term "democracy" had no meaning to them and 43 per cent said they could not think of an example of a benefit that democracy would bring them personally. Less than half demonstrated a basic and qualified understanding of human rights (Asia Foundation 2001: 3, 30).

There was also confusion about the relationship between democracy and the law, as Bishop Belo pointed out when he argued that "[d]emocracy demands being open to everyone, respecting everyone. But it also demands law. The idea getting around that the advent of democracy means one has the right to do whatever one likes, is not democracy" (*Cidadaun* 2001).

Traditional values and systems of justice were at times very different from western concepts. A domestic violence workshop conducted in Viqueque district in 2002 reflected the extent of the cultural divide:

> [I]t became apparent that both men and women disputed the fundamental values being propagated by the two European UN women and their local assistants. Some men virtually described their ideas as a new form of colonialism saying that the Timorese were now free and laws should reflect their values not those of the UN. Women told me, in the absence of any other men, that a reasonable level of violence towards a wife was acceptable if she misbehaved. Some of the women involved were well educated and very articulate but they remained committed to a worldview that the western women found incomprehensible. This extended to the desire to keep a brideprice system "because this shows how our parents value us". However they were prepared to concede that current rates (around 30 buffalo and other payments) were probably too high. Clearly, the value systems inherent in village people's understandings and their systems of justice remain significantly at odds with those of the western educated social transformers employed by the UN. (Mearns 2002: 50–51)

By not taking sufficient steps to bridge the disconnect between its conception of the rule of law and Timorese cultural understandings of justice, UNTAET generated resentment amongst some Timorese that values were being imposed upon them. Concerns also arose that the Timorese would absorb values and standards they did not necessarily understand. Gusmao reflected both this concern and his doubts about the legitimacy of UNTAET as a vehicle to disseminate new values when he argued:

> We are witnessing another phenomenon in East Timor; that of an obsessive acculturation to standards that hundreds of international experts try to convey to the East Timorese, who are hungry for values: - democracy (many of those who teach US never practised it in their own countries because they became UN staff members); - human rights (many of those who remind US of them forget the situation in their own countries); - gender (many of the women who attend the workshops know that in their countries this issue is no example for others); - NGOs (numerous NGOs live off the aid "business" to poor countries); - youth (all those who remind US of this issue know that in their countries most of the youth are unemployed) ...

It might sound as though I am speaking against these noble values of democratic participation. I do not mind if it happens in the democratic minds of people. What seems to be absurd is that we absorb standards just to pretend we look like a democratic society and please our masters of independence.

What concerns me is the non-critical absorption of (universal) standards given the current stage of the historic process we are building ... What concerns me is that the Timorese may become detached from their reality and, above all, try to copy something which is not yet clearly understood by them. (Gusmao 2000b: 1)

UNTAET struggled to engage with Timorese notions of justice, many of which were not accommodated in UNTAET's more legalistic conception. A recurrent theme in Timorese discourse was that justice should be conceptualised not as a narrow legal process but as "social justice" – the creation of a "fair" society offering basic socio-economic security. Influential Timorese as diverse as the head of the Timorese Socialist Party, the chair of the Catholic Peace and Justice Commission and District Administrators in remote areas emphasised to me that success in implementing new justice processes and changing modes of conflict resolution depended on placing "justice" in the broader context of socio-economic imperatives, including employment. UNTAET could conduct education to change people's understanding of the law, but this would not translate into changed beliefs and behaviour unless the right socio-economic conditions were in place. Gusmao agreed: "We have to find a balance between social rights and the right to justice narrowly defined in the formal sense of the law, judiciary, trials, punishment and prison. If we only narrowly define justice in this formal way we will have ignored much that is important to people's lives" (Gusmao 2001b).

UNTAET failed to make a clear link between these concepts of "social justice" and its rule of law policies, or to seek to demonstrate the causal link between the establishment of the rule of law and the achievement of socio-economic objectives. On a local level, this meant that socio-economic and justice objectives were seen as not mutually supportive but as competing demands. The District Administrator in Maliana, the site of some of the worst violence of 1999, argued for example that militia killers should be punished and people should have regular access to justice, but his priorities were those of the majority of villagers: the economy, water, health and education. They could not afford to spend time worrying about justice when there were so many other pressing needs. In this respect, programmes such as that instituted by the Cambodia Resettlement and Reintegration programme that explicitly linked reconciliation and the rule of law to economic development objectives might have helped bridge the gap.

Rebuilding social relationships

Although East Timorese social networks were traumatised and displaced by the violence of 1999 and the abuses of Indonesian rule, some important and robust collective social relationships proved resilient (Patrick 2001: 51). At village level, although disrupted by the mass deportation of the population and the rifts caused by militia violence, social networks based around the village *liurai* and the *adat* system remained relatively intact. Routines, conceptions of status and patronage networks resumed relatively quickly after September 1999. In terms of civil society, the CNRT resistance network and the Catholic Church stood out as engendering cohesion and trust and promoting many values consistent with democratisation objectives. Encompassing some 90 per cent of the population, the Catholic Church was the most active civil society organisation under Indonesian rule and all early NGOs under Indonesian rule were Church based. The Church played a leading role in conflict resolution and the provision of public services such as education and healthcare. It provided a locus for resistance and during the violence offered protection to thousands of Timorese. Similarly, the underground CNRT network established deep connections across East Timorese society, relying on the trust of whole communities for its survival. Beyond mobilising the resistance movement, it provided an umbrella for strategic development planning for possible independence.[13]

State–society linkages on the other hand were weak and characterised by a high degree of mistrust. East Timorese perceived the state as an external imposition and society was generally reluctant to engage the state constructively (Meden 2002). Civil society groups, notably the Church and the CNRT, mobilised the population in "resistance" to, not cooperation with, the state. Ordinary Timorese avoided contact with the state wherever possible. The Indonesian authorities marginalised East Timorese from most areas of the administration, relied on coercion as the primary means of control and suppressed most channels for interest representation beyond the *liurai*, who were often rewarded for their compliance through corruption. Local political leadership had evolved and functioned in a non-state environment and was contingent on a hierarchical system based on ancestral legitimacy. The concept of a state whose citizens enjoyed equal rights and in which state bodies divided along executive, legislative and judicial lines was thus alien (Hohe 2002: 582).

UNTAET was, therefore, faced with a situation where the erosion of social networks and trust was not as severe as it had been in Cambodia, but where state–society linkages upon which western concepts of the rule of law relied were weak. Unlike UNTAC, UNTAET made some key efforts to build trust, particularly through support for reconciliation processes. By working with the Church and supporting the growth of the NGO community, it also attempted to support the development of civil society and with it the growth of constructive state–society relations, although it arguably could have done so in a more strategic and organised fashion.

The Church maintained a strong social influence after 1999 and participated in a wide range of development activities during the UNTAET period (Meden 2002). The extent of its importance in organised social activity was reflected in a survey that found that 49 per cent of respondents belonged to a religious volunteer group, but only 4 per cent participated in an NGO (Asia Foundation 2001: 55). In the lead-up to the 1999 ballot, the United Nations strongly supported Church involvement in reconciliation work and the search for a political solution to the East Timor question. UNTAET continued to work closely with the Church to build political legitimacy and trust, for example by including a representative of the Catholic Church on the National Consultative Council and ensuring that Church leaders were visibly represented at major events. The UNTAET-sponsored Commission for Reception, Truth and Reconciliation (Commissao de Acolhimento Verdade e Reconciliacao, CAVR) worked hard to gain the Church's support for its work.

Meanwhile, the Church continued its close involvement with donor agencies in the delivery of community development assistance and undertook its own reconciliation work, including using Church services and events to "socialise" concepts of peaceful conflict management (K. Robertson 2000). Both UNTAET and the Timorese leadership strongly supported the Church's role in the democratisation process, including confidence-building and civic education regarding elections and human rights issues (Catholic News Service 2002). UNTAET provided a supportive environment for these contributions; however, it is an open question whether UNTAET could have been more proactive and systematic in using Church networks as a legitimising force. Again, the limiting factor appears to have been UNTAET's desire to maintain a balance between utilising the Church and maintaining the separation between Church and state. Many Church leaders were reluctant to involve themselves too deeply in "political" activities at the expense of religious duties, so it is debatable whether UNTAET could have tipped the balance further.

With the politicisation factor much greater, UNTAET struggled to find any constructive way to harness the CNRT network as a means by which to encourage the growth of supportive social relationships. The CNRT, however, took matters into its own hands and used its status and networks to develop community groups and consultation mechanisms that remained after independence. Although the political bias of the CNRT network introduced its own set of problems, it is arguable that it contributed significantly to the building of trust between the new state administration and the population and the development of citizen participation in political processes. As CNRT's head, Gusmao in particular was a critical asset in building trust across Timorese society and between society and the state. To the extent that UNTAET developed any policy to deal with the CNRT network, it could be characterised as benign tolerance rather than active support. UNTAET and other organisations such as the National Democratic Institute for International Affairs (NDI) meanwhile established their own grassroots civic education programmes to build citizen participation in political processes.

NGOs

UNTAET's key strategy for building state–society linkages was to support the growth of civil society through the NGO movement. With UNTAET's help, longstanding human rights NGOs such as Yayasan Hak and Fokupers were re-established and the NGO community grew exponentially. The East Timor NGO Forum was re-established in late 1999 as the key umbrella group for NGOs, and by 2002 it had over 200 members (East Timor NGO Forum 2002). It included a number of legal aid NGOs, such as Ukun Rasik An, Liberta and Lembaga Bantuan Hukum Timor Lorosae, as well as a Bar Association. An East Timorese National Jurists Association was founded in February 2000, comprising some 100 East Timorese law graduates and human rights activists. The rapid growth of the NGO sector and its ability to play a successful advocacy role, including on rule of law issues, suggests that UNTAET made a significant contribution to the development of civil society.

UNTAET and ETTA made a number of positive efforts to institutionalise NGO–state relations. NGOs participated in the first World Bank Joint Assessment Mission in October 1999 and attended donors' conferences from the very first meeting at Tokyo in December 1999. In 2001, ETTA established a National Planning Commission and a Consultative Commission on Civil Society (led by Gusmao), which provided opportunities for the government and civil society to cooperate on national development planning. There was some degree of interchange between prominent civil society members and government or quasi-government organisations: the NGO Forum's Executive Director, Arsenio Bano, was appointed as a government minister, for example, and the head of Yayasan Hak, Aniceto Guterres Lopes, was appointed the chair of the CAVR. Little direct engagement occurred in the justice sector until the establishment in March 2004 of a National Dialogue on Justice, in which senior judicial officials engaged civil society in debate about the justice system through a series of public meetings across East Timor (USAID 2004; Gusmao 2004).

Despite this support, UNTAET and the international donor community underestimated the capacity and expectations of Timorese civil society to play a role. During the critical opening phase of the mission in particular, civil society actors tended to be marginalised by international actors in the humanitarian response, causing resentment and criticism (Patrick 2001: 56; East Timor NGO Forum 2001a). Disgruntled civil society groups refused to participate in East Timor's first civic education programme and it was not until early 2001 that they agreed to play a role (Chesterman 2001a: 17). UNTAET, UNDP and other donors provided capacity-building programmes and human rights workshops to help address the lack of experience and capacity of most NGOs (Patrick 2001: 62). However, as Patrick (2001) argues, they paid insufficient attention to this need. This was particularly the case in rural areas, where most of the population lived. Furthermore, insufficient attention was given to helping civil society adjust from a stance of resistance to one of constructive partnership with the state (UNDP 2001b).

Strengthening state capacity

As discussed above, UNTAET under-prioritised capacity-building in the judicial sector itself. More broadly, UNTAET made few efforts to equip the fledgling state apparatus to cope with the demands of finishing and operating the legal regime it had begun. UNTAET undertook only limited transition planning to help create the conditions for legal policy formulation by the government, including unsuccessful attempts to create a body of government lawyers and civil servants with specialised legal drafting skills. The UNTAET Judicial Affairs Unit attempted training and mentoring activities, and discussed but did not follow through with creating a Law Commission. Similarly, the office of the Deputy Special Representative of the Secretary-General undertook only limited planning for the administration of justice following the transition (KCL 2003: para. 237).

There appear to have been several reasons why most of these initiatives stalled. First, less tangible priorities gave way to more pressing visible needs such as the restoration of court infrastructure and the appointment of a judiciary. Second, UNTAET officials were reluctant to be seen to be predetermining a future legal regime and thus usurping the sovereign rights of the future East Timorese government (KCL 2003: para. 237). Third, after the Second Transitional Government was created in September 2001, responsibility for justice policy and institution-building tasks fell to the East Timorese Minister for Justice, who appears to have been concerned less with justice initiatives than with power issues in what was a fluid political situation.

More broadly, UNTAET was criticised for its failure to establish a modern state administrative system at district level and below, where the majority of the population lived. UNTAET retained the 13-district state administrative structure imposed by Indonesia and installed international District Field Officers and later Timorese understudies who served as the main contact point between UNTAET and the bulk of the population. Hohe (2002: 582–583) provides an insightful study of how UNTAET's district administration system, particularly the system of appointing Timorese district officials, did not conform to the population's traditional ideas of political legitimacy and thus had difficulty gaining acceptance. It was further hampered by inadequate efforts to build the administrative capacity of district officials. As the Timorese District Administrator in Liquica noted, "There are problems between the internationals and the locals, although cooperation with CIVPOL is alright. Most people are farmers; we do not know how to write proposals or to get funding for community ideas. They do it but they do not teach us ... There are language courses but they do not give us very much" (A. Ximenes, personal communication, 23 November 2001; my translation from Bahasa Indonesia). In the face of such problems, the Head of Administration for Local Government and Development, the body responsible for administering the 13 districts, concluded that UNTAET had done so little to build the capacity of ETTA that it faced being only a "marginally viable administration" after independence (Nixon 2002: 15).

UNTAET had even more limited administrative reach below district capitals, with little structure or legal basis for local government below village level. Local governance systems varied by village and remained the responsibility of village chiefs and elders, intertwined with the CNRT's parallel clandestine structures (NDI et al. 2002: 18, 22). This tended to perpetuate traditional local socio-political structures, which were not designed to support the needs of a modern democratic state – including rule of law institutions. In some cases, UNTAET's attempts to create democratic state structures caused collapse or anarchy in the existing social system. Some aid projects, for example, undermined traditional communal work systems, and civic education on democracy was at times interpreted to condone ignoring the village chief or authority, leading to anarchy in the village (Hohe 2002: 582–583). In either case, by not developing a more considered strategy to deal with state administration at the level that affected the majority of the population, UNTAET denied itself the opportunity to influence processes and systems that had an integral bearing on justice at grassroots level.

Restoring security

Deployed into a much more benign security environment than was the case for UNTAC or UNMIK, UNTAET had greater opportunity to promote the rule of law through effecting a transition from violent to nonviolent forms of power acquisition and conflict management. Even so, some persistent internal security issues undermined the rule of law. The politicisation of the F-FDTL and the democratic model introduced under UNTAET polarised alliances and the security apparatus, threatening future instability. As described above, this was dramatically manifested in the unrest of April–May 2006 and revealed the ease with which the executive politicised not only the security agencies but the ministries charged with their oversight. It also revealed the absence of adequate regulatory frameworks, as well as capacity deficits (UNSC 2006b: 9).

The INTERFET intervention and the presence of the UNTAET peacekeeping force ensured a relatively stable security environment during the UNTAET mandate. Militia activity was contained; internally, crime was reduced to relatively low levels, particularly given the high unemployment rate and the longstanding climate of violence endured under Indonesian rule. However, some internal security issues had a bearing on law and order, including disturbances by marginalised former guerrilla fighters and the unemployed, the creation of gangs in the towns, and petty crime resulting from the slow introduction of law and order (Babo-Soares 2001: 3). Each posed a moderate threat to social stability.

UNTAET oversaw the development of the F-FDTL, ultimately extending its military mandate in East Timor until it was fully prepared to stand alone. Although UNTAET made creditable progress in this task, a lack of clarity persisted in the delineation of military and police responsibilities, and an adequate legal framework governing the F-FDTL's activities was never fully developed. These problems were exacerbated by the reluctance of former Falintil fighters in the F-FDTL to accept ETPS authority in civilian law enforcement and by a lack of government confidence in the ETPS that saw it call in the F-FDTL to undertake policing roles (AI 2003b). Further, as the crisis of 2006 demonstrated, the perceived bias towards Falintil members from the east in the recruitment of the first F-FDTL battalion in February 2001 was never fully resolved (UNSC 2006b: paras 57–58). The F-FDTL also continued to suffer from many of the same problems of other fledgling institutions in East Timor, such as poor training, lack of resources and continued resort to human rights abuses.

The issue of parallel security groups posed a further threat to security and the rule of law. Small unofficial security cadres composed of former CNRT members and demobilised and disaffected Falintil fighters emerged in 2000 in some areas, performing a "security role" that included unlawful arrests, assault and murder (UNTAET Human Rights Unit 2001: 4). Although these groups never developed into a fully fledged parallel security structure, they threatened the legitimacy and efficacy of CIVPOL, the ETPS and the F-FDTL as the sole organisations responsible for maintaining law and order (Mobekk 2001: 55; Shoesmith 2003: 249). UNTAET monitored and sought to disband these groups, but security gangs, particularly those aligned with the Popular Council for the Defence of the Democratic Republic of East Timor (CPD-RDTL), remained in East Timor after independence. Some old clandestine groups established under Indonesia were also revived (Wainright 2002: 12–13).

The dual presidential/prime ministerial leadership system formalised in the constitution institutionalised the political struggle between Gusmao and Alkatiri. The intense friction between the two personalities had a destabilising effect, culminating in public rioting in December 2002 after a public attack by Gusmao on the government. Political alliances were polarised and by late 2001 it was apparent to UNTAET that the two arms of the security apparatus – the Gusmao-controlled F-FDTL and the Fretilin-controlled ETPS – had become caught up in the struggle (Shoesmith 2003: 246). This posed a threat to the rule of law, both in terms of undermining the separation of powers and in terms of strained relations and violent clashes between the two groups in 2002. Some veterans' groups also perpetrated attacks on police in late 2002, culminating in riots in Dili. Again, this seems to have partly resulted from allegations that the Interior Minister (Rogerio Lobato) had sought to politicise the ETPS through recruitment policy, although this appeared to have been resisted by the Timorese and UNTAET police commissioners (Shoesmith 2003: 250).

Reflecting the inverse relationship between rule of law and security, the legal vacuum that persisted for many months after UNTAET's arrival allowed continued room for crime, violence and retaliations. This undermined the public's sense of security and, with it, their confidence to conduct daily life. The frustration caused by a lack of access to justice also exacerbated the potential for violent conflict.

One such instance involved tensions between two communities in Oecussi over unresolved justice for the 85 victims of the Passabe massacre of September 1999. Although investigations were completed by April 2000, the Serious Crimes Investigation Unit (SCIU) did not issue an indictment until September 2001, leaving both sides confused and dissatisfied. Both communities expressed a strong desire to resolve the conflict, but threatened to withdraw from the formal justice system because of the delays. Numerous alleged militia members suspected of perpetrating serious crimes enjoyed continued impunity. By mid-2001, the victim

communities had begun to vent their frustration by stoning vehicles, setting up road blocks and severing relations with Passabe village leaders.
UNTAET district staff sought to draw the parties into a reconciliation
process, but the victim villages demanded justice first. The parties resorted to an *adat* process but, after failing to resolve the first killing case,
concluded that *adat* was not appropriate and they would wait for the formal justice system. Tensions grew. A mass held by Bishop Belo in Tumin
in October 2001 nearly triggered a violent eruption, after which 10 men
from one of the victim villages assaulted a man from Passabe. Although
UNTAET district officials reported their concern that frustration had
grown to such a level that violent conflict between the villages had become a very real prospect, no steps appear to have been taken to resolve
the problem (UNTAET 2001b: 1–4).

Addressing informal justice structures

The issue of informal or "traditional" justice or dispute resolution structures commanded a higher profile in the minds of UNTAET policy
makers than of those in UNTAC or UNMIK. A wide variety of such
structures existed across East Timor, particularly in rural areas (Mearns
2002: 28–29). Customary leaders retained significant influence in their
communities despite Portuguese, Indonesian and then UNTAET efforts
to introduce new patterns of governance and political authority. The
vast majority of disputes in East Timor during the UNTAET period
were dealt with outside the formal justice system; in some rural areas
with little or no access to the formal justice system, 99 to 100 per cent
of cases were resolved through *adat* (Mearns 2002: 26). According to
UNTAET officials working on "traditional justice" issues, domestic violence and rape, which constituted an estimated 50–70 per cent of all
crime in East Timor, were usually resolved through *adat*. In general, it
was only if *adat* did not succeed that cases were reported to CIVPOL,
although even in remote areas there was a consensus that for very serious
cases – usually murder or a serious injury – CIVPOL should be informed
at the outset.

Although traditional justice systems were not formally sanctioned,
UNTAET condoned and at times encouraged their use. UNTAET's
National Security Adviser viewed traditional justice systems as "the
fundamental social fabric that binds communities together and ensures
community stability", observing that "to ignore traditional East Timor
could disturb the rule of law continuum and unsettle security both at a
community and national level" (National Security Adviser 2001a: 1). It
was also the view of officials working in the Adviser's office that all major

problems in East Timor, with the exception of militia incursions in late 2000, had resulted from a breakdown in law and order, and that traditional justice could be very important in addressing this in the absence of sufficient capacity in the formal justice sector. Workshops discussed the potential of traditional justice as cost-effective, efficient, flexible, acceptable to traditional authorities and supportive of reconciliation objectives. On the ground, CIVPOL and the judiciary pragmatically encouraged the use of traditional justice, recognising that the formal justice system could not deal in a timely and visibly just fashion with the number and nature of local complaints (Mearns 2002: 29, 39).

UNTAET recognised a systemic gap in failing to develop a principled, informed approach to traditional justice, but did not address it. It did not thoroughly investigate the desirable spheres of operation of traditional justice systems with modern approaches to the rule of law or develop a mechanism to harmonise the two (National Security Adviser 2001a: 1; Coy 2001). Although the idea of incorporating traditional structures was raised, including by East Timorese, at the planning and initial stages of UNTAET, concrete proposals were never developed (KCL 2003: para 253). The Office of the National Security Adviser initiated broad-ranging justice consultations, but they died out owing to the lack of a sustained focus within UNTAET. The longer-term need for detailed research was identified but not addressed, constrained by a lack of time, resources and relevant expertise in UNTAET and by the difficulty of finding Timorese who understood regional and vernacular variations in *adat*.

UNTAET's continued ad hoc reliance on traditional justice undermined its own rule of law objectives. First, the lack of consistency with which various elements of UNTAET, notably CIVPOL, referred issues to traditional justice mechanisms undermined the integrity of the rule of law regime they were trying to develop. As the National Security Adviser noted:

> In the absence of clear political direction, arbitrary decisions are often being made at the local level as to what falls within the purview of customary law. This can further damage the credibility and effectiveness of the rule of law. Additionally, the credibility of the police services is often undermined by alternate figures of authority. (National Security Adviser 2001a: 1–2)

In most districts, CIVPOL freely encouraged villagers to resolve domestic violence and minor issues within the traditional justice system. In some cases, the refusal of CIVPOL to intervene despite requests to do so led to the retaliatory torture and murder of suspects (Mearns 2002: 46). In many other instances, UNTAET officials felt that the police and formal justice system lost credibility because victims did not understand

why CIVPOL would not intervene. Given that cases were seldom referred to CIVPOL until *adat* had already failed, victims found being referred back to *adat* extremely frustrating. As reported by one UNTAET
District Human Rights Officer:

> At its most basic, it's about lazy policing. It's obviously much easier for the
> police to not keep any formal record of cases if they can just refer it to adat.
> The other factor is that there are many issues which the community believe
> are police issues and not social issues. Most are associated with family law
> issues, such as adultery ... issues about child support ... marriage disputes ...
> The community find it difficult to understand why the formal justice system
> will not or cannot assist with these cases. Women advocating for the rights of
> other women are particularly mystified.

Judges also blurred traditional dispute resolution mechanisms with
their authority in the formal justice system, particularly with respect to
domestic violence, where in some instances judges ordered payment of
compensation rather than fully prosecuting cases (Halliday 2001). The
civilian administration was also confused about the delineation. For example, the Maliana District Administrator admitted that, although he
was clear on the delineation of serious crimes and ordinary crimes, he
was not clear about which ordinary crimes could be referred to the formal justice system and which were meant to be resolved informally.

Second, the use of traditional justice systems did not necessarily deliver
justice for the victims in accordance with international human rights principles. Examples included community pressuring of individuals to confess
crimes, the use of the bride price, domestic violence rulings that did not
give equal rights to women and children, the lack of a right to appeal and
punishments involving torture and murder (Mearns 2002: 46). Moreover,
most local justice processes rested on the central organising principles of
consensus and the restoration of normal social relations between conflicting parties, neither of which necessarily amounted to justice for the victim (Mearns 2002: 49).

At the same time, insufficiently accounting for the incompatibility of
western concepts of justice with key elements of local justice, particularly
reciprocity and compensation, undermined the legitimacy of the formal
justice system. Removing the perpetrator from the scene through imprisonment or imposing fines payable to the state rather than direct reparation to the victim or victim's family, for example, did not lead to full
resolution at the local level, raising the prospect of ongoing conflict
(Mearns 2002: 54). Local communities also resisted justice processes
that potentially threatened traditional mores. One District Human Rights
Officer, for example, observed a high degree of resistance to the CAVR

because it was believed to undermine the use of *adat*. Senior CIVPOL officers also reported that, despite conducting awareness programmes, they found it extremely difficult to supplant traditional justice measures involving domestic violence, to influence local views or to get the village *liurai* to cooperate.

The question of how to deal with traditional justice remained unresolved by the time of UNTAET's departure. In response to a sizeable domestic lobby, traditional justice systems were formally recognised in the constitution (Mearns 2002: 63–69). However, the East Timor government did not make efforts to determine the appropriate use of traditional justice vis-à-vis the formal justice system, and the problems described above continued.

Dealing with the past

If Bosnian Serbs had returned soon after Dayton and sought a public meeting, they would have been slaughtered. Eighteen months ago, militia commanders were brought back from West Timor to Baucau, Viqueque and Los Palos. The militia leader who returned to Los Palos attended a town meeting in Los Palos. He had blood on his hands ... he was a militia killer. He made a public confession and the population cried. Timorese have an innate sense of how to do justice and an incredible capacity to forgive. If wrongdoers ask for forgiveness and are ready to face justice, theoretically they could be pardoned by Gusmao, return to Los Palos and truly be forgiven. That is why I am optimistic about finding credible justice in East Timor.

(Sergio Vieira de Mello, personal communication, 21 November 2001)

UNTAET made a concerted effort to seek "credible justice" for the past in East Timor in response to strong expectations by Timorese and international actors and a consensus at the United Nations that dealing with the past was vital to secure a lasting resolution of the conflict and to establish the rule of law (UNGA 1999a: para. 42). There was a strong consensus from an early stage that Timorese people were "crying out for justice", although attitudes within and outside UNTAET differed as to how this should be achieved (Interim Office of the Commission for Reception, Truth and Reconciliation 2001: 2; Robinson 2002; Babo-Soares 2001: 10; Christian Solidarity Worldwide 2001; *Cidadaun* 2001). A wide range of actors in the Timorese political elite and civil society concurred that security and democratisation objectives, such as building the rule of law, depended on delivering justice for past crimes. Resentment and unfinished business between pro-independence and pro-integration actors continued to breed insecurity, fears of recrimination and uncertainty about multi-party democracy, whereas failing to pursue justice sent a damaging signal about the future direction of the country. As the head of the Timorese Socialist Party Avelino Coelho put it:

> Pursuing justice and reconciliation is part of building the principles, values and instruments of our new society. It will help regulate society. We need a justice process. How can you set killers free while you enforce traffic regulations? You will never be able to convince people of the advantages of obeying the law this way. It creates a confused situation. If you want to enforce the laws, there must be a clear philosophy behind them. (Avelino Coelho, personal communication, 26 November 2001)

UNTAET developed an innovative approach that sought to balance the principle of individual criminal accountability with the imperative of promoting reconciliation, recognising the practical realities of an over-stretched court system and the need to work with the militia in West Timor to repatriate some 250,000 refugees. It established three key initiatives, each of which represented a first for the United Nations: an UNTAET-run tribunal to prosecute serious crimes, including crimes against humanity, murder and torture; a truth and reconciliation commission to conduct truth-seeking and to establish community reconciliation processes to handle lesser crimes; and reconciliation processes to deal with refugee returns. The United Nations also supported the establishment of an Indonesian tribunal to try perpetrators of the 1999 atrocities. Although an international tribunal was also mooted, support progressively waned at the United Nations and this option was never pursued.

The success of these initiatives was impeded by severely limited administrative capacity in the justice system; reliance on Indonesia to fulfil its obligations regarding the repatriation of refugees and the ad hoc tribunal; UNTAET incompetence; and difficulties in accommodating and balancing the actions of East Timorese leaders and local notions of justice. To the extent that the process was seen as a litmus test of UNTAET's commitment to the rule of law, it was not an overall success, although some advances were made in delivering acceptable justice for the past. These initiatives are discussed in turn below.

Serious crimes

Created under UNTAET Regulation No. 2000/15 in June 2000, the Special Panels for Serious Crimes were unprecedented in UN history. Established in the Dili District Court, the panels had universal jurisdiction over the "serious crimes" of genocide, war crimes, crimes against humanity, murder, sexual offences and torture perpetrated between 1 January and 25 October 1999. The panels were of mixed jurisdiction and composition:

each panel comprised two international and one East Timorese judge and applied a combination of Indonesian and international law. The legal provisions incorporated many key elements of the Rome Statute of the International Criminal Court.

As the only body in a position to prosecute crimes in accordance with international standards, the Special Panels disappointed many in their failure to deliver timely outcomes or bring to justice the majority of perpetrators. Trials began in January 2001, but by December 2001, two years after UNTAET's establishment, only one case had been completed, with 10 Timorese sentenced in relation to killings in Los Palos. By February 2004, the Special Panels had made 81 indictments and charged 369 persons, but had made only 44 judgments and 46 convictions (UNTAET Serious Crimes Unit 2003; UNSC 2004a: 6). Of those charged, 281 remained at large in Indonesia, including the alleged ringleaders of the 1999 violence – former Minister of Defence General Wiranto and other high-ranking military and police officers (UNTAET Serious Crimes Unit 2003).

Indonesian obstructionism was only partly to blame for the failure of the panels to deliver comprehensive justice. UNTAET's own organisational dysfunction played a key role (Hirst and Varney 2005: 1). First, logistical support for the Serious Crimes Investigation Unit (SCIU, which later became the Serious Crimes Unit, or SCU) was inadequate. Despite the obvious major legal and financial burden of the panels, and in stark contrast to other international war crimes tribunals, the SCIU did not have its own budget and it suffered from severe shortages of human and material resources.

Second, continuity and momentum were lost as responsibility for investigations was repeatedly shifted. Responsibility initially rested with Australian military police during the INTERFET operation; it was then transferred to CIVPOL in December 1999, to the UNTAET Human Rights Unit in March 2000, to an UNTAET prosecutorial service in the Judicial Affairs department from June to August 2000, then to the Serious Crimes Investigation Unit. After independence, the SCU worked under the legal authority of the Prosecutor General (UNTAET Human Rights Unit 2001: 2; *La'o Hamutuk* 2001a).

Third, the SCIU fell into serious disarray for extended periods, suffering from vacancies and changes in leadership, low morale and other personnel problems. Strategic policy-making was poor and the SCIU became notoriously opaque and difficult to deal with. It made little effort to undertake community outreach activities or to cooperate with other areas of UNTAET such as the Human Rights Unit and the CAVR, which complained of "power games" and the difficulty of accessing information and coordinating policy. Members of the unit were accused of striking secret deals with militia leaders and putting brakes on the prosecutions (Jolliffe 2002: 5). A highly critical internal UN review in March 2001 recommended sweeping changes (*La'o Hamutuk* 2001b), and the unit's performance improved after it was revamped following the appointment of a new Deputy Special Representative in July 2001. By this stage, however, the unit's poor reputation was well established and it never fully recovered its credibility.

A further problem was UNTAET's failure adequately to integrate Timorese counterparts into the serious crimes process. Timorese political leaders were brought on board and expressed strong rhetorical support for the process (Ramos-Horta 2002), but the Timorese judiciary was neglected. East Timorese judges and other judicial officials, particularly in the Dili District Court where the panels were convened, publicly objected that they had not been included meaningfully in the consultation process prior to the establishment of the Serious Crimes Panels (Linton 2001). Only one Timorese worked in the SCIU. The loss of a sense of ownership over a critical process undermined its legitimacy by compounding public criticism and making the process less transparent to Timorese; an opportunity was also missed to build capacity in dealing with serious crimes.

Finally, the serious crimes process was hamstrung by Indonesia's lack of cooperation. The panels were not empowered to order the surrender of suspects in third states, and Indonesia did not uphold the terms of a Memorandum of Understanding on Cooperation in Legal Judicial and Human Rights signed with UNTAET in April 2000 that provided for co-operation in prosecuting the crimes of 1999. As a result, UNTAET was able to prosecute only individuals remaining in East Timor, and Indonesian military and police officers and Timorese militia leaders were quarantined from the process. A Timorese judge who heard East Timor's first case of crimes against humanity summed up the sense of injustice felt by Timorese about the whole process:

> As a judge, it's my duty to enforce the law ... Every individual must be responsible for his crimes. But speaking as a Timorese and not as a judge, I think this system is not fair. Is it fair to prosecute the small Timorese and not the big ones who gave them orders? Personally, I'm worried about this. (Maria Natercia Pereira, quoted in Mydans 2001)

Reconciliation and the question of amnesty

Both UNTAET and Timorese leaders recognised that reconciliation between pro-independence and pro-integration supporters, particularly militia elements, was a pressing imperative. Much was seen to depend on it:

the Foreign Minister, Jose Ramos-Horta, argued that not reconciling with the past would spell political "bankruptcy" for East Timorese leaders (Ramos-Horta 2002). Gusmao stressed the importance of reconciliation to heal community fissures and to defuse ongoing border security threats and the refugee problem. Others stressed that the economic viability of the state depended on reconciliation: to continue to have the country split would ruin any chance of recovery and put off donors. Bishop Belo pointed to the interdependence of justice and reconciliation: "For me reconciliation and justice are like a double-sided coin. Reconciliation with justice, justice with reconciliation. Justice without reconciliation is not complete. Neither is it humane. On the other hand, reconciliation without justice will not resolve the problem" (*Cidadaun* 2001).

Reconciliation initiatives were established on several levels across a variety of organisations well before UNTAET's deployment. Guterres (2003) describes in detail the political reconciliation processes initiated by Gusmao and others during 1999, including the role of external intermediaries. Grassroots reconciliation initiatives were undertaken by a variety of local and international civil society organisations such as the Catholic Peace and Justice Commission.

UNTAET supported these efforts in principle, but senior officials admitted that they struggled to develop a coherent political and legal mechanism to deal with reconciliation. Much depended on the cooperation of Indonesia, which was not forthcoming. Other problems related to trying to balance the competing imperatives of reconciliation and justice.

The question of how to deal with militia leaders was foremost amongst these challenges. The Deputy Special Representative, Dennis McNamara, likened the East Timor situation to Cambodia, in which he and Vieira de Mello had been forced to deal with the Khmer Rouge in order to repatriate refugees. In East Timor, UNTAET needed to deal with the militia leaders who controlled the refugee camps in West Timor, while at the same time pursuing justice for their crimes (Jolliffe 2002: 5). UNTAET in conjunction with Gusmao embarked on an active policy of reconciliation with militias to secure the repatriation of refugees through the return of moderate militia leaders who controlled them and were ready to face justice, and later devising a strategy to deal with hardcore militia leaders. In these circumstances, it was difficult not only to maintain policy consistency but also to keep all factions on board, including within UNTAET itself. Peacekeeping forces, for example, were frustrated at a ban on arresting senior militia leaders crossing the border for talks with UNTAET officials (Jolliffe 2002: 5), and pro-justice groups criticised the talks for undermining their goal of accountability for the past.

The case of the militia leader Remesio Lopes de Carvalho highlighted the difficulty of balancing reconciliation imperatives with the integrity of justice processes. Facilitated by Gusmao, UNTAET's Chief of Staff Nagalingam Parameswaran negotiated Remesio's return to East Timor. In a high-profile reconciliation ceremony, Remesio crossed the border in October 2001, bringing with him nearly 1,000 refugees. He was arrested on suspicion of crimes against humanity and murder and transferred to Dili. After appearing before an investigating judge in Dili District Court, Remesio was conditionally released and returned to his home village in Ainaro District, where he remained, unindicted, under house arrest (UNTAET 2001d). This was not, however, before Parameswaran had been observed dining with Remesio in Dili following the latter's release, a move that was criticised not only for its insensitivity but for undermining principles of justice. The opacity of Parameswaran's negotiations fuelled accusations that UNTAET had been cutting deals with militia leaders and damaging confidence in the integrity of justice processes (DAGAinfo 2002; Jolliffe 2002: 5). It also confused refugees about justice processes, conferred legitimacy on militia leaders and raised questions about the United Nations' overall approach:

> If UNTAET were to persuade Indonesian authorities to bring militia leaders to justice, the refugees under their control would be free to come home. Instead, the refugees observe UN officials negotiating with militia leaders, and the UN loses the refugees' trust. Genuine refugees remain in West Timor, while militia followers and leaders, as well as East Timorese TNI [Indonesian armed forces] soldiers, return to East Timor with impunity. Many refugees, already misled about the situation in East Timor, fear that those who have been oppressing them for the past two years will resume that role if and when the refugees finally go home. (*La'o Hamutuk* 2001c)

In January 2002, Parameswaran was disciplined by the Transitional Administrator after the Commission on Human Rights expressed concerns about his actions (CHR 2002b). He subsequently resigned, accusing UNTAET of racism, management problems and interference in his reconciliation work. Remesio was not indicted by the SCU for crimes against humanity until 2003, by which time he was again at large in West Timor.

Xanana Gusmao's dominant role in the reconciliation issue illustrated the challenges faced by external actors in dealing with the divergent views of powerful local actors. UNTAET was greatly assisted by Gusmao in fulfilling its reconciliation mandate, but at the same time had to contend with the risk that Gusmao's support for amnesty would undermine rule of law goals through compromising the principle of individual criminal accountability. UNTAET firmly opposed amnesty for serious crimes as incompatible with international law (F. Martin, personal communication, 21 November 2001). In contrast, Gusmao supported accountability for past crimes but argued that peace and stability were the overriding priorities and that "justice" was a tool for reconciliation rather than a cause in its own right. Gusmao's views were pragmatic rather than idealistic: his emphasis on reconciliation and amnesty was designed to facilitate large-scale refugee returns from West Timor and to avoid further jeopardising relations with Indonesia and West Timor (*Suara Timor Lorosae* 2001). Gusmao also questioned the appropriateness of formal criminal procedures to deliver justice in the face of pressing development priorities:

> These men, they will go to trial, they will go to prison. Who will pay for their daily life in prison? The money that you pay in taxation, instead of going to teachers and nurses, will go to prisoners. Do you accept this? What we have discussed is that if we need to repair buildings, the people who burned the buildings will repair them. (*Time Asia* 2001)

Gusmao thus began to promote the idea of limited amnesty for militia crimes, having declared in 1999 a "general amnesty for all political crimes" (Stein 1999). UNTAET officials were concerned that Gusmao's stance would undermine the rule of law principles it was trying to promote and eventually succeeded in persuading Gusmao to moderate his stance to preclude amnesty before justice (*Time Asia* 2001; Bull 2001) and to support the second-track justice process of the CAVR. UNTAET for its part accepted the inclusion of a presidential pardon clause in the constitution, the details of which it was not in a position to influence. This process of mutual accommodation relied partly on the close and productive relationship Vieira de Mello had developed with Gusmao. Primarily, however, it appeared to develop from Gusmao's own nuanced consideration of the issues, and it is questionable to what extent UNTAET might have influenced the direction of the amnesty question had it been dealing with a different leader.

Commission for Reception, Truth and Reconciliation

UNTAET established the Commission for Reception, Truth and Reconciliation (CAVR) in July 2001. Another first for the United Nations, it reflected emerging perceptions of the merits of restorative justice approaches as a healing mechanism and a successful model for conflict management (Stahn 2001a: 957). The Commission's objectives were to deal with the perpetrators of lower-level crimes, to end cycles of recrimination, to facilitate the return of refugees from West Timor and to relieve pressure on the judicial system by extending immunity for lesser crimes.

It was established as an independent statutory authority with three ambitious mandates: truth-seeking, community reconciliation and policy recommendations to government.

The Commission's truth-seeking mandate involved enquiry into the pattern of human rights violations committed in the context of political conflict in East Timor between 25 April 1974 and 25 October 1999, through the taking of statements in public hearings and the compilation of a major report. The community reconciliation mandate established a public apology and reparation system that centred on quasi-judicial Community Reconciliation Procedures (CRPs) covering criminal or non-criminal acts committed between the above dates. Each Community Reconciliation Agreement was negotiated and registered as an order of the relevant district court and, once its terms were fulfilled, the perpetrator was granted immunity from further civil or criminal liability. The granting of immunities strictly excluded serious crimes, which remained the exclusive jurisdiction of the Serious Crimes Panels. The Commission's recommendations function required it to submit a report to the government by October 2004 recommending further action to prevent future human rights violations and promote reconciliation.

The CAVR's seven Timorese National Commissioners were appointed in January 2002 and commenced work the following month. The bulk of the Commission's work was conducted after UNTAET's departure: the first community reconciliation hearings were held in August 2002 and the first public truth-seeking hearing in November 2002. By October 2003, the CAVR had taken 6,000 truth-seeking statements and held 89 community reconciliation hearings, of which 89 per cent had resulted in CRAs (*La'o Hamutuk* 2003). By December 2003, it had completed 600 of 1,500 applications for CRPs. Although still small relative to the overall number of violations, this was impressive progress compared with the Serious Crimes Panels. The CAVR completed its work in late 2005.

It was evident from the level of participation and support that the CAVR enjoyed that it was perceived as a legitimate process that contributed to delivering justice for past crimes and healing individual communities. A strong sense of Timorese ownership and the calibre of international staff appear to have been key factors in its success. The Commission originated as a CNRT proposal in 2000 and was largely driven by Timorese from the outset. Key CAVR executive bodies, including the steering committee and the selection panel that chose the Commissioners, were virtually all Timorese and from relatively early on more than 90 per cent of CAVR staff were Timorese (*La'o Hamutuk* 2003). Reconciliation officials in the villages were all Timorese.

The CAVR's international staff were relatively unusual: most had had a long association with East Timor and brought knowledge, empathy and language skills of a calibre well above those of most other UNTAET officials. International staff in control of policy and funding made strategic decisions to limit the recruitment of internationals and to minimise their own involvement where they felt it might dilute the spirit of the process. Despite being elected as a National Commissioner under a provision allowing for the appointment of non-Timorese, for example, a senior Human Rights Unit official working at the CAVR declined the offer in order to keep the Commission a Timorese process.

Although overall a successful balance was reached, the CAVR nonetheless experienced many of the same problems between internationals and locals apparent in other areas of the mission. It was difficult to build an equitable working environment in the face of widely disparate salaries, experience and expectations. The CAVR relied heavily on international funding, expertise and leadership and some Timorese staff complained that international staff dominated decision-making. Decisions were sometimes made without consulting the relevant Timorese staff member, and internationals continued to perform line functions when they were meant to be acting in a mentor role. On the other side of the coin, some Timorese staff perceived that highly paid internationals should be doing the "hard work", whereas internationals felt that the locals were not proactive enough in moving the work of the Commission forward and acquiring skills (*La'o Hamutuk* 2003).

The CAVR model was premised on the view that openness, transparency and community participation were integral outcomes of the process, and it appears to have succeeded in implementing these principles to a credible degree. The steering committee held broad national consultations, including with pro-autonomy supporters in West Timor, at most stages of the CAVR's work, including on such issues as the nomination and short-listing of commissioners. CRP panels were initiated from within communities and comprised community representatives. The CAVR conducted a range of healing workshops for survivors of human rights violations and set up programmes to work with civil society to develop recommendations to carry the healing processes forward. Victim hearings were held in the sub-districts and national-level public hearings were conducted as part of the truth-seeking function. Such efforts to involve local communities were generally well received, although communities in some areas were still reluctant to buy in to the process (*La'o Hamutuk* 2003).

Another factor in the CAVR's success appears to have been its ability to navigate the political situation, albeit not without difficulty. UNTAET officials and their Timorese counterparts invested significant efforts in building political support for the CAVR, including from Gusmao, Fretilin leaders and the two bishops. Gusmao's support in particular was viewed as critical for the credibility of the process with both the population and donors. The CAVR demonstrated the importance of an informed strategic approach in its handling of the potential for divergence between UNTAET and Gusmao on the question of amnesty. CAVR staff mobilised senior channels in UNTAET and Timorese leaders to successfully persuade key figures to support the Commission publicly.

Despite its successes, the Commission experienced many problems typical of the UNTAET mission. Progress was impeded by resource shortfalls, which caused a backlog in processing applications and limited the amount of time information-gathering teams could spend in each sub-district (*La'o Hamutuk* 2003). As with the Serious Crimes Panels, the justice function of the Commission was compromised by Indonesia's lack of cooperation, which led to a lack of information on key events and perpetrators and the absence of many perpetrators at hearings. In the context of the dysfunctional judicial system and the incompetence of the SCIU, the Commission had ongoing difficulties clarifying CRPs. In particular, the weak judicial system proved a disincentive for perpetrators to submit themselves to the CAVR process, because they knew that the formal justice system did not have the capacity to prosecute them anyway. Although relatively successful in garnering the participation of petty criminals, the CAVR therefore struggled to get militias to become involved in what was ultimately a voluntary process. Without strong incentives to participate, such as the threat of prosecution, the CAVR was unable to overcome this weakness.

Indonesian ad hoc tribunal on East Timor

The Indonesian Ad Hoc Human Rights Court on East Timor completed its hearings in August 2003. Although the tribunal was an important first step in Indonesia's assumption of responsibility for pursuing accountability for human rights violations in East Timor, the process was deeply flawed. Its failure to deliver justice in the face of an incompetent judicial system, interference by the Indonesian armed forces in the judiciary and insufficient political will to prosecute senior Indonesian officials has been well documented.[14] The court's mandate was excessively narrow, examining only 2 months in a 24-year occupation and 3 of East Timor's 13 districts. Of the 18 suspects tried, all but 6 were acquitted and all but one of those convicted received less than the legal minimum sentence. None of the most senior officials named in the Indonesian inquiry report in January 2000 were seriously investigated, let alone indicted. The highest-ranking military officer to be tried, Major General Adam Damiri, was sentenced to 3 years – well under the 10-year minimum sentence under Indonesian law for crimes against humanity. All remained free at the time of writing.

Like the Serious Crimes process, the Indonesian tribunal exacerbated Timorese cynicism about UN-sponsored "justice" that saw low-ranking East Timorese punished but higher-ranking Timorese and Indonesians sentenced lightly, acquitted or never brought to trial. The UN Security Council made a deliberate strategic decision not to pursue an international tribunal or make provision for Indonesian suspects to be tried in East Timor in absentia in the knowledge that this would almost inevitably result in impunity for those most responsible for the atrocities in East Timor.[15] Although there were valid policy considerations on both sides, UN member states could have pushed for a different solution that more fully supported its own rhetoric about bringing to justice those responsible for the crimes of 1999. In failing to do so, it missed an opportunity to bring to life key principles of the rule of law: accountability and equality under the law.

Performing effectively

It is beyond the scope of this study to provide a full analysis of the internal workings of UNTAET. However, it is evident from the preceding discussion that efforts in the rule of law sector proceeded without a coordinated strategy and in the face of systemic mission deficiencies. Three themes with particular relevance to the rule of law are discussed in further detail here: strategic planning failures, including the results-driven versus developmental focus of the mission; the problem of mission cohesion; and UNTAET's exit strategy, including the UNMISET successor mission.

Strategic planning failures

The lack of contingency planning for worst-case scenarios following the August 1999 ballot has been discussed widely in the literature.[16] Plans for "Phase III" of the United Nations Assistance Mission in East Timor (UNAMET) – the genesis of UNTAET – were barely formulated by the time of the ballot (Martin 2001: 126; Chopra 2000: 28). Planning for rule of law issues was scant and completely failed to provide for the breakdown in the rule of law that followed the ballot. Planning was premised on the dubious assumption that Indonesia would fulfil its obligations to maintain security, including in the event of a transfer of sovereignty. It was therefore assumed that, during a peaceful transition period, Indonesian law would continue to apply and an orderly transfer of the administration of the judiciary would occur. UNAMET's mandate was subsequently extended to include the recruitment and training of an independent East Timorese police force, but not to prepare for a new East Timorese judiciary, despite the fact that UNAMET had requested this (KCL 2003: para. 222).

UNTAET thus deployed grossly under-prepared into a vastly more difficult situation than it had envisaged. Planning in UNTAET's early phase was similarly inadequate and, as Suhrke (2001: 13) notes, guided by the flawed assumption that the United Nations was dealing with a *tabula rasa*. The inaccuracy of this assumption and the difficulties UNTAET encountered in dealing with East Timor's complex political and social landscape have been described above.

Lack of developmental focus

The mission systemically prejudiced strategic development goals in favour of emergency responses. Its few judicial resources were directed entirely to "emergency issues" and the UN Secretary-General's 4 October recommendation for detailed strategic assessments and planning fell by the wayside. The pressing demands of the emergency phase of the operation made the initial lack of coherent planning excusable, but it is more difficult to account for UNTAET's later failure to implement a more considered strategy for the development of justice institutions envisaged in the Secretary-General's 4 October report (KCL 2003: para 224).

Much can perhaps be explained by the difficulty of trying to fit a complex governance mandate within a peacekeeping planning structure (Suhrke 2001). Organisationally, the planning and implementation of UNTAET objectives were compromised by a messy handover and the ongoing power struggle between the Departments of Peacekeeping Operations and Political Affairs in New York. Planning and the allocation of resources and funding for the military and emergency humanitarian phase were not smoothly redirected to longer-term state-building priorities. The mission did not devote attention to planning state-building tasks during the initial phase, and funding and resource allocations for civilian mandate areas such as the justice sector were neglected (Katzenstein 2003: 257).

Perhaps most significantly, there was an inherent tension between UNTAET's results-driven rather than developmental focus and the nature of state-building goals as time-dependent, resource-intensive developmental processes. UNTAET was essentially driven by the demand for expediency and compromised its own development goals in the constant drive for "results" that would fit into the reporting cycle and secure funding. How to build the rule of law was a secondary issue that did not fit easily into mission performance indicators. There was a significant degree of awareness of this problem in the UN system, but it had not yet found a way to overcome it by the time of the UNTAET mission.

Mission cohesion

Problems with mission cohesion affected UNTAET's efforts to build the rule of law on several counts. First, the lack of strategic coordination between the courts, police and prisons undermined the performance of each of those organisations (KCL 2003: para. 250). Interlocutors complained of communications difficulties, police records were not transferred to the courts and different sections of UNTAET operated under different (or no) understandings of prevailing policy. The development of different agencies proceeded at different paces, such that a suspect could be arrested but not locked up owing to the lack of a prison, or locked up but not tried owing to the lack of a court.

Second, management of rule of law initiatives was transferred clumsily between several different organisations. In policing, for example, first INTERFET, then CIVPOL and then the East Timor Police Service had responsibility for maintaining law and order, but there were no established protocols for the orderly transfer of resources or other matters, such as evidence. In the field, these issues were dealt with in an ad hoc fashion that often resulted in delays, loss of evidence and confusion (KCL 2003: para. 242).

Third, it was difficult to build a common vision within UNTAET about its objectives and modus operandi. UNTAET's disparate personnel had very different conceptual viewpoints on what constituted the rule of law, let alone how it should be established. The ongoing tensions between the "Anglo" and "Portuguese" factions in the mission over the judicial sector exemplified the highly disruptive impact of differing visions. Similarly, CIVPOL and legal officers came from vastly different jurisdictional and professional backgrounds and regularly disputed the "proper" way to do things.

For example, the Baucau CIVPOL team leader referred to above observed a wide disparity in the quality of officers and found it difficult to deal with different jurisdictional backgrounds in the broader Baucau contingent, which consisted of 38 officers from 16 nations. Some CIVPOL were illiterate and could not drive, and generally good levels of trust between CIVPOL and the community were undermined by the involvement of some individuals in corruption, child sex offences, forced evictions and black market operations. Levels of training varied, as did attitudes towards the use of firearms. At the same time as they battled with problems of internal cohesion, CIVPOL experienced difficulties with other elements of the UNTAET mission. In Baucau, the UNTAET District Administrator did not understand the CIVPOL mandate and regularly obstructed their operations.

Exit strategies and UNMISET

Compared with its chaotic entry, the United Nations performed better in devising an exit strategy for UNTAET that balanced the political imperative of transferring power to Timorese with the practical one of maintaining an adequate level of assistance through a successor mission, UNMISET. Emphasis was placed on the imperative of addressing rule of law issues, as reflected in UNMISET's three "pillars": "stability, democracy and justice", "public security and law enforcement", and "external security and border control". The Security Council recognised that fragile emerging institutions required continuing assistance, singling out "difficulties which have had a negative impact on the effectiveness of the judicial system" (UNSC 2002e: 1). A significant portion of the mission's resources was allocated to assist administration of the justice sector under the "stability, democracy and justice" pillar.[17] The UNMISET Office of the Special Representative maintained a Serious Crimes Unit and a Human Rights Unit, a CIVPOL component of 1,250 officers remained to oversee the development of the ETPS, and a scaled-down peacekeeping force was maintained until defence functions could be assumed by the F-FDTL.

Implementation, however, was another matter, and the chaos that had surrounded rule of law issues under UNTAET was exacerbated on its departure. UNMISET's failure to recruit key positions in the rule of law area, including those of Prisons Adviser, Senior Adviser to the Inspector General, Public Prosecutor and Public Defender, had a detrimental effect on its ability to carry out critical support functions (UNSC 2002b: 11). Administrative mismanagement stemming from a lack of coordination and cooperation between UNTAET and the Minister for Justice caused an almost complete breakdown in the legal framework for the judiciary on UNTAET's departure. Concern among the judiciary over the absence of a professional code and an independent judicial appointments system, and the lapsing of the appointments of most judges and prosecutors on 20 May 2002, saw the entire court system plunged into disarray from late May to mid-July. The impasse was resolved when Gusmao signed a decree allowing judges appointed by UNTAET to continue in their roles until permanent appointments could be made, but further progress in addressing the fundamental issues was slow. The National Parliament passed a Judicial Magistrates Statute in September 2002 providing for the composition and functioning of the Superior Council for the Judiciary and the appointment of judges. However progress on appointments, including to the Court of Appeal, was stymied because the Council did not become operational for some months (UNSC 2002d: 4). Other issues neglected by UNTAET, such as land and property, remained in a similar state of limbo.

Discussion of UNMISET's efforts to address these problems is beyond the scope of this chapter, although it is noteworthy that UNMISET continued to recognise the need for greater emphasis on human rights and rule of law elements, including such issues as training needs, inadequate access to justice for the population, and lack of facilities and case management procedures (UNSC 2003a). It is also worth noting that the critical outstanding issues towards the end of UNMISET's mandate remained rule of law and security-related issues. The Secretary-General emphasised that, beyond UNMISET, international assistance would continue to be "indispensable" in providing "further guidance and advice in the areas of civil administration, justice and policing, as well as in such areas as human rights training. It is likely that the new country's capacity to ensure security in the border area will not have reached an optimal level, and that the serious crimes process will not be complete" (UNSC 2003b: 11).

Relegating the United Nations' post-UNMISET assistance primarily to technical assistance, he also underscored the responsibility of East Timorese leaders to nurture respect for the rule of law, civil society, political dialogue, a non-political civil service, a free press and an independent judiciary (UNSC 2003b).

Observations

In thus highlighting Timorese responsibilities, the question arises of how and where to draw a line between UN and "local" responsibilities for rule of law creation, as with other aspects of state-building. UNTAET implemented an untested model in East Timor that raised many questions about the appropriate UN response. Should a brief visitor such as UNTAET have been expected to take responsibility for key determinants of rule of law creation that were clearly time dependent and ultimately relied on domestic processes? Was it sensible to set the bar so high that expectations were inevitably disappointed? Conversely, had UNTAET not set ambitious rule of law targets, who would have? Would aspirations and action have fallen further behind the democratic ideal?

Linton (2001) argues that, in designing judicial institutions for East Timor, UNTAET gave insufficient attention to the question of what was feasible, appropriate and consistent with the expectations and aspirations of the population. It is arguable that UNTAET's blueprint for rule of law development was indeed destined for failure given the environment into which it deployed, coupled with resource and time constraints. However, a basic level of justice with the potential for ongoing development might have been in reach had some basic pitfalls been avoided – for example, had UNTAET from the outset put more physical and political resources into pursuing the development of legal, judicial and other rule of law institutions in an informed and strategically coherent manner. The potential value of transitional off-the-shelf designs arises in this respect. A strategy could have been devised that took a longer-term developmental approach to pursuing ambitious targets, clearly defining discrete tasks for UNTAET in the context of a long-term strategy to be implemented by a successor mission, the donor community and the Timorese. This might have produced a more sustainable outcome that edged towards those impossibly high targets and also managed expectations.

Pursuing such a strategy, however, would not necessarily address the fundamental challenge highlighted by UNTAET's experience: how to engage the recipient population in a volatile, highly charged environment. Although, as Vieira de Mello envisaged, UNTAET could have worked harder and more sensitively to make its initiatives the "property of the East Timorese", its experience pointed ultimately to how difficult it is for an external actor to do so in the context of issues that cut to the political and cultural core of community structures and aspirations.

Notes

1. UNSC (2002b: 1) also makes this claim.
2. For coverage of these problems, see Strohmeyer (2001).
3. UNTAET regulations that specifically related to the justice sector included Regulations 1999/3 and 2000/25 on the Transitional Judicial Services Commission, Regulations 2000/11, 2000/14, 2001/18, and 2001/25 on the Organization of the Courts, Regulation 2000/5 on Panels with Jurisdiction Over Serious Criminal Offences, Regulation 2000/16 on the Public Prosecution Service, Regulation 2000/30 on Transitional Rules of Criminal Procedure, and Regulation 2001/22 on the Police Service.
4. This was reflected in the fact that the third regulation (Regulation 1999/3) – and first sectoral regulation – recognised the urgent need for (and established) a transitional judicial services commission to appoint a judiciary. See UNTAET (1999b).
5. See, for example, Mobekk (2001).
6. See also *La'o Hamutuk* (2002: 2, 11).
7. On independence, the ETPS was renamed Policia Nacional de Timor-Leste (National Police of Timor-Leste).
8. See, for example, a speech by Mari Alkatiri (2001), in which he pledged respect for human rights, the rule of law and the independence of the judiciary.
9. Any disputes were resolved by the Dili District Court, which made some highly controversial decisions (Pritchard 2001: 188).

10. Community policing may be defined as a cooperative partnership between the law enforcement agency and the community to solve problems of crime and disorder (Mobekk 2001: 10).
11. See, for example, Gorjao (2002: 317–320); Suhrke (2001); and Chopra (2002).
12. In September 2001, following the August 2001 Constituent Assembly elections, responsibility for the Justice portfolio was devolved to Timorese with the appointment of the all-Timorese Second Transitional Cabinet.
13. See, for example, CNRT (1998) and the *Proceedings of the Strategic Development Planning for East Timor Conference, Melbourne 5–9 April 1999.*
14. See HRW (2002a); East Timor Action Network (2003); AI (2003c); JSMP (2003c).
15. In January 2000, the UN Secretary-General recommended to the Security Council that, contrary to recommendations for an international tribunal made by the human rights investigator, Sonia Picardo, Indonesia should be given the opportunity to try its own transgressors. This decision was strongly supported by Australia.
16. See, for example, Martin (2001: 126) and Chopra (2000: 28).
17. Of 100 core civilian positions, 14 were allocated to legal/justice jobs (UNSC 2002b: 11, para. 70).

7

No entry without strategy

Operational context can make or break a mission. As the case studies have illustrated, the disrupted states into which the United Nations Transitional Authority in Cambodia (UNTAC), the United Nations Interim Administration Mission in Kosovo (UNMIK) and the United Nations Transitional Administration in East Timor (UNTAET) deployed were hostile intervention environments that might have proven inhospitable to even the most sophisticated efforts to establish the rule of law. As stated at the outset of this book, UN transitional administrations were charged with performing extremely complex tasks in difficult situations with few resources. Such challenges could cripple even the best-laid plans.

In these circumstances, the UN Security Council may need to consider whether, in fact, *no* entry is the only real strategy. That said, once the decision is made to intervene, the prospects for a successful mission must surely depend on comprehensive, appropriate response strategies informed by a clear vision of what "success" would look like and how this is going to be attempted. The conclusions of this chapter are offered in that spirit.

Case-study findings

All three case studies confirmed the significance – and interconnectedness – of the key areas of enquiry identified in Chapter 3 in explaining the difficulties faced by UN transitional administrations in establishing

No entry without strategy: Building the rule of law under UN transitional administration, Bull, United Nations University Press, 2008, ISBN 978-92-808-1151-3

the rule of law. Three factors emerged as "deal breakers" that critically undermined the United Nations' rule of law objectives: the failure of missions to establish effective state rule of law institutions, to build commitment and to address informal justice structures. The remaining six factors could more appropriately be considered "deal makers" that, depending on the extent to which they were advanced or neglected, enhanced or undermined attempts to establish the rule of law. This section summarises the findings regarding each of the nine areas of enquiry, before considering their relative significance.

Setting the parameters: The mission mandate

The extent to which the Security Council mandate set appropriate parameters for rule of law work proved important, as did the way in which each mission interpreted that mandate in practice. In Cambodia, the failure of the Paris Agreements to provide for a specific rule of law mandate constrained UNTAC's ability to pursue critical changes, discouraged the adoption of rule of law initiatives and condoned a "line of least resistance" approach. In contrast, the expansive mandates given to UNMIK and UNTAET offered broad scope for rule of law initiatives but lacked clarity regarding rule of law priorities and guidance on how ambitious targets were to be achieved. This resulted in a less robust and focused intervention than was necessary to achieve substantial progress in establishing the rule of law.

Establishment of state rule of law institutions

State rule of law institutions are the cornerstone of the United Nations' rule of law strategy, and it is telling that none of the three missions examined in this study were able to establish well-functioning institutions that were perceived as just, reliable and accessible, and were adopted accordingly by the population as their preferred means of resolving disputes.

A protracted justice vacuum in the opening phases of the Kosovo and East Timor missions, and in Cambodia's case for most of the mission, spawned violence, retaliations and the growth of new criminal threats. The lack of a holistic approach that recognised synergies between legal, judicial, police and correctional bodies caused systemic dysfunction. In both East Timor and Kosovo, hybrid legal systems were developed that, although closer to international standards than their predecessors, were nonetheless incomplete and proved difficult to implement, both practically and politically. Legal flaws and procedural shortcomings became institutionalised as permanent deficiencies, leaving a legacy of problems that successor governments were ill equipped to resolve. In both East Timor and Kosovo, insufficient attention was paid to what was feasible, appropriate and consistent with the expectations and aspirations of the population.

Building commitment

In all three cases, the transitional administration struggled to build meaningful domestic support for rule of law reforms at either elite or mass level. This appeared to be a function of the disempowerment of key constituencies; poor management of expectations for consultation and ownership; the difficulty of bridging disconnects between western and local conceptions of justice and the rule of law; and scepticism about the ability of new systems to deliver benefits to the community. These problems caused resentment, eroded support and sometimes prompted local actors to circumvent state processes or to challenge the United Nations' authority. Conversely, where efforts were made to build confidence in and ownership over rule of law processes, better results were recorded. New indigenous police services enjoyed a relatively high level of support, which appeared to stem from their visibility as a symbol of change and close ties with the community.

The case studies highlight the dilemma of how to strike a successful balance between devolution and control that both satisfies indigenous demands for "ownership" and ensures mission objectives are met. In the face of immature institutional safeguards, devolving power saw justice processes fall hostage to local politics. Not devolving power generated resistance from important elite actors. Either way, the United Nations lost influence.

Rebuilding social relationships

In each case study, the United Nations operated in a society lacking in robust collective social relationships, where state–society linkages were weak and debilitated by mistrust, and the prevailing channel for interest representation was a politically or ethnically biased and corrupt patronage system. Such environments proved an unsound basis for the development of sustainable rule of law institutions. Anonymous trust was slow to emerge in all three case studies, with much of the population continuing to avoid interaction with the authorities, including state justice structures.

Strategies to address these issues were weak, although in each case some positive steps were taken in the form of trauma counselling, community or political reconciliation processes and civil society development, particularly through the establishment of non-governmental organisations (NGOs). In Cambodia, UNTAC made progress in police community trust-building initiatives and NGO development. In East Timor, UNTAET worked with the Catholic Church to build political legitimacy and trust, though was less successful in harnessing the National Council of Timorese Resistance (CNRT). In Kosovo, very little effort was made to encourage the growth of robust civil society networks. In all cases, UN actors either underestimated, or were powerless to address, the capacity and expectations of local civil society to play a role. This marginalised and often alienated these actors.

State capacity

In some respects, the UN transitional administration contributed to an improvement in the capacity of the state to undertake initiatives to develop the rule of law. In each case, it helped to establish a more stable government structure and to disempower destabilising influences on the state – regional hegemons in Cambodia and militia elements in East Timor, for example. Nonetheless, post-UN Cambodia and East Timor remained weak states, as did Kosovo under UNMIK. In Cambodia, the State of Cambodia relied on coercion to maintain social control and arguably remained the key threat to the rule of law. In East Timor and Kosovo, the successor "state" was ill equipped to continue rule of law work after the United Nations' departure, in terms of both logistical capacity and the commitment of state actors to basic principles such as the separation of powers.

In all cases, the United Nations made insufficient effort to equip fledgling state apparatuses to cope with the demands of refining and consolidating the rule of law institutions it had begun to establish. UNTAET and UNMIK under-prioritised the building of government capacity for justice policy formulation and modern responsive administrations, including at the district level and below, where the majority of the population lived.

Restoring security

In all three case studies, UN intervention arguably proved an effective "circuit breaker" in intrastate security dilemmas, restoring security to a level sufficient to create "space" for the mission to promote the rule of law through assisting the transition from violent to non-violent forms of power acquisition and conflict management. Nevertheless, the incomplete restoration of security contributed to new outbreaks of continued violence and complicated access to, trust in and willingness to use new justice systems. Missions were only partly successful in neutralising spoilers whose behaviour undermined the rule of law. In both Kosovo and East Timor, for example, Transitional Administrators struggled with parallel security groups that unilaterally assumed a "security role" that included unlawful arrests, assault and murder. The missions also proved unable to defuse destabilising local political struggles, which saw the Cambodian coup of 1997, violent riots in Kosovo in 2004 and the redeployment of foreign troops to East Timor in 2006.

Informal justice structures

The neglect in all three missions of non-state processes such as alternative dispute resolution, restorative justice and reconciliation mechanisms increased the burden on state systems and undermined the potential for informal processes, as the fundamental fabric binding communities together, to support rule of law objectives. UN transitional administrations made insufficient effort to dismantle or promote informal structures, link them with the formal justice system or otherwise incorporate them into a broader rule of law strategy. Local justice regimes thus remained as competitors to the state justice system and at times contradicted core principles of the rule of law. The prevalence of summary and mob justice in Cambodia and domestic violence in East Timor are two examples. Failing to integrate informal and formal structures in some way created confusion and inconsistency, and this undermined the legitimacy of the state justice system, which in many cases was less accessible, less effective and less trusted than its informal alternatives.

In cases where informal justice processes were harnessed more effectively, such as the use of restorative justice processes by the Civilian Police in Cambodia and the Commission for Reception, Truth and Reconciliation in East Timor, they appeared to assist in embedding justice processes consistent with or complementary to the western liberal model.

Dealing with the past

The case studies demonstrate that unreconciled grievances may impede the ability of a society to move beyond patterns of violence and adopt regularised institutional patterns supportive of the rule of law. In Cambodia, the continued impunity of political figures directly implicated in the genocide remained a divisive social issue a decade later. In Kosovo, the election of a suspected war criminal as Prime Minister in November 2004 pushed ethnic reconciliation even further off the political agenda.

Reconciliation processes tended to be more effective where they enjoyed strong domestic backing and were combined with the development process. The East Timor mission proved the most successful attempt at reckoning credibly with the past. UNTAET sought to balance the principle of individual accountability with reconciliation, recognising the practical limitations of an overstretched court system and the need to work with Indonesia and the militia. Some advances were made in delivering an acceptable justice for the past, including through community reconciliation processes, which appeared to have a positive impact at the village and national level. Nonetheless, UNTAET's efforts were severely impeded by limited administrative capacity in the justice system, Indonesian recalcitrance, the weakness of the UNTAET Serious Crimes Unit itself and difficulties in accommodating local notions of justice.

Performing effectively

Mission performance in all three cases undermined rule of law objectives. Resource constraints were often debilitating, but perhaps even more striking were strategic management shortcomings. In a telling disconnect between broader UN rhetoric and action on the ground, rule of law issues remained peripheral to strategic transition planning. Other problems more closely related to the inherent structural weaknesses of UN missions included the difficulties faced by mission leaders in creating a common vision of the mission's rule of law objectives, and poor coordination between mission rule of law components, particularly where these involved several UN agencies or, indeed, more than one international organisation. This was most striking in Kosovo, where two mission pillars with key responsibilities for rule of law issues were run by separate international organisations with limited coordination.

The East Timor and Cambodia missions suffered from a short deployment period, emphasising the tension between the short-run results-driven focus of peacekeeping missions and state-building as a time-dependent, resource-intensive developmental process. This made it difficult for overstretched missions to invest in areas that required a longer-term "developmental" outlook. Missions were characterised by poor entry and exit strategies, leaving them grossly under-prepared to meet both immediate and long-term challenges.

Finally, in some respects missions failed to lead by example in terms of adherence, both in policy and in individual behaviour, to their own rule of law principles. This undermined the credibility not just of the mission but of the rule of law principles at stake.

Ranking the factors

Although more extensive research into each of the above areas of enquiry would potentially enable more precise judgements to be made, the case studies suggest that these factors could usefully be grouped into two tiers: "deal breakers", which virtually guaranteed the failure of the UN transitional administration to meet its rule of law objectives; and "deal makers", which enhanced or, conversely, limited the quality of mission outcomes.

The "deal breakers"

Three factors emerged as "deal breakers": the failure of missions to establish effective state justice systems, to build commitment, and to address informal justice institutions. The criticality of these factors derived from their centrality to the United Nations' state-based enforcement approach to building the rule of law. Having positioned the state as the primary agent of justice, a commodity to be delivered primarily through the state justice system, it follows that any strategy that did not successfully establish legitimate state structures for the peaceful redress of disputes, discredit or harness alternative justice structures, and generate a sufficient level of commitment on the part of the recipient population could not expect to succeed. In short, missions did not create the fundamental conditions under which their transitional subjects would be induced to follow the trajectory laid down as the means by which the rule of law was to be established.

The "deal makers"

In each of the case studies, the other six factors proved important but not demonstrably critical to the overall success of the United Nations in meeting its objectives. The issue of security is one example. Ensuring security against violence proved important in enabling individuals to engage confidently with the state justice system without fear for their safety. It also created the space for supportive social relationships to develop, enabled more effective UN mission performance and helped to provide political certainty. Nonetheless, some level of insecurity appeared to be tolerable. Participation in the judicial system, for example, remained a contemplatable prospect for many Timorese despite outbreaks of violence and a general rise in criminality. Similarly, the high degree of insecurity faced by Kosovo Serbs did not appear to deter Kosovo Albanians from embracing their new police force. Given that, in all three missions, the United Nations made creditable if not complete progress in restoring security, it is difficult to establish from these case studies the threshold at which lack of security would completely prevent the pursuit of rule of law objectives. Lack of security did, nonetheless, have a negative effect, especially for very vulnerable segments of the population.

Similarly, the other factors hindered the effectiveness of the mission but did not demonstrably derail it. Low state capacity, a lack of supportive social relationships and a failure to deal with the past arguably constrained the extent to which future progress on rule of law initiatives could be sustained and deepened, yet the case studies are not conclusive as to the extent of the overall damage this caused. Poor overall mission performance had a similarly detrimental effect, yet in some areas progress was made with very few resources and in the face of deficient mission management, suggesting that high performance by certain individuals or groups within the mission was able to have a positive impact. The case studies demonstrate the limitations imposed by inappropriate mandates, but these limitations were not necessarily fatal.

Although the critical importance of these factors could not be established from the case studies, their cumulative effect should perhaps not be underestimated. The case studies demonstrate the importance of a holistic approach to establishing the rule of law, suggesting that the prospects for success might be significantly reduced unless due attention is given to each of the factors identified. This underscores the well-recognised fact that justice sector reform cannot be divorced from political or social context. This point is particularly salient when examining whether the United Nations' state-based enforcement model is, in fact, a useful approach to establishing the rule of law. This is considered in the next section.

Towards a state-building strategy

This section discusses what insights the case studies may provide on fundamental questions regarding the United Nations' state-building enterprise: whether the United Nations' state-based enforcement model may be an ineffective approach to establishing the rule of law; whether the liberal normative template that underpins the United Nations' self-declared state-building agenda is fundamentally ill suited to the hostile intervention environment of the disrupted state; and what, therefore, is a realistic role for external actors such as the United Nations seeking to engage in rule of law promotion.

The state-based enforcement approach

Chapter 3 argued that the principal means by which UN transitional administrations attempted to establish the rule of law was through a state-based enforcement model that focused on creating or strengthening state legal, judicial and law enforcement bodies. The case studies would suggest that, in the context of the disrupted state, this formalistic approach to the rule of law may have been defective and the assumption implicit in the United Nations' approach that state-based institutions are the key to establishing the rule of law is misplaced. In this sense, the case studies add weight to the existing body of literature, reviewed in Chapter 3, which casts doubt on this assumption.

Each of the case studies demonstrates flaws in the United Nations' state-based enforcement model for establishing the rule of law. When the rule of law is thought of as a normative value scheme constituted by the "rules of the game" and adherence to those rules, the case studies suggest that it does not make sense to equate the rule of law directly with the establishment of state-based coercive mechanisms, especially when these are more formalist than substantive in nature.

Each UN transitional administration sought to establish the rule of law by defining a set of formal rules (the legal system) and constructing state organisations (judiciaries, police forces and prisons) following liberal models found in western states. In Cambodia, Kosovo and East Timor, these rules and organisations were often poorly designed, inadequately established, inaccessible and inappropriate to local mores. They proved ineffective in making and enforcing rules governing cooperative patterns of social behaviour because relevant actors did not believe they provided real solutions to real problems. In short, the "form" was deficient and the "substance" lacking.

In each of the case studies, it is clear that the prevailing "rules of the game" did not reside only in state institutions. Failing to acknowledge this undermined the United Nations' efforts to establish the rule of law. A range of informal institutions that arguably amounted to or at least strongly influenced "law" existed. In some instances informal rules were codified in quite structured informal institutions – the parallel structures in Kosovo or "traditional justice" systems in East Timor – and were significantly more entrenched than their state counterparts. As described above, by not developing a principled, informed approach to such informal sources, the United Nations missed a critical opportunity either to harness them in support of core rule of law principles or to ensure that they did not undermine them.

Similarly, each of the case studies demonstrates that adherence to the desired rule system depended critically on the voluntary commitment of local actors, particularly given the weakness of state sanction mechanisms. Embryonic and poorly functioning state enforcement mechanisms established by the UN mission often proved ineffective in ensuring adherence to the law, particularly when such adherence required significant shifts in normative behaviour. In the face of a dysfunctional coercive apparatus, the subjects of new legal systems often believed that there were viable and sometimes more legitimate alternatives to obeying the new laws.

Adherence to the rule of law as a value system thus appeared to depend significantly on the extent to which local actors were prepared and able to accept it as legitimate and commit voluntarily to it. The legitimacy of the rule of law was undermined where it was not perceived to be compatible with pre-existing social values, where local actors did not have a sense of "ownership" over processes designed to construct the new value system or where the new system did not deliver desired or reliable outcomes. The capacity to commit was undermined by security disincentives, such as the threat of violent retribution for going to court; access disincentives, such as excessive financial or logistical constraints; and education shortfalls, whereby communities were sometimes completely unaware that a new way of doing things was even being offered.

The state enforcement approach did not adequately account for the importance of power issues. The case studies demonstrate the profound influence that power structures, formal or informal, had on efforts to establish the rule of law and the relative ineffectiveness of UN transitional administrations in dealing with this issue. The threat posed by rule of law reform was extremely high for powerful spoiler groups and for some players in the political elite bent on taking advantage of a period of flux to consolidate their authority.

Finally, the ability of the United Nations to establish substantive rule of law institutions depended critically on appropriate institutional design choices. In a sense, all the above factors may be thought of as institutional choice issues that deeply influenced the extent to which state rule of law structures developed that were robust, reliable and ultimately capable of achieving their objectives.

In practical terms, there are thus good reasons why a formalist approach to institution-building should give way to a more substantive approach. This needs to be pursued both through appropriate institutional design of state institutions as well as consideration of the extent to which state institutions alone will achieve the desired outcomes.

The liberal normative template and the disrupted state

The experience of transitional administration in Cambodia, East Timor and Kosovo raises a significant question mark over whether the liberal normative template underpinning the United Nations' self-declared state-building agenda is fundamentally ill suited to post-conflict environments.

First, moving from the conditions of the disrupted state to the fundamentally different liberal normative template is exceedingly difficult. The disrupted states in which UN transitional administrations were deployed clearly represented an extreme and, in many ways, hostile intervention environment characterised by high levels of state incompetence, social trauma and violence. Such features are self-evidently the antithesis of the desired objectives of UN state-building enterprises as outlined in Chapter 2, and as such may present significant challenges to external intervention. Low state capacity, the presence of ongoing hostilities, the fragility of social relationships and the challenges posed by informal political and institutional alternatives to the UN model made it extremely difficult for UN transitional administrations to implement rule of law initiatives in each of the case studies. The potential for this to constrain the extent to which peace operations can realistically pursue rule of law objectives needs to be carefully assessed and built into mission strategy before over-ambitious programmes are attempted, particularly in short missions.

Second, it may be destabilising to attempt ambitious liberalising reforms in the inherently unstable environment of the disrupted state. Just as holding democratic elections may set up dangerous "win–lose" conditions in a highly combustible environment, so too rule of law interventions may exacerbate conflicts rather than moving towards more peaceful modes of dispute resolution. The difficulties of establishing the Extraordinary Chambers in Cambodia and the risk of pursuing serious crimes investigations in delicate stages of reconciliation between militia groups and their communities in East Timor are examples of where rule of law interventions may have inflamed tensions.

Similarly, allowing too much devolution of authority may risk jeopardising key mission objectives, as experienced in East Timor with UNTAET's loss of control over important justice sector outcomes following the establishment of the Ministry of Justice. This became even clearer after independence, when the lack of fully developed institutional discipline over powerful elites enabled those elites to engage security and bureaucratic apparatuses in violent power struggles – as witnessed by the involvement of senior security sector, ministry and political heads in East Timor in the violence of 2006.

The case studies therefore point to the need for careful sequencing of reforms and clear recognition that, in the disrupted state, attempting too much too soon may risk diverging further from the trajectory to democracy and the rule of law.

The role for external actors

Both the theoretical debates and the empirical experience discussed in this book cast doubt on the UN approach, considered in Chapter 3, to establishing the rule of law. Together, they caution against an operational approach that equates building the rule of law too closely with the establishment of state institutions, or imagines that a new law will perform the functions expected of it. Empirically, even the most sanguine interpretation of the history of attempts by external actors to establish the rule of law suggests a rocky path with high prospects of failure, particularly in the extreme environment of the post-conflict disrupted state. External actors have consistently struggled to identify, let alone respond to, the intricate social and political networks that underpin rules-based behaviour or to heal the fundamental fractures of disrupted states.

As with other external attempts at rule of law promotion, the experience of UN transitional administration leaves little room for optimism about the role for external actors in promoting the rule of law in the hostile environment of the disrupted state. As Upham has described, rather than truly promoting the rule of law, transitional administrations appear to have gone little further than to replicate "[a] formalist model of law detached from the social and political interconnections that form actual legal systems anywhere" (2002: 10).

Systemic resource constraints on UN missions – including money, time and expertise – have always been well acknowledged in the UN system. Although they inevitably restricted the range of options open to UN Transitional Administrators, many of the most intractable challenges stemmed from a failure to deal with fundamental questions about context and the role of external actors. In none of the case studies did a sufficient number of UN actors give strategic consideration to how an alien, transient and highly intrusive governing authority could address contextual issues relating to culture, conflict, power and the role of the state. Critically, Transitional Administrators never fully confronted the central question of whether giving real substance to rule of law institutions could be achieved only through internal processes of change and, if so, whether there was a role for external assistance.

Transitional Administrators thus never determined the most appropriate role for themselves in supporting the establishment of the rule of law. The above discussion offers some lessons on how such a role might be configured, in terms of confirming a range of issues that must be considered and addressed. Further, several broad themes emerged from the case studies as having a significant bearing on the extent to which the transitional administration proved a positive force for change. These are discussed below.

Create an enabling "space"

The idea that external actors may create an enabling environment for internal societal transformations has underlined their role in facilitating local processes and providing resources, thereby creating the space for local actors to "start a conversation that will define and redefine their polity" (Chesterman 2004a: 31). The literature has also emphasised the role of institutional reform as a "lever of change" that pushes culture and politics in the desired direction (Kleinfeld-Belton 2005: 22; Bastian and Luckham 2003: 312).

As an administering body with extensive political authority, the UN transitional administration demonstrated the potential for external actors to create either an enabling or a disabling environment in which domestic processes of change could occur. Central to this was the ability of the UN transitional administration to provide a secure environment in which domestic processes of change could begin to take place. For example, the presence of a benign authority willing to support and protect civil society groups provided the "space" for NGOs to develop as a check on the state. Similarly, improvements in personal security deriving from the presence of peacekeepers allowed ordinary people to resume ordinary interactions, including those in the legal arena. Within the space thus created, the provision of resources such as technical expertise and training facilities provided local actors with the means to acquire knowledge and skills in the rule of law field.

Conversely, failing to provide an enabling "space" risked crowding out local actors, introducing distortions or further exacerbating social divisions. In particular, the transitional administration experience underscored the difficulty of overcoming the paradoxical tension between "control" by an external authority and the aspirations for "ownership" and "participation" embedded in the liberal normative template. As Chesterman (2003, 2007) has pointed out, "benevolent autocracy" makes for an uncertain foundation for the sort of liberalising transformation envisaged in the UN state-building agenda. The difficulties of stimulating a genuinely indigenous civil society and the resentment felt by local actors whose participation in the rule of law arena was overly circumscribed are two examples. In Kosovo, for instance, imposing a liberal template for democracy and the rule of law proved impossible when local actors could not participate fully in justice processes in which they had no authoritative role and felt deeply disempowered by UNMIK's "reserved powers", coupled with a lack of resolution on Kosovo's final status. Instead of engaging in internal processes of state–society interaction integral to the democratic normative transformation at hand, local actors rejected or sought to undermine key processes.

Importantly, the enforcement of a political settlement acceptable to all key players proved a crucial enabling parameter over which the United Nations had considerable influence. In East Timor, a decisive political settlement regarding the future sovereign status of the territory enabled UNTAET and East Timorese leaders to set firm goals within a defined time frame and to begin to approach long-term rule of law goals such as reconciliation, without being dragged down by internal political turmoil or damaging confrontation with Indonesia. In Kosovo, the lack of a decision on its final status paralysed efforts to build the rule of law and inflamed political agendas that ran counter to rule of law objectives. In Cambodia, continued conflict between the parties to the Paris Agreements had a negative impact across the mission, including on rule of law objectives. The factions blocked UNTAC's rule of law initiatives at the highest levels and politicised the justice sector, and their mutual mistrust undermined the potential for cooperative activity.

These experiences suggest that, in fulfilling this enabling role, UN transitional administrations needed to pay close attention to both creating and constraining the "space" in ways that helped push change in the right direction.

Engage local populations

The political settlement example reinforces the point that creating "space" is not enough if local actors are not willing or able to move in to fill it in constructive ways. The "commitment" issues examined in the case studies demonstrate clearly that any attempt by an external actor to promote social transformation in pursuit of the rule of law requires much fuller integration of local populations at all levels and across all initiatives. As argued in Chapter 3, building the rule of law – where it is absent – is fundamentally about transforming norms of social behaviour, and thus the social interactions of the recipient population must be at the centre of any strategy.

Empowering local actors to participate in strategies designed to promote the rule of law proved particularly challenging for transitional administrations because of their inherently intrusive and autocratic nature. Being required to govern a territory under tenuous notions of local consent, while also being expected to promote local "ownership", placed Transitional Administrators in a paradoxical situation. Although aware of the issue, none of the missions successfully resolved the dilemma of where to draw the line between UN and local responsibilities for rule of law creation, including how much authority to devolve and when and in what order this should be done.

The case studies illustrate that there is unlikely to be a simple or consistent answer to questions about power devolution. They do, however, underscore that failing to adopt a principled approach to this dilemma from the outset, or to manage the expectations of local political elites and the broader population, complicated almost every rule of law initiative. Situations need to be managed actively from the outset and in as transparent a manner as possible. Doing so allows for the possibility of generating and retaining local commitment to reforms without actually conferring "ownership" where this is thought of as executive authority (Chesterman 2004a: 143–144).

The case studies also illustrate that, ultimately, an external administration may have only limited control over the pace at which it devolves power. In each of the case studies, the UN transitional administration's ability to control the pace of the transition depended not only on the machinations of the UN system and its member states, which tended to push the mission towards rapid transition and exit, but critically on the extent to which local players were willing to continue to support the administration's presence. This underscores further the need for decisive, well-planned efforts from the outset to build commitment to UN transitional authority and to make the most of the narrow window of opportunity in which the United Nations could realistically "call the shots".

Confront the tyranny of time

The case studies confirm that embedding stable and durable rule of law institutions is a long-term enterprise ill suited to truncated interventions. Although many UN mission staff expressed intense frustration at the lack of time to implement comprehensive rule of law strategies, UN transitional administrations nonetheless failed to give adequate consideration to which aspects of rule of law establishment could be supported in the short term and handled by an external player, as opposed to time-dependent processes that ultimately relied on intricate and long-term domestic interactions. It is conceivable that, by attempting to work across the entire range of justice sector activities in a very short time, less progress was made towards establishing the rule of law than might have been achieved by a more modest agenda. This goal might have been better served had the United Nations restricted its activities to a core set of appropriately sequenced objectives supported by clearly articulated follow-on strategies.

A stronger commitment by the Security Council to support a targeted UN presence for the long haul would perhaps have made the greatest difference. As the Secretary-General stated in response to the 2006 East Timor crisis:

> Much has been achieved since [Timor-Leste's] independence in major areas of institutional capacity building. But the UN and the international community have learned from lessons elsewhere, and have now been starkly reminded by the Timor-Leste crisis, that nation-building and peacebuilding are long-term tasks. This is especially true of the time required to build a new police service and justice system. We now have a responsibility not only to remain committed to assist Timor-Leste, but to show that we commit ourselves to do so on a long-term basis. (UNSC 2006b: 42)

Develop front-end strategies

Deploying at short notice into unpredictable emergency situations necessarily restricted the time available to devise a nuanced strategy appropriate to local context. However, as the case studies demonstrate, the resulting ad hoc and strategically flawed responses struck serious blows to the legitimacy and authority of the United Nations, creating a negative impression at the outset from which missions never fully recovered. Being unable to act swiftly to establish effective law enforcement and judicial presences, for example, only reinforced the breakdown in the rule of law and the impunity this entailed. Similarly, choosing one set of laws and then abandoning these for another, or implementing hastily conceived legislation that was technically deficient and poorly received, only further undermined confidence in the legal system.

The entry phase proved the critical point at which respect for and commitment to the rule of law objectives of the mission were won or lost. It would follow that the principal opportunity for the United Nations as an external actor to create constructive parameters for change lies in demonstrating a principled, strategic approach to state-building from the outset. Such an approach would address, at a minimum, the questions of how to create an enabling space, how to engage local populations and how to ensure an adequate deployment period.

No entry without strategy

Is it all too hard? The above discussion inevitably poses the question of whether the flaws in strategy and implementation exposed by these case studies may be addressed by better strategy and better implementation, or whether they are, in fact, inseparable from the structural dynamics of the United Nations itself. Does the chaotic raft of actors, relationships and political agendas that come together in UN state-building missions render them fundamentally ineffectual instruments for social and political transformation of the extent required to establish the rule of law?

It is tempting to conclude that, given the magnitude of both the challenges and the constraints, establishing the rule of law is a "mission impossible", but this may not be the case. Similarly, it does not necessarily follow that UN peace operations should confine themselves to straightforward stabilisation objectives and simply forget broader state-building ambitions.

Although international and domestic pressure for the United Nations to engage in state-building activities may wax and wane, it seems unlikely to disappear. Such pressure has been, and might usefully continue to be, applied in support of relevant UN reform. This study, along with many others, has suggested that UN state-building policy and practice have both lagged behind theory. This gap is only partially attributable to human and physical resource constraints. The case studies presented in this book were enriched by the knowledge and observations of a wide range of capable and dedicated UN mission staff, many of whom are acknowledged experts in their field. Their work was often frustrated by the politics of UN decision-making, the structural constraints of a reactive, ad hoc and fragmented UN bureaucracy and the disparate interests and power relations of the UN conglomerate of member states, political organs and agencies. Although it was not a feature of this study, the case studies nonetheless back the contention that the prospects for successful state-building strategies depend on broader UN reform issues – from reconfiguring the Security Council and other UN organs, to better coordination, resourcing and commitment to long-term interventions. In this respect, continuing to refine the roles and capacity of the UN system through such measures as the establishment of the Secretariat's Rule of Law Coordination and Research Group could play a key role.

Further, adopting a principle of "no entry without strategy" might improve the prospects for contributing to meaningful change. Entry strategies should be formulated with particular reference to context, based on a robust and revisable theory of change and sequenced carefully. Crucially, they should be communicated to and accepted by a critical mass of key local players.

Strategies should not try to do too much. The transitional administration experience cautions against adopting an over-ambitious state-building agenda that exceeds the political will or organisational capability of the UN system. Successful strategies are likely to be those that strike an acceptable trade-off between pursuing lofty notions of the rule of law – which might require extensive social and political engineering that tackles not just state structures but social mores, norms and state–society relations – and what can realistically be achieved. Although the parameters of what is "realistic" will depend on the intervention context, this study suggests that trying to establish a fully fledged state justice sector from scratch is a high-risk strategy that is unlikely to be achievable or even relevant to the real needs of the community being asked to accept it. Strategists may need to think outside the box.

Perhaps the most compelling reason to keep chasing the elusive goal is the belief, supported by this study, that a sustained peace cannot be achieved without the rule of law. The core aspirations embodied in the UN conception of "the rule of law" remain of critical importance to both international society and those smaller constellations of persons most affected by state disruption. Whatever the odds, UN interventions should strive to offer security against violence, to promote legitimate structures to redress agreements dishonoured and to encourage state practices worthy of society's trust. These should be at the centre of any state-building strategy.

Bibliography

ADHOC, LICADHO and Human Rights Watch (1999), "Impunity in Cambodia: how human rights offenders escape justice", *Human Rights Watch*, vol. 11, no. 3 (C), Phnom Penh.

Advocacy Project (2000), "Series conclusion: the power of advocacy, part 2", *On the Record Kosovo*, 15 September, vol. 10, issue 12/2, accessed 12 August 2004, at ⟨http://www.advocacynet.org/news_view/news_68.html⟩.

AFP (2000a), "Hashim Thaci: 'The Snake' faces make or break electoral challenge", 25 October, accessed 11 August 2004, at ⟨http://www.balkanpeace.org/hed/archive/oct00/hed1008.shtml⟩.

AFP (2000b), "Ramush Haradinaj: Kosovo's heavyweight outsider", 25 October, accessed 11 August 2004, at ⟨http://www.balkanpeace.org/hed/archive/oct00/hed1008.shtml⟩.

Agreements on a Comprehensive Political Settlement of the Cambodia Conflict (1991), enacted 23 October 1991 [Paris Agreements].

AI [Amnesty International] (2000), *Amnesty International's recommendations to UNMIK on the judicial system*, February, London.

——— (2001), *East Timor: justice at risk*, 26 July, London, report no. ASA 57/002/2001.

——— (2002a), *Kingdom of Cambodia: urgent need for judicial reform*, 19 June, London, report no. ASA 23/004/2002, accessed 6 June 2003, at ⟨http://web.amnesty.org/library/Index/ENGASA230042002?open&of=ENG-KHM⟩.

——— (2002b), *Federal Republic of Yugoslavia (Kosovo): international officials flout international law*, 1 September, London, accessed 20 June 2004, at ⟨http://web.amnesty.org/library/Index/ENGEUR700082002?open&of=ENG-YUG⟩.

——— (2003a), *Kingdom of Cambodia: a human rights review based on the Convention against Torture*, London, accessed 1 September 2003, at ⟨http://web.amnesty.org/library/print/ENGASA230072003⟩.

—— (2003b), *Timor-Leste: briefing to Security Council members on policing and security in Timor-Leste*, London, report no. ASA 57/001/2003.

—— (2003c), *Indonesia: guilty verdict insufficient to deliver justice and truth*, 5 August, London, accessed 20 February 2004, at ⟨http://www.amnestyusa.org/news/2003/indonesia08052003.html⟩.

—— (2004a), *Kosovo: facts and figures on trafficking of women and girls for forced prostitution in Kosovo*, 6 May, London, report no. EUR 70/013/2004, accessed 20 August 2004, at ⟨http://www.amnesty.org/library/Index/ENGEUR700132004⟩.

—— (2004b), *Serbia and Montenegro (Kosovo): the legacy of past human rights abuses*, 1 April, London, report no. EUR 70/009/2004, accessed 20 June 2004, at ⟨http://web.amnesty.org/library/Index/ENGEUR700092004⟩.

Akashi, Y (1992a), "Statement by the Special Representative of the Secretary-General for Cambodia on further accession by the SNC to international human rights instruments", United Nations Transitional Authority in Cambodia.

—— (1992b), "Statement by the Special Representative of the Secretary-General on the adoption of the text of Provisions Relating to the Judiciary and Criminal Law and Procedure", 10 September 1992, United Nations Transitional Authority in Cambodia.

—— (1993), "Neutral political environment: statement by Mr Akashi", 10 February, Phnom Penh.

Alkatiri, M (2001), "Speech by Mari Alkatiri, Head of Government, on the occasion of the ceremony of the swearing in of members of the Transitional Government of East Timor", 20 September, Dili.

An agenda for peace. See UNGA (1992).

Anleu, S (2000), *Law and social change*, Sage Publications, London.

Annan, K (1998), "Peacekeeping, military intervention and national sovereignty in internal armed conflict", in Moore, J (ed) *Hard choices: moral dilemmas in humanitarian intervention*, Rowman & Littlefield, Lanham, MD, pp. 55–69.

Aron, L (2002), "Russia reinvents the rule of law", *Russian Outlook*, 20 March, accessed 26 April 2006, at ⟨http://www.aei.org/publications/pubID.13781,filter.all/pub_detail.asp⟩.

Ashley, D (1998), "The failure of conflict resolution in Cambodia: causes and lessons", in Brown, F and Timberman, D (eds) *Cambodia and the international community: the quest for peace, development and democracy*, Asia Society, New York, pp. 49–78.

Asia Foundation (2001), *East Timor National Survey of Voter Knowledge (Preliminary Findings)*, May, Dili, accessed 29 March 2001, at ⟨http://www.asiafoundation.org/pdf/EastTimorVoterEd.pdf⟩.

—— (2003), *Democracy in Cambodia – 2003: a survey of the Cambodian electorate*, draft, 16 May, accessed 12 December 2003, at ⟨http://www.asiafoundation.org/pdf/DemocracyinCambodia.pdf⟩.

Babo-Soares, D (2001), "Law and order: judiciary development in East Timor", paper presented to the conference Comparing Experiences with State Building in Asia and Europe: The Cases of East Timor, Bosnia and Kosovo, October, Bali.

Barnett, M (1995), "The UN and global security: the norm is mightier than the sword", *Ethics and International Affairs*, vol. 9, accessed 8 October 2000, at ⟨http://www.cceia.org/barnett9.htm⟩.

Bastian, S and Luckham, R (eds) (2003), *Can democracy be designed? The politics of institutional choice in conflict-torn societies*, 2ed Books, London.

Berry, K (1997), *From red to blue: Australia's initiative for peace*, Allen & Unwin Australia, Sydney.

Biebesheimer, C and Payne, J (2001), *IDB experience in justice reform*, International Development Bank, Washington DC.

Bloomfield, K (1998), "How should we remember?", speech at the conference Dealing with the past: reconciliation processes and peacebuilding, INCORE, 8–9 June, Belfast, accessed 10 October 2007, at ⟨http://www.incore.ulst.ac.uk/research/projects/thepast/bloom.htm⟩.

Bolton, J (2001), "United States policy on United Nations peacekeeping", *World Affairs*, vol. 163, no. 3, pp. 129–147, accessed 29 July 2004, at ⟨http://www.findarticles.com/p/articles/mi_m2393/is_3_163/ai_69752065/pg_1⟩.

Boothby, D (2004), "The political challenges of administering Eastern Slavonia", *Global Governance*, vol. 10, pp. 37–51.

Boraine, A (2005), "Transitional justice", in Chesterman, S, Ignatieff, M and Thakur, R (eds) *Making states work: state failure and the crisis of governance*, United Nations University Press, Tokyo, pp. 318–338.

Borbely, M, Carlsson, H, Chastenay, C, Felgenhauer, T, Fung, C, Hykl, R, Pentony, P, Sachs, N and Sieber-Messick, M (1999), *Project report on the role of foreign aid for legal reform programs in the Russian Federation*, Woodrow Wilson School of Public and International Affairs, Princeton University, Princeton, NJ, January, accessed 3 February 2001, at ⟨http://www1.worldbank.org/publicsector/legal/projectreport.pdf⟩.

Borg-Olivier, A (2003), "Criminal codes sent for review", *Focus Kosovo*, April, accessed 18 June 2004, at ⟨http://www.unmikonline.org/pub/focuskos/apr03/focusklaw1.htm⟩.

Bouloukos, A and Dakin, B (2001), "Toward a universal declaration of the rule of law: implications for criminal justice and sustainable development", *International Journal of Comparative Sociology*, vol. 42, no. 1–2, pp. 145–162.

Brahimi Report. See UNGA (2000f).

Braibanti, R (1968), *The role of law in political development*, Center for Commonwealth Studies, Duke University, Durham, NC.

Braithwaite, J (2000), "Repentance rituals and restorative justice", *Journal of Political Philosophy*, vol. 8, no. 1, pp. 115–131.

Brookes, D (2000), "Evaluating restorative justice programs", paper presented to the United Nations Crime Congress, Ancillary Meetings, Vienna.

Brown, F and Timberman, D (1998), *Cambodia and the international community: the quest for peace, development and democracy*, Asia Society, New York.

Brown, M and Zasloff, J (1998), *Cambodia confounds the peacemakers: 1979–1998*, Cornell University Press, Ithaca, NY.

Brownlie, I (1998), *The rule of law in international affairs: international law at the fiftieth anniversary of the United Nations*, Martinus Nijhoff, The Hague.

Bull, C (2001), *Xanana Gusmao's views on justice*, Commission for Reception, Truth and Reconciliation, November, Dili, accessed 2 May 2006, at ⟨http://www.easttimor-reconciliation.org/Gusmao_Justice-E.htm⟩.

Bull, H (1977), *The anarchical society: a study of order in world politics*, Macmillan, London.

Burgerman, S (2000), "Building the peace by mandating reform: United Nations-mediated human rights agreements in El Salvador and Guatemala", *Latin American Perspectives*, vol. 27, no. 3, pp. 63–87.

Burkle, F (2003), "Complex emergencies and military capabilities", in Maley, W, Sampford, C and Thakur, R (eds) *From civil strife to civil society: civil and military responsibilities in disrupted states*, United Nations University Press, Tokyo, pp. 96–108.

Callahan, M (1999), *Mandates and empire: the League of Nations and Africa 1914–1931*, Sussex Academic Press, Brighton.

Caplan, R (2002), *A new trusteeship? The international administration of war-torn territories*, Oxford University Press, New York.

—— (2004a), "Partner or patron? international civil administration and local capacity building", *International Peacekeeping*, vol. 11, no. 2, pp. 229–247.

—— (2004b), "International authority and state-building: the case of Bosnia and Herzegovina", *Global Governance*, vol. 10, pp. 53–65.

Carlson, S N (2006), *Legal and judicial rule of law work in multi-dimensional peacekeeping operations: lessons-learned study*, United Nations Department of Peacekeeping Operations Peacekeeping Best Practices Unit, March, New York, accessed 14 March 2006, at ⟨http://pbpu.unlb.org/pbps/Pages/Public/viewdocument.aspx?id=2&docid=739⟩.

Carothers, T (1998), "The rule of law revival", *Foreign Affairs*, vol. 77, no. 2, pp. 95–106.

—— (1999), *Aiding democracy abroad: the learning curve*, Carnegie Endowment for International Peace, Washington DC.

—— (2003), *Promoting the rule of law abroad: the problem of knowledge*, Carnegie Endowment for International Peace, January, Washington DC.

—— (2006a), "The rule of law revival", in Carothers, T (ed) *Promoting the rule of law abroad: in search of knowledge*, Carnegie Endowment for International Peace, Washington DC, pp. 3–14.

—— (2006b), "Promoting the rule of law abroad: are we there yet?", presentation made to the Carnegie Endowment for International Peace, 1 February, Washington DC, accessed 10 March 2006, at ⟨http://www.carnegieendowment.org/events/index.cfm?fa=eventDetail&id=849&&prog=zgp&proj=zdrl⟩.

—— (2006c), *Promoting the rule of law abroad: in search of knowledge*, Carnegie Endowment for International Peace, Washington DC.

Cassese, A (1998), "On the current trends towards criminal prosecution and punishment of breaches of international humanitarian law", *European Journal of International Law*, vol. 9, pp. 2–17.

Catholic News Service (2002), "East Timor's president says church plays large role in reconstruction", accessed 29 March 2004, at ⟨http://www.etan.org/et2002b/may/26-31/24etpres.htm⟩.

Charlesworth, H (2003), "The constitution of East Timor, May 20th, 2002", *International Journal of Constitutional Law*, vol. 1, no. 2, pp. 325–334.

Chesterman, S (2001a), *East Timor in transition: from conflict prevention to statebuilding*, International Peace Academy, May, New York, accessed 15 December 2003, at ⟨http://www.ipacademy.org⟩.

—— (2001b), *Kosovo in Limbo: state-building and "substantial autonomy"*, International Peace Academy, August, New York, accessed 15 December 2003, at ⟨www.ipacademy.org⟩.

—— (2002a), *Justice under international administration: Kosovo, East Timor and Afghanistan*, International Peace Academy, September, New York, accessed 15 December 2003, at ⟨http://www.ipacademy.org⟩.

—— (2002b), "Walking softly in Afghanistan: the future of UN state-building", *Survival*, vol. 44, no. 3, pp. 37–46.

—— (2003), *You, the people: The United Nations, transitional administration, and state-building*, International Peace Academy, November, New York, accessed 6 April 2006, at ⟨http://www.ipacademy.org⟩.

—— (2004a), *You, the people: The United Nations, transitional administration, and state-building*, Oxford University Press, New York.

—— (2004b), "UN state-building: challenges and contradictions", paper presented to the conference Strengthening of Civilian Administration in Post-conflict Societies and Failed States, International Peace Academy, 21 June, New York, accessed 2 May 2006, at <http://www.ipacademy.org/Publications/Publications.htm>.

—— (2007), "Ownership in theory and in practice: transfer of authority in UN statebuilding operations", *Journal of Intervention and Statebuilding*, vol. 1, no. 1, March.

Chesterman, S, Ignatieff, M and Thakur, R (2004), *Making states work: from state failure to state-building*, International Peace Academy, July, New York.

—— (2005a), "Introduction: making states work", in Chesterman, S, Ignatieff, M and Thakur, R (eds) *Making states work: state failure and the crisis of governance*, United Nations University Press, Tokyo, pp. 1–12.

Chopra, J (1997), "Peace-maintenance: the last stage of development", *Journal of Humanitarian Assistance*, accessed 27 February 2002, at ⟨http://www.jha.ac/articles/a023.htm⟩.

—— (1999), *Peace maintenance: the evolution of international political authority*, Routledge, London.

—— (2000), "The UN's kingdom of East Timor", *Survival*, vol. 42, no. 3, pp. 27–39.

—— (2002), "Building state failure in East Timor", *Development and Change*, vol. 33, no. 5, pp. 979–1000.

CHR [Commission on Human Rights] (2000), *Promoting and consolidating democracy*, 25 April, Geneva, E/CN.4/RES/2000/47.

—— (2002a), *Report of the UN High Commissioner for Human Rights on the situation of human rights in East Timor*, 1 March, Geneva, E/CN.4/2002/39.

—— (2002b), *Report of the Special Rapporteur on the independence of judges and lawyers, Dato' Param Cumaraswamy, submitted in accordance with Commission on Human Rights Resolution 2001/39*, 11 February, Geneva, E/CN.4/

2002/72, accessed 24 March 2004, at ⟨http://www.hri.ca/fortherecord2002/documentation/commission/e-cn4-2002-72.htm⟩.

—— (2003), *Question of the violation of human rights and fundamental freedoms in any part of the world: situation of human rights in parts of south-eastern Europe*, 26 March, E/CN.4/2003/38/Add.1.

Christian Solidarity Worldwide (2001), *Mission to East Timor 28 April to 5 May 2001*.

Cidadaun (2001), "Interview" [with Bishop Belo], October, vol. 10, accessed 15 April 2004, at ⟨http:/www.easttimor-reconciliation.org/Belo_Interview_E.htm⟩.

Clark, H (2002), *Kosovo: work in progress: closing the cycle of violence*, Centre for the Study of Forgiveness and Reconciliation, January, Coventry, accessed 5 August 2004, at ⟨http://legacy.www.coventry.ac.uk/legacy/acad/isl/forgive/images/kosovo.pdf⟩.

Cliffe, L (1994), *The transition to independence in Namibia*, Lynne Rienner, Boulder, CO.

CNRT [National Council of East Timorese Resistance] (1998), *Magna Carta concerning freedoms, rights, and duties for the people of East Timor*, 25 April, Peniche, accessed 4 May 2006, at ⟨http://www.geocities.com/CapitolHill/Senate/7112/cnrt2.htm⟩.

Cockell, J (2002), "Civil-military responses to security challenges in peace operations: ten lessons from Kosovo", *Global Governance*, vol. 8, no. 4, pp. 483–502.

Cocozzelli, F (2003), *Kosovo at the crossroads: competing solidarities, 2003*, Social Sciences Research Council, New York.

Cohen, D and Prusak, L (2001), *In good company. How social capital makes organisations work*, Harvard Business School Press, Boston, MA.

Coram, B (1996), "Second best theories and implications for institutional design", in Goodin, R (ed) *The theory of institutional design*, Press Syndicate of the University of Cambridge, Cambridge, pp. 90–102.

Cousens, E (2001), "Introduction", in Cousens, E and Kumar, C (eds) *Peacebuilding as politics: cultivating peace in fragile societies*, Lynne Rienner, Boulder, CO, pp. 1–20.

Cousens, E and Kumar, C (eds) (2001), *Peacebuilding as politics: cultivating peace in fragile societies*, Lynne Rienner, Boulder, CO.

Coy, J (2001), *Internal memorandum*, United Nations Transitional Administration in East Timor, 17 August, Dili.

Crosby, A (2000), "Policing Timor Lorosa'e", *Peacekeeping and International Relations*, vol. 29, no. 3/4, pp. 1–3.

Curtis, G (1993), "Transition to What? Cambodia, UNTAC and the peace process", UNRISD Discussion Paper No. 48, November.

—— (1998), *Cambodia reborn? The transition to democracy and development*, Brookings Institution, Washington DC.

DAGAinfo (2002), "UN diplomat cites racism as he quits", *DAGAinfo*, vol. 128, 30 January, accessed 26 February 2004, at ⟨http://www.daga.org/res/dagainfo/di128.htm⟩.

Dahl, R (1998), *On democracy*, Yale University Press, New Haven, CT, and London.

Dauvergne, P (1998a), "Weak states, strong states: a state-in-society perspective", in Dauvergne, P (ed) *Weak and strong states in Asia-Pacific societies*, Allen & Unwin in association with the Department of International Relations, Research School of Pacific and Asian Studies, Australian National University, Canberra, pp. 1–10.

―――― (ed) (1998b), *Weak and strong states in Asia-Pacific societies*, Allen and Unwin in association with the Department of International Relations, Research School of Pacific and Asian Studies, Australian National University, Canberra.

Denoon, D (2005), *A trial separation: Australia and the decolonisation of Papua New Guinea*, Pandanus Books, Canberra.

Diamond, L (1993a), "The globalization of democracy", in Slater, R, Schulz, B and Dorr, S (eds) *Global transformation and the third world*, Lynne Rienner, Boulder, CO, pp. 31–70.

―――― (1993b), "Introduction: political culture and democracy", in Diamond, L (ed) *Political culture and democracy in developing countries*, Lynne Rienner, Boulder, CO, pp. 1–33.

Diamond, L, Linz, J and Lipset, S (eds) (1998–1999), *Democracy in developing countries*, Lynne Rienner, Boulder, CO.

Dicey, A (1889), *Introduction to the study of the law of the constitutions*, 3rd edn, Macmillan, London.

Dobbins, J, Jones, S, Crane, K, Rathmell, A, Steele, B, Teltschik, R and Timilsina, A (2005), *The UN's role in nation-building: from Congo to Iraq*, RAND Corporation, Santa Monica, Arlington and Pittsburgh, accessed 9 February 2006, at ⟨http://www.rand.org/pubs/monographs/2005/RAND_MG304.pdf⟩.

Donnelly, J (1999), "The social construction of human rights", in Dunne, T and Wheeler, N (eds) *Human rights in global politics*, Cambridge University Press, Cambridge, pp. 71–102.

Donovan, D (1993), "The Cambodian legal system: an overview", in Donovan, D, Jones, S, Pokemper, D and Muscat, R (eds) *Rebuilding Cambodia: human resources, human rights, and law: three essays*, Johns Hopkins Foreign Policy Institute, Washington DC, pp. 69–108.

Donovan, D, Jones, S, Pokemper, D and Muscat, R (1993), *Rebuilding Cambodia: human resources, human rights, and law: three essays*, Johns Hopkins Foreign Policy Institute, Washington DC.

Dorff, R (1999), "Responding to the failed state: what to do and what to expect", paper presented at the Failed States Conference, Purdue University, West Lafayette.

Doyle, K (2001a), "Atrocities trial struggles with politics of justice", *Cambodia Daily*, 30 January.

Doyle, M (1995), *UN peacekeeping in Cambodia: UNTAC's civil mandate*, Lynne Rienner, Boulder, CO.

Dryzek, J (1996), "The informal logic of institutional design", in Goodin, R (ed) *The theory of institutional design*, Press Syndicate of the University of Cambridge, Cambridge, pp. 103–125.

Dunne, T and Wheeler, N (1999a), "Introduction: human rights and the fifty years' crisis", in Dunne, T and Wheeler, N (eds) *Human rights in global politics*, Cambridge University Press, Cambridge, pp. 1–28.

Dunne, T and Wheeler, N (eds) (1999b), *Human rights in global politics*, Cambridge University Press, Cambridge.

Du Toit, A (2000), "The moral foundations of the South African TRC: truth as acknowledgement and justice as recognition", in Rotberg, R and Thompson, D (eds) *Truth versus justice: the morality of truth commissions*, Princeton University Press, Princeton, pp. 122–140.

Dworkin, R (1986), *Law's empire*, Harvard University Press, Cambridge, MA.

Dziedzic, M (2002), "Policing from above: executive policing and peace implementation in Kosovo", in Dwan, R (ed) *Executive policing: enforcing the law in peace operations*, Oxford University Press, New York, pp. 33–52.

East Timor Action Network (2003), "Indonesian court's final East Timor sentence 'a joke': East Timor Action Network urges international tribunal", 5 August, accessed 20 February 2004, at ⟨http://etan.org/news/2003a/08verdict.htm⟩.

East Timor NGO Forum (2001a), *Building an independent East Timor: critical issues for donors*, Oslo, accessed 25 February 2004, at ⟨http://www.geocities.com/etngoforum/ngos.xls⟩.

———— (2002), *List of NGOs*, Dili, accessed 10 March 2004, at ⟨http://www.geocities.com/etngoforum/ngos.xls⟩.

Eaton, C (1994), "Police in institution building", in Smith, H (ed) *International peacekeeping: building on the Cambodian experience*, Australian Defence Studies Centre, Canberra, pp. 59–63.

Edelman, L and Cahill, M (1998), "How law matters in dispute and dispute processing (or, the contingency of legal matter in informal dispute processes)", in Garth, B and Sarat, A (eds) *How does law matter?*, Northwestern University Press, Evanston, IL, pp. 15–44.

Ehrlich, I (1975), "The deterrent effect of capital punishment: a question of life and death", *American Economic Review*, vol. 65, no. 3, pp. 397–417.

Ellickson, R (1991), *Order without law: how neighbours settle disputes*, Harvard University Press, Cambridge, MA.

Evans, G (1993), *Cooperating for peace: the global agenda for the 1990s and Beyond*, Allen & Unwin, St Leonards.

Evans, P (1997), "The eclipse of the state? Reflections on stateness in an era of globalisation", *World Politics*, vol. 50, no. 1, October, pp. 62–87.

Falk, R (2000a), *Human rights horizons: the pursuit of justice in a globalizing world*, Routledge, New York.

———— (2000b), "Kosovo revisited", *The Nation*, vol. 270, issue 14, accessed 28 October 2007, at ⟨http://www.thenation.com/doc/20000410/falk⟩.

Falt, J (1998), "The growth of an independent private bar in Cambodia in the context of development", paper presented at the International Conference on Cambodian Legal and Judicial Reform in the Context of Sustainable Development, Cambodian Legal Resources Development Centre, 8–10 June, Phnom Penh.

Farrall, J (2007), *United Nations peacekeeping and the rule of law*, Issues paper, 1 March, Centre for International Governance and Justice, Regulatory Institutions Network, Australian National University, Canberra.

FBIS [Foreign Broadcast Information Service] (1993a), "Commission chairman rejects UNTAC's law changes", 12 March, Washington DC, p. 42.

—— (1993b), "Sihanouk discusses form of new government", 16 June, Washington DC, p. 31.

—— (1993c), "Hun Sen makes statement after SNC meeting", 6 April, p. 36.

Fearon, J (1991), "Counterfactuals and hypothesis testing in political science", *World Politics*, vol. 43, no. 2, pp. 169–195.

Fernando, B (1998), *Problems facing the Cambodian legal system*, Asian Human Rights Commission, Hong Kong.

Findlay, T (1995), *Cambodia: the legacy and lessons of UNTAC*, Oxford University Press, New York.

Fishman, R (1990), "Rethinking state and regime: southern Europe's transition to democracy", *World Politics*, vol. 42, no. 3 pp. 422–440.

Fitzpatrick, D (2002), *Land claims in East Timor*, Asia Pacific Press, Canberra.

Fitzpatrick, P (1980), *Law and state in Papua New Guinea*, Academic Press, London and New York.

Flatham, R (1992), "Liberalism and the suspect enterprise of political institutionalization: the case of the rule of law", in Shapiro, I (ed) *The rule of law*, New York University Press, New York, pp. 297–327.

Fokupers (2001), "Statement of concern regarding the appeal hearing", 25 July, Dili, accessed 5 May 2006, at ⟨http://www.etan.org/et2001c/july/22-28/25drser.htm⟩.

Forst, R (2001), "Towards a critical theory of transnational justice", *Metaphilosophy*, vol. 32, no. 1, pp. 160–179.

Franck, T (1972), "The new development: can American law and legal institutions help developing countries?", *Wisconsin Law Review*, vol. 1972, no. 3, pp. 767–801.

Freedom House (2004), *Nations in transit 2004: Serbia and Montenegro (Kosovo)*, Freedom House, New York, accessed 6 August 2004, at ⟨http://www.freedomhouse.org/research/nattransit.htm⟩.

Fukuyama, F (2004), "The imperative of state-building", *Journal of Democracy*, vol. 15, no. 2, pp. 17–31, accessed 9 February 2006, at ⟨http://ezproxy.libadfa.adfa.edu.au:2634/journals/journal_of_democracy/vol5/15.2fukuyama.pdf⟩.

Gantchev, G (1993), "Outstanding warrant for the arrest of Brigadier-General Phorn Salin (CPAF)", United Nations Transitional Authority in Cambodia, Civil Administration Component, 13 August, Battambang.

Garth, B and Sarat, A (eds) (1998a), *How does law matter?*, Northwestern University Press, Evanston, IL.

Garth, B and Sarat, A (1998b), "Studying how law matters: an introduction", in Garth, B and Sarat, A (eds) *How does law matter?*, Northwestern University Press, Evanston, IL, pp. 1–14.

Geertz, C (1983), *Local knowledge: further essays in interpretive anthropology*, Basic Books, New York.

Germanos, G (1992), *Report covering the period 29 July–12 August 1992*, United Nations Transitional Authority in Cambodia, Civil Administration Component, 12 August, Kompong Thom.

Ghani, A, Lockhart, C and Carnahan, M (2005), *Closing the sovereignty gap: an approach to state-building*, Overseas Development Institute, London, accessed 2 April 2005, at ⟨http://www.odi.org.uk/publications/working_papers/wp253.pdf⟩.

Goldstone, R (1996), "Justice as a tool for peace-making: truth commissions and international criminal tribunals", *New York Journal of International Law and Politics*, vol. 28, pp. 485–503.

—— (2002), "Whither Kosovo? Whither democracy?", *Global Governance*, vol. 8, no. 2, pp. 143–147.

Golub, S (2003), *Beyond rule of law orthodoxy: the legal empowerment alternative*, Carnegie Endowment for International Peace, October, Washington DC.

Goodin, R (ed) (1996), *The theory of institutional design*, Press Syndicate of the University of Cambridge, Cambridge.

Government of Serbia (2004), *A plan for the political solution to the situation in Kosovo and Metohija*, Belgrade, accessed 6 August 2004, at ⟨http://www.srbija.sr.gov.yu/extfile/en/1987/plan_kosovo_metohija2004.doc⟩.

Greenberg, D (1980), "Law and development in light of dependency theory", *Research in Law and Sociology*, vol. 3, pp. 129–159.

Gusmao, X (2000a), Address to the National Press Club, 5 May, Canberra.

—— (2000b), "New Year's message by Kay Rala Xanana Gusmao", 31 December, Dili.

—— (2001a), "Conflict resolution and East Timor," 2 April.

—— (2001b), "Inaugural human rights oration", October, Melbourne.

—— (2004), "National Dialogue on Justice: opening address", 5 March, Dili, accessed 22 March 2004, at ⟨http://www.jsmp.minihub.org/News/mar04/05mar04_XG_natDialog_eng.htm⟩.

Guterres, F d C (2003), *Reconciliation in East Timor: building peace and stability*, Brisbane, accessed 29 March 2004, at ⟨http://www.pcr.uu.se/research/program/EastTimor031008.pdf⟩.

Guterres Lopes, A (2002), "From the ashes: building a new legal system in East Timor", paper presented at the Indigenous Law Conference, December, University of Sydney, accessed 5 May 2006, at ⟨http://www.gaje.net.au/aniceto.htm#_ftn1⟩.

Halliday, K (2001), "Women and justice", *La'o Hamutuk Bulletin*, vol. 2, issue 6, October, accessed 30 October 2001, at ⟨http://www.etan.org/lh/bulletins/bulletinv2n6a.html⟩.

Hamber, B (1998), "How should we remember? Issues to consider when establishing commissions and structures for dealing with the past", paper presented at the conference Dealing with the past: reconciliation processes and peacebuilding, INCORE, 8–9 June, Belfast, accessed 10 October 2007, ⟨http://www.incore.ulst.ac.uk/research/projects/thepast/hamber.html⟩.

Hammergren, L (1998a), *Institutional strengthening and justice reform*, United States Agency for International Development, August, Washington DC, accessed 27 April 2006, at ⟨http://pdf.dec.org/pdf_docs/PNACD020.pdf⟩.

—— (1998b), *Political will, constituency building, and public support in justice reforms*, United States Agency for International Development, August, Washington DC, accessed 27 April 2006, at ⟨http://pdf.dec.org/pdf_docs/PNACD023.pdf⟩.

—— (1998c), *Judicial training and justice reform*, United States Agency for International Development, August, Washington DC, accessed 27 April 2006, at ⟨http://pdf.dec.org/pdf_docs/PNACD021.pdf⟩.

—— (1998d), *Code reform and law revision*, United States Agency for International Development, August, Washington DC.

Hampton, J (1992), "Democracy and the rule of law", in Shapiro, I (ed) *The rule of law*, New York University Press, New York, pp. 13–44.

Hart, H (1961), *The concept of law*, Oxford University Press, London.

Hartmann, M (2003a), *International judges and prosecutors in Kosovo: a new model for post-conflict peacekeeping*, United States Institute of Peace, October, Washington DC, accessed 18 June 2004, at ⟨www.usip.org⟩.

—— (2003b), "International judges and prosecutors: the lessons learned", *Focus Kosovo*, December, accessed 18 June 2004, at ⟨http://www.unmikonline.org/pub/focuskos/dec03/focusklaw3.htm⟩.

Hayashi (2001), "Collective conflict management", *Harvard International Review*, vol. 22, no. 4, pp. 82–83.

—— (1960), *The constitution of liberty*, University of Chicago Press, Chicago.

—— (1976), *Law, legislation and liberty: a new statement of the liberal principles of justice and political economy*, Routledge & Kegan Paul, London.

Hayner, P (1996), "Commissioning the truth: further research questions", *Third World Quarterly*, vol. 17, no. 1, pp. 19–29.

Heder, S and Ledgerwood, J (eds) (1996a), *Propaganda, politics, and violence in Cambodia: democratic transition under United Nations peace-keeping*, M. E. Sharpe, Armonk, NY.

Heder, S and Ledgerwood, J (1996b), "Politics of violence: an introduction", in Heder, S and Ledgerwood, J (eds) *Propaganda, politics and violence in Cambodia: democratic transition under United Nations peace-keeping*, M. E. Sharpe, Armonk, NY, pp. 3–33.

Heininger, J (1994), *Peacekeeping in transition: the United Nations in Cambodia*, Twentieth Century Fund Press, New York.

Hendrickson, D (1998), "Safeguarding peace: Cambodia's constitutional challenge", *Accord*, November, Conciliation Resources, London, accessed 24 October 2007, at ⟨http://www.c-r.org/our-work/accord/cambodia/contents.php⟩.

Hinsley, F (1986), *Sovereignty*, Cambridge University Press, Cambridge and New York.

Hirst, M and Varney, H (2005), *Justice abandoned? An assessment of the serious crimes process in East Timor*, International Center for Transitional Justice, New York, accessed 6 August 2007, at ⟨http://www.ictj.org/en/news/pubs/index.html⟩.

Hohe, T (2002), "The clash of paradigms: international administration and local political legitimacy in East Timor", *Contemporary Southeast Asia*, vol. 24, no. 3, pp. 569–589.

House of Commons [United Kingdom] (2004), *Mrs Alice Mahon (Halifax), Column 1128 Commons Hansard Debates 25 March 2004*, accessed 11 August 2004, at ⟨http://www.publications.parliament.uk/pa/cm200304/cmhansrd/cm040325/debindx/40325-x.htm⟩.

HRW [Human Rights Watch] (2002a), *Justice denied for East Timor: Indonesia's sham prosecutions, the need to strengthen the trial process in East Timor, and the imperative of UN action*, December, New York, accessed 20 February 2004, at ⟨http://www.hrw.org/backgrounder/asia/timor/etimor1202bg.htm⟩.

—— (2002b), *Human Rights Watch World Report 2002*, New York, accessed 29 July 2004, at ⟨http://hrw.org/wr2k2/⟩.

HRW Asia (1995), *Cambodia at war*, Human Rights Watch, New York.

Hughes, C (1996), *UNTAC in Cambodia: the impact on human rights*, Institute of Southeast Asian Studies, Singapore.

—— (2001), *An investigation of conflict management in Cambodian villages*, Centre for Peace and Development, Cambodia Development Resource Institute, October, Phnom Penh.

Huntington, S (1991), *The third wave: democratization in the late twentieth century*, University of Oklahoma Press, Norman.

ICG [International Crisis Group] (2002), *Finding the balance: the scales of justice in Kosovo*, 12 September, Pristina and Brussels.

—— (2004), *Collapse in Kosovo*, 22 April, Pristina, Belgrade, Brussels, accessed 1 June 2004, at ⟨http://www.crisisweb.org/library/documents/europe/balkans/155_collapse_in_kosovo_revised.pdf⟩.

ICISS [International Commission on Intervention and State Sovereignty] (2001), *The responsibility to protect: report of the International Commission on Intervention and State Sovereignty*, December, accessed 28 May 2002, at ⟨http://www.iciss.ca/Report-English.asp⟩.

Ignatieff, M (2002), "Intervention and state failure", *Dissent*, vol. 49, no. 1, pp. 114–123.

—— (2003), *Empire lite: nation-building in Bosnia, Kosovo and Afghanistan*, Vintage, London.

IICK [Independent International Commission on Kosovo] (2000), *The Kosovo Report*, accessed 6 March 2002, at ⟨http://www.kosovocommission.org/reports/1.pdf⟩.

Inglehart, R (1988), "The renaissance of political culture", *American Political Science Review*, vol. 82, no. 4, pp. 1203–1230.

In larger freedom. See UNGA (2005a).

Inoguchi, T, Newman, E and Keane, J (eds) (1998a), *The changing nature of democracy*, United Nations University Press, Tokyo.

Interim Office of the Commission for Reception, Truth and Reconciliation (2001), *Report on reconciliation meetings in Bali and Kupang, 22–25 August 2001*, Commission for Reception, Truth and Reconciliation, Dili.

International Institute for Democracy and Electoral Assistance (2000), *Democracy and global co-operation at the United Nations*, International IDEA, Stockholm, accessed 23 May 2001, at ⟨http://www.idea.int/publications/democracy_and_global_cooperation/introduction.htm⟩.

International Rehabilitation Council for Torture Victims (2000), "Health and human rights torture and trauma in post-conflict East Timor", *Lancet*, vol. 356, no. 9243, 18 November, pp. 1–3.

IPA [International Peace Academy] (2003a), "State-building", accessed 5 May 2006, at ⟨http://www.ipacademy.org/Programs/Research/ProgReseState_Building.htm⟩.

—— (2003b), *The future of UN state-building: strategic and operational challenges and the legacy of Iraq*, November, New York.

Islam Online (2002), "Kosovo parliament elects Rugova as president", 4 March, accessed 13 August 2004, at ⟨http://www.islam-online.net/English/ News/2002-03/04/article22.shtml⟩.

Jackson, R (1999a), "Surrogate sovereignty? Great power responsibility and 'failed' states", paper presented to the Failed States Conference, Purdue University, West Lafayette.

Jacoby, W (2001), "Institutional transfer: method or mirage?", presentation to the Carnegie Endowment for International Peace Second Rule of Law Roundtable, Carnegie Endowment for International Peace, 5 October, Washington DC, accessed 26 April 2006, at ⟨http://www.carnegieendowment.org/events/ index.cfm?fa=eventDetail&id=404⟩.

Jolliffe, J (2002), "Timor's enduring pain on the slow road to justice", *The Age*, 5 January, p. 5.

Jones, D (1994), "The League of Nations experiment in international protection", *Ethics and International Affairs*, vol. 8, pp. 77–95.

JSMP [Judicial System Monitoring Program] (2001), *Justice in practice: human rights in court administration*, November, Dili.

—— (2002a), *The right to appeal in East Timor*, October, Dili.

—— (2002b), *Findings and recommendations: workshop on formal and local justice systems in East Timor*, July, Dili.

—— (2002c), *Policy paper for the draft law on domestic violence*, November, Dili, accessed 27 April 2006, at ⟨http://www.jsmp.minihub.org/Legislation/ Policy%20Paper%20%20for%20the%20Draft%20Law%200n%20Domestic %20Violence.pdf⟩.

—— (2003a), *JSMP background paper on the justice sector*, 4 June, Dili, accessed 16 January 2004, at ⟨http://www.jsmp.minihub.org/News/04_06_03.htm⟩.

—— (2003b), *The Court of Appeal decision on the applicable subsidiary law in Timor-Leste*, August, Dili.

—— (2003c), *JSMP: court in Jakarta completes theatrical performance*, 6 August, Dili, accessed 20 February 2004, at ⟨http://www.jsmp.minihub.org/News/ 06_8_3.htm⟩.

Katzenstein, S (2003), "Hybrid tribunals: searching for justice in East Timor", *Harvard Human Rights Journal*, vol. 16, pp. 245–278.

KCL [King's College London] (2003), *A review of peace operations: a case for change*, Conflict Security and Development Group, King's College London, University of London, and International Policy Institute, 28 February, London, accessed 5 May 2006, at ⟨http://ipi.sspp.kcl.ac.uk/rep006/s05.html⟩.

Kelsen, H (1946), *General Theory of Law and State*, translated by Anders Wedberg, Harvard University Press, Cambridge, MA.

Kirste, K (2001), *Administrative capacity building in Kosovo. An assessment of UNMIK/OSCE's civil administration policy*, 13 December, Denpasar.

Kiss, E (2000), "Moral ambition within and beyond political constraints", in Rotberg, R and Thompson, D (eds) *Truth versus justice: the morality of truth commissions*, Princeton University Press, Princeton, NJ, pp. 68–98.

Kleinfeld Belton, R (2005), *Competing definitions of the rule of law: implications for practitioners*, Carnegie Endowment for International Affairs, January, Washington DC, accessed 10 March 2006, at ⟨http://www.carnegieendowment. org/events/index.cfm?fa=eventDetail&id=849&&prog=zgp&proj=zdrl⟩.

Knopic, J (2004), "Corruption in Kosovo: perceptions versus experiences; potential investigative techniques", paper prepared for a Seminar on the Law of Nationbuilding, Chicago-Kent College of Law, May, accessed 19 July 2004, at ⟨http://operationkosovo.kentlaw.edu/resources/legal/kosovo/knopic-final.htm⟩.

Kohli, A, Evans, P, Katzenstein, P, Przeworski, A, Hoeber Rudolph, S, Scott, J and Skocppol, T (1996), "The role of theory in comparative politics: a symposium", *World Politics*, vol. 48, no. 1, pp. 1–49.

Kostunica, V (2004), "Statement of Serbian prime minister Vojislav Kostunica following the murder of Dimitrije Popovic in Gracanica", 5 June, Belgrade, accessed 5 May 2006, at ⟨http://www.srbija.sr.gov.yu/vesti/vest.php?id=2769⟩.

Krasner, S (ed) (1999), *Sovereignty: organised hypocrisy*, Princeton University Press, Princeton, NJ.

Kritz, N (2006), "Remarks by Neil Kritz", presentation at the seminar Promoting the rule of law abroad: are we there yet?, 1 February, Washington DC.

Krygier, M (2000), "Ethical positivism and the liberalism of fear", in Campbell, T and Goldsworthy, J (eds) *Judicial power, democracy and legal positivism*, Dartmouth Publishing Company, Aldershot, pp. 59–88.

La'o Hamutuk (2001a), "Introduction: justice for East Timor?" *La'o Hamutuk Bulletin*, vol. 2, issue 6, October, accessed 30 October 2001, at ⟨http://www. etan.org/lh/bulletins/bulletinv2n6.html⟩.

——— (2001b), "UNTAET and 'serious crimes'", *La'o Hamutuk Bulletin*, vol. 2, issue 6, October, accessed 30 October 2001, at ⟨http://www.etan.org/lh/ bulletins/bulletinv2n6.html⟩.

——— (2001c), "La'o Hamutuk responds: refugee returns too slow, strategy still misguided", *La'o Hamutuk Bulletin*, vol. 2, issue 6, October, accessed 30 October 2001, at ⟨http://www.etan.org/lh/bulletins/bulletinv2n6a.html⟩.

——— (2002), "An assessment of the UN's police mission in East Timor", *La'o Hamutuk Bulletin*, vol. 3, no. 1, pp. 1–3, 11.

——— (2003), "Reviewing the East Timor Commission for Reception, Truth and Reconciliation", *La'o Hamutuk Bulletin*, vol. 4, accessed 18 February 2004, at ⟨http://www.etan.org/lh/bulletins/bulletinv4n5.html⟩.

Latifi, B and Mekolli, N (2001), "Investigative report: trial and error: Kosovo's fledgling justice system", Institute for War and Peace Reporting, London, accessed 6 March 2002, at ⟨http://www.iwpr.net/index.pl?archive/bcr2/ bcr2_20011116_1_ir_eng.txt⟩.

Law adopted by the National Assembly on October 21, 1994 on the Common Statute of Civil Servants of the Kingdom of Cambodia, accessed 20 October 2007, at ⟨http://www.bigpond.com.kh/council_of_jurists/Foncpubl/fpl014g.htm⟩.

Law on Criminal Procedure (1993), 24th session of the 1st Legislature of the State Assembly of Cambodia, enacted 28 January 1993, accessed 1 April 2006, at ⟨http://www.bigpond.com.kh/Council_of_Jurists/Penal/pen002g.htm⟩.

Lawson, S (1993), "Conceptual issues in the comparative study of regime change and democratization", *Comparative Politics*, vol. 26, pp. 183–205.

Lawyers' Committee for Human Rights (1999), "A fragile peace: laying the foundation for justice in Kosovo", October accessed 3 October 2007, at ⟨http://www.humanrightsfirst.org/pubs/descriptions/kosovofull1099.htm⟩.

―――― (2000), "Building on quicksand: the collapse of the World Bank's judicial reform project in Peru", April, accessed 3 October 2007, at ⟨http://www.humanrightsfirst.org/pubs/descriptions/perubuilding.htm⟩.

League of Nations (1931), *League of Nations Official Journal*, November, Geneva.

Lijphart, A (1995), "The Southern European examples of democratization: six lessons for Latin America", in Pridham, G (ed) *Transitions to democracy: comparative perspectives from Southern Europe, Latin America and Eastern Europe*, Dartmouth Publishing Company, Aldershot, pp. 173–189.

Linton, S (2001), "Rising from the ashes: the creation of a viable criminal justice system in East Timor", *Melbourne University Law Review*, vol. 25, no. 1, pp. 122–180, accessed 6 February 2003, at ⟨http://www.austlii.edu.au/au/journals/MULR/2001/5.htm⟩.

Little, D (1999), "A different kind of justice: dealing with human rights violations in transitional societies", *Ethics and International Affairs*, vol. 13, accessed 27 April 2006, at ⟨http://www.cceia.org/viewMedia.php/prmTemplateID/8/prmID/457⟩.

Lizee, P (1993), "The challenge of conflict resolution in Cambodia", *Cambodia Defence Quarterly*, vol. 23, pp. 35–38, 40, 42, 44.

―――― (2000), *Peace, power and resistance in Cambodia*, Macmillan Press, London.

Lopez-de-Silanes, F (2002), *The politics of legal reform*, UN Centre for International Development, April.

Lorenz, F (2000a), "A series of reports from Kosovo: five months in the field", *Peacekeeping and International Relations*, vol. 29, no. 5/6, pp. 8–11.

―――― (2000b), "The rule of law in Kosovo: problems and prospects", *Criminal Law Forum*, vol. 11, no. 2, pp. 127–142.

―――― (2001), "A series of reports from Kosovo: five months in the field", *Peacekeeping and International Relations*, vol. 30, no. 1–3, pp. 13–16.

Lyon, T (2002), "Combating conflict entrepreneurs", presentation at the event Combating Conflict Entrepreneurs, Carnegie Endowment for International Peace, 7 February, accessed 27 April 2002, at ⟨http://www.carnegieendowment.org/events/index.cfm?fa=eventDetail&id=453&⟩.

McAdams, J (1997), *Transitional justice and the rule of law in new democracies*, University of Notre Dame Press, Notre Dame.

McAuslan, P (1997), "Law, governance, and the development of the market: practical problems and possible solutions", in Faundez, J (ed) *Good governance and law: legal and institutional reform in developing countries*, St. Martin's Press, New York, pp. 25–44.

McClymount, M and Golub, S (eds) (2000), *Many roads to justice: the law-related work of Ford Foundation grantees around the world*, The Ford Foundation, New York.

McDonald, C (2001), "Out of the ashes – a new criminal justice system for East

Timor", paper presented at the International Society for the Reform of Criminal Law 15th International Conference, 30 August, Canberra.

McFarlane, J and Maley, W (2001), *Civilian police in United Nations police operations*, Australian Defence Studies Centre, Canberra.

McHugh, Heather (1996), "The truth about truth commissions", *USAID Research and Reference Services Project*, Washington DC, March.

Mackinlay, J, Chopra, J and Minear, L (1992), *An interim report on the Cambodian peace process*, Norwegian Institute of International Affairs, December.

McLean, L (1992), *Report for July 1992*, United Nations Transitional Authority in Cambodia, 2 August, Phnom Penh.

McNamara, D (1992a), "Proposal for Special Prosecutor's office", United Nations Transitional Authority in Cambodia, Human Rights Component, 26 November, Phnom Penh.

—— (1992b), "Office of the Special Investigator (Prosecutor)", United Nations Transitional Authority in Cambodia, Human Rights Component, 24 December, Phnom Penh.

—— (1992c), "Proposal for the establishment of UNTAC's Special Prosecutor's office", United Nations Transitional Authority in Cambodia, Human Rights Component, 9 December, Phnom Penh.

—— (1992d), *Report of the Human Rights Component: June and July 1992*, United Nations Transitional Authority in Cambodia, Human Rights Component, 17 August, Phnom Penh.

—— (1993), "Address to the World Conference on Human Rights by the Director of UNTAC's Human Rights Component", United Nations Transitional Authority in Cambodia.

—— (1994), *UN peacekeeping and human rights in Cambodia: a critical evaluation*, August, Geneva.

—— (1995a), "The protection and promotion of human rights", in United Nations Institute for Training and Research (ed) *The United Nations Transitional Authority in Cambodia (UNTAC): Debriefing and lessons: report and recommendations of the international conference, Singapore, August 1994*, Kluwer Law International, London and Boston, pp. 165–170.

—— (1995b), "UN human rights activities in Cambodia: an evaluation", in Henkin, A (ed) *Honoring human rights and keeping the peace: lessons from El Salvador, Cambodia and Haiti: recommendations for the United Nations*, Aspen Institute Justice and Society Program, Washington DC, pp. 57–82.

McPhedran, I (1993), "Strange and difficult task of policing in a lawless land", *Canberra Times*, 4 June, p. 11.

Maley, W (2000), "The UN and East Timor", *Pacifica Review*, vol. 12, no. 1, pp. 63–76.

—— (2001), "The impact of external military intervention: political, economic and social", paper presented at the International Commission on Intervention and State Sovereignty Roundtable, 10 June, New Delhi.

—— (2003), "Institutional design and the rebuilding of trust", in Maley, W, Sampford, C and Thakur, R (eds) *From civil strife to civil society: civil and military responsibilities in disrupted states*, United Nations University Press, Tokyo, pp. 163–179.

Maley, W, Sampford, C and Thakur, R (2003a), "Introduction", in Maley, W, Sampford, C and Thakur, R (eds) *From civil strife to civil society: civil and military responsibilities in disrupted states*, United Nations University Press, Tokyo, pp. 1–13.

—— (eds) (2003b), *From civil strife to civil society: civil and military responsibilities in disrupted states*, United Nations University Press, Tokyo.

Manuel, S (2001), "A case of executive order", *Focus Kosovo*, December, accessed 18 June 2004, at ⟨http://www.unmikonline.org/pub/focuskos/dec01/focusklaw2.htm⟩.

—— (2002), "Justice seen to apply to all: interview with Clint Williamson", *Focus Kosovo*, April, accessed 18 June 2004, at ⟨http://www.unmikonline.org/pub/focuskos/apr02/focusklaw1.htm⟩.

Marks, S (1994a), "Forgetting 'the policies and practices of the past': impunity in Cambodia", in Peou, S (ed) *Cambodia: change and continuity in contemporary politics*, Ashgate Publishing, Aldershot, pp. 233–260.

—— (1994b), "The new Cambodian constitution: from civil war to a fragile democracy", in Peou, S (ed) *Cambodia: change and continuity in contemporary politics*, Ashgate Publishing, Aldershot, pp. 109–174.

Marshall, D and Inglis, S (2003), "The disempowerment of human rights-based justice in the United Nations Mission in Kosovo", *Harvard Human Rights Journal*, vol. 16, pp. 95–146, accessed 30 July 2004, at ⟨http://www.harvard.law.edu/students/orgs/hrj/iss16/index.shtml⟩.

Martin, I (2001), *Self-determination in East Timor: the United Nations, the ballot, and international intervention*, Lynne Rienner, Boulder, CO.

Mearns, D (2002), *Looking both ways: models for justice in East Timor*, Australian Legal Resources International, November.

Meden, N (2002), "From resistance to nation building: the changing role of civil society in East Timor", *Development Outreach*, Winter, accessed 29 March 2004, at ⟨http://wwww.reliefweb.int/w/Rwb.nsf/0/7fc1cc5b8cd274a585256bb9006fa389?OpenDocument⟩.

Mendez, J (1997a), "In defence of transitional justice", in McAdams, J (ed) *Transitional justice and the rule of law in new democracies*, University of Notre Dame Press, Notre Dame, pp. 1–26.

—— (1997b), "Accountability for past abuses", *Human Rights Quarterly*, vol. 19, no. 2, pp. 255–282.

Merry, S (1988), "Legal pluralism", *Law and Society Review*, vol. 22, no. 5, pp. 869–896.

Merryman, J (1977), "Comparative law and social change: on the origins, style, decline and revival of the law and development movement", *American Journal of Comparative Law*, vol. 25, pp. 457–491.

Migdal, J (1998a), *Strong societies and weak states: state-society relations and state capabilities in the third world*, Princeton University Press, Princeton, NJ.

—— (1998b), "Why do so many states stay intact?", in Dauvergne, P (ed) *Weak and strong states in Asia-Pacific societies*, Allen & Unwin in association with the Department of International Relations, Research School of Pacific and Asian Studies, Australian National University, Canberra, pp. 11–37.

Milliken, J and Krause, K (2002), "State failure, state collapse, and state reconstruction: concepts, lessons and strategies", *Development and Change*, vol. 33, no. 5, pp. 753–774.

Ministry of Justice/UNDP (2002), *Joint assessment: Ministry of Justice-UNDP on the judiciary system: mission report Timor Leste November 2002*, Dili, Ministry of Justice of the Democratic Republic of East Timor and United Nations Development Programme.

Minow, M (2000), "The hope for healing: what can truth commissions do?", in Rotberg, R and Thompson, D (eds) *Truth versus justice: the morality of truth commissions*, Princeton University Press, Princeton, NJ, pp. 235–256.

Mobekk, E (2001), *Policing peace operations: United Nations civilian police in East Timor*, King's College, London and John D. and Catherine T. MacArthur Foundation Programme on Peace and International Cooperation, October, London.

Morison, M (1996), "Cambodia and the United Nations: an interview with Justice Michael Kirby, former Special Representative of the Secretary-General for Human Rights in Cambodia", *Human Rights Defender*, September, accessed 5 April 2006, at ⟨http://www.austlii.edu.au/au/other/ahric/hrd/Sept96/hrd05304.html⟩.

Mydans, S (2001), "Modest beginnings for East Timor's justice system", *New York Times*, 4 March.

Nagle, J and Mahr, A (1999), *Democracy and democratization*, Sage Publications, London.

National Security Adviser [UNTAET] (2001a), *Traditional justice concept paper: background paper for discussion*, United Nations Transitional Administration in East Timor, 19 September, Dili.

——— (2001b), *Traditional justice workshop: 25 September 2001*, UNTAET, 25 September, Dili.

NDI [National Democratic Institute for International Affairs] (1990), *Nation building: the UN and Namibia*, Washington DC.

NDI, University of East Timor, and Abrantes, M (2002), *Carrying the people's aspirations: a report on focus group discussions in East Timor*, February, Dili.

Nee, M (1995), *Towards restoring life: Cambodian villages*, Jesuit Service Cambodia, Phnom Penh.

Neou, K and Gallup, G (1997), "The state of human rights in Cambodia", in *Legal and Political Development in Cambodia*, Cambodian Center for Advanced Study, Phnom Penh.

Nixon, R (2002), "The United Nations mission in rural East Timor: the case of the enclave district of Oecusse", research paper, Northern Territory University, Darwin.

No exit without strategy. See UNSC (2001a).

North, D (1990), *Institutions, institutional change and economic performance*, Cambridge University Press, Cambridge.

——— (1993), "Economic performance through time: lecture to the memory of Alfred Nobel, December 9, 1993", accessed 6 April 2006, at ⟨http://nobelprize.org/economics/laureates/1993/north-lecture.html⟩.

Northedge, F (1986), *The League of Nations: its life and times 1920–1946*, Leicester University Press, Leicester.

Nyberg, A (1993), *Activity report for January 1993*, United Nations Transitional Authority in Cambodia, Civil Administration Component, 7 February, Phnom Penh.

O'Donnell, G (1993), "On the state, democratisation and some conceptual problems: a Latin American view with glances at some post-communist countries", *World Development*, vol. 21, no. 8, pp. 1355–1369.

Offe, C (1996), "Designing institutions in East European transitions", in Goodin, R (ed) *The theory of institutional design*, Press Syndicate of the University of Cambridge, Cambridge, pp. 199–226.

Office of the United Nations Special Coordinator in the Occupied Territories (1999), *Rule of law development in the West Bank and Gaza strip: survey and state of the development effort*, May, Gaza, accessed 10 July 2002, at ⟨http://www.arts.mcgill.ca/programs/polisci/faculty/rexb/unsco-ruleoflaw⟩.

OHCHR [Office of the United Nations High Commissioner for Human Rights] (2003), *Asia and Pacific region: quarterly reports of field offices (last quarter of 2003)*, December, Bangkok, accessed 6 February 2004, at ⟨http://www.ohchr.org/english/countries/field/docs/asia4.doc⟩.

————— (2006a), *Rule of law tools for post-conflict states: mapping the justice sector*, Geneva, HR/PUB/06/2, accessed 6 August 2007, at ⟨http://www.ohchr.org/english/about/publications/⟩.

————— (2006b), *Rule of law tools for post-conflict states: monitoring legal systems*, Geneva, HR/PUB/06/3, accessed 6 August 2007, at ⟨http://www.ohchr.org/english/about/publications/⟩.

————— (2006c), *Rule of law tools for post-conflict states: prosecution initiatives*, Geneva, HR/PUB/06/4, accessed 6 August 2007, at ⟨http://www.ohchr.org/english/about/publications/⟩.

————— (2006d), *Rule of law tools for post-conflict states: truth commissions*, Geneva, HR/PUB/06/1, accessed 6 August 2007, at ⟨http://www.ohchr.org/english/about/publications/⟩.

Ohmae, K (1995), *The end of the nation state: rise of regional economies*, Free Press Paperbacks, New York.

OIK [Ombudsperson Institution in Kosovo] (2003), *Third annual report 2002–2003*, 10 July, Pristina.

————— (2004), *Fourth annual report 2003–2004*, 12 July, Pristina.

OMIK [Organization for Security and Co-operation in Europe Mission in Kosovo] (2000), *The Criminal Justice System in Kosovo (February–July 2000)*, Pristina, 10 August, accessed 20 October 2007, at ⟨http://www.osce.org/kosovo/documents.html?lsi=true&src=8&limit=10&y=2000&pos=10⟩.

————— (2001), *Strategy for justice*, OSCE, June, Pristina, accessed 11 February 2002, at ⟨http://www.osce.org/kosovo/documents/reports/justice/strategy_justice_e.pdf⟩.

OMIK (2002a), Department of Human Rights and Rule of Law, Legal Systems Monitoring Section *Report 9 – on the administration of justice*, OSCE, March, Pristina.

——— (2002b), Department of Human Rights and Rule of Law, Legal Systems Monitoring Section *Kosovo's war crimes trials: a review*, OSCE, September, Pristina.

——— (2003a), Department of Human Rights and Rule of Law, Legal Systems Monitoring Section *Kosovo: review of the criminal justice system (March 2002–April 2003): protection of witnesses in the criminal justice system*, OSCE, Pristina.

——— (2003b), Department of Human Rights and Rule of Law, Legal Systems Monitoring Section *Property rights in Kosovo: 2002–2003*, OSCE, Pristina.

——— (2003c), Department of Human Rights and Rule of Law, Legal Systems Monitoring Section *Parallel structures in Kosovo: October 2003*, OSCE, Pristina.

——— (2004a), Department of Human Rights and Rule of Law, Legal Systems Monitoring Section *Human rights challenges following the March riots*, OSCE, Pristina.

——— (2004b), Department of Human Rights and Rule of Law, Legal Systems Monitoring Section *Kosovo review of the criminal justice system: "the administration of justice in the municipal courts"*, OSCE, March, Pristina.

——— (2006), *OSCE Mission in Kosovo: mandate*, accessed 1 May 2006, at ⟨http://www.osce.org/kosovo/13197.html⟩.

O'Neill, W (2002), *Kosovo: an unfinished peace*, Lynne Rienner, Boulder, CO.

Orucu, E (1996), "Mixed and mixing systems: a conceptual search", in Orucu, E, Attwooll, E and Coyle, S (eds) *Studies in legal systems: mixed and mixing*, Kluwer Law International, London, pp. 335–352.

OSCE DIIIR [Organization for Security and Co-operation in Europe Office for Democratic Institutions and Human Rights] (1999), *Kosovo/Kosova: as seen, as told: an analysis of the human rights findings of the OSCE Kosovo Verification Mission October 1998 to June 1999*, OSCE, Warsaw, accessed 27 March 2001, at ⟨http://www/osce.org/kosovo/reports/hr/part1/index.htm⟩.

Ospina, S and Hohe, T (2001), *Traditional power structures and the community empowerment and local governance project*, September, Dili.

Ottaway, M (2002), "Rebuilding state institutions in collapsed states", *Development and Change*, vol. 33, no. 5, pp. 1001–1024.

Palan, A (1994), "NGO in first Khmer criticism of UNTAC", *Phnom Penh Post*, 23 September 23–6 October, p. 19.

Paris Agreements (1991), *Agreements on a Comprehensive Political Settlement of the Cambodia Conflict*, enacted 23 October.

Paris, R (2004), *At war's end: building peace after civil conflict*. Cambridge University Press, Cambridge.

Parsons, T (1962), "Law and social control", in Evan, W (ed) *Law and sociology: exploratory essays*, Free Press of Glencoe, New York, pp. 56–72.

Patrick, I (2001), "East Timor emerging from conflict: the role of local NGOs and international assistance", *Disasters*, vol. 25, no. 1, pp. 48–66.

Peake, G (2004), *Policing the peace: police reform experiences in Kosovo, Southern Serbia and Macedonia*, Saferworld, January.

Peerenboom, R (2004), "Varieties of rule of law: an introduction and provisional conclusion" in Peerenboom, R (ed) *Asian discourses of rule of law: theories and implementation of rule of law in 12 Asian countries, France and the US*, Routledge Curzon, London, pp. 1–55.

Peou, S (ed) (1997), *Conflict neutralization in the Cambodia war: from battlefield to ballot-box*, Oxford University Press, New York.

Perito, R (2002), "National police training within an executive police operation", in Dwan, R (ed) *Executive policing: enforcing the law in peace operations*, Oxford University Press, New York, pp. 85–101.

Perriello, T and Wierda, M (2006), *Lessons from the deployment of international judges and prosecutors in Kosovo*, International Center for Transitional Justice, New York, accessed 6 August 2007, at ⟨http://www.ictj.org/en/news/pubs/index.html⟩.

Pettifer, J (2002), "Kosovo economy and society after 1945 – some observations", Conflict Studies Research Centre, Camberley, accessed 12 August 2004, at ⟨http://www.da.mod.uk/CSRC/documents/balkans/G103⟩.

Pettit, P (1996), 'Institutional design and rational choice', in Goodin, R (ed) *The theory of institutional design*, Press Syndicate of the University of Cambridge, Cambridge, pp. 54–89.

Plunkett, M (1993), *Decision on the future of UN prosecutions of crimes involving human rights breaches during the transitional period*, United Nations Transitional Authority in Cambodia, Special Prosecutor's Office, 1 February, Phnom Penh.

——— (1994), "The establishment of the rule of law in post-conflict peacekeeping", in Smith, H (ed) *International peacekeeping: building on the Cambodian experience*, Australian Defence Studies Centre, Canberra, pp. 65–75.

Poletti, E (1998), "Working for human rights in Cambodian prisons", *Law Institute Journal*, vol. 72, no. 3, pp. 52–53.

Porcell, G (1992), *Activity report of civil administration*, United Nations Transitional Authority in Cambodia, Civil Administration Component, 11 December, Phnom Penh.

Pritchard, S (2001), "United Nations involvement in post-conflict reconstruction efforts: new and continuing challenges in the case of East Timor", *University of New South Wales Law Journal*, vol. 24, no. 1, pp. 183–190.

Proceedings of the Strategic Development Planning for East Timor Conference, Melbourne 5–9 April 1999 (1999), Melbourne.

Provisions dated September 10, 1992 Relating to the Judiciary and Criminal Law and Procedure Applicable in Cambodia during the Transitional Period (1992), Supreme National Council, enacted 10 September 1992, accessed 1 April 2006, at ⟨http://www.bigpond.com.kh/Council_of_Jurists/Judicial/jud005g.htm⟩.

Przeworski, A (1995), *Sustainable democracy*, Cambridge University Press, Cambridge.

Pugh (1998), "Post-conflict rehabilitation: social and civil dimensions", *Journal of Humanitarian Assistance*, December, accessed 1 May 2006, at ⟨http://www.jha.ac/articles/a034.htm⟩.

Putnam, R (1993), "The prosperous community: social capital and public life", *The American Prospect*, vol. 13, pp. 35–42.

——— (2000), *Bowling alone: the collapse and revival of American community*, Simon and Schuster, New York.

Puymbroeck, R (ed) (2001), *Comprehensive legal and judicial development*, International Bank for Reconstruction and Development/World Bank, Washington DC.

Ramos-Horta, J (2002), "Address to the Foreign Correspondents Club", 26 July, Hong Kong.

Ratner, S (1993), "The Cambodia settlement agreements", in Peou, S (ed) *Cambodia: change and continuity in contemporary politics*, Ashgate Publishing, Aldershot, pp. 3–44.

——— (1995), *The new UN peacekeeping: building peace in lands of conflict*, St. Martin's Press and Council on Foreign Relations, New York.

——— (2000), "Democracy and accountability: the criss-crossing paths of two emerging norms", in Fox, G and Roth, B (eds) *Democratic governance and international law*, Cambridge University Press, Cambridge, pp. 449–490.

Rausch, C (2002), "The assumption of authority in Kosovo and East Timor: legal and practical implications", in Dwan, R (ed) *Executive policing: enforcing the law in peace operations*, Oxford University Press, New York, pp. 11–32.

Raz, J (1979), *The authority of law: essays on law and morality*, Clarendon Press, Oxford.

Rees, E (2006), *Security sector reform (SSR) and peace operations: "improvisions and confusion" from the field*, UN Department of Peacekeeping Operations Peacekeeping Best Practices Section, New York, accessed 17 May 2006, at ⟨http://pbpu.unlb.org/pbpu/view/viewdocument.aspx?id=2&docid=750⟩.

Reiger, C and Wierda, M (2006), *The serious crimes process in Timor-Leste: in retrospect*, International Center for Transitional Justice, New York, accessed 6 August 2007, at ⟨http://www.ictj.org/en/news/pubs/index.html⟩.

Rengger, N (1997), "Towards a culture of democracy? Democratic theory and democratisation in Eastern and Central Europe", in Pridham, G, Herring, E and Sanford, G (eds) *Building democracy? the international dimension of democratisation in Eastern Europe*, Leicester University Press, London, pp. 56–80.

Renouf, G (2002), "Some features of the legal system in East Timor", paper presented at the East Timor Legal Coordination Symposium, 11–12 March, Darwin.

Reus-Smit, C (1998), "Changing patterns of governance: from absolutism to global multilateralism", in Paolini, A, Jarvis, A and Reus-Smit, C (eds) *Between sovereignty and global governance: the United Nations, the state and civil society*, Macmillan Press, London, pp. 1–28.

Roberts, D (2001), *Political transition in Cambodia 1991–99: power, elitism and democracy*, Curzon Press, Richmond, Surrey.

Robertson, G (2000), *Crimes against humanity: the struggle for global justice*, Penguin Books, Ringwood.

Robertson, K (2000), "Peacebuilding in East Timor", paper presented at the Fourth annual peacebuilding consultations, Asia-Pacific Working Group (Indonesia and East Timor Sub-group), Canadian Council for International Cooperation, 29 February.

Robinson, M (2000), "Transitional justice: defining the quality of Indonesia's future democracy", speech on 22–24 November, Surabaya, accessed 26 April 2006, at ⟨http://www.unhchr.ch/huricane/huricane.nsf/0/027E8971704EA4BDC 12569AB0059007F?opendocument⟩.

——— (2002), "Statement by Mary Robinson, United Nations High Commissioner for Human Rights" at the 55th Annual DPI/NGO Conference: Rebuilding Societies Emerging from Conflict: A Shared Responsibility, 9 September, New York, accessed 20 February 2004, at ⟨http://www.unhchr.ch/ huricane/huricane.nsf/view01/E26D0A6E2C1874EBC1256C310039C47F ?opendocument⟩.

Roht-Arriaza, N (1997), "Combating impunity: some thoughts on the way forward", *Law and Contemporary Problems*, vol. 59, no. 4, pp. 93–102.

Rome Statute of the International Criminal Court, 17 July 1998, accessed 13 August 2007, at ⟨http://www.un.org/law/icc/statute/romefra.htm⟩.

Rotberg, R (2000), "Truth commissions and the provision of truth, justice and reconciliation", in Rotberg, R and Thompson, D (eds) *Truth versus justice: the morality of truth commissions*, Princeton University Press, Princeton, NJ, pp. 3–21.

Rotberg, R and Thompson, D (eds) (2000), *Truth versus justice: the morality of truth commissions*, Princeton University Press, Princeton, NJ.

Rothstein, B (1998), *Just institutions matter: the moral and political logic of the universal welfare state*, Press Syndicate of the University of Cambridge, Cambridge.

Rubin, B (2006), "Peace building and state-building in Afghanistan: constructing sovereignty for whose security?", *Third World Quarterly*, vol. 27, no. 1, pp. 175–185.

Saikal, A (2003), "The dimensions of state disruption", in Maley, W, Sampford, C and Thakur, R (eds) *From civil strife to civil society: civil and military responsibilities in disrupted states*, United Nations University Press, Tokyo, pp. 17–30.

Salla, M (2000), "Promoting reconciliation in East Timor: imperatives for transition to self-government", *Pacifica Review*, vol. 12, no. 1, pp. 33–46.

Saltford, J (2000), "UNTEA and UNWRI: United Nations involvement in West New Guinea during the 1960s", PhD thesis, University of Hull, accessed 5 May 2006, at ⟨http://papuaweb.org/dlib/s123/saltford/phd.pdf⟩.

Sanderson, J (n.d.), paper in General Sanderson's personal archives held at the Australian Defence Force Academy in Canberra.

Savic, M (2002), "Serbia minister: U.N. lawyer incompetent", *Associated Press*, 30 December, accessed 2 May 2006, at ⟨http://www.balkanpeace.org/hed/ archive/dec02/hed5400.shtml⟩.

Schabas, W and Kritz, N (n.d.), "The model codes for post-conflict criminal justice", accessed 11 May 2006, at ⟨http://www.aiad-icdaa.org/Inci/DRAFT %20MODEL%20CODES%20Intro.pdf⟩.

Schedler, A (1998), "What is democratic consolidation?", *Journal of Democracy*, vol. 9, no. 2, pp. 91–107.

——— (2001), "Measuring democratic consolidation", *Studies in Comparative International Development*, vol. 36, no. 1, pp. 66–86.

Schneider, M (1999), "The intellectual origins of colonial trusteeship in East Asia: Nitobe Inazo, Paul Reinsch and the end of empire", *American Asian Review*, vol. 17, no. 1, pp. 1–48.

Seidman, R (1978), *The state, law and development*, Croom Helm, London.

Shain, Y and Linz, J (1995), *Between states: interim governments and democratic transitions*, Cambridge University Press, Cambridge.

Shalom, S (1990), "The United States and Libya Part 1: Before Qaddafi", in *Zmag*, May, accessed 15 October 2007, at ⟨http://www.zmag.org/zmag/articles/Shalomlyb1.html⟩.

Sharlet, R (1998), "Legal transplants and political mutations: the reception of constitutional law in Russia and the Newly Independent States", *East European Constitutional Review*, vol. 7, no. 4, pp. 107–123, accessed 27 April 2006, at ⟨http://www.law.nyu.edu/eecr/v017num4/index.html⟩.

Shawcross, W (1994), *Cambodia's new deal: a report*, Carnegie Endowment for International Peace, Washington DC.

Sheikhi, S (2001), *Disciplining the judges of Kosovo*, United Nations Interim Administration Mission in Kosovo, 22 June, Pristina, accessed 26 February 2002, at ⟨http://www.unmikonline.org/pub/features/fr048.html⟩.

Shoesmith, D (2003), "Timor-Leste: divided leadership in a semi-presidential system", *Asian Survey*, vol. 43, no. 2, pp. 231–252.

Sieff, M and Wright, L (1999), "Reconciling order and justice? New institutional solutions in post-conflict states", *Journal of International Affairs*, vol. 52, no. 2, pp. 757–779.

Sok, S (ed) (1998), *International conference on "Cambodian Legal and Judicial Reform in the Context of Sustainable Development"*, Cambodian Legal Resources Development Center, Phnom Penh.

Sok, S and Sarin, D (1998), *Legal system of Cambodia*, Cambodian Legal Resources Development Centre, Phnom Penh.

Sorensen, G (1998), "Democratisation in the third world: the role of western politics and research", paper presented at the conference Failed States and International Security: Causes, Prospects and Consequences, Purdue University, West Lafayette, accessed 27 April 2006, at ⟨http://www.ippu.purdue.edu/failed_states/1998/papers/sorensen.html⟩.

Spruyt, H (1994), *The sovereign state and its competitors: an analysis of systems change*, Princeton University Press, Princeton, NJ.

Stahn, C (2001a), "Accommodating individual criminal responsibility and national reconciliation: the UN Truth Commission for East Timor", *American Journal of International Law*, vol. 95, no. 4, pp. 952–966.

Stahn, C (2001b), "Constitution without a state? Kosovo under the United Nations Constitutional Framework for Self-Government", *Leiden Journal of International Law*, vol. 14, pp. 531–561.

Stein, G (1999), *East Timor: Xanana Gusmao/Amnesty*, ABC Radio, 26 August, accessed 13 April 2004, at ⟨http://www.abc.net.au/am/s46725.htm⟩.

Stohl, L (1998), "Westphalia, the end of the Cold War and the new world order: old roots to a 'new' problem", paper presented at the conference Failed States and International Security: Causes, Prospects and Consequences, Purdue University, West Lafayette.

Strohmeyer, H (2001), "Collapse and reconstruction of a judicial system: the United Nations missions in Kosovo and East Timor", *American Journal of International Law*, vol. 95, no. 46, pp. 46–63.

Suara Timor Lorosae (2001), "Xanana: UNTAS not a defeated group", 29 March, accessed 14 May 2001, at ⟨http://www.etan.org/et2001a/march/25-31/29etnews.htm⟩.

Suhrke, A (2001), "Peacekeepers as nation-builders: dilemmas of the UN in East Timor", *International Peacekeeping*, vol. 8, no. 4, pp. 1–20.

Summerfield, D (2002), "Effects of war: moral knowledge, revenge, reconciliation, and medicalised concepts of 'recovery'", *British Medical Journal*, vol. 325, accessed 12 August 2004, at ⟨http://bmj.bmjjournals.com/cgi/reprint/325/7372/1105⟩.

Tamanaha, B (2001), *A general jurisprudence of law and society*, Oxford University Press, New York.

Tan, B T (1995), "Drafting the Cambodian constitution", in United Nations Institute for Training and Research (ed) *The United Nations Transitional Authority in Cambodia (UNTAC): debriefing and lessons: report and recommendations of the international conference, Singapore, August 1994*, pp. 205–210.

Teitel, R (2000), *Transitional justice*, Oxford University Press, New York.

The rule of law and transitional justice in conflict and post-conflict societies. See UNSC (2004e).

Thier, A and Chopra, J (2002), *Considerations for political and institutional reconstruction in Afghanistan*, Watson Institute of International Studies, Brown University, January, Providence, RI.

Thome, J (1997), "Comment, on McAuslan, P: law, governance and the development of the market: practical problems and possible solutions", in Faundez, J (ed) *Good government and law: legal and institutional reform in developing countries*, St. Martin's Press, New York, pp. 45–50.

Thornberry, C (1995), *Peacekeeping, peacemaking and human rights*, INCORE, Coleraine, Northern Ireland.

Time Asia (2001), "Interview: what happens next?", 3 September, accessed 2 August 2002, at ⟨http://www.pcug.org.au/~wildwood/01augnext.htm⟩.

Traub, J (2000), "Inventing East Timor", *Foreign Affairs*, vol. 79, no. 4, pp. 74–89.

Trubek, D (1972), "Toward a social theory of law: an essay on the study of law and development", *Yale Law Journal*, vol. 82, no. 1, pp. 1–50.

Trubek, D and Galanter, M (1974), "Scholars in self-estrangement: some reflections on the crisis in law and development", *Wisconsin Law Review*, vol. 4, pp. 1062–1101.

UNDP [United Nations Development Programme] (1997), *Governance for sustainable human development: a UNDP policy document*, January, accessed 11 July 2002, at ⟨http://magnet.undp.org/policy/chapter2.htm#a⟩.

——— (2001a), *Peace-building from the ground-up: a case study of UNDP's CARERE programme in Cambodia 1991–2000*, UNDP, March, Phnom Penh.

——— (2001b), *Support to the judiciary system in East Timor: project review final report*, UNDP, October, Dili.

—— (2002a), *The Timor-Leste correctional service: setting the course*, UNDP, accessed 7 March 2004, at ⟨http://www.undp.east-timor.org/documentsreports/governance_capacitydevelopment/Correctional%20Service%20English.pdf⟩.

—— (2002b), *Project for employment and reconciliation in Kosovo (PERK)*, UNDP, Pristina, accessed 12 August 2004, at ⟨http://www.kosovo.undp.org/Projects/PERK/perk.htm⟩.

—— (2004), *Conflict Prevention and Reconciliation Initiative (CPR)*, UNDP, Pristina, accessed 12 August 2004, at ⟨http://www.kosovo.undp.org/Projects/CPR/cpr.htm⟩.

UNFPA [United Nations Population Fund] (2001), *Just as spoon and fork always touch each other: domestic violence in East Timor*, UNFPA, Dili.

UNGA [United Nations General Assembly] (1992), *An agenda for peace: preventive diplomacy, peacemaking and peace-keeping*, 17 June, New York, A/47/277-8/24111.

—— (1993), *Vienna declaration and program of action*, 12 July, New York, A/CONF.157/23.

—— (1994a), *Report of the Secretary-General to the General Assembly on strengthening the rule of law*, New York, A/49/512.

—— (1994b), *Strengthening of the rule of law*, 23 December, New York, A/RES/49/194.

—— (1999a), *Question of East Timor: progress report of the Secretary-General*, 13 December, New York, A/54/654.

—— (1999b), *Support by the United Nations system of the efforts of Governments to promote and consolidate new or restored democracies*, 5 January, New York, A/RES/53/31.

—— (2000a), *Strengthening the rule of law*, 20 July, New York, A/55/177.

—— (2000b), *Resolution adopted by the General Assembly: 54/163 human rights in the administration of justice*, 23 February, New York, A/RES/54/163.

—— (2000c), *Report of the Secretary-General on the implementation of the report of the Panel on United Nations Peace Operations*, 20 October, New York, A/55/502.

—— (2000d), *United Nations Millennium Declaration*, 8 September, New York, A/55/L.2.

—— (2000e), *Support by the United Nations System of the efforts of governments to promote and consolidate new or restored democracies*, 13 October, New York, A/55/489.

—— (2000f), *Report of the Panel on United Nations Peace Operations [Brahimi Report]*, 21 August, New York, A/55/305-S/2000/809.

—— (2000g), *Support by the United Nations system of the efforts of Governments to promote and consolidate new or restored democracies*, 20 January, New York, A/RES/54/36.

—— (2001), *Support by the United Nations system of the efforts of Governments to promote and consolidate new or restored democracies*, 18 January, New York, A/RES/55/43.

—— (2003), *Investigation into the fraudulent diversion of $4.3 million by a senior staff member of the reconstruction pillar of the United Nations Interim Administration Mission in Kosovo*, 13 November, New York, A/58/592.

―――― (2004), *A more secure world: our shared responsibility. Report of the Secretary-General's High-level Panel on Threats, Challenges and Change*, 2 December, New York, A/59/565, accessed 3 February 2006, at ⟨http://www.un.org/secureworld/report2.pdf⟩.

―――― (2005a), *In larger freedom: towards development, security and human rights for all*, 21 March, New York, A/59/2005.

―――― (2005b), *2005 World Summit Outcome*, 24 October, New York, A/RES/60/1.

―――― (2007), *Report of the Special Representative of the Secretary-General for human rights in Cambodia, Yash Ghai*, 30 January, New York, A/HRC/4/36.

UNHCHR [United Nations High Commissioner for Human Rights] (1999), *Independence and impartiality of the judiciary, jurors and assessors and the independence of lawyers: Commission on Human Rights Resolution 1999/31*, 26 April, Geneva, 1999/31.

―――― (2002), *Integrity of the judicial system*, 22 April, Geneva, E/CN.4/RES/2002/37.

United Nations (1995a), *The United Nations and Cambodia, 1991–95*, United Nations Department of Public Information, New York.

―――― (1995b), *The United Nations and Mozambique, 1992–95*, United Nations Department of Public Information, New York.

―――― (2004), *A more secure world: Our shared responsibility: Report of the High-level Panel on Threats, Challenges and Change, Executive Summary*, at ⟨http://www.un.org/secureworld/brochure.pdf⟩.

United States Department of State (2000a), *Country reports on human rights practices: Federal Republic of Yugoslavia*, Bureau of Democracy, Human Rights and Labor, US Department of State, Washington DC, accessed 1 May 2005, at ⟨http://www.state.gov/⟩.

―――― (2000b), *Kosovo Judicial Assessment Mission Report*, Department of State, April, Washington DC, accessed 11 February 2002, at ⟨http://www.state.gov/www/global/human-rights/kosovoii/042000-kosovo-rpt.pdf⟩.

United States General Accounting Office (2002), *Cambodia: governance reform progressing, but key efforts are lagging*, June, Washington DC.

Uniting our strengths. See UNSC (2006a).

UNMIK [United Nations Interim Administration Mission in Kosovo] (1999), *Regulation No 1999/1 on the authority of the Interim Administration in Kosovo*, 25 July, Pristina, UNMIK/REG/1999/1, accessed 11 May 2001, at ⟨http://www.un.org/peace/kosovo/pages/regulations/reg1.htm⟩.

―――― (2001a), *UNMIK at two: the way forward*, June, Pristina, accessed 31 May 2002, at ⟨http://www.unmikonline.org/2ndyear/unmikat2p2.htm⟩.

―――― (2001b), *Constitutional Framework for Provisional Self-Government*, 15 May, Pristina, UNMIK/REG/2001/19.

―――― (2001c), "Kosovo: KTC discusses Constitutional Framework", 16 May, Pristina, UNMIK/PR/582.

―――― (2001d), "Objective justice on trial: Regulation 2000/64 in action", *UNMIK News*, vol. 78, 5 February, accessed 23 August 2004, at ⟨http://www.unmikonline.org/pub/news/n178.html⟩.

——— (2001e), *On the executive branch of the PISG in Kosovo*, 13 September.

——— (2001f), "Interview: Police Commissioner Christopher Albiston", UNMIK, 2 February, Pristina, accessed 26 February 2002, at ⟨http://www.unmikonline.org/pub/features/fr013.html⟩.

——— (2002a), "Address to the Kosovo Assembly by SRSG Michael Steiner", 9 May, Pristina, UNMIK/PR/732, accessed 1 June 2002, at ⟨http://www.unmikonline.org/press/2002/pressr/pr732.htm⟩.

——— (2002b), "Address to the Security Council by Michael Steiner, SRSG", 24 April, Pristina, UNMIK/Pr719, accessed 1 June 2002, at ⟨http://www.unmikonline.org/press/2002/pressr/pr719.htm⟩.

——— (2002c), "UN envoy urges Kosovars to work together towards 'fair society for all'", *UNMIK news*, 15 February, accessed 26 April 2006, at ⟨http://www.unmikonline.org/archives/ncws02_02full.htm#1902⟩.

——— (2003a), "Standards for Kosovo", 10 December, Pristina, UNMIK/PR/1078.

——— (2003b), *Pillar 1: police and justice: presentation paper: third quarter, July 2003*, UNMIK, July, Pristina, accessed 18 June 2004, at ⟨http://www.unmikonline.org/justice/documents/PillarI_Report_Ju103.pdf⟩.

——— (2003c), "Press briefing notes, 1 April 2003", UNMIK, 1 April, Pristina, accessed 30 July 2004, at ⟨http://www.unmikonline.org/press/2003/trans/tr010403.htm⟩.

——— (2004a), *Kosovo standards implementation plan*, UNMIK, 31 March, Pristina, accessed 18 June 2004, at ⟨http://www.unmikonline.org/pub/misc/KSIP-Eng.pdf⟩.

——— (2004b), "UNMIK police daily press update: 4 August 2004", UNMIK, 5 August, Pristina, accessed 6 August 2004, at ⟨http://www.unmikonline.org/civpol/archive/DPU050804.htm⟩.

——— (2004c), "UNMIK's statement on today's session of the Kosovo Assembly", 8 July, Pristina, UNMIK/PR/1202, accessed 25 August 2004, at ⟨http://www.unmikonline.org/press/2004/pressr/pr1202.pdf⟩.

UNSC [United Nations Security Council] (1997), *Resolution 1145 (1997)*, 19 December, New York, S/RES/1145 (1997).

——— (1999a), *Report of the Secretary-General on the United Nations Interim Administration Mission in Kosovo*, 12 July, New York, S/1999/779.

——— (1999b), *Report of the Secretary-General on the United Nations Interim Administration Mission in Kosovo*, 16 September, S/1999/987, accessed 28 August 2001, at ⟨http://www.un.org/docs/sc/reports/1999/s1999779.htm⟩.

——— (1999c), *Report of the Secretary-General on the situation in East Timor*, 4 October, New York, S/1999/1024.

——— (1999d), *Resolution 1244 (1999)*, 10 June, New York, S/RES/1244 (1999), accessed 24 August 2001, at ⟨http://www.un.org/docs/scres/1999/99sc1244.htm⟩.

——— (1999e), *Report of the Secretary-General on the United Nations Interim Administration Mission in Kosovo*, S/1999/987, accessed 28 August 2001, at ⟨http://www/un/org/docs/sc/reports/1999/s1999987.htm⟩.

——— (1999f), *Report of the Secretary-General pursuant to paragraph 10 of Security Council Resolution 1244 (1999)*, 12 June, New York, S/1999/672.

────── (1999g), *Report of the Secretary-General on the United Nations Interim Administration Mission in Kosovo*, 23 December, S/1999/1250, accessed 28 August 2001, at ⟨www.un.org/docs/sc/reports/1999/s19991250.htm⟩.

────── (1999h), *Resolution 1272 (1999)*, 25 October, New York, S/RES/1272 (1999), accessed 11 October 2007, at ⟨http://www.un.org/peace/etimor/docs/9931277E.htm⟩.

────── (2000a), *Report of the Secretary-General on the United Nations Interim Administration Mission in Kosovo*, 29 April, S/2000/363.

────── (2000b), *Report of the Secretary-General on the United Nations Interim Administration Mission in Kosovo*, 3 March, S/2000/177.

────── (2000c), *Report of the Secretary-General on the United Nations Transitional Administration in East Timor*, 26 January, S/2000/53.

────── (2000d), *Report of the Secretary-General on the United Nations Transitional Administration in East Timor*, 26 July, New York, S/2000/738.

────── (2000e), *Report of the Secretary-General on the United Nations Interim Administration Mission in Kosovo*, 6 June, S/2000/538.

────── (2000f), *Resolution 1327 (2000)*, 13 November, New York, S/RES/1327 (2000).

────── (2000g), *Report of the Secretary-General on the United Nations Interim Administration Mission in Kosovo*, 18 September, S/2000/878.

────── (2000h), *Report of the Secretary-General on the United Nations Interim Administration Mission in Kosovo*, 15 December, S/2000/1196.

────── (2000i), *Report of the Secretary-General on the United Nations Transitional Administration in East Timor (for the period 27 January–26 July 2000)*, 26 July, New York, S/2000/738.

────── (2001a), *No exit without strategy: Security Council decision-making and the closure or transition of United Nations peacekeeping operations*, 20 April, New York, S/2001/394.

────── (2001b), *Report of the Secretary-General on the United Nations Interim Administration Mission in Kosovo*, 7 June, New York, S/2001/565.

────── (2001c), *Report of the Secretary-General on the United Nations Interim Administration Mission in Kosovo*, 2 October, New York, S/2001/926.

────── (2002a), *Statement by the President of the Security Council*, 20 May, New York, S/PRST/2002/13.

────── (2002b), *Report of the Secretary-General on the United Nations Transitional Administration in East Timor*, 17 April, New York, S/2002/432.

────── (2002c), *Report of the Secretary-General on the United Nations Interim Administration Mission in Kosovo*, 22 April, New York, S/2002/436.

────── (2002d), *Report of the Secretary-General on the United Nations Mission of Support in East Timor*, 6 November, New York, S/2002/1223.

────── (2002e), *Resolution 1410 (2002)*, 17 May, New York, S/RES/1410 (2002).

────── (2002f), *Report of the Secretary-General on the United Nations Interim Administration Mission in Kosovo*, 15 January, New York, S/2002/62.

────── (2002g), *Report of the Secretary-General on the United Nations Interim Administration Mission in Kosovo*, 9 October, New York, S/2002/1126.

────── (2002h), *Report of the Security Council Mission to Kosovo and Belgrade, Federal Republic of Yugoslavia*, 19 December, New York, S/2002/1376.

————— (2003a), *Resolution 1473 (2003)*, 4 April, New York, S/RES/1473 (2003).

————— (2003b), *Report of the Secretary-General on the United Nations Mission of Support in East Timor*, 6 October, New York, S/2003/944.

————— (2003c), *Report of the Secretary-General on the United Nations Mission of Support in East Timor*, 21 April, New York, S/2003/449.

————— (2003d), *Report of the Secretary-General on the United Nations Interim Administration Mission in Kosovo*, 29 January, New York, S/2003/113.

————— (2003e), *Report of the Secretary-General on the United Nations Interim Administration Mission in Kosovo*, 14 April, New York, S/2003/421.

————— (2003f), *Report of the Secretary-General on the United Nations Interim Administration Mission in Kosovo*, 26 June, New York, S/2003/675.

————— (2003g), *Report of the Secretary-General on the United Nations Interim Administration Mission in Kosovo*, 15 October, New York, S/2003/996.

————— (2004a), *Special Report of the Secretary-General on the United Nations Mission of Support in East Timor*, 13 February, New York, S/2004/117.

————— (2004b), *Report of the Secretary-General on the United Nations Interim Administration Mission in Kosovo*, 26 January, New York, S/2004/71.

————— (2004c), *Report of the Secretary-General on the United Nations Interim Administration Mission in Kosovo*, 30 April, New York, S/2004/348.

————— (2004d), *Report of the Secretary-General on the United Nations Interim Administration Mission in Kosovo*, 30 July, New York, S/2004/613.

————— (2004e), *The rule of law and transitional justice in conflict and post-conflict societies*, 23 August, New York, S/2004/616.

————— (2006a), *Uniting our strengths: enhancing United Nations support for the rule of law*, 14 December, New York, S/2006/980.

————— (2006b), *Report of the Secretary-General on Timor-Leste pursuant to Security Council Resolution 1690 (2006)*, 8 August, New York, S/2006/628.

————— (2007a), *Report of the Secretary-General on the United Nations Integrated Mission in Timor-Leste (for the period from 9 August 2006 to 26 January 2007)*, 1 February, S/2007/50.

————— (2007b), *Report of the Secretary-General on the United Nations Interim Administration Mission in Kosovo*, 29 June, New York, S/2007/395.

UNTAC [United Nations Transitional Authority in Cambodia] (1992a), *Analysis report: Kandal Province*, UNTAC, 9 November, Phnom Penh.

————— (1992b), "Report on the SNC 24 August 1992", UNTAC, Phnom Penh.

————— (1993a), *The prosecution policy of the UNTAC Special Prosecutor*, Phnom Penh.

————— (1993b), "Urgent decision of Special Representative of the Secretary-General required today on the reluctance of Cambodian judges to hear cases prosecuted by the Special Prosecutor", UNTAC, 28 January, Phnom Penh.

————— (1993c), "Daily press briefing", UNTAC, 30 June, Phnom Penh.

————— (1993d), "Daily press briefing", UNTAC, 8 March, Phnom Penh.

————— (1993e), "Special press briefing", UNTAC, 9 March, Phnom Penh.

————— (1993f), *UNTAC fact sheet*, 29 March, Phnom Penh.

————— (1993g), "Note for the file: meeting regarding actions to be taken after the Phnom Penh municipal judge refused to hear the case of the PDK suspect", UNTAC, Phnom Penh.

——— (1993h), "Report on the meeting of the SNC in Beijing 28 January 1993", UNTAC, Phnom Penh.

——— (1993i), "Report on the working meeting of the SNC on 9 March 1993", UNTAC, Phnom Penh.

——— (1993j), "Discussion with Minister for Justice", UNTAC, 29 January, Phnom Penh.

——— (1993k), "Report on the special SNC meeting with the Core Group, 18 June 1993", UNTAC, Phnom Penh.

——— (1993l), "Preliminary report on the attack against the FPC party office of Baphnum district, 15 January 1993", UNTAC, Baphnum.

——— (1993m), "Summary/follow-up report on Baphnum FUNCINPEC office incident, 15 January 1993", UNTAC, Baphnum.

——— (1993n), "Progress report no 1 regarding the assault to the district office of FUNCINPEC in Baphnum on 11.01.93, 24 January 1993", UNTAC, Baphnum.

——— (1993o), *Evaluation report: UN CIVPOL: UNTAC Cambodia*, UNTAC, Phnom Penh.

UNTAC Civil Administration Component (1992), *Second civil administration training seminar*, 21–23 July, Phnom Penh.

UNTAC Human Rights Component (1992), *Proceedings of the International Symposium on Human Rights in Cambodia*, 30 November–2 December, Phnom Penh.

UNTAC Information/Education Division (1993), *Visit to Kampong Cham Province, 15–18 June 1993*, UNTAC, Phnom Penh.

UNTAET [United Nations Transitional Administration in East Timor] (1999a), *UNTAET Regulation No 1999/1 on the Authority of the Transitional Administration in East Timor*, 27 November, Dili, UNTAET/REG/1999/1.

——— (1999b), *UNTAET Regulation No 1999/3 on the establishment of a Transitional Judicial Service Commission*, 3 December, Dili, UNTAET/REG/1999/3.

——— (2001a), *Regulation No. 2001/10 on the establishment of a Commission for Reception, Truth and Reconciliation in East Timor*, 13 July, Dili, UNTAET/REG/2001/10.

——— (2001b), "Escalation of Passabe/Tumin conflict in Oecussi", UNTAET, 18 October, Oecussi.

——— (2001c), "Meeting on a strategy for reconciliation efforts", UNTAET, Dili.

——— (2001d), "Daily briefing 17 October 2001: refugees, militia leader return from West Timor", UNTAET, Dili.

——— (2001e), "UNTAET daily briefing 18 October 2001: Over 500 Covalima refugees return from West Timor", UNTAET, Dili.

——— (2001f), *UNTAET Regulation 2001/18 on the amendment of UNTAET Regulation No 2000/11 on the organization of the courts in East Timor*, 21 July, Dili, UNTAET/REG/2001/18.

——— (2001g), *UNTAET Regulation 2001/22 on the establishment of the East Timor Police Service*, 10 August, Dili, UNTAET/REG/2001/22.

——— (2001h), *UNTAET Regulation No 2001/23 on the establishment of a prison service in East Timor*, 28 August, Dili, UNTAET/REG/2001/23.

—— (2001i), *UNTAET Regulation 2001/24 on the establishment of a legal aid service in East Timor*, 5 September, Dili, UNTAET/REG/2001/24.

UNTAET Human Rights Unit (2001), *UNTAET Human Rights Unit March 2001*, UNTAET, Dili.

Upham, F (2002), *Mythmaking in the rule of law orthodoxy*, Carnegie Endowment for International Peace, September, Washington DC, accessed 5 May 2006, at ⟨http://www.carnegieendowment.org/files/wp30.pdf⟩.

USAID [United States Agency for International Development] (2004), *National debate focuses on justice system issues*, 11 March, Dili, accessed 22 March 2004, at ⟨http://www.jsmp.minihub.org/News/mar04/17mar04_usaid_nationaldebated _eng.htm⟩.

USIP [United States Institute of Peace] (2002), *Lawless rule versus rule of law in the Balkans*, United States Institute of Peace, December, Washington DC, accessed 18 July 2004, at ⟨http://www.usip.org⟩.

Van Creveld, M (1999), *The use and decline of the state*, Cambridge University Press, Cambridge.

Vasconcelos, C (2001), "Briefing to the Annual Conference of the International Association of Prosecutors", 25 August, Brazil, accessed 24 February 2004, at ⟨http://www.pcug.org.au/~wildwood/01augsystem.htm⟩.

Vecernje Novosti (2001a), "Reward for violence", 16 May, accessed 29 July 2004, at ⟨http://news.serbianunity.net/bydate/2001/May_17/1.html⟩.

Vecernje Novosti (2001b), "Vladan Batic on Haekkerup's project", 16 May, accessed 29 July 2004, at ⟨http://news.serbianunity.net/bydate/2001/May_16/14. html⟩.

Vickery, M (1984), *Cambodia 1975–1982*, Silkworm Books, Chiang Mai.

—— (2001b), *Presentation to the Commission on Human Rights: Fifty Seventh Session, by Sergio Vieira de Mello, Special Representative of the Secretary-General to East Timor and Transitional Administrator. Agenda item 9: Violation of human rights – the situation in East Timor*, Geneva, accessed 10 October 2007, at ⟨http://www.jsmp.minihub.org/resources/2001/SRSG_Statement.htm⟩.

—— (2001c), "Address to the National Council", 28 June, Dili.

—— (2002), "Statement to the UNSC Open Debate on East Timor", 30 January, New York.

Villmoare, E (2002), "Ethnic crimes and UN justice in Kosovo: the trial of Igor Simic", *Texas International Law Journal*, vol. 37, no. 2, pp. 373–386.

Von Einsiedel, S (2005), "Policy responses to state failure", in Chesterman, S, Ignatieff, M and Thakur, R (eds) *Making states work: state failure and the crisis of governance*, United Nations University Press, Tokyo, pp. 13–35.

Walker, G (1988), *The rule of law*, Melbourne University Press, Melbourne.

Wainright, E (2002), *New neighbour, new challenge: Australia and the security of East Timor*, Australian Strategic Policy Institute, Canberra.

Walsh, D (1999), "KLA leader Thaci ordered rivals executed, rebel commanders say", *World Socialist Website*, 29 June, accessed 6 August 2004, at ⟨http://www. wsws.org/articles/1999/jun1999/kla-j29.shtml⟩.

Walters, F P (1952), *A history of the League of Nations*, Oxford University Press, London.

Wartorn Societies Project (2000c), *Rebuilding after war: lessons from WSP: what we learned about the challenges of rebuilding after war*, United Nations Research Institute for Social Development, accessed 3 May 2006, at ⟨http://www.unrisd.org/wsp/rebuilding/rebu-02.htm⟩.

Waters, C (2001), "Legal education in Kosovo", *Peacekeeping and International Relations*, vol. 30, no. 4, pp. 7–8.

Watson, A (1974), *Legal transplants*, Scottish Academic Press, Edinburgh.

——— (1993), *Legal transplants: an approach to comparative law*, University of Georgia Press, Athens.

Weber, M (1922), *The theory of social and economic organisation*, Oxford University Press, Oxford, 1947.

——— (1946), *Essays in sociology*, Oxford University Press, New York.

Wheeler, N and Dunne, T (2001), "East Timor and the new humanitarian interventionism", *International Affairs*, vol. 77, no. 4, pp. 805–827.

Wicremasinghe, T (1998), "Confession as a technique of proof in criminal proceedings", in Fernando, B (ed) *Problems facing the Cambodian legal system*, Asian Human Rights Commission, Hong Kong, pp. 71–78.

Widner, J (2001), *Building the rule of law*, W. W. Norton, New York.

Wilde, R (2001a), "From Danzig to East Timor and beyond: the role of international territorial administration", *American Journal of International Law*, vol. 95, no. 3, pp. 583–606, accessed 3 April 2002, at ⟨http://ezproxy.libadfa.edu.au:2093/pdqweb?TS=1015211838&RQT=309&CC=1&Dtp=1⟩.

——— (2001b), "The complex role of the legal adviser when international organizations administer territory", paper presented at the Annual Meeting of the American Society of International Law, Washington DC.

World Bank (2002), *Participation*, accessed 12 December 2003, at ⟨http://www4.worldbank.org/legal/leglr/access_pa.html⟩.

Yahmed, J (1992), *Province of Kampong Thom, activity report, 27 July–12 August 1992*, UNTAC, Civil Administration Component, 13 August, Kompong Thom.

——— (1993), *Activity report, Kompong Thom, 1–21 March 1993*, UNTAC, Civil Administration Component, 26 March, Kompong Thom.

Yannis, A (2002), "State collapse and its implications for peace-building and reconstruction", *Development and Change*, vol. 33, no. 5, pp. 817–836.

——— (2004), "The UN as government in Kosovo", *Global Governance*, vol. 10, pp. 67–81.

Yayasan HAK (2001), *Serious concerns regarding the independence of the judiciary under United Nations Transitional Administration in East Timor*, Yayasan HAK, 24 July, Dili.

Zagaris, B (1988), "Law and development or comparative law and social change – the application of old concepts in the Commonwealth Caribbean", *Inter-American Law Review*, vol. 19, no. 3, pp. 549–586.

Zerner, C (1994), "Through a green lens: the construction of customary environmental law and community in Indonesia's Maluku islands", *Law and Society Review*, vol. 28, no. 5, pp. 1079–1122.

Index